THE CATHEDRAL

THE
LONDON NOVELS

Fortitude
The Duchess of Wrexe
The Green Mirror
The Captives
The Joyful Delaneys

The Young Enchanted
Wintersmoon
Hans Frost
Captain Nicholas

SCENES FROM
PROVINCIAL LIFE

The Cathedral
The Old Ladies
Harmer John

HERRIES

Rogue Herries
The Fortress
The Bright Pavilions

Judith Paris
Vanessa
Katherine Christian

The Wooden Horse
Mr. Perrin and Mr. Traill
The Prelude to Adventure
Maradick at Forty
A Prayer for My Son
John Cornelius
The Sea Tower
The Blind Man's House

The Dark Forest
The Secret City
Portrait of a Man with Red Hair
Above the Dark Circus
Jeremy
Jeremy and Hamlet
Jeremy at Crale
The Killer and the Slain

SHORT STORIES

The Golden Scarecrow
The Silver Thorn

The Thirteen Travellers
All Souls' Night

Head in Green Bronze

Joseph Conrad (*A Critical Study*)
Anthony Trollope (*English Men of Letters*)
The Apple Trees (*Golden Cockerel Press*)
The Crystal Box

The English Novel (*Rede Lecture*)
Reading (*An Essay*)
The Waverley Pageant
The Cathedral (*A Play*)

Roman Fountain

(*With J. B. Priestley*)
Farthing Hall (*A Novel in Letters*)

THE CATHEDRAL

A NOVEL

BY

HUGH WALPOLE

MACMILLAN AND CO., LIMITED
ST. MARTIN'S STREET, LONDON
1944

TO

JESSIE AND JOSEPH CONRAD

WITH MUCH LOVE

"Thou shalt have none other gods but Me."

CONTENTS

BOOK I

PRELUDE

BOOK II

THE WHISPERING GALLERY

BOOK III

JUBILEE

BOOK IV

THE LAST STAND

BOOK I

PRELUDE

CHAPTER I

ADAM BRANDON was born at Little Empton in Kent
in 1839. He was educated at the King's School,
Canterbury, and at Pembroke College, Cambridge.
Ordained in 1863, he was first curate at St. Martin's,
Portsmouth, then Chaplain to the Bishop of Wor-
cester; in the year 1875 he accepted the living of
Pomfret in Wiltshire and was there for twelve years.
It was in 1887 that he came to our town; he was
first Canon and afterwards Archdeacon. Ten years
later he had, by personal influence and strength of
character, acquired so striking a position amongst
us that he was often alluded to as 'the King of
Polchester.' His power was the greater because
both our Bishop (Bishop Purcell) and our Dean
(Dean Sampson) during that period were men of
retiring habits of life. A better man, a greater saint
than Bishop Purcell has never lived, but in 1896 he
was eighty-six years of age and preferred study and
the sanctity of his wonderful library at Carpledon
to the publicity and turmoil of a public career;
Dean Sampson, gentle and amiable as he was, was
not intended by nature for a moulder of men. He
was, however, one of the best botanists in the

County and his little book on 'Glebeshire Ferns' is, I believe, an authority in its own line.

Archdeacon Brandon was, of course, greatly helped by his magnificent physical presence. 'Magnificent' is not, I think, too strong a word. Six feet two or three in height, he had the figure of an athlete, light blue eyes, and his hair was still, when he was fifty-eight years of age, thick and fair and curly like that of a boy. He looked, indeed, marvellously young, and his energy and grace of movement might indeed have belonged to a youth still in his teens. It is not difficult to imagine how startling an effect his first appearance in Polchester created. Many of the Polchester ladies thought that he was like 'a Greek God' (the fact that they had never seen one gave them the greater confidence), and Miss Dobell, who was the best read of all the ladies in our town, called him 'the Viking.' This stuck to him, being an easy and emphatic word and pleasantly cultured.

Indeed, had Brandon come to Polchester as a single man there might have been many broken hearts ; however, in 1875 he had married Amy Broughton, then a young girl of twenty. He had by her two children, a boy, Falcon, now twenty-one years of age, and a girl, Joan, just eighteen. Brandon therefore was safe from the feminine Polchester world ; our town is famous among Cathedral cities for the morality of its upper classes.

It would not have been possible during all these years for Brandon to have remained unconscious of the remarkable splendour of his good looks. He was very well aware of it, but any one who called him conceited (and every one has his enemies) did him a grave injustice. He was not conceited at all—he simply regarded himself as a completely exceptional person. He was not elated that he was exceptional, he did not flatter himself because it was so ; God had seen fit (in a moment of boredom, perhaps, at the number of insignificant and mis-shaped human beings He was forced to create) to fling into the world, for once, a truly Fine Specimen, Fine in Body, Fine in Soul, Fine in Intellect. Brandon had none of the sublime egoism of Sir Willoughby Patterne—he thought of others and was kindly and often unselfish—but he did, like Sir Willoughby, believe himself to be of quite another clay from the rest of mankind. He was intended to rule, God had put him into the world for that purpose, and rule he would—to the glory of God and a little, if it must be so, to the glory of himself. He was a very simple person, as indeed were most of the men and women in the Polchester of 1897. He did not analyse motives, whether his own or any one else's ; he was aware that he had ' weaknesses ' (his ungovernable temper was a source of real distress to him at times —at other times he felt that it had its uses). On the whole, however, he was satisfied with himself, his appearance, his abilities, his wife, his family, and, above all, his position in Polchester. This last was very splendid.

His position in the Cathedral, in the Precincts, in the Chapter, in the Town, was unshakable.

He trusted in God, of course, but, like a wise man, he trusted also in himself.

It happened that on a certain wild and stormy afternoon in October 1896 Brandon was filled with a great exultation. As he stood, for a moment, at the door of his house in the Precincts before crossing the Green to the Cathedral, he looked up at the sky obscured with flying wrack of cloud, felt the rain drive across his face, heard the elms in the neighbouring garden creaking and groaning, saw the lights of the town far beneath the low wall that bounded the Precincts sway and blink in the storm, his heart beat with such pride and happiness that it threatened to burst the body that contained it. There had not been, perhaps, that day anything especially magnificent to elate him ; he had won, at the Chapter Meeting that morning, a cheap and easy victory over Canon Foster, the only Canon in Polchester who still showed, at times, a wretched pugnacious resistance to his opinion ; he had met Mrs. Combermere afterwards in the High Street and, on the strength of his Chapter victory, had dealt with her haughtily ; he had received an especially kind note from Lady St. Leath asking him to dinner early next month ; but all these events were of too usual a nature to excite his triumph.

No, there had descended upon him this afternoon that especial ecstasy that is surrendered once and again by the gods to men to lead them, maybe, into some especial blunder or to sharpen, for Olympian humour, the contrast of some swiftly approaching anguish.

Brandon stood for a moment, his head raised, his chest out, his soul in flight, feeling the sharp sting of the raindrops upon his cheek ; then, with a little breath of pleasure and happiness, he crossed the Green to the little dark door of Saint Margaret's Chapel.

The Cathedral hung over him, as he stood, feeling in his pocket for his key, a huge black shadow, vast indeed to-day, as it mingled with the grey sky and

seemed to be taking part in the directing of the wildness of the storm. Two little gargoyles, perched
on the porch of Saint Margaret's door, leered
down upon the Archdeacon. The rain trickled
down over their naked twisted bodies, running in
rivulets behind their outstanding ears, lodging for a
moment on the projection of their hideous nether
lips. They grinned down upon the Archdeacon,
amused that he should have difficulty, there in the
rain, in finding his key. 'Pah!' they heard him
mutter, and then, perhaps, something worse. The
key was found, and he had then to bend his great
height to squeeze through the little door. Once
inside, he was at the corner of the Saint Margaret
Chapel and could see, in the faint half-light, the
rosy colours of the beautiful Saint Margaret window
that glimmered ever so dimly upon the rows of
cane-bottomed chairs, the dingy red hassocks, and
the brass tablets upon the grey stone walls. He
walked through, picking his way carefully in the
dusk, saw for an instant the high, vast expanse of
the nave with its few twinkling lights that blew in
the windy air, then turned to the left into the Vestry,
closing the door behind him. Even as he closed
the door he could hear high, high up above him the
ringing of the bell for Evensong.

In the Vestry he found Canon Dobell and
Canon Rogers. Dobell, the Minor Canon who
was singing the service, was a short, round, chubby
clergyman, thirty-eight years of age, whose great
aim in life was to have an easy time and agree
with every one. He lived with a sister in a little
house in the Precincts and gave excellent dinners.
Very different was Canon Rogers, a thin aesthetic
man with black bushy eyebrows, a slight stoop and

thin brown hair. He took life with grim seriousness. He was a stupid man but obstinate, dogmatic,
and given to the condemnation of his fellow-men.
He hated innovations as strongly as the Archdeacon
himself, but with his clinging to old forms and rituals
there went no self-exaltation. He was a cold-
blooded man, although his obstinacy seemed sometimes to point to a fiery fanaticism. But he was not
a fanatic any more than a mule is one when he
plants his feet four-square and refuses to go forward.
No compliments nor threats could move him ; he
would have lived, had he had a spark of asceticism,
a hermit far from the haunts of men, but even that
withdrawal would have implied devotion. He was
devoted to no one, to no cause, to no religion, to no
ambition. He spent his days in maintaining things
as they were, not because he loved them, simply
because he was obstinate. Brandon quite frankly
hated him.

In the farther room the choir-boys were standing
in their surplices, whispering and giggling. The
sound of the bell was suddenly emphatic. Canon
Rogers stood, his hands folded, motionless, gazing
in front of him. Dobell, smiling so that a dimple
appeared in each cheek, said in his chuckling whisper
to Brandon :

'Ronder comes to-day, doesn't he ?'

'Ronder ?' Brandon repeated, coming abruptly
out of his secret exultation.

'Yes . . . Hart-Smith's successor.'

'Oh, yes—I believe he does. . . .

Cobbett, the Verger, with his gold staff, appeared in the Vestry door. A tall handsome man,
he had been in the service of the Cathedral as
man and boy for fifty years. He had his

private ambitions, the main one being that old
Lawrence, the head Verger, in his opinion a
silly old fool, should die and permit his own
legitimate succession. Another ambition was that
he should save enough money to buy another three
cottages down in Seatown. He owned already
six there. But no one observing his magnificent
impassivity (he was famous for this throughout
ecclesiastical Glebeshire) would have supposed that
he had any thought other than those connected with
ceremony. As he appeared the organ began its
voluntary, the music stealing through the thick
grey walls, creeping past the stout grey pillars that
had listened, with so impervious an immobility, to
an endless succession of voluntaries. The Archdeacon prayed, the choir responded with a long
Amen, and the procession filed out, the boys with
faces pious and wistful, the choir-men moving
with nonchalance, their restless eyes wandering
over the scene so absolutely known to them.
Then came Rogers like a martyr; Dobell gaily
as though he were enjoying some little joke of his
own; last of all, Brandon, superb in carriage, in
dignity, in his magnificent recognition of the value
of ceremony.

Because to-day was simply an ordinary afternoon
with an ordinary Anthem and an ordinary service
(Martin in F) the congregation was small, the gates
of the great screen closed with a clang behind the
choir, and the nave, purple grey under the soft
light of the candle-lit choir, was shut out into twilight. In the high carved seats behind and beyond
the choir the congregation was sitting; Miss Dobell,
who never missed a service that her brother was
singing, with her pinched white face and funny old-

fashioned bonnet, lost between the huge arms of her seat; Mrs. Combermere, with a friend, stiff and majestic; Mrs. Cole and her sister-in-law, Amy Cole; a few tourists; a man or two; Major Drake, who liked to join in the psalms with his deep bass; and little Mr. Thompson, one of the masters at the School, who loved music and always came to Evensong when he could.

There they were then, and the Archdeacon, looking at them from his stall, could not but feel that they were rather a poor lot. Not that he exactly despised them; he felt kindly towards them and would have done no single one of them an injury, but he knew them all so well—Mrs. Combermere, Miss Dobell, Mrs. Cole, Drake, Thompson. They were shadows before him. If he looked hard at them they seemed to disappear. . . .

The exultation that he had felt as he stood outside his house-door increased with every moment that passed. It was strange, but he had never, perhaps, in all his life been so happy as he was at that hour. He was driven by the sense of it to that, with him, rarest of all things, introspection. Why should he feel like this ? Why did his heart beat thickly, why were his cheeks flushed with a triumphant heat ? It could not but be that he was realising to-day how everything was well with him. And why should he not realise it ? Looking up to the high vaulted roofs above him, he greeted God, greeted Him as an equal, and thanked Him as a fellow-companion who had helped him through a difficult and dusty journey. He thanked Him for his health, for his bodily vigour and strength, for his beauty, for his good brain, for his successful married life, for his wife (poor Amy), for his house and furniture, for his garden and tennis-lawn, for his carriage and horses, for his son, for his position in the town, his dominance in the Chapter, his authority on the School Council, his importance in the district. . . . For all these things he thanked God, and he greeted Him with an outstretched hand.

'As one power to another,' his soul cried, 'greetings! You have been a true and loyal friend to me. Anything that I can do for You I will do. . . .'

The time came for him to read the First Lesson. He crossed to the Lectern and was conscious that the tourists were whispering together about him. He read aloud, in his splendid voice, something about battles and vengeance, plagues and punishment, God's anger and the trembling Israelites. He might himself have been an avenging God as he read. He was uplifted with the glory of power and the exultation of personal dominion. . . .

He crossed back to his seat, and, as they began the 'Magnificat,' his eye alighted on the tomb of the Black Bishop. In the volume on Polchester in Chimes' Cathedral Series (4th edition, 1910), page 52, you will find this description of the Black Bishop's Tomb: 'It stands between the pillars at the far east end of the choir in the eighth bay from the choir screen. The stone screen which surrounds the tomb is of most elaborate workmanship, and it has, in certain lights, the effect of delicate lace; the canopy over the tomb has pinnacles which rise high above the level of the choir-stalls. The tomb itself is made from a solid block of a dark blue stone. The figure of the bishop, carved in black marble, lies with his hands folded across his breast, clothed

in his Episcopal robes and mitre, and crozier on his
shoulder.   At his feet are a vizor and a pair of
gauntlets, these also carved in black marble.   On
one finger of his right hand is a ring carved from
some green stone.   His head is raised by angels
and at his feet beyond the vizor and gauntlets are
tiny figures of four knights fully armed.   A small
arcade runs round the tomb with a series of shields
in the spaces, and these shields have his motto,
" God giveth Strength," and the arms of the See
of Polchester.   His epitaph in brass round the edge
of the tomb has thus been translated:

' " Here, having surrendered himself back to God,
lies Henry of Arden.   His life, which was dis-
tinguished for its great piety, its unfailing generosity,
its noble statesmanship, was rudely taken in the
nave of this Cathedral by men who feared neither
the punishment of their fellows nor the just vengeance of an irate God.

' " He died, bravely defending this great house
of Prayer, and is now, in eternal happiness, fulfilling
the reward of all good and faithful servants, at his
Master's side." '

It has been often remarked by visitors to the
Cathedral how curiously this tomb catches light
from all sides of the building, but this is undoubtedly
in the main due to the fact that the blue stone of
which it is chiefly composed responds immediately
to the purple and violet lights that fall from the
great East window.   On a summer day the blue of
the tomb seems almost opaque as though it were
made of blue glass, and the gilt on the background
of the screen and the brasses of the groins glitter
and sparkle like fire.

Brandon to-day, wrapped in his strange mood of

almost mystical triumph, felt as though he were, indeed, a reincarnation of the great Bishop.

As the 'Magnificat' proceeded, he seemed to enter into the very tomb and share in the Bishop's dust. 'I stood beside you,' he might almost have cried, 'when in that last savage encounter you faced them on the very steps of the altar, striking down two of them with your fists, falling at last, bleeding from a hundred wounds, but crying at the very end, "God is my right ! "'

As he stared across at the tomb, he seemed to see the great figure, deserted by all his terrified adherents, lying in his blood in the now deserted Cathedral ; he saw the coloured dusk creep forward and cover him. And then, in the darkness of the night, the two faithful servants who crept in and carried away his body to keep it in safety until his day should come again.

Born in 1100, Henry of Arden had been the first Bishop to give Polchester dignity and power. What William of Wykeham was to Winchester, that Henry of Arden was to the See of Polchester. Through all the wild days of the quarrel between Stephen and Matilda he had stood triumphant, yielding at last only to the mad overwhelming attacks of his private enemies. Of those he had had many. It had been said of him that 'he thought himself God—the proudest prelate on earth.' Proud he may have been, but he had loved his Bishopric. It was in his time that the Saint Margaret's Chapel had been built, through his energy that the two great Western Towers had risen, because of him that Polchester now could boast one of the richest revenues of any Cathedral in Europe. Men said that he had plundered, stolen the land of powerless men, himself headed forays against neighbouring villages and even castles. He had done it for the greater glory of God. They had been troublous times. It had been every man for himself. . . .

He had told his people that he was God's chief servant ; it was even said that he had once, in the plenitude of his power, cried that he was God Himself. . . .

His figure remained to this very day dominating Polchester, vast in stature, black-bearded, rejoicing in his physical strength. He could kill, they used to say, an ox with his fist. . . .

The 'Gloria' rang triumphantly up into the shadows of the nave. Brandon moved once more across to the Lectern. He read of the casting of the money-changers out of the Temple.

His voice quivered with pride and exultation so that Cobbett, who had acquired, after many years' practice, the gift of sleeping during the Lessons and Sermon with his eyes open, woke up with a start and wondered what was the matter.

Brandon's mood, when he was back in his own drawing-room, did not leave him ; it was rather intensified by the cosiness and security of his home. Lying back in his large arm-chair in front of the fire, his long legs stretched out before him, he could hear the rain beating on the window-panes and beyond that the murmur of the organ (Brockett, the organist, was practising, as he often did after Evensong).

The drawing-room was a long narrow one with many windows ; it was furnished in excellent taste. The carpet and the curtains and the dark blue coverings to the chairs were all a little faded, but this only gave them an additional dignity and repose. There were two large portraits of himself and Mrs. Brandon painted at the time of their marriage, some low white bookshelves, a large copy of 'Christ in the Temple '—plenty of space, flowers, light.

Mrs. Brandon was, at this time, a woman of forty-two, but she looked very much less than that. She was slight, dark, pale, quite undistinguished. She had large grey eyes that looked on to the ground when you spoke to her. She was considered a very shy woman, negative in every way. She agreed with everything that was said to her and seemed to have no opinions of her own. She was simply ' the wife of the Archdeacon.' Mrs. Combermere considered her a ' poor little fool.' She had no real friends in Polchester, and it made little difference to any gathering whether she were there or no. She had been only once known to lose her temper in public—once in the market-place she had seen a farmer beat his horse over the eyes. She had actually gone up to him and struck him. Afterwards she had said that ' she did not like to see animals ill-treated.' The Archdeacon had apologised for her, and no more had been said about it. The farmer had borne her no grudge.

She sat now at the little tea-table, her eyes screwed up over the serious question of giving the Archdeacon his tea exactly as he wanted it. Her whole mind was apparently engaged on this problem, and the Archdeacon did not care to-day that she did not answer his questions and support his comments because he was very, very happy, the whole of his being thrilling with security and success and innocent pride.

Joan Brandon came in. In appearance she was,

as Mrs. Sampson said, 'insignificant.' You would
not look at her twice any more than you would have
looked at her mother twice. Her figure was slight
and her legs (she was wearing long skirts this year
for the first time) too long. Her hair was dark
brown and her eyes dark brown. She had nice
rosy cheeks, but they were inclined to freckle. She
smiled a good deal and laughed, when in company,
more noisily than was proper. 'A bit of a tomboy,
I'm afraid,' was what one used to hear about her.
But she was not really a tomboy ; she moved quietly,
and her own bedroom was always neat and tidy.
She had very little pocket-money and only seldom
new clothes, not because the Archdeacon was mean,
but because Joan was so often forgotten and left
out of the scheme of things. It was surprising
that the only girl in the house should be so often
forgotten, but the Archdeacon did not care for girls,
and Mrs. Brandon did not appear to think very often
of any one except the Archdeacon. Falk, Joan's
brother, now at Oxford, when he was at home had
other things to do than consider Joan. She had
gone, ever since she was twelve, to the Polchester
High School for Girls, and there she was popular,
and might have made many friends, had it not been
that she could not invite her companions to her
home. Her father did not like ' noise in the house.'
She had been Captain of the Hockey team ; the
small girls in the school had all adored her. She
had left the place six months ago and had come
home to ' help her mother.' She had had, in honest
fact, six months' loneliness, although no one knew
that except herself. Her mother had not wanted
her help. There had been nothing for her to do,
and she had felt herself too young to venture into

the company of older girls in the town. She had been rather ' blue ' and had looked back on Seafield House, the High School, with longing, and then suddenly, one morning, for no very clear reason she had taken a new view of life. Everything seemed delightful and even thrilling, commonplace things that she had known all her days, the High Street, keeping her rooms tidy, spending or saving the minute monthly allowance, the Cathedral, the river. She was all in a moment aware that something very delightful would shortly occur. What it was she did not know, and she laughed at herself for imagining that anything extraordinary could ever happen to any one so commonplace as herself, but there the strange feeling was and it would not go away.

To-day, as always when her father was there, she came in very quietly, sat down near her mother, saw that she made no sort of interruption to the Archdeacon's flow of conversation. She found that he was in a good humour to-day, and she was glad of that because it would please her mother. She herself had a great interest in all that he said. She thought him a most wonderful man, and secretly was swollen with pride that she was his daughter. It did not hurt her at all that he never took any notice of her. Why should he? Nor did she ever feel jealous of Falk, her father's favourite. That seemed to her quite natural. She had the idea, now most thoroughly exploded but then universally held in Polchester, that women were greatly inferior to men. She did not read the more advanced novels written by Mme. Sarah Grand and Mrs. Lynn Linton. I am ashamed to say that her favourite authors were Miss Alcott and Miss Charlotte Mary Yonge. Moreover, she herself admired Falk extremely. He seemed to her a hero and always right in everything that he did.

Her father continued to talk, and behind the reverberation of his deep voice the roll of the organ like an approving echo could faintly be heard.

'There was a moment when I thought Foster was going to interfere. I've been against the garden-roller from the first—they've got one and what do they want another for? And, anyway, he thinks I meddle with the School's affairs too much. Who wants to meddle with the School's affairs? I'm sure they're nothing but a nuisance, but some one's got to prevent the place from going to wrack and ruin, and if they all leave it to me I can't very well refuse it, can I? Hey?'

'No, dear.'

'You see what I mean?'

'Yes, dear.'

'Well, then—' (As though Mrs. Brandon had just been overcome in an argument in which she'd shown the greatest obstinacy.) 'There you are. It would be false modesty to deny that I've got the Chapter more or less in my pocket. And why shouldn't I have? Has any one worked harder for this place and the Cathedral than I have?'

'No, dear.'

'Well, then. . . . There's this new fellow Ronder coming to-day. Don't know much about him, but he won't give much trouble, I expect—trouble in the way of delaying things, I mean. What we want is work done expeditiously. I've just about got that Chapter moving at last. Ten years' hard work. Deserve a V.C. or something. Hey?'

'Yes, dear, I'm sure you do.'

The Archdeacon gave one of his well-known

roars of laughter—a laugh famous throughout the county, a laugh described by his admirers as 'Homeric,' by his enemies as 'ear-splitting.' There was, however, enemies or no enemies, something sympathetic in that laugh, something boyish and simple and honest.

He suddenly pulled himself up, bringing his long legs close against his broad chest.

'No letter from Falk to-day, was there?'

'No, dear.'

'Humph. That's three weeks we haven't heard. Hope there's nothing wrong.'

'What could there be wrong, dear?'

'Nothing, of course. . . . Well, Joan, and what have you been doing with yourself all day?'

It was only in his most happy and resplendent moods that the Archdeacon held jocular conversations with his daughter. These conversations had been, in the past, moments of agony and terror to her, but since that morning when she had suddenly woken to a realisation of the marvellous possibilities in life her terror had left her. There were other people in the world besides her father. . . .

Nevertheless, a little, her agitation was still with her. She looked up at him, smiling.

'Oh, I don't know, father. . . . I went to the Library this morning to change the books for mother——'

'Novels, I suppose. No one ever reads anything but trash nowadays.'

'They hadn't anything that mother put down. They never have. Miss Milton sits on the new novels and keeps them for Mrs. Sampson and Mrs. Combermere.'

'Sits on them?'

' Yes—really sits on them. I saw her take one from under her skirt the other day when Mrs. Sampson asked for it. It was one that mother has wanted a long time.'

The Archdeacon was angry. ' I never heard anything so scandalous. I'll just see to that. What's the use of being on the Library Committee if that kind of thing happens ? That woman shall go.'

' Oh no ! father ! . . .'

' Of course she shall go. I never heard anything so dishonest in my life ! . . .'

Joan remembered that little conversation until the end of her life. And with reason.

The door was flung open. Some one came hurriedly in, then stopped, with a sudden arrested impulse, looking at them. It was Falk.

Falk was a very good-looking man—fair hair, light blue eyes like his father's, slim and straight and quite obviously fearless. It was that quality of courage that struck every one who saw him ; it was not only that he feared, it seemed, no one and nothing, but that he went a step further than that, spending his life in defying every one and everything, as a practised dueller might challenge every one he met in order to keep his play in practice. ' I don't like young Brandon,' Mrs. Sampson said. ' He snorts contempt at you. . . .'

He was only twenty-one, a contemptuous age. He looked as though he had been living in that house for weeks, although, as a fact, he had just driven up, after a long and tiresome journey, in an ancient cab through the pouring rain. The Archdeacon gazed at his son in a bewildered, confused amaze, as though he, a convinced sceptic, were suddenly

confronted, in broad daylight, with an undoubted
ghost.

' What's the matter ? ' he said at last.   ' Why
are you here ? '

' I've been sent down,' said Falk.

It was characteristic of the relationship in that
family that, at that statement, Mrs. Brandon and
Joan did not look at Falk but at the Archdeacon.

' Sent down ! '

' Yes, for ragging !   They wanted to do it last
term.'

' Sent down ! '   The Archdeacon shot to his
feet ; his voice suddenly lifted into a cry.   ' And
you have the impertinence to come here and tell
me !   You walk in as though nothing had
happened !   You walk in ! . . .'

' You're angry,' said Falk, smiling.   ' Of course
I knew you would be.   You might hear me out
first.   But I'll come along when I've unpacked
and you're a bit cooler.   I wanted some tea, but
I suppose that will have to wait.   You just listen,
father, and you'll find it isn't so bad.   Oxford's a
rotten place for any one who wants to be on his
own, and, anyway, you won't have to pay my bills
any more.'

Falk turned and went.

The Archdeacon, as he stood there, felt a dim
mysterious pain as though an adversary whom he
completely despised had found suddenly with his
weapon a joint in his armour.

CHAPTER II

THE train that brought Falk Brandon back to
Polchester brought also the Ronders—Frederick
Ronder, newly Canon of Polchester, and his aunt,
Miss Alice Ronder. About them the station
gathered in a black cloud, dirty, obscure, lit by
flashes of light and flame, shaken with screams,
rumblings, the crashing of carriage against carriage,
the rattle of cab-wheels on the cobbles outside.
To-day also there was the hiss and scatter of the
rain upon the glass roof. The Ronders stood,
not bewildered, for that they never were, but
thinking what would be best. The new Canon
was a round man, round-shouldered, round-faced,
round-stomached, round-legged. A fair height, he
was not ludicrous, but it seemed that if you laid
him down he would roll naturally, still smiling, to
the farthest end of the station. He wore large,
very round spectacles. His black clerical coat and
trousers and hat were scrupulously clean and smartly
cut. He was not a dandy, but he was not shabby.
He smiled a great deal, not nervously as curates
are supposed to smile, not effusively, but simply
with geniality. His aunt was a contrast, thin,
straight, stiff white collar, little black bow-tie,

coat like a man's, skirt with no nonsense about it. No nonsense about her anywhere. She was not unamiable, perhaps, but business came first.

'Well, what do we do?' he asked.

'We collect our bags and find the cab,' she answered briskly.

They found their bags, and there were a great many of them ; Miss Ronder, having seen that they were all there and that there was no nonsense about the porter, moved off to the barrier followed by her nephew.

As they came into the station square, all smelling of hay and the rain, the deluge slowly withdrew its forces, recalling them gradually so that the drops whispered now, patter-patter—pit-pit. A pigeon hovered down and pecked at the cobbles. Faint colour threaded the thick blotting-paper grey.

Old Fawcett himself had come to the station to meet them. Why had he felt it to be an occasion? God only knows. A new Canon was nothing to him. He very seldom now, being over eighty, with a strange 'wormy' pain in his left ear, took his horses out himself. He saved his money and counted it over by his fireside to see that his old woman didn't get any of it. He hated his old woman, and in a vaguely superstitious, thoroughly Glebeshire fashion half-believed that she had cast a spell over him and was really responsible for his 'wormy' ear.

Why had he come? He didn't himself know. Perhaps Ronder was going to be of importance in the place ; he had come from London and they all had money in London. He licked his purple protruding lips greedily as he saw the generous man. Yes, kindly and generous he looked. . . .

They got into the musty cab and rattled away over the cobbles.

' I hope Mrs. Clay got the telegram all right.' Miss Ronder's thin bosom was a little agitated beneath its white waistcoat. ' You'll never forgive me if things aren't looking as though we'd lived in the place for months.'

Alice Ronder was over sixty and as active as a woman of forty. Ronder looked at her and laughed.

' Never forgive you ! What words ! Do I ever cherish grievances ? Never . . . but I do like to be comfortable.'

' Well, everything was all right a week ago. I've slaved at the place, as you know, and Mrs. Clay's a jewel—but she complains of the Polchester maids—says there isn't one that's any good. Oh, I want my tea, I want my tea ! '

They were climbing up from the market-place into the High Street. Ronder looked about him with genial curiosity.

' Very nice,' he said ; ' I believe I can be comfortable here.'

' If you aren't comfortable you certainly won't stay,' she answered him sharply.

' Then I *must* be comfortable,' he replied, laughing.

He laughed a great deal, but absent-mindedly, as though his thoughts were elsewhere. It would have been interesting to a student of human nature to have been there and watched him as he sat back in the cab, looking through the window, indeed, but seeing apparently nothing. He seemed to be gazing through his round spectacles very short-sightedly, his eyes screwed up and dim. His fat soft hands were planted solidly on his thick knees.

The observer would have been interested because he would soon have realised that Ronder saw everything ; nothing, however insignificant, escaped him, but he seemed to see with his brain as though he had learnt the trick of forcing it to some new function that did not properly belong to it. The broad white forehead under the soft black clerical hat was smooth, unwrinkled, mild and calm. . . . He had trained it to be so.

The High Street was like any High Street of a small Cathedral town in the early evening. The pavements were sleek and shiny after the rain ; people were walking with the air of being unusually pleased with the world, always the human expression when the storms have withdrawn and there is peace and colour in the sky. There were lights behind the solemn panes of Bennett's the bookseller's, that fine shop whose first master had seen Sir Walter Scott in London and spoken to Byron. In his window were rows of the classics in calf and first editions of the Surtees books and *Dr. Syntax*. At the very top of the High Street was Mellock's the pastry-cook's, gay with its gas, rich with its famous saffron buns, its still more famous gingerbread cake, and, most famous of all, its lemon biscuits. Even as the Ronders' cab paused for a moment before it turned to pass under the dark Arden Gate on to the asphalt of the Precincts, the great Mrs. Mellock herself, round and rubicund, came to the door and looked about her at the weather. An errand-boy passed, whistling, down the hill, a stiff military-looking gentleman with white moustaches mounted majestically the steps of the

Conservative Club; then they rattled under the black archway, echoed for a moment on the noisy cobbles, then slipped into the quiet solemnity of the Precincts asphalt. It was Brandon who had insisted on the asphalt. Old residents had complained that to take away the cobbles would be to rid the Precincts of all its atmosphere.

'I don't care about atmosphere,' said the Archdeacon, 'I want to sleep at night.'

Very quiet here; not a sound penetrated. The Cathedral was a huge shadow above its darkened lawns; not a human soul was to be seen.

The cab stopped with a jerk at Number Eight. The bell was rung by old Fawcett, who stood on the top step looking down at Ronder and wondering how much he dared to ask him. Ask him too much now and perhaps he would not deal with him in the future. Moreover, although the man wore large spectacles and was fat he was probably not a fool. . . . Fawcett could not tell why he was so sure, but there was something. . . .

Mrs. Clay was at the door, smiling and ordering a small frightened girl to 'hurry up now.' Miss Ronder disappeared into the house. Ronder stood for a moment looking about him as though he were a spy in enemy country and must let nothing escape him.

'Whose is that big place there?' he asked Fawcett, pointing to a house that stood by itself at the farther corner of the Precincts.

'Archdeacon Brandon's, sir.'

'Oh! . . .' Ronder mounted the steps. 'Good night,' he said to Fawcett. 'Mrs. Clay, pay the cabman, please.'

The Ronders had taken this house a month ago;

for two months before that it had stood desolate, wisps of paper and straw blowing about it, its ' To let ' notice creaking and screaming in every wind. The Hon. Mrs. Pentecoste, an eccentric old lady, had lived there for many years, and had died in the middle of a game of patience ; her worn and tattered furniture had been sold at auction, and the house had remained unlet for a considerable period because people in the town said that the ghost of Mrs. Pentecoste's cat (a famous blue Persian) walked there. The Ronders cared nothing for ghosts ; the house was exactly what they wanted. It had two panelled rooms, two powder-closets, and a little walled garden at the back with fruit trees.

It was quite wonderful what Miss Ronder had done in a month ; she had abandoned Eaton Square for a week, worked in the Polchester house like a slave, then retired back to Eaton Square again, leaving Mrs. Clay, her aide-de-camp, to manage the rest. Mrs. Clay had managed very well. She would not have been in the service of the Ronders for nearly fifteen years had she not had a gift for managing. . . .

Ronder, washed and brushed, came down to tea, looked about him, and saw that all was good.

' I congratulate you, Aunt Alice,' he said— ' excellent ! '

Miss Ronder very slightly flushed.

' There are a lot of things still to be done,' she said ; nevertheless she was immensely pleased.

The drawing-room was charming. The stencilled walls, the cushions of the chairs, the cover of a gate-legged table, the curtains of the mullioned windows were of a warm dark blue. And whatever in the room was not blue seemed to be white,

or wood in its natural colour, or polished brass.
Books ran round the room in low white book-cases.
In one corner a pure white Hermes stood on a
pedestal with tiny wings outspread. There was
only one picture, an excellent copy of ' Rembrandt's
mother.' The windows looked out to the garden,
now veiled by the dusk of evening. Tea was on
a little table close to the white tiled fireplace. A
little square brass clock chimed the half-hour as
Ronder came in.

' I suppose Ellen will be over,' Ronder said.
He drank in the details of the room with a quite
sensual pleasure. He went over to the Hermes
and lifted it, holding it for a moment in his podgy
hands.

' You beauty ! ' he whispered aloud. He put
it back, turned round to his aunt.

' Of course Ellen will be over,' he repeated.

' Of course,' Miss Ronder repeated, picking up
the old square black lacquer tea-caddy and peering
into it.

He picked up the books on the table—two
novels, *Sentimental Tommy*, by J. M. Barrie, and
Sir George Tressady, by Mrs. Humphry Ward,
Mr. Swinburne's *Tale of Balen*, and *The Works of
Max Beerbohm*. Last of all, Leslie Stephen's *Social
Rights and Duties*.

He looked at them all, with their light yellow
Mudie labels, their fresh bindings, then, slowly
and very carefully, put them back on the table.

He always handled books as though they were
human beings.

He came and sat down by the fire.

' I won't see over the place until to-morrow,' he
said. ' What have you done about the other books ? '

'The book-cases are in. It's the best room in the house. Looks over the river and gets most of the light. The books are as you packed them. I haven't dared touch them. In fact, I've left that room entirely for you to arrange.'

'Well,' he said, 'if you've done the rest of this house as well as this room, you'll do. It's jolly—it really is. I'm going to like this place.'

'And you hated the very idea of it.'

'I hated the discomfort there'd be before we settled in. But the settling in is going to be easier than I thought. Of course we don't know yet how the land lies. Ellen will tell us.'

They were silent for a little. Then he looked at her with a puzzled, half-humorous, half-ironical glance.

'It's a bit of a blow to you, Aunt Alice, burying yourself down here. London was the breath of your nostrils. What did you come for? Love of me?'

She looked steadily back at him.

'Not love exactly. Curiosity, perhaps. I want to see at first hand what you'll do. You're the most interesting human being I've ever met, and that isn't prejudice. Aunts do not, as a rule, find their nephews interesting. And what have you come here for? I assure you I haven't the least idea.'

The door was opened by Mrs. Clay.

'Miss Stiles,' she said.

Miss Stiles, who came in, was not handsome. She was large and fat, with a round red face like a sun, and she wore colours too bright for her size. She had a slow soft voice like the melancholy moo of a cow. She was not a bad woman, but, temperamentally, was made unhappy by the success or good fortune of others. Were you in distress, she would love you, cherish you, never abandon you. She would share her last penny with you, run to the end of the world for you, defend you before the whole of humanity. Were you, however, in robust health, she would hint to every one of a possible cancer ; were you popular, it would worry her terribly and she would discover a thousand faults in your character ; were you successful in your work, she would pray for your approaching failure lest you should become arrogant. She gossiped without cessation, and always, as it were, to restore the proper balance of the world, to pull down the mighty from their high places, to lift the humble only that they in their turn might be pulled down. She played fluently and execrably on the piano. She spent her day in running from house to house.

She had independent means, lived four months of the year in Polchester (she had been born there and her family had been known there for many generations before her), four months in London, and the rest of the year abroad. She had met Alice Ronder in London and attached herself to her. She liked the Ronders because they never boasted of their successes, because Alice had a weak heart, because Ronder, who knew her character, half-humorously deprecated his talents, which were, as he knew well enough, no mean ones. She bored Alice Ronder, but Ronder found her useful. She told him a great deal that he wanted to know, and, although she was never accurate in her information, he could separate the wheat from the chaff. She was a walking mischief-maker, but meant no harm to a living soul. She prided herself on her honesty, on saying exactly what she thought to every one. She was kindness itself to her servants, who adored her, as did railway-porters, cabmen and newspaper men. She over-tipped wherever she went because 'she could not bear not to be liked.' In our Polchester world she was an important factor. She was always the first to hear any piece of news in our town, and she gave it a wrong twist just as fast as she could.

She was really delighted to see the Ronders, and told them so with many assurances of affection, but she was a little distressed to find the room so neat and settled. She would have preferred them to be 'in a thorough mess' and badly in need of her help.

'My dear Alice, how quick you've been ! How clever you are ! At the same time I think you'll find there's a good deal to arrange still. The Polchester girls are so slow and always breaking things. I suppose some things have been smashed in the move—nothing very valuable, I hope.'

'Lots of things, Ellen,' said Ronder, laughing. 'We've had the most awful time and badly need your help. It's only this room that Aunt Alice got straight—just to have something to show, you know. And our journey down ! I can't tell you what it was, hardly room to breathe and coming up here in the rain ! '

'Oh, you poor things ! What a welcome to Polchester ! You must simply have hated the look of the whole place. *Such* a bad introduction, and everything looking as gloomy and depressing as possible. I expect you wished yourselves well out of it. I don't wonder you're depressed. I hope you're not feeling your heart, Alice dear.'

'Well, I am a little,' acknowledged Miss Ronder. 'But I shall go to bed early and get a good night.'

'You poor dear! I was afraid you'd be absolutely done up. Now, you're *not* to get up in the morning and I'll run about and do your shopping for you. I *insist*. How's Mrs. Clay?'

'A little grumpy at having so much to do,' said Ronder, 'but she'll get over it.'

'I'm afraid she's a little ill-tempered at times,' said Miss Stiles with satisfaction. 'I thought when I came in that she looked out of sorts. Troubles never come singly, of course.'

All was well now and Miss Stiles completely satisfied. She admired the room and the Hermes, and prophesied that, after a week or two, they would probably find things not so bad after all. She drank several cups of tea and passed on to general conversation. It was obvious, very soon, that she was bursting with a piece of news.

'I can see, Ellen,' said Ronder, humorously observing her, 'that you're longing to tell us something.'

'Well, it is interesting. What do you think? Falk Brandon has been sent down from Oxford for misbehaviour.'

'And who is Falk Brandon?' asked Ronder.

'The Archdeacon's son. His only boy. I've told you about Archdeacon Brandon many times. He thinks he runs the town and has been terribly above himself for a long while. This will pull him down a little. I must say, although I don't want to be uncharitable, that I'm glad of it. It's too absurd the way that he's been having everything his own way here. All the Canons are over ninety and simply give in to him about everything.'

'When did this happen?'

'Oh, it's only just happened. He arrived by

your train.   I saw young George Lascelles as I was
on my way up to you.   He met him at the station—
Falk, I mean—and he didn't pretend to disguise it.
George said " Hullo, Brandon, what are you doing
here ? " and Falk said " Oh, I've been sent down "—
just like that.   Didn't pretend to disguise it.   He's
always been as brazen as anything.   He'll give his
father a lot of trouble before he's done.'

' There's nothing very terrible,' said Ronder,
laughing, ' in being sent down from Oxford.   I've
known plenty of good fellows who were.'

Miss Stiles looked annoyed.   ' Oh, but you
don't know.   It will be terrible for his father.   He's
the proudest man in England.   Some people call it
conceit, but, however that may be, he thinks there's
nothing like his family.   Even poor Mrs. Brandon
he's proud of when she isn't there.   It will be awful
for him that every one should know.'

Ronder said nothing.

' You know,' said Miss Stiles, who felt that her
news had fallen flat, ' you'll have to fight him or
give in to him.   There's no other way here.   I hope
you'll fight him.'

' I ? ' said Ronder.   ' Why, I never fight anybody.   I'm much too lazy.'

' Then you'll never be comfortable here, that's
all.   He can't bear being crossed.   He must have
his way about everything.   If the Bishop weren't so
old and the Dean so stupid. . . . What we want here
is a little life in the place.'

' You needn't look to us for that, Ellen,' said
Ronder.   ' We've come here to rest——

' Peace, perfect peace. . . .'

' I don't believe you,' said Miss Stiles, tossing her
head.   ' I'd be disappointed to think it of you.'

Alice Ronder gave her nephew a curious look, half of amusement, half of expectation.

'It's quite true, Ellen,' she said. 'Now, if you've finished your tea, come and look at the rest of the house.'

CHAPTER III

ONE OF JOAN'S DAYS

I FIND it difficult now to realise how apart from the life of the world Polchester was in those days. Even now, when the War has shaken up and jostled together every small village in Great Britain, Polchester still has some shreds of its isolation left to it ; but then——why, it might have been a walled-in fortress of mediaeval times, for all its connection with the outside world !

This isolation was quite deliberately maintained. I don't mean, of course, that Mrs. Combermere and Brandon and old Bentinck-Major and Mrs. Sampson said to themselves in so many words, ' We will keep this to ourselves and defend its walls against every new invader, every new idea, new custom, new impulse. We will all be butchered rather than allow one old form, tradition, superstition to go ! ' It was not as conscious as that, but in effect it was that that it came to. And they were wonderfully assisted by circumstances. It is true that the main line ran through Polchester from Drymouth, but its travellers were hurrying south, and only a few trippers, a few Americans, a few sentimentalists stayed to see the Cathedral ; and those who stayed found ' The Bull ' an impossibly inconvenient and uncomfortable hostelry and did not come again. It is true that even then, in 1897, there were many agitations by sharp business men like Crosbie and John Allen, Croppet and Fred Barnstaple, to make the place more widely known, more commercially attractive. It was not until later that the golf course was laid out and the St. Leath Hotel rose on Pol Hill. But other things were tried—steamers on the Pol, char-à-bancs to various places of local interest, and so on—but, at this time, all these efforts failed. The Cathedral was too strong for them, above all Brandon and Mrs. Combermere were too strong for them. Nothing was done to encourage strangers ; I shouldn't wonder if Mrs. Combermere didn't pay old Jolliffe of ' The Bull ' so much a year to keep his hotel inconvenient and insanitary. The men on the Town Council were for the most part like the Canons, aged and conservative. It is true that it was in 1897 that Barnstaple was elected Mayor, but without Ronder I doubt whether even he would have been able to do very much.

The town then revolved, so to speak, entirely on its own axis ; it revolved between the two great events of the year, the summer Polchester Fair, the winter County Ball, and those two great affairs were conducted, in every detail and particular, as they had been conducted a hundred years before. I find it strange, writing from the angle of to-day, to conceive it possible that so short a time ago anything in England could have been so conservative. I myself was only thirteen years of age when Ronder came to our town, and saw all grown figures with the exaggerated colour and romance that local inquisitive age bestows. About my own contemporaries, young Jeremy Cole for instance, there was

no colour at all, but the older figures were strange—
gigantic, almost mythological. Mrs. Combermere,
the Dean, the Archdeacon, Mrs. Sampson, Canon
Ronder, moved about the town, to my young eyes,
like gods and goddesses, and it was not until after
my return to Polchester at the end of my first Cambridge year that I saw clearly how small a town it
was and how tiny the figures in it.

Joan Brandon thought her father a marvellous
man, as I have already said, but she had seen him
too often lose his temper, too often snub her mother,
too often be upset by trivial and unimportant details,
to conceive him romantically. Falk, her brother,
was romantic to her because she had seen so much
less of him ; her father she knew too well. For
some time after Falk's return from Oxford nothing
happened. Joan did not know what exactly she
had expected to happen, but she had an uneasy
sense that more was going on behind the scenes
than she knew.

The Archdeacon did not speak to Falk unless he
were compelled, but Falk did not seem to mind this
in the least. His handsome defiant face flashed
scorn at the whole family.

He was out of the house most of the day, came
down to breakfast when every one else had finished,
and often was not present at dinner in the evening.
The Archdeacon had said that breakfast was not to
be kept for him, but nevertheless breakfast was there,
on the table, however late he was. The cook and,
indeed, all the servants adored him because, I
suppose, he had no sense of class-difference at all
and laughed and joked with any one if he was
in a good temper. All these first days he spoke
scarcely one word to Joan ; it was as though

the whole family were in his black books for some disgraceful act — they were the guilty ones and not he.

Joan blamed herself for feeling so light-hearted and gay during this family crisis, but she could not help it. A very short time ago the knowledge that battle was engaged in the very heart of the house would have made her miserable and apprehensive, but now it seemed to be all outside her and unconnected with her as though she had a life of her own that no one could touch. Her courage seemed to grow with every half-hour of her life. Some months passed, and then one morning she came into the drawing-room and found her mother rather bewildered and distressed.

' Oh dear, I really don't know what to do ! ' said her mother.

It was so seldom that Joan was appealed to for advice that her heart now beat with pride.

' What's the matter, mother ? ' she asked, trying to look dignified and unconcerned.

Mrs. Brandon looked at her with a frightened and startled look as though she had been speaking to herself and had not wished to be overheard.

' Oh, Joan ! . . . I didn't know that you were there ! '

' What's the matter ?　Is it anything I can help about ? '

' No, dear, nothing . . . really I didn't know that you were there.'

' No, but you must let me help, mother.' Joan marvelled at her own boldness as she spoke.

' It's nothing you can do, dear.'

' But it's sure to be something I can do.　Do you know that I've been home for months and

months simply with the idea of helping you, and I'm
never allowed to do anything ? '

'Really, Joan—I don't think that's quite the
way to speak.'

'No, but, mother, it's true. I *want* to help. I'm
grown up. I'm going to dinner at the Castle, and
I *must* help you, or—or—I shall go away and earn
my own living ! '

This last was so startling and fantastic that
both Joan and her mother stared at one another in
a kind of horrified amazement.

'No, I didn't mean that, of course,' Joan said,
hurriedly recovering herself. 'But you must see
that I must have some work to do.'

'I don't know what your father would say,'
said Mrs. Brandon, still bewildered.

'Oh, never mind father,' said Joan quickly;
'this is a matter just between you and me. I'm
here to help you, and you must let me do something.
Now, what's the trouble to-day ? '

'I don't know, dear. There's no trouble exactly.
Things are so difficult just now. The fact is that
I promised to go to tea with Miss Burnett this afternoon and now your father wants me to go with
him to the Deanery. So provoking ! Miss Burnett
caught me in the street, where it's always so difficult
to think of excuses.'

'Let me go to Miss Burnett's instead,' said Joan.
'It's quite time I took on some of the calling for
you. I've never seen Mr. Morris, and I hear he's
very nice.'

'Very well, dear,' said Mrs. Brandon, suddenly
beginning, as her way was when there was any
real opposition, to capitulate on all sides at once.
'Suppose you do go, dear. I'm sure it's very kind

of you. And you might take those books back to
the Circulating Library as well. It's Market-Day.
Are you sure you won't mind the horses and cows
and dogs ? '

Joan laughed. ' I believe you think I'm still
five years old, mother. That's splendid. I'll start
off after lunch.'

Joan went up to her room, elated. Truly, this
was a great step forward. It occurred to her
on further reflection that something very serious
indeed must be going on behind the scenes to
cause her mother to give in so quickly. She sat
on her old faded rocking-chair, her hands crossed
behind her head, thinking it all out. Did she once
begin calling on her own account she was grown-up
indeed. What would these Morrises be like ?

She found now that she was beginning to be a
little frightened. Mr. Morris was the new Rector
of St. James', the little church over by the cattle
market. He had not been in Polchester very long,
and was said to be a shy timid man, but a good
preacher. He was a widower, and his sister-in-law
kept house for him. Joan considered further on the
great importance of these concessions ; it made all
the difference to everything. She was now to have
a life of her own, and every kind of adventure and
romance was possible for her. She was suddenly
so happy that she sprang up and did a little dance
round her room, a sort of polka, that became so
vehement that the pictures and the little rickety
table rattled.

' I'll be so grown-up at the Morrises' this afternoon that they'll think I've been calling for years,'
she said to herself.

She had need of all her courage and optimism at

luncheon, for it was a gloomy meal. Only her father and mother were present. They were all very silent.

After lunch she went upstairs, put on her hat and coat, picked up the three Library books, and started off. It was a sunny day, with shadows chasing one another across the Cathedral green. There was, as there so often is in Polchester, a smell of the sea in the air, cold and invigorating. She paused for a moment and looked across at the Cathedral. She did not know why, but she had been always afraid of the Cathedral. She had never loved it, and had always wished that they could go on Sundays to some little church like St. James'.

For most of her conscious life the Cathedral had hung over her with its dark menacing shadow, forbidding her, as it seemed to her, to be gay or happy or careless. To-day the thought suddenly came to her, 'That place is going to do us harm. I hate it,' and for a moment she was depressed and uneasy; but when she came out from the Arden Gate and saw the High Street all shining with the sun, running down the hill into glittering distance, she was gloriously cheerful once more. There the second wonderful thing that day happened to her. She had taken scarcely a step down the hill when she came upon Mrs. Sampson. There was nothing wonderful about that ; Mrs. Sampson, being the wife of a Dean who was much more retiring than he should be, was to be seen in public at all times and seasons, having to do, as it were, the work of two rather than one. No, the wonderful thing was that Joan suddenly realised that her terror of Mrs. Sampson—a terror that had always been a real thorn in her flesh—was completely gone It was as though a charm, an Abracadabra, had been whispered over Mrs. Sampson and she had been changed immediately into a rabbit. It had never been Mrs. Sampson's fault that she was alarming to the young. She was a good woman, but she was cursed with two sad burdens—a desperate shyness and a series, unrelenting, unmitigating, mysterious, desperate, of nervous headaches.

Her headaches were a feature of Polchester life, and those who were old enough to understand pitied her and offered her many remedies. But the young cannot be expected to realise that there can be anything physically wrong with the old, and Mrs. Sampson's sharpness of manner, her terrifying habit of rapping out a ' Yes ' or a ' No,' her gloomy view of boisterous habits and healthy appetites, made her one most truly to be avoided. Before to-day Joan would have willingly walked a mile out of her way to escape her ; to-day she only saw a nervous, pale-faced little woman in an ill-fitting blue dress, for whom she could not be anything but sorry.

' Good morning, Mrs. Sampson.'

' Good morning, Joan.'

' Isn't it a nice day ? '

' It's cold, I think. Is your mother well ? '

' Very well, thank you.'

' Give her my love.'

' I will, Mrs. Sampson.'

' Good-bye.'

' Good-bye.'

Mrs. Sampson's nose, that would take on a blue colour on a cold day, quivered, her thin mouth shut with a snap, and she was gone.

' But I wasn't afraid of her ! ' She was almost

frightened at this new spirit that had come to her, and, feeling rather that in another moment she would be punished for her piratical audacity, she turned up the steps into the Circulating Library.

It was the custom in those days that far away from the dust of the grimy shelves, in the very middle of the room, there was a table with all the latest works of fiction in their gaudy bindings, a few volumes of poetry and a few memoirs. Close to this table Miss Milton sat, wrapped, in the warmest weather, in a thick shawl and knitting endless stockings. She hated children, myself in particular. She was also a Snob of the Snobs, and thanked God on her knees every night for Lady St. Leath, Mrs. Combermere and Mrs. Sampson, by whose graces she was left in her present position.

Joan was still too near childhood to be considered very seriously, and it was well known that her father did not take her very seriously either. She was always, therefore, on the rare occasions when she entered the Library, snubbed by Miss Milton. It must be confessed that to-day, in spite of her success with Mrs. Sampson, she was nervous. She was nervous partly because she hated Miss Milton's red-rimmed eyes, and never looked at them if she could help it, but, in the main, because she knew that her mother was returning the Library books too quickly, and had, moreover, insisted that she should ask for Mr. Barrie's *Sentimental Tommy* and Mr. Seton Merriman's *The Sowers*, both of them books that had been asked for for weeks and as steadily and persistently refused.

Joan knew what Miss Milton would say, ' That they might be in next week, but that she couldn't be sure.' Was Joan strong enough now, in her new-found glory, to fight for them ?   She did not know.

She advanced to the table smiling.   Miss Milton did not look up, but continued to knit one of her horrible stockings.

' Good-morning, Miss Milton. Mother has sent back these books.   They were not quite what she wanted.'

' I'm sorry for that.'   Miss Milton took the books into her chilblained protection.   ' It's a little difficult, I must say, to know what Mrs. Brandon prefers.'

' Well, there's *Sentimental Tommy*,' began Joan.

But Miss Milton was an old general.

' Oh, that's out, I'm afraid.   Now, here's a sweetly pretty book—*Roger Vanbrugh's Wife*, by Adeline Sergeant.   It's only just out. . . .'

' Or there's *The Sowers*,' said Joan, caught against her will by the red-rimmed eyes and staring at them.

' Oh, that's out, I'm afraid.   There are several books here—— '

' You promised mother,' said Joan, ' that she should have *Sentimental Tommy* this week.   You promised her a month ago.   It's about time that mother had a book that she cares for.'

' Really,' said Miss Milton, wide-eyed at Joan's audacity.   ' You seem to be charging me with some remissness, Miss Brandon.   If you have any complaint, I'm sure the Library Committee will attend to it.   It's to them I have to answer.   When the book is in you shall have it.   I can promise no more.   I am only human.'

' You have said that now for three months,' said Joan, beginning, to her own surprised delight, to be angry. 'Surely the last reader hasn't been three months over it. I thought subscribers were only allowed to keep a book a week.'

Miss Milton's crimson colouring turned to a deep purple.

'The book is out,' she said. 'Both books are out. They are in great demand. I have no more to say.'

The Library door opened, and a young man came in. Joan was still too young to wish for scenes in public. She must give up the battle for to-day. When, however, she saw who it was, she blushed. It was young Lord St. Leath—Johnny St. Leath, as he was known to his familiars, who were many and of all sorts and conditions. Joan hated herself for blushing, especially before the odious Miss Milton, but there was a reason. One day in last October after morning service Joan and her mother had waited in the Cloisters to avoid a shower of rain. St. Leath had also waited and very pleasantly had talked to them both. There was nothing very alarming in this, but as the rain cleared and Mrs. Brandon had moved forward across the Green, he had suddenly, with a confusion that had seemed to her charming, asked Joan whether one day they mightn't meet again. He had given her one look straight in the eyes, tried to say something more, failed, and turned away down the Cloisters.

Joan had never before been asked by any young man to meet him again. She had told herself that this was nothing and the merest, most obvious politeness ; nevertheless the look that he had given her remained.

Now, as she saw him advancing towards her, there was the thought, was it not on that very morning that her new courage and self-confidence had come to her? The thought was so absurd that she flung it at Miss Milton. But the blush remained.

Johnny was an ungainly young man, with a red face, freckles, a large mouth, and a bull-terrier—a conventional British type, I suppose, saved, nevertheless, from conventionality by his affection for his three plain sisters, his determination to see things as they were, and his sense of humour, the last of these something quite his own, and always appearing in unexpected places. The bull-terrier, in spite of the notice on the Library door that no dogs were admitted, advanced breathlessly and dribbling with excitement for Miss Milton's large black felt slippers.

'Here, Andrew, old man. Heel! Heel!' said Johnny. Andrew, however, quite naturally concluded that this was only an approval of his intentions, and there might have followed an awkward scene had his master not caught him by the collar and held him suspended in mid-air, to his own indignant surprise and astonishment.

Joan laughed, and Miss Milton, quivering between indignation, fear and snobbery, dropped the stocking that she was knitting.

Andrew burst from his master's clutches, rushed the stocking into the farthest recesses of the Library, and proceeded there to enjoy it.

Johnny apologised.

'Oh, it's quite all right, Lord St. Leath,' said Miss Milton. 'What a fine animal!'

'Yes, he is,' said Johnny, rescuing the stocking. 'He's as strong as Lucifer. Here, Andrew, you devil, I'll break every bone in your body.'

During this little scene Johnny had smiled at Joan, and in so pleasant a way that she was compelled to smile back at him.

'How do you do, Miss Brandon?' He had recalled Andrew now, and the dog was slobbering happily at his feet. 'Jolly day, isn't it?'

'Yes,' said Joan, and stood there awkwardly, feeling that she ought to go but not knowing quite how to do so. He also seemed embarrassed, and turned abruptly to Miss Milton.

'I say, look here. . . . Mother asked me to come in and get that book you promised her. What's the name of the thing? . . . I've got it written down.'

He fumbled in his pocket and produced a bit of paper.

'Here it is. *Sentimental Tommy*, by a man called Barrie. Silly name, but mother's always reading the most awful stuff.'

Joan turned towards Miss Milton.

'How funny!' she said. 'That's the book I've just been asking for. It's out.'

Miss Milton's face was a curious purple.

'Well, that's odd,' said Johnny. 'Mother told me that you'd sent her a line to say it was in whenever she sent for it.'

'It's been out three months,' said Joan, staring now straight into Miss Milton's angry eyes.

'I've been keeping . . .' said Miss Milton. 'That is, there's a special copy. . . . Lady St. Leath specially asked——'

'Is it in, or isn't it?' asked Johnny.

'There *is* a copy, Lord St. Leath——' With confused fingers Miss Milton searched in a drawer. She produced the book.

'You told me,' said Joan, forgetting now in her anger St. Leath and all the world, 'that there wouldn't be a copy for weeks. If you'd told me you were keeping one for Lady St. Leath, that would have been different. You shouldn't have told me a lie.'

'Do you mean to say,' said Johnny, opening his eyes very widely indeed, 'that you refused this copy to Miss Brandon ?'

'Certainly,' said Miss Milton, breathing very hard as though she had been running a long distance. 'I was keeping it for your mother.'

'Well, I'm damned !' said Johnny. 'I beg your pardon, Miss Brandon, . . . but I never heard such a thing. Does my mother pay a larger subscription than other people ?'

'Certainly not.'

'Then what right had you to tell Miss Brandon a lie ?'

Miss Milton, in spite of long training in the kind of warfare attaching, of necessity, to Circulating Libraries, was very near to tears—also murder. She would have been delighted to pierce Joan's heart with a bright stiletto, had such a weapon been handy. She saw the softest, easiest, idlest job in the world slipping out of her fingers ; she saw herself, a desolate and haggard virgin, begging her bread on the Polchester streets. She saw . . . but never mind her visions. They were terrible ones. She had recourse to her only defence.

'If I have misunderstood my duty,' she said in a trembling voice, 'there is the Library Committee.'

'Oh, never mind,' said Joan whose anger had disappeared. 'It doesn't matter a bit. We'll have the book after Lady St. Leath.'

'Indeed you won't,' said Johnny, seizing the volume and forcing it upon Joan. 'Mother can wait. I never heard of such a thing.' He turned fiercely upon Miss Milton. 'My mother shall know exactly what has happened. I'm sure she'd be horrified if she understood that you were keeping books from other subscribers in order that she might have them. . . . Good afternoon.'

He strode from the room. At the door he paused.

'Can I—— Shall we—— Are you going down the High Street, Miss Brandon ?'

'Yes,' said Joan. They went out of the room and down the Library steps together.

In the shiny, sunny street they paused. The dark cobwebs of the Library hung behind Joan's consciousness like the sudden breaking of a mischievous spell.

She was so happy that she could have embraced Andrew, who was, however, already occupied with the distant aura of a white poodle on the other side of the street.

Johnny was driven by the impulse of his indignation down the hill. Joan, rather breathlessly, followed him.

'I say !' said Johnny. 'Did you ever hear of such a woman ! She ought to be poisoned. She ought indeed. No, poisoning's too good for her. Hung, drawn and quartered. That's what she ought to be. She'll get into trouble over that.'

'Oh no,' said Joan. 'Please, Lord St. Leath, don't say any more about it. She has a difficult time, I expect, everybody wanting the same books. After all, a promise is a promise.'

'But she'd promised your mother——'

'No, she never really did. She always said that

it would be in in a day or two. She never properly promised. . I expect we'd have had it next.'

' The snob, the rotten snob ! ' Johnny paused and raised his stick. ' I hate women like that. No, she's not doing her job properly. She oughtn't to be there.'

So swift had been their descent that they arrived in a moment at the market.

Because to-day was market-day there was a fine noise, confusion and splendour — carts rattling in and out, sheep and cows driven hither and thither, the wooden stalls bright with flowers and vegetables, the dim arcades looming behind the square filled with mysterious riches. They could not talk very much here, and Joan was glad. She was too deeply excited to talk. At one moment St. Leath took her arm to guide her past a confused mob of bewildered sheep. The Glebeshire peasant on marketing-day has plenty of conversation. Old wrinkled women, stout red-faced farmers, boys and girls all shouted together, and above the scene the light driving clouds flung their transparent shadows, like weaving shuttles across the sun.

' Oh, do let's stop here a moment,' said Joan, peering into one of the arcades. ' I've always loved this one all my life. I've never been able to resist it.'

This was the Toy Arcade, now, I'm afraid, gone the way of so many other romantic things. It had been to all of us the most wonderful spot in Polchester from the very earliest days, this partly because of the toys themselves, partly because it was the densest and darkest of all the Arcades, never utterly to be pierced by our youthful eyes, partly because only two doors away were the sinister rooms of Mr. Dawson, the dentist. Here not only was there every kind of toy—dolls, soldiers, horses, carts, games, tops, hoops, dogs, elephants—but also sweets —chocolates, jujubes, caramels, and the best sweet in the whole world, the Polchester Bull's-eye.

They went in together. Mrs. Magnet, now with God, an old woman like a berry, always in a bonnet with green flowers, smiled and bobbed. The colours of the toys jumbled against the dark walls were like patterns in a carpet.

' What do you say, Miss Brandon ? ' said Johnny. ' If I give you a toy will you give me one ? '

' Yes,' said Joan, afraid a little of Mrs. Magnet's piercing black eye.

' You're not to see what I get. Turn your back a moment.'

Joan turned round. As she waited she could hear the ' Hie ! . . . Hie ! Woah ! ' of the market-cries, the bleating of the sheep, the lowing of a cow.

' Here you are, then. She turned. He presented her with a Japanese doll, gay in a pink cotton frock, his waist girdled with a sash of gold tissue.

' Now you turn your back,' she said.

In a kind of happy desperation she seized a nigger with bold red cheeks, a white jacket and crimson trousers.

Mrs. Magnet wrapped the presents up. They paid, and walked out into the sun again.

' I'll keep that doll,' said Johnny, ' just as long as you keep yours.'

' Good-bye,' said Joan hurriedly. ' I've got to call at a house on the other side of the market. . . . Good-bye.'

She felt the pressure of his hand on hers, then,

clutching her parcel, hurried, almost ran, indeed, through the market-stalls. She did not look back.

When she had crossed the Square she turned down into a little side street. The plan of Polchester is very simple. It is built, as it were, on the side of a rock, running finally to a flat top, on which is the Cathedral. Down the side of the rock there are broad ledges, and it is on one of these that the market-place is built. At the bottom of the rock lies the jumble of cottages known most erroneously as Seatown, and round the rock runs the river Pol, slipping away at last through woods and hills and valleys into the sea. At high tide you can go all the way by river to the sea, and, in the summer, this makes a pleasant and beautiful excursion. It is because of this that Seatown has, perhaps, some right to its name, because in one way and another sailors collect in the cottages and at the ' Dog and Pilchard,' that pleasant and democratic hostelry of which, in 1897, Samuel Hogg was landlord. Many visitors have been known to declare that Seatown was 'too sweet for anything,' and that 'it would be really wicked to knock down the ducks of cottages,' but 'the ducks of cottages' were the foulest and most insanitary dwelling-places in the south of England, and it has always been to me amazing that the Polchester Town Council allowed them to stand so long as they did. In 1902, as all the Glebeshire world knows, there was the great battle of Seatown, ending in the cottages' destruction. In 1897 those evil dwelling-places gloried in their full magnificence of sweet corruption, nor did the periodical attacks of typhoid alarm in the least the citizens of the Upper Town. Once and again gentlemen from other parts paid mysterious official visits, but we had ways, in old times, of dealing with inquisitive meddlers from the outside world.

Because the market-place was half-way down the Rock, and because the Rectory of St. James' was just below the market-place, the upper windows of that house commanded a wonderful view both of the hill, High Street and Cathedral above it, and of Seatown, river and woods below it. It was said that it was up this very rocky street from the river, through the market, and up the High Street that the armed enemies of the Black Bishop had fought their way to the Cathedral on that great day when the Bishop had gone to meet his God, and a piece of rock is still shown to innocent visitors as the place whence some of his enemies, in full armour, were flung down, many thousand feet, to the waters of the Pol.

Joan had often longed to see the view from the windows of St. James' Rectory, but she had not known old Dr. Burroughs, the former Rector, a cross man with gout and rheumatism. She walked up some steps and found the house the last of three all squeezed together on the edge of the hill. The Rectory, because it was the last, stood square to all the winds of heaven, and Joan fancied what it must be in wild wintry weather. Soon she was in the drawing-room shaking hands with Miss Burnett, who was Mr. Morris' sister-in-law, and kept house for him.

Miss Burnett was a stout negative woman, whose whole mind was absorbed in the business of house-keeping, prices of food, wickedness and ingratitude of servants, maliciousness of shopkeepers and so on. The house, with all her managing, was neither tidy nor clean, as Joan quickly saw ; Miss Burnett was not, by temperament, methodical, nor had she ever received any education. Her mind, so far as a perception of the outside world and its history went, was some way behind that of a Hottentot or a South Sea Islander. She had, from the day of her birth, been told by every one around her that she was stupid, and, after a faint struggle, she had acquiesced in that judgment. She knew that her younger sister, afterwards Mrs. Morris, was pretty and accomplished, and that she would never be either of those things. She was not angry nor jealous at this. The note of her character was acquiescence, and when Agatha had died of pleurisy it had seemed the natural thing for her to come and keep house for the distressed widower. If Mr. Morris had since regretted the arrangement he had, at any rate, never said so.

Miss Burnett's method of conversation was to say something about the weather and then to lapse into a surprised and distressed stare. If her visitor made some statement she crowned it with, ' Well, now, that was just what I was going to say.'

Her nose, when she talked, twinkled at the nostrils apprehensively, and many of her visitors found this fascinating, so that they suddenly, with hot confusion, realised that they too had been staring in a most offensive manner. Joan had not been out in the world long enough to enable her to save a difficult situation by brilliant talk, and she very quickly found herself staring at Miss Burnett's nose and longing to say something about it, as, for instance, ' What a strange nose you've got, Miss Burnett—see how it twitches ! ' or, ' If you'll allow me, Miss Burnett, I'd just like to study your nose for a minute.' When she realised this horrible

desire in herself she blushed crimson and gazed
about the untidy and entangled drawing-room in
real desperation. She could see nothing in the
room that was likely to save her. She was about to
rise and depart, although she had only been there
five minutes, when Mr. Morris came in.

Joan realised at once that this man was quite
different from any one whom she had ever known.
He was a stranger to her Polchester world in body,
soul and spirit, as though, a foreigner from some
far-distant country, he had been shipwrecked and
cast upon an inhospitable shore. So strangely did
she feel this that she was quite surprised when he
did not speak with a foreign accent. 'Oh, he must
be a poet !' was her second thought about Mr.
Morris, not because he dressed oddly or had long
hair. She could not tell whence the impression
came, unless it were in his strange, bewildered, lost
blue eyes. Lost, bewildered—yes, that was what
he was ! With every movement of his slim,
straight body, the impulse with which he brushed
back his untidy fair hair from his forehead, he seemed
like a man only just awake, a man needing care and
protection, because he simply would not be able to
look after himself. So ridiculously did she have
this impression that she almost cried ' Look out !'
when he moved forward, as though he would certainly knock himself against a chair or a table.

'How strange,' she thought, 'that this man
should live with Miss Burnett ! What does he
think of her ?' She was excited by her discovery
of him, but that meant very little, because just now
she was being excited by everything. She found
at once that talking to him was the easiest thing in
the world. Mr. Morris did not say very much ;

he smiled gently, and when Miss Burnett, awaking suddenly from her torpor, said, ' You'll have some tea, Miss Brandon, won't you ? ' he, smiling, softly repeated the invitation.

' Thank you,' said Joan, ' I will. How strange it is,' she went on, ' that you are so close to the market and, even on market-day, you don't hear a sound ! '

And it was strange ! as though the house were bewitched and had suddenly, even as Joan entered it, gathered around it a dark wood for its protection.

' Yes,' said Mr. Morris. ' We found it strange at first. But it's because we are the last house, and the three others protect us. We get the wind and rain, though. You should hear this place in a storm. But the house is strong enough ; it's very stoutly built ; not a board creaks in the wildest weather. Only the windows rattle and the wind comes roaring down the chimneys.'

' How long have you been here ? ' asked Joan.

' Nearly a year—and we still feel strangers. We were near Ashford in Kent for twelve years, and the Glebeshire people are very different.'

' Well,' said Joan, who was a little irritated because she felt that his voice was a little sadder than it ought to be, ' I think you'll like Polchester. I'm *sure* you will. And you've come in a good year, too. There's sure to be a lot going on this year because of the Jubilee.'

Mr. Morris did not seem to be as thrilled as he should be by the thought of the Jubilee, so Joan went on :

' It's so lucky for us that it comes just at the Polchester Fair time. We always have a tremendous week at the Fair — the Horticultural Show and a

Ball in the Assembly Rooms, and all sorts of things. It's going to be my first ball this year, although I've really come out already.' She laughed. 'Festivities start to-morrow with the arrival of Marquis.'

'Marquis?' repeated Mr. Morris politely.

'Oh, don't you know Marquis? His is the greatest Circus in England. He comes to Polchester every year, and they have a procession through the town—elephants and camels, and Britannia in her chariot, and sometimes a cage with the lions and the tigers. Last year they had the sweetest little ponies—four of them, no higher than St. Bernards—and there are the clowns too, and a band.'

She was suddenly afraid that she was talking too much—silly too, in her childish enthusiasms. She remembered that she was in reality deputising for her mother, who would never have talked about the Circus. Fortunately at that moment the tea came in ; it was brought by a flushed and contemptuous maid, who put the tray down on a little table with a bang, tossed her head as though she despised them all, and slammed the door behind her.

Miss Burnett was upset by this, and her nose twitched more violently than ever. Joan saw that her hand trembled as she poured out the tea, and she was at once sorry for her.

Mr. Morris talked about Kent and London, and tea was drunk and the saffron cake praised, and Joan thought it was time to go. At the last, however, she turned to Mr. Morris and said :

'Do you like the Cathedral?'

'It's wonderful,' he answered. 'You should see it from our window upstairs.'

'Oh, I hate it——' said Joan.

'Why?' Morris asked her.

c

There was a curious challenge in his voice. They were both standing facing one another.

'I suppose that's a silly thing to say. Only you don't live as close to it as we do, and you haven't lived here so long as we have. It seems to hang right over you, and it never changes, and I hate to think it will go on just the same, years after we're dead.'

'Have you seen the view from our window?' Morris asked her.

'No,' said Joan, 'I was never in this house before.'

'Come and see it,' he said.

'I'm sure,' said Miss Burnett heavily, 'Miss Brandon doesn't want to be bothered—when she's seen the Cathedral all her life, too.'

'Of course I'd love to see it,' said Joan, laughing. 'To tell you the truth, that's what I've always wanted. I looked at this house again and again when old Canon Burroughs was here, and thought there must be a wonderful view.'

She said good-bye to Miss Burnett.

'My mother does hope you will soon come and see us,' she said.

'I have just met Mrs. Brandon for a moment at Mrs. Combermere's,' said Mr. Morris. 'We'll be very glad to come.'

She went out with him.

'It's up these stairs,' he said. 'Two flights. I hope you don't mind.'

They climbed on to the second landing. At the end of the passage there was a window. The evening was grey and only little faint wisps of blue still lingered above the dusk, but the white sky threw up the Cathedral towers, now black and sharp-edged in magnificent relief. Truly it *was* a view !

The window was in such a position that through it you gazed behind the neighbouring houses, above some low roofs, straight up the twisting High Street to the Cathedral. The great building seemed to be perched on the very edge of the rock, almost, you felt, swinging in mid-air, and that so precariously that with one push of the finger you might send it staggering into space. Joan had never seen it so dominating, so commanding, so fierce in its disregard of the tiny clustered world beneath it, so near to the stars, so majestic and alone.

' Yes—it's wonderful,' she said.

' Oh, but you should see it,' he cried, ' as it can be. It's dull to-day, the sky's grey and there's no sunset,—but when it's flaming red with all the windows shining, or when all the stars are out or in moonlight . . . it's like a great ship sometimes, and sometimes like a cloud, and sometimes like a fiery palace. Sometimes it's in mist and you can only see just the top of the towers. . . ."

' I don't like it,' said Joan, turning away. ' It doesn't care what happens to us.'

' Why should it ? ' he answered. ' Think of all it's seen—the battles and the fights and the plunder —and it doesn't care ! We can do what we like and it will remain just the same.'

' People could come and knock it down,' Joan said.

' I believe it would still be there if they did. The rock would be there and the spirit of the Cathedral. . . . What do people matter beside a thing like that ? Why, we're ants . . . !'

He stopped suddenly.

'You'll think me foolish, Miss Brandon,' he said. 'You have known the Cathedral so long——' He paused. 'I think I know what you mean about fearing it——'

He saw her to the door.

'Good-bye,' he said, smiling. 'Come again.'

'I like him,' she thought as she walked away. What a splendid day she had had !

CHAPTER IV

THE IMPERTINENT ELEPHANT

ARCHDEACON BRANDON had surmounted with surprising celerity the shock of Falk's unexpected return. He was helped to this firstly by his confident belief in a God who had him especially in His eye and would, on no account, do him any harm. As God had decided that Falk had better leave Oxford, it was foolish to argue that it would have been wiser for him to stay there. Secondly, he was helped by his own love for, and pride in, his son. The independence and scorn that were so large a part of Falk's nature were after his own heart. He might fight and oppose them (he often did), but always behind the contest there was appreciation and approbation. That was the way for a son of his to treat the world—to snap his fingers at it! The natural thing to do, the good old world being as stupid as it was. Thirdly, he was helped by his family pride. It took him only a night's reflection to arrive at the decision that Falk had been entirely right in this affair and Oxford entirely in the wrong. Two days after Falk's return he wrote (without saying anything to the boy) Falk's tutor a very warm letter, pointing out that he was sure the tutor would agree with him that a little more tact and diplomacy might have prevented so unfortunate an issue. It was not for him, Brandon, to suggest that the authorities in Oxford were perhaps a little behind the times, a little out of the world. Nevertheless it was probably true that long residence in Oxford had hindered the aforesaid authorities from realising the trend of the day, from appreciating the new spirit of independence that was growing up in our younger generation. It seemed obvious to him, Archdeacon Brandon, that you could no longer treat men of Falk's age and character as mere boys and, although he was quite sure that the authorities at Oxford had done their best, he nevertheless hoped that this unfortunate episode would enable them to see that we were not now living in the Middle Ages, but rather in the last years of the nineteenth century. It may seem to some a little ironical that the Archdeacon, who was the most conservative soul alive, should write thus to one of the most conservative of our institutions, but—' Before Oxford the Brandons were. . . .'

What the tutor remarked when he read this letter is not recorded. Brandon said nothing to Falk about all this. Indeed, during the first weeks after Falk's return he preserved a stern and dignified silence. After all, the boy must learn that authority was authority, and he prided himself that he knew, better than any number of Oxford Dons, how to train and educate the young. Nevertheless light broke through. Some of Falk's jokes were so good that his father, who had a real sense of fun if only a slight sense of humour, was bound to laugh. Very soon father and son resumed their old relations of sudden tempers and mutual admiration, and a strange, rather pathetic, quite uneloquent love that was none the less real because it was, on either side, completely selfish.

But there was a fourth reason why Falk's return caused so slight a storm. That reason was that the Archdeacon was now girding up his loins before he entered upon one of his famous campaigns. There had been many campaigns in the past. Campaigns were indeed as truly the breath of the Archdeacon's nostrils as they had been once of the great Napoleon's —and in every one of them had the Archdeacon been victorious.

This one was to be the greatest of them all, and was to set the sign and seal upon the whole of his career.

It happened that, three miles out of Polchester, there was a little village known as Pybus St. Anthony. A very beautiful village it was, with orchards and a stream and old-world cottages and a fine Norman church. But not for its orchards nor its stream nor its church was it famous. It was famous because for many years its living had been regarded as one of the most important in the whole diocese of Polchester. It was the tradition that the man who went to Pybus St. Anthony had the world in front of him. When likely men for preferment were looked for it was to Pybus St. Anthony that men looked. Heaven alone knows how many Canons and Archdeacons had made their first bow there to the Glebeshire world ! Three Deans and a Bishop had, at different times, made it their first stepping-stone to fame. Canon Morrison (Honorary Canon of the Cathedral) was its present incumbent. Less intellectual than some of the earlier incumbents, he was nevertheless a fine fellow. He had been there only three years when symptoms of cancer of the throat had appeared. He had been operated on in

London, and at first it had seemed that he would recover. Then the dreaded signs had reappeared ; he had wished, poor man, to surrender the living, but because there was yet hope the Chapter, in whose gift the living was, had insisted on his remaining.

A week ago, however, he had collapsed. It was feared now that at any moment he might die. The Archdeacon was very sorry for Morrison. He liked him, and was deeply touched by his tragedy ; nevertheless one must face facts ; it was probable that at any moment now the Chapter would be forced to make a new appointment.

He had been aware—he did not disguise it from himself in the least—for some time now of the way that the appointment must go. There was a young man, the Rev. Rex Forsyth by name, who, in his judgment, could be the only possible man. Young Forsyth was, at the present moment, chaplain to the Bishop of St. Minworth. St. Minworth was only a Suffragan Bishopric, and it could not honestly be said that there was a great deal for Mr. Forsyth to do there. But it was not because the Archdeacon thought that the young man ought to have more to do that he wished to move him to Pybus St. Anthony. Far from it ! The Archdeacon, in the deep secrecy of his own heart, could not honestly admit that young Forsyth was a very hard worker—he liked hunting and whist and a good bottle of wine . . . he was that kind of man.

Where, then, were his qualifications as Canon Morrison's successor ? Well, quite honestly—and the Archdeacon was one of the honestest men alive —his qualifications belonged more especially to his ancestors rather than to himself. In the Archdeacon's opinion there had been too many *clever* men at

Pybus. Time now for a *normal* man. Morrison was normal, and Forsyth would be more normal still.

He was in fact first cousin to young Johnny St. Leath and therefore a very near relation of the Countess herself. His father was the fourth son of the Earl of Trewithen, and, as every one knows, the Trewithens and the St. Leaths are, for all practical purposes, one and the same family, and divide Glebeshire between them. No one ever quite knew what young Rex Forsyth became a parson for. Some people said he did it for a wager; but however true that might be, he was not very happy with dear old Bishop Clematis and very ready for preferment.

Now the Archdeacon was no snob; he believed in men and women who had long and elaborate family-trees simply because he believed in institutions and because it had always seemed to him a quite obvious fact that the longer any one or anything remained in a place, the more chance there was of things being done as they always had been done. It was not in the least because she was a Countess that he thought the old Lady St. Leath a wonderful woman; not wonderful for her looks certainly—no one could call her a beautiful woman—and not wonderful for her intelligence; the Archdeacon had frequently been compelled to admit to himself that she was a little on the stupid side— but wonderful for her capacity for staying where she was like a rock and allowing nothing whatever to move her. In these dangerous days—and what dangerous days they were!—the safety of the country simply depended on a few such figures as the Countess. Queen Victoria was another of them, and for her the Archdeacon had a real and very touching devotion. Thank God he would be able to show a little of it in the prominent part he intended to play in the Polchester Jubilee festivals this year !

Any one could see then that to have young Rex Forsyth close at hand at Pybus St. Anthony was the very best possible thing for the good of Polchester. Lady St. Leath saw it, Mrs. Combermere saw it, Mrs. Sampson saw it, and young Forsyth himself saw it. The Archdeacon entirely failed to understand how there could be any one who did not see it. However, he was afraid that there were one or two in Polchester. . . . People said that young Forsyth was stupid ! Perhaps he was not very bright ; all the easier then to direct him in the way that he should go, and throw his forces into the right direction. People said that he cared more for his hunting and his whist than for his work—well, he was young and, at any rate, there was none of the canting hypocrite about him. The Archdeacon hated canting hypocrites !

There had been signs, once and again, of certain anarchists and devilish fellows, who crept up and down the streets of Polchester spreading their wicked mischief, their lying and disintegrating ideas. The Archdeacon was determined to fight them to the very last breath in his body, even as the Black Bishop before him had fought *his* enemies. And the Archdeacon had no fear of his victory.

Rex Forsyth at Pybus St. Anthony would be a fine step forward. Have one of these irreligious radicals there, and Heaven alone knew what harm he might wreak. No, Polchester must be saved. Let the rest of the world go to pieces, Polchester would be preserved.

On how many earlier occasions had the Archdeacon surveyed the Chapter, considered it in all its details and weighed up judiciously the elements, good and bad, that composed it. How well he knew them all ! First the Dean, mild and polite and amiable, his mind generally busy with his beloved flora and fauna, his flowers and his butterflies, very easy indeed to deal with. Then Archdeacon Witheram, most nobly conscientious, a really devout man, taking his work with a seriousness that was simply admirable, but glued to the details of his own half of the diocese, so that broader and larger questions did not concern him very closely. Bentinck-Major next. The Archdeacon flattered himself that he knew Bentinck-Major through and through — his snobbery, his vanity, his childish pleasure in his position and his cook, his vanity in his own smart appearance ! It would be difficult to find words adequate for the scorn with which the Archdeacon regarded that elegant little man. Then Ryle, the Precentor. He was, to some extent, an unknown quantity. His chief characteristic perhaps was his hatred of quarrels —he would say or do anything if only he might not be drawn into a ' row.' ' Peace at any price ' was his motto, and this, of course, as with the famous Vicar of Bray, involved a good deal of insincerity. The Archdeacon knew that he could not trust him, but a masterful policy of terrorism had always been very successful. Ryle was frankly frightened by the Archdeacon, and a very good thing too ! Might he long remain so ! Lastly there was Foster, the Diocesan Missioner. Let it be said at once that the Archdeacon hated Foster. Foster had been a thorn in the Archdeacon's side ever since his arrival in Polchester—a thin, shambly-kneed, untidy, pale-faced prig, that was what Foster was ! The Arch-deacon hated everything about him—his grey hair, his large protruding ears, the pimple on the end of his nose, the baggy knees to his trousers, his thick heavy hands that never seemed to be properly washed.

Nevertheless beneath that hatred the Arch-deacon was compelled to a reluctant admiration. The man was fearless, a fanatic if you please, but devoted to his religion, believing in it with a fervour and sincerity that nothing could shake. An able man too, the best preacher in the diocese, better read in every kind of theology than any clergyman in Glebeshire. It was especially for his open mind about new religious ideas that the Arch-deacon mistrusted him. No opinion, however heterodox, shocked him. He welcomed new thought and had himself written a book, *Christ and the Gospels*, that for its learning and broad-mindedness had created a considerable stir. But he was a dull dog, never laughed, never even smiled, lived by himself and kept to himself. He had, in the past, opposed every plan of the Arch-deacon's, and opposed it relentlessly, but he was always, thanks to the Archdeacon's efforts, in a minority. The other Canons disliked him ; the old Bishop, safely tucked away in his Palace at Carpledon, was, except for his satellite Rogers, his only friend in Polchester.

So much for the Chapter. There was now only one unknown element in the situation—Ronder. Ronder's position was important because he was Treasurer to the Cathedral. His predecessor, Hart-Smith, now promoted to the Deanery of Norwich, had been an able man, but one of the old school, a great friend of Brandon's, seeing eye to eye with him in everything. The Archdeacon then had had his finger very closely upon the Cathedral purse, and Hart-Smith's departure had been a very serious blow. The appointment of the new Canon had been in the hands of the Crown, and Brandon had, of course, had nothing to say to it. However, one glance at Ronder—he had seen him and spoken to him at the Dean's a few days after his arrival —had reassured him. Here, surely, was a man whom he need not fear—an easy, good-natured, rather stupid fellow by the look of him. Brandon hoped to have his finger on the Cathedral purse as tightly in a few weeks' time as he had had it before.

And all this was in no sort of fashion for the Archdeacon's personal advancement or ambition. He was contented with Polchester, and quite prepared to live there for the rest of his days and be buried, with proper ceremonies, when his end came. With all his soul he loved the Cathedral, and if he regarded himself as the principal factor in its good governance and order he did so with a sort of divine fatalism—no credit to him that it was so. Let credit be given to the Lord God who had seen fit to make him what he was and to place in his hands that great charge.

His fault in the matter was, perhaps, that he took it all too simply, that he regarded these men and the other figures in Polchester exactly as he saw them, did not believe that they could ever be anything else. As God had created the world, so did Brandon create Polchester as nearly in his own likeness as might be—there they all were and there, please God, they would all be for ever!

Bending his mind then to this new campaign, he thought that he would go and see the Dean. He knew by this time, he fancied, exactly how to prepare the Dean's mind for the proper reception of an idea, although, in truth, he was as simple over his plots and plans as a child brick-building in its nursery.

About three o'clock one afternoon he prepared to sally forth. The Dean's house was on the other side of the Cathedral, and you had to go down the High Street and then to the left up Orange Street to get to it, an irrational roundabout proceeding that always irritated the Archdeacon. Very splendid he looked, his top-hat shining, his fine high white collar, his spotless black clothes, his boots shapely and smart. (He and Bentinck-Major were, I suppose, the only two clergymen in Polchester who used boot-trees.) But his smartness was in no way an essential with him. Clothed in rags he would still have the grand air. 'I often think of him,' Miss Dobell once said, 'as one of those glorious gondoliers in Venice. How grand he would look !'

However that might be, it is beyond question that the ridiculous clothes that a clergyman of the Church of England is compelled to wear did not make him absurd, nor did he look an over-dressed fop like Bentinck-Major.

Miss Dobell's gondolier was, on this present occasion, in an excellent temper ; and meeting his daughter Joan, he felt very genial towards her. Joan had observed, several days before, that the family crisis might be said to be past, and very thankful she was.

She had, at this time, her own happy dreams,

Street he saw that the pavement on both sides of the street was black with people. He was not a man who liked to be jostled, and he was the more uncomfortable in that he discovered that his immediate neighbour was Samuel Hogg, the stout and rubicund landlord of the 'Dog and Pilchard' of Seatown. With him was his pretty daughter Annie. Near to them were Mr. John Curtis and Mr. Samuel Croppet, two of the Town Councillors. With none of these gentlemen did the Archdeacon wish to begin a conversation.

And yet it was difficult to know what to do. The High Street pavements were narrow, and the crowd seemed continually to increase. There was a good deal of pushing and laughter and boisterous good-humour. To return up the street again seemed to have something ignominious about it. Brandon decided to satisfy his curiosity, support his dignity, and indulge his amiability by staying where he was.

'Good afternoon, Hogg,' he said. 'What's the disturbance for?'

'Markisses Circus, sir.' Hogg lifted his face like a large round sun. 'Surely you'd 'eard of it, Archdeacon?'

'Well, I didn't know,' said Brandon in his most gracious manner, 'that it was this afternoon. . . . Of course, how stupid of me!'

He smiled round good-naturedly upon them all, and they all smiled back upon him. He was a popular figure in the town; it was felt that his handsome face and splendid presence did the town credit. Also, he always knew his own mind. *And* he was no coward.

He nodded to Curtis and Croppet and then

stared in front of him, a fixed genial smile on his face, his fine figure triumphant in the sun. He looked as though he were enjoying himself and was happy because he liked to see his fellow-creatures happy; in reality he was wondering how he could have been so foolish as to forget Marquis' Circus? Why had not Joan said something to him about it? Very careless of her to place him in this unfortunate position.

He looked around him, but he could see no other dignitary of the Church close at hand. How tiresome — really, how tiresome! Moreover, as the timed moment of the procession arrived the crowd increased, and he was now most uncomfortably pressed against other people. He felt a sharp little dig in his stomach, then, turning, found close beside him the flushed, anxious, meagre little face of Samuel Bond, the Clerk of the Chapter. Bond's struggle to reach his dignified position in the town had been a severe one, and had only succeeded because of a multitude of self-submissions and abnegations, humilities and contempts, flatteries and sycophancies that would have tired and defeated a less determined soul. But, in the background, there were the figures of Mrs. Bond and four little Bonds to spur him forward. He adored his family. 'Whatever I am, I'm a family man,' was one of his favourite sayings. In so worthy a cause much sycophancy may be forgiven him. To no one, however, was he so completely sycophantic as to the Archdeacon. He was terrified of the Archdeacon; he would wake up in the middle of the night and think of him, then tremble and cower under the warm protection of Mrs. Bond until sleep rescued him once more.

It was natural, therefore, that however numerous the people in Polchester might be whom the Archdeacon despised, he despised little Bond most of all. And here was little Bond pressed up against him, with the large circumference of the cheerful Mr. Samuel Hogg near by, and the ironical town smartness of Messrs. Curtis and Croppet close at hand. Truly a horrible position.

'Ah, Archdeacon! I didn't see you—indeed I didn't!' The little breathless voice was like a child's penny whistle blown ignorantly. 'Just fancy!—meeting you like this! Hot, isn't it, although it's only February. Yes. . . . Hot indeed. I didn't know you cared for processions, Archdeacon——'

'I don't,' said Brandon. 'I hadn't realised that there *was* a procession. Stupidly, I had forgotten——'

'Well, well,' came the good-natured voice of Mr. Hogg. 'It'll do us no harm, Archdeacon—no harm at all. I forget whether you rightly know my little girl. This is Annie—come out to see the procession with her father.'

The Archdeacon was compelled to shake hands. He did it very graciously. She was certainly a fine girl—tall, strong, full-breasted, with dark colour and raven black hair; curious, her eyes, very large and bright. They stared full at you, but past you, as though they had decided that you were of insufficient interest.

Annie thus gazed at the Archdeacon and said no word. Any further intimacies were prevented by approach of the procession. To the present generation Marquis' Circus would not appear, I suppose, very wonderful. To many of us, thirty years ago, it seemed the final expression of Oriental splendour and display.

There were murmurs and cries of ' Here they come ! Here they come ! 'Ere they be ! ' Every one pressed forward ; Mr. Bond was nearly thrown off his feet and caught at the lapel of the Archdeacon's coat to save himself. Only the huge black eyes of Annie Hogg displayed no interest. The procession had started from the meadows beyond the Cathedral and, after discreetly avoiding the Precincts, was to plunge down the High Street, pass through the Market-place and vanish up Orange Street—to follow, in fact, the very path that the Archdeacon intended to pursue.

A band could be heard, there was an astounded hush (the whole of the High Street holding its breath), then the herald appeared.

He was, perhaps, a rather shabby fellow, wearing the tarnished red and gold of many a procession, but he walked confidently, holding in his hand a tall wooden truncheon gay with paper-gilt, having his round cap of cloth of gold set rakishly on one side of his head. After him came the band, also in tarnished cloth of gold and looking as though they would have been a trifle ashamed of themselves had they not been deeply involved in the intricacies of their music. After the band came four rather shabby riders on horseback, then some men dressed apparently in admiring imitation of Charles II.; then, to the wonder and whispered incredulity of the crowd, Britannia on her triumphal car. The car—an elaborate cart, with gilt wheels and strange cardboard figures of dolphins and Father Neptune —had in its centre a high seat painted white and perched on a kind of box. Seated on this throne was Britannia herself—a large, full-bosomed, flaxen-haired lady in white flowing robes, and having a very anxious expression of countenance, as, indeed, poor thing, was natural enough, because the cart rocked the box and the box yet more violently rocked the chair. At any moment, it seemed, might she be precipitated, a fallen goddess, among the crowd, and the fact that the High Street was on a slope of considerable sharpness did not add to her ease and comfort. Two stout gentlemen, perspiration bedewing their foreheads, strove to restrain the ponies, and their classic clothing, that turned them into rather tattered Bacchuses, did not make them less incongruous.

Britannia and her agony, however, were soon forgotten in the ferocious excitements that followed her. Here were two camels, tired and dusty, with that look of bored and indifferent superiority that belongs to their tribe, two elephants, two clowns, and last, but of course the climax of the whole affair, a cage in which there could be seen behind the iron bars a lion and a lioness, jolted haplessly from side to side, but too deeply shamed and indignant to do more than reproach the crowd with their burning eyes. Finally, another clown bearing a sandwich-board on which was printed in large red letters, 'Marquis' Circus—the Finest in the World—Renowned through Europe—Come to the Church Meadows and see the Fun '—and so on.

As this glorious procession passed down the High Street the crowd expressed its admiration in silent whispering. There was no loud applause ; nevertheless, Mr. Marquis, were he present, must have felt the air electric with praise. It was murmured that Britannia was Mrs. Marquis, and, if that were true, she must have given her spouse afterwards, in the sanctity of their privacy, a very grateful account of her reception.

When the band had passed a little way down the street and their somewhat raucous notes were modified by distance, the sun came out in especial glory, as though to take his own peep at the show, the gilt and cloth of gold shone and gleamed, the chair of Britannia rocked as though it were bursting with pride, and the Cathedral bells, as though they too wished to lend their dignified blessing to the scene, began to ring for Evensong. A sentimental observer, had he been present, might have imagined that the old town was glad to have once again an excuse for some display, and preened itself and showed forth its richest and warmest colours and wondered, perhaps, whether after all the drab and interesting citizens of to-day were not minded to return to the gayer and happier old times. Quite a noise, too, of chatter and trumpets and bells and laughter. Even the Archdeacon forgot his official smile and laughed like a boy.

It was then that the terrible thing happened. Somewhere at the lower end of the High Street the procession was held up and the chariot had suddenly to pull itself back upon its wheels, and the band were able to breathe freely for a minute, to gaze about them and to wipe the sweat from their brows ; even in February blowing and thumping ' all round the town ' was a warm business.

Now, just opposite the Archdeacon were the two elephants, checked by the sudden pause. Behind them was the cage with the lions, who, now that the jolting had ceased, could collect their scattered indignities and roar a little in exasperated protest.

The elephants, too, perhaps felt the humility of their
position, accustomed though they might be to it by
many years of sordid slavery. It may be, too, that
the sight of that patronising and ignorant crowd,
the crush and pack of the High Street, the silly
sniggering, the triumphant jangle of the Cathedral
bells, thrust through their slow and heavy brains
some vision long faded now, but for an instant
revived, of their green jungles, their hot suns, their
ancient royalty and might. They realised perhaps
a sudden instinct of their power, that they could
with one lifting of the hoof crush these midgets
that hemmed them in back to the pulp whence they
came, and so go roaming and bellowing their
freedom through the streets and ways of the city.
The larger of the two suddenly raised his head and
trumpeted ; with his dim uplifted eyes he caught
sight of the Archdeacon's rich and gleaming top-
hat shining, as an emblem of the city's majesty,
above the crowd. It gleamed in the sun, and he
hated it. He trumpeted again and yet again, then,
with a heavy lurching movement, stumbled towards the pavement, and with little fierce eyes and
uplifted trunk heaved towards his enemies.

The crowd, with screams and cries, fell back in
agitated confusion. The Archdeacon, caught by
surprise, scarcely realising what had occurred,
blinded a little by the sun, stood where he was. In
another moment his top-hat was snatched from his
head and tossed into air. . . .

He felt the animal's hot breath upon his face,
heard the shouts and cries around him, and, in very
natural alarm, started back, caught at anything for
safety (he had tumbled upon the broad and protective chest of Samuel Hogg), and had a general

impression of whirling figures, of suns and roofs and
shining faces and, finally, the high winds of heaven
blowing upon his bare head.

In another moment the incident was closed.
The courtier of Charles II. had rushed up ; the
elephant was pulled and hustled and kicked ;
for him swiftly the vision of power and glory
and vengeance was over, and once again he was
the tied and governed prisoner of modern civilisation. The top-hat lay, a battered and hapless
remnant, beneath the feet of the now advancing
procession.

Once the crowd realised that the danger was over
a roar of laughter went up to heaven. There were
shouts and cries. The Archdeacon tried to smile.
He heard in dim confusion the cheery laugh of
Samuel Hogg, he caught the comment of Croppet
and the rest.

With only one thought that he must hide himself, indignation, humiliation, amazement that such
a thing could be in his heart, he backed, turned,
almost ran, finding at last sudden refuge in Bennett's
book-shop. How wonderful was the dark rich
security of that enclosure ! The shop was always
in a half-dusk and the gas burnt in its dim globes
during most of the day. All the richer and hand-
somer gleamed the rows of volumes, the morocco
and the leather and the cloth. Old Mr. Bennett
himself, the son of the famous man who had known
Scott and Byron, was now a prodigious age (in the
town his nickname was Methusalem), but he still
liked to sit in the shop in a high chair, his white
beard in bright contrast with the chaste selection
of the newest works arranged in front of him.
He might himself have been the Spirit of Select

Literature summoned out of the vasty deep by the Cultured Spirits of Polchester.

Into this splendid temple of letters the Archdeacon came, halted, breathless, bewildered, tumbled. He saw at first only dimly. He was aware that old Mr. Bennett, with an exclamation of surprise, rose in his chair. Then he perceived that two others were in the shop ; finally, that these two were the Dean and Ronder, the men of all others in Polchester whom he least wished to find there.

' Archdeacon ! ' cried the Dean.

' Yes — om — ah — an extraordinary thing has occurred—I really—oh, thank you, Mr. Wilton. . . ."

Mr. Frank Wilton, the young assistant, had offered a chair.

' You'll scarcely believe me—really, I can hardly believe myself.' Here the Archdeacon tried to laugh. ' As a matter of fact, I was coming out to see you . . . on my way . . . and the elephant. . . ."

' The elephant ? ' repeated the Dean, who, in the way that he had, was nervously rubbing one gaitered leg against the other.

' Yes—I'm a little incoherent, I'm afraid. You must forgive me . . . breathless too. . . . It's too absurd. So many people . . ."

' A little glass of water, Mr. Archdeacon ? ' said young Wilton, who had a slight cast in one eye, and therefore gave the impression that he was watching round the corner to see that no one ran off with the books.

' No, thank you, Wilton. . . . No, thank you. . . . Very good of you, I'm sure. But really it was a monstrous thing. I was coming to see you, as I've just said, Dean, having forgotten all about this ridiculous procession. I was held up by the crowd

just below the shop here. Then suddenly, as the
animals were passing, the elephant made a lurch
towards me—positively, I'm not exaggerating—
seized my hat and—ran off with it ! '

The Archdeacon had, as I have already said,
a sense of fun. He saw, for the first time, the
humour of the thing. He began to laugh ; he
laughed more loudly ; laughter overtook him
altogether, and he roared and roared again, sitting
there, his hands on his knees, until the tears ran
down his cheek.

' Oh dear . . . my hat . . . an elephant . . .
Did you ever hear——? My best hat . . . ! ' The
Dean was compelled to laugh too, although, being a
shy and hesitating man, he was not able to do it
very heartily. Young Mr. Wilton laughed, but in
such a way as to show that he knew his place and
was ready to be serious at once if his superiors
wished it. Even old Mr. Bennett laughed as
distantly and gently as befitted his great age.

Brandon was conscious of Ronder. He had,
in fact, been conscious of him from the very
instant of his first perception of him. He was
giving himself away before their new Canon ; he
thought that the new Canon, although he was
smiling pleasantly and was standing with becoming
modesty in the background, looked superior. . . .

The Archdeacon pulled himself up with a jerk.
After all, it was nothing of a joke. A multitude of
townspeople had seen him in a most ludicrous position, had seen him start back in terror before a
tame elephant, had seen him frightened and hatless.
No, there was nothing to laugh about.

' An elephant ? ' repeated the Dean, still gently
laughing.

'Yes, an elephant,' answered Brandon rather testily.   That was enough of the affair, quite enough. 'Well, I must be getting back.   See you to-morrow, Dean.'

'Anything important you wanted to see me about?' asked the Dean, perceiving that he had laughed just a little longer than was truly necessary.

'No, no . . . nothing.   Only about poor Morrison.   He's very bad, they tell me . . . a week at most.'

'Dear, dear—is that so?' said the Dean.   'Poor fellow, poor fellow!'

Brandon was now acutely conscious of Ronder. Why didn't the fellow say something instead of standing silently there with that superior look behind his glasses?   In the ordinary way he would have greeted him with his usual hearty patronage. Now he was irritated.   It was really most unfortunate that Ronder should have witnessed his humiliation.   He rose, abruptly turning his back upon him.   The fellow was laughing at him—he was sure of it.

'Well—good-day, good-day.'   As he advanced to the door and looked out into the street he was aware of the ludicrousness of going even a few steps up the street without a hat.

Confound Ronder!

But there was scarcely any one about now.   The street was almost deserted.   He peered up and down.

In the middle of the road was a small, shapeless, black object.

. . . His hat!

CHAPTER V

MRS. BRANDON hated her husband. No one in
Polchester had the slightest suspicion of this;
certainly her husband least of all. She herself had
been first aware of it one summer afternoon some
five or six years ago when, very pleasantly and in
the kindest way, he had told her that she knew
nothing about primroses. They had been having
tea at the Dean's, and, as was often the case then,
the conversation had concerned itself with flowers
and ferns. Mrs. Brandon was quite ready to admit
that she knew nothing about primroses—there were
for her yellow ones and other ones, and that was
all. The Archdeacon had often before told her
that she was ignorant, and she had acquiesced without a murmur. Upon this afternoon, just as Mrs.
Sampson was asking her whether she liked sugar,
revelation came to her. That little scene was often
afterwards vividly in front of her—the Archdeacon,
with his magnificent legs spread apart in front of
the fireplace; Miss Dobell trying to look with
wisdom upon a little bundle of primulas that the
Dean was showing to her; the sunlight upon the
lawn beyond the window; the rooks in the high
elms busy with their nests; the May warmth striking

through the misty air,—all was painted for ever afterwards upon her mind.

'My dear, you may as well admit at once that you know nothing whatever about primroses.'

'No, I'm afraid I don't — thank you, Mrs. Sampson. One lump, please.'

She had been coming to it. Of course, a very long time before this—very, very far away, now an incredible memory, seemed the days when she had loved him so passionately that she almost died with anxiety if he left her for a single night. Almost too passionate it had been, perhaps. He himself was not capable of passionate love, or, at any rate, had been quite satisfied to be *not* passionately in love with *her*. He pursued other things—his career, his religion, his simple beneficence, his health, his vigour. His love for his son was the most passionately personal thing in him, and over that they might have met had he been able to conceive her as a passionate being. Her ignorance of life— almost complete when he had met her—had been but little diminished by her time with him. She knew now, after all those years, little more of the world and its terrors and blessings than she had known then. But she did know that nothing in her had been satisfied. She knew now of what she was capable, and it was perhaps the thought that he had, by taking her, prevented her fulfilment and complete experience that caused her, more than anything else, to hate him.

She very quickly discovered that he had married her for certain things—to have children, to have a companion. He had soon found that the latter of these he was not to obtain. She had in her none of the qualities that he needed in a companion, and so he had, with complete good-nature and kindliness, ceased to consider her. He should have married a bold ambitious woman who would have wanted the things that he wanted—a woman something like Falk, his son. On the rare occasions when he analysed the situation he realised this. He did not in any way vent his disappointment upon her—he was only slightly disappointed. He treated her with real kindness save on the occasions of his violent loss of temper, and gave her anything that she wanted. He had, on the whole, a great contempt for women save when, as for instance with Mrs. Combermere, they were really men.

It was to her most humiliating of all that nothing in their relations worried him. He was perfectly at ease about it all, and fancied that she was the same. Meanwhile her real life was not dead, only dormant. For some years she tried to change the situation ; she made little appeals to him, endeavoured timidly to force him to need her, even on one occasion threatened to sleep in a separate room. The memory of *that* little episode still terrified her. His incredulity had only been equalled by his anger. It was just as though some one had threatened to deprive him of his morning tub. . . .

Then, when she saw that this was of no avail, she had concentrated herself upon her children, and especially upon Falk. For a while she had fancied that she was satisfied. Suddenly—and the discovery was awful—she was aware that Falk's affection all turned towards his father rather than towards her. Her son despised her and disregarded her as his father had done. She did not love Falk the less, but she ceased to expect anything from him—and this new loss she put down to her husband's account.

It was shortly after she made this discovery that the affair of the primroses occurred.

Many a woman now would have shown her hostility, but Mrs. Brandon was, by nature, a woman who showed nothing. She did not even show anything to herself, but all the deeper, because it found no expression, did her hatred penetrate. She scored now little marks against him for everything that he did. She did not say to herself that a day of vengeance was coming, she did not think of anything so melodramatic, she expected nothing of her future at all—but the marks were there.

The situation was developed by Falk's return from Oxford. When he was away her love for him seemed to her simply all in the world that she possessed. He wrote to her very seldom, but she made her Sunday letters to him the centre of her week, and wrote as though they were a passionately devoted mother and son. She allowed herself this little gentle deception—it was her only one.

But when he returned and was in the house it was more difficult to cheat herself. She saw at once that he had something on his mind, that he was engaged in some pursuit that he kept from every one. She discovered, too, that she was the one of whom he was afraid, and rightly so, the Archdeacon being incapable of discovering any one's pursuits so long as he was engaged on one of his own. Falk's fear of her perception brought about a new situation between them. He was not now oblivious of her presence as he had been. He tried to discover whether she knew anything. She found him often watching her, half in fear and half in defiance.

The thought that he might be engaged now upon

some plan of his own in which she might share excited her and gave her something new to live for. She did not care what his plan might be ; however dangerous, however wicked, she would assist him. Her moral sense had never been very deeply developed in her.   Her whole character was based on her relations with individuals ; for any one she loved she would commit murder, theft or blasphemy. She had never had any one to love except Falk.

She despised the Archdeacon the more because he now perceived nothing. Under his very nose the thing was, and he was sublimely contented. How she hated that content, and how she despised it !

About a week after the affair of the elephant, Mrs. Combermere asked her to tea. She disliked Mrs. Combermere, but she went to tea there because it was easier than not going. She disliked Mrs. Combermere especially because it was in her house that she heard silly, feminine praise of her husband. It amused her, however, to think of the amazed sensation there would be, did she one day burst out before them all and tell them what she really thought of the Archdeacon.

Of course she would never do that, but she had often outlined the speech in her mind.

Mrs. Combermere also lived in the Precincts, so that Mrs. Brandon had not far to go. Before she arrived there a little conversation took place between the lady of the house, Miss Stiles, Miss Dobell and Dr. Puddifoot, that her presence would most certainly have hindered. Mrs. Combermere was once described by some one as ' constructed in concrete ' ; and that was not a bad description of her, so solid, so square and so unshakable and unbeatable was she. She wore stiff white collars like a man's, broad thick boots, short skirts and a belt at her waist. Her black hair was brushed straight back from her forehead, she had rather small brown eyes, a large nose and a large mouth. Her voice was a deep bass. She had some hair on her upper lip, and thick, strong, very white hands. She liked to walk down the High Street, a silver-topped cane in her hand, a company of barking dogs at her heels, and a hat, with large hat-pins, set a little on one side of her head. She had a hearty laugh, rather like the Archdeacon's. Dr. Puddifoot was our doctor for many years and brought many of my generation into the world. He was a tall, broad, loose-set man, who always wore tweeds of a bright colour.

Mrs. Combermere cared nothing for her surroundings, and her house was never very tidy. She bullied her servants, but they liked her because she gave good wages and fulfilled her promises. She was the first woman in Polchester to smoke cigarettes. It was even said that she smoked cigars, but no one, I think, ever saw her do this.

On this afternoon she subjected Miss Stiles to a magisterial inquiry ; Miss Stiles had on the preceding evening given a little supper party, and no one in Polchester did anything of the kind without having to render account to Mrs. Combermere afterwards. They all sat round the fire, because it was a cold day. Mrs. Combermere sat on a straight-backed chair, tilting it forward, her skirt drawn up to her knees, her thick-stockinged legs and big boots for all the world to see.

' Well, Ellen, whom did you have ? '

' Ronder and his aunt, the Bentinck-Majors, Charlotte Ryle and Major Drake.'

D

'Sorry I couldn't have been there. What did you give them?'

'Soup, fish salad, cutlets, chocolate soufflé, sardines on toast.'

'What drink?'

'Sherry, claret, lemonade for Charlotte, whisky.'

'Any catastrophes?'

'No, I don't think so. Bentinck-Major sang afterwards.'

'Hum—not sorry I missed *that*. When was it over?'

'About eleven.'

'What did you ask them for?'

'For the Ronders.'

Mrs. Combermere, raising one foot, kicked a coal into blaze.

'Tea will be in in a minute. . . . Now, I'll tell you for your good, my dear Ellen, that I don't like your Ronder.'

Miss Stiles laughed. 'Oh, you needn't mind me, Aggie. You never have. Why don't you?'

'In the first place, he's stupid.'

Miss Stiles laughed again.

'Never wronger in your life. I thought you were smarter than that.'

Mrs. Combermere smacked her knee. 'I may be wrong. I often am. I take prejudices, I know. Secondly, he's fat and soft—too like the typical parson.'

'It's an assumed disguise—however, go on.'

'Third, I hear he agrees with everything one says.'

'You hear? You've not talked to him yourself, then?'

Mrs. Combermere raised her head as the door opened and the tea came in.

'No. I've only seen him in Cathedral. But I've called, and he's coming to-day.'

Miss Stiles smiled in her own dark and mysterious way. 'Well, Aggie, my dear, I leave you to find it all out for yourself. . . . I keep my secrets.'

'If you do,' said Mrs. Combermere, getting up and going to the tea-table, 'it's the first time you ever have. *And*, Ellen,' she went on, 'I've a bone to pick. I won't have you laughing at my dear Archdeacon.'

'Laughing at your Archdeacon?' Miss Stiles' voice was softer and slower than any complaining cow's.

'Yes. I hear you've all been laughing about the elephant. That was a thing that might have happened to any one.'

Puddifoot laughed. 'The point is, though, that it happened to Brandon. That's the joke. *And* his new top hat.'

'Well, I won't have it. Milk, doctor? Miss Dobell and I agree that it's a shame.'

Miss Dobell, who was in appearance like one of those neat silk umbrellas with the head of a parrot for a handle, and whose voice was like the running brook both for melody and monotony, thus suddenly appealed to, blushed, stammered, and finally admitted that the Archdeacon was, in her opinion, a hero.

'That's not exactly the point, dear Mary,' said Miss Stiles. 'The point is, surely, that an elephant straight from the desert ate our best Archdeacon's best hat in the High Street. You must admit that that's a laughable circumstance in this the sixtieth year of our good Queen's reign. I, for one, intend to laugh.'

'No, you don't, Ellen,' and, to every one's

surprise, Mrs. Combermere's voice was serious. 'I mean what I say. I'm not joking at all. Brandon may have his faults, but this town and everything decent in it hangs by him. Take him away and the place drops to pieces. I suppose you think you're going to introduce your Ronders as up-to-date rivals. We prefer things as they are, thank you.'

Miss Stiles' already bright colouring was a little brighter. She knew her Aggie Combermere, but she resented rebukes before Puddifoot.

'Then,' she said, 'if he means all that to the place, he'd better look after his son more efficiently.'

'*And* exactly what do you mean by that?' asked Mrs. Combermere.

'Oh, everybody knows,' said Miss Stiles, looking round to Miss Dobell and the doctor for support, 'that young Brandon is spending the whole of his time down in Seatown, and that Miss Annie Hogg is not entirely unconnected with his visits.'

'Really, Ellen,' said Mrs. Combermere, bringing her fist down upon the table, 'you're a disgusting woman. Yes, you are, and I won't take it back, however much you ask me to. All the worst scandal in this place comes from you. If it weren't for you we shouldn't be so exactly like every novelist's Cathedral town. But I warn you, I won't have you talking about Brandon. His son's only a boy, and the handsomest male in the place, by the way—present company, of course, excepted. He's only been home a few months, and you're after him already with your stories. I won't have it——'

Miss Stiles rose, her fingers trembling as she drew on her gloves.

'Well, I won't stay here to be insulted, anyway.

You may have known me a number of years, Aggie, but that doesn't allow you *all* the privileges. The only matter with me is that I say what I think. You started the business, I believe, by insulting my friends.'

'Sit down, Ellen,' said Mrs. Combermere, laughing. 'Don't be a fool. Who's insulting your friends? You'd insult them yourself if they were only successful enough. You can have your Ronder.'

The door opened and the maid announced : 'Canon Ronder.'

Every one was conscious of the dramatic fitness of this, and no one more so than Mrs. Combermere. Ronder entered the room, however, quite unaware of anything apparently, except that he was feeling very well and expected amusement from his company. He presented precisely the picture of a nice contented clergyman who might be baffled by a school treat but was thoroughly " up " to afternoon tea. He seemed a little stouter than when he had first come to Polchester, and his large spectacles were as round as two young moons.

'How do you do, Mrs. Combermere? I do hope you will forgive my aunt, but she has a bad headache. She finds Polchester a little relaxing.'

Mrs. Combermere did not get up, but stared at him from behind her tea-table. That was a stare that has frightened many people in its time, and to-day it was especially challenging. She was annoyed with Ellen Stiles, and here, in front of her, was the cause of her annoyance.

They faced one another, and the room behind them was aware that Mrs. Combermere, at any rate, had declared battle. Of what Ronder was aware no one knew.

'How do you do, Canon Ronder? I'm delighted that you've honoured my poor little house. I hear that you're a busy man. I'm all the more proud that you can spare me half an hour.'

She kept him standing there, hoping, perhaps, that he would be consciously awkward and embarrassed. He was completely at his ease.

'Oh no, I'm not busy. I'm a very lazy man.' He looked down at her smiling, aware, apparently, of no one else in the room. 'I'm always meaning to pull myself up. But I'm too old for improvement.'

'We're all busy people here, although you mayn't think it, Canon Ronder. But I'm afraid you're giving a false account of yourself. I've heard of you.'

'Nothing but good, I hope.'

'Well, I don't know. That depends. I expect you're going to shake us all up and teach us improvement.'

'Dear me, no! I come to you for instruction. I haven't an idea in the world.'

'Too much modesty is a dangerous thing. Nobody's modest in Polchester.'

'Then I shall be Polchester's first modest man. But I'm not modest. I simply speak the truth.'

Mrs. Combermere smiled grimly. 'There, too, you will be the exception. We none of us speak the truth here.'

'Really, Mrs. Combermere, you're giving Polchester a dreadful character.' He laughed, but did not take his eyes away from her. 'I hope that you've been here so long that you've forgotten what the place is like. I believe in first impressions.'

'So do I,' she said, very grimly indeed.

'Well, in a year's time we shall see which of us is right. I'll be quite willing to admit defeat.'

'Oh, a year's time!' She laughed more pleasantly. 'A great deal can happen in a year. You may be a bishop by then, Canon Ronder.'

'Ah, that would be more than I deserve,' he answered quite gravely.

The little duel was over. She turned round, introduced him to Miss Dobell and Puddifoot, both of whom, however, he had already met. He sat down, very happily, near the fire and listened to Miss Dobell's shrill proclamation of her adoration of Browning. Conversation became general, and was concerned first with the Jubilee and the preparations for it, afterwards with the state of South Africa, Lord Penrhyn's quarries, and bicycling. Every one had a good deal to say about this last topic, and the strange costumes which ladies, so the papers said, were wearing in Battersea Park when out on their morning ride.

Miss Dobell said that 'it was too disgraceful,' to which Mrs. Combermere replied, 'Fudge! As though every one didn't know by this time that women had legs!'

Everything, in fact, went very well, although Ellen Stiles observed to herself with a certain malicious pleasure that their hostess was not entirely at her ease, was 'a little ruffled about something.'

Soon two more visitors arrived—first Mr. Morris, then Mrs. Brandon. They came close upon one another's heels, and it was at once evident that they would, neither of them, alter very considerably the room's atmosphere. No one ever paid any attention to Mrs. Brandon in Polchester, and although Mr. Morris had been some time now in the town, he was so shy and retiring and quiet that no one was, as yet, very distinctly aware of him. Mrs. Combermere was occupied with her own thoughts and the others were talking very happily beside the fire, so it soon happened that Morris and Mrs. Brandon were sitting by themselves in the window.

There occurred then a revelation. . . . That is perhaps a portentous word, but what else can one call it? It is a platitude, of course, to say that there is probably no one alive who does not remember some occasion of a sudden communion with another human being that was so beautiful, so touching, so transcendentally above human affairs that a revelation was the only definition for it. Afterwards, when analysis plays its part, one may talk about physical attractions, about common intellectual interests, about spiritual bonds, about what you please, but one knows that the essence of that meeting is undefined.

It may be quite enough to say about Morris and Mrs. Brandon that they were both very lonely people. You may say, too, that there was in both of them an utterly unsatisfied longing to have some one to protect and care for. Not her husband nor Falk nor Joan needed Mrs. Brandon in the least—and the Archdeacon did not approve of dogs in the house. Or you may say, if you like, that these two liked the look of one another, and leave it at that. Still the revelation remains—and all the tragedy and unhappiness and bitterness that that revelation involved remains too. . . .

This was, of course, not the first time that they

had met. Once before at Mrs. Combermere's they had been introduced and talked together for a moment ; but on that occasion there had been no revelation.

They did not say very much now. Mrs. Brandon asked Morris whether he liked Polchester and he said yes. They talked about the Cathedral and the coming Jubilee. Morris said that he had met Falk. Mrs. Brandon, colouring a little, asked was he not handsome ? She said that he was a remarkable boy, very independent, that was why he had not got on very well at Oxford. . . . He was a tremendous comfort to her, she said. When he went away . . . but she stopped suddenly.

Not looking at him, she said that sometimes one felt lonely even though there was a great deal to do, as there always was in a town like Polchester.

Yes, Morris said that he knew that. And that was really all. There were long pauses in their conversation, pauses that were like the little wooden hammerings on the stage before the curtain rises.

Mrs. Brandon said that she hoped that he would come and see her, and he said that he would. Their hands touched, and they both felt as though the room had suddenly closed in upon them and become very dim, blotting the other people out.

Then Mrs. Brandon got up to go. Afterwards, when she looked back to this, she remembered that she had looked, for some unknown reason, especially at Canon Ronder, as she stood there saying good-bye.

She decided that she did not like him. Then she went away, and Mrs. Combermere was glad that she had gone.

Of all the dull women. . . .

CHAPTER VI

SEATOWN MIST AND CATHEDRAL DUST

FALK BRANDON knew quite well that his mother was watching him.

It was a strange truth that until this return of his from Oxford he had never considered his mother at all. It was not that he had grown to disregard her, as do many sons, because of the monotonous regularity of her presence. Nor was it that he despised her because he seemed so vastly to have outgrown her. He had not been unkind nor patronising nor contemptuous—he had simply not yet thought about her. The circumstances of his recent return, however, had forced him to consider every one in the house. He had his secret preoccupation that seemed so absorbing and devastating to him that he could not believe that every one around him would not guess it. He soon discovered that his father was too cock-sure and his sister too innocent to guess anything. Now he was not himself a perceptive man ; he had, after all, seen as yet very little of the world, and he had a great deal of his father's self-confidence ; nevertheless, he was just perceptive enough to perceive that his mother was thinking about him, was watching him, was waiting to see what he would do. . . .

His secret was quite simply that, for the last year, he had been devastated by the consciousness of Annie Hogg, the daughter of the landlord of ' The Dog and Pilchard.' Yes, devastated was the word. It would not be true to say that he was in love with her or, indeed, had any analysed emotion for her— he was aware of her always, was disturbed by her always, could not keep away from her, wanted something in connection with her far deeper than mere love-making——

What he wanted he did not know. He could not keep away from her, and yet when he was with her nothing occurred. She did not apparently care for him ; he was not even sure that he wanted her to. At Oxford during his last term he had thought of her—incessantly, a hot pain at his heart. He had not invited the disturbance that had sent him down, but he had welcomed it.

Every day he went to ' The Dog and Pilchard.' He drank but little and talked to no one. He just leaned up against the wall and looked at her. Sometimes he had a word with her. He knew that they must all be speaking of it. Maybe the whole town was chattering. He could not think of that. He had no plans, no determination, no resolve—and he was desperately unhappy. . . .

Into this strange dark confusion the thought of his mother drove itself. He had from the very beginning been aware of his father in this connection. In his own selfish way he loved his father, and he shared in his pride and self-content. He was proud of his father for being what he was, for his good-natured contempt of other people, for his handsome body and his dominance of the town. He could understand that his father should feel as he did, and he did honestly consider him a magnificent man and far above every one else in the place. But that did not mean that he ever listened to anything that his father said. He pleased himself in what he did, and laughed at his father's temper.

He had perceived from the first that this connection of his with Annie Hogg might do his father very much harm, and he did not want to harm him. The thought of this did not mean that for a moment he contemplated dropping the affair because of his father—no, indeed—but the thought of the old man, as he termed him, added dimly to his general unhappiness. He appreciated the way that his father had taken his return from Oxford. The old man was a sportsman. It was a great pity that he should have to make him unhappy over this business. But there it was—you couldn't alter things.

It was this fatalistic philosophy that finally ruled everything with him. 'What must be must.' If things went wrong he had his courage, and he was helped too by his contempt for the world. . . .

He knew his father, but he was aware now that he knew nothing at all about his mother.

'What's *she* thinking about?' he asked himself.

One afternoon he was about to go to Seatown when, in the passage outside his bedroom, he met his mother. They both stopped as though they had something to say to one another. He did not look at all like her son, so fair, tall and aloof, as though even in his own house he must be on his guard, prepared to challenge any one who threatened his private plans.

'She's like a little mouse,' he thought to himself, as though he were seeing her for the first time, 'preparing to run off into the wainscot.' He was conscious, too, of her quiet clothes and shy pre-occupied timidity—all of it he seemed to see for the first time, a disguise for some purpose as secret, perhaps, as his own.

' Oh, Falk,' she said, and stopped, and then went on with the question that she so often asked him :

' Is there anything you want ? '

' No, mother, thank you.   I'm just going out.'

' Oh, yes. . . .'   She still stayed there nervously looking up at him.

' I was wondering——   Are you going into the town ? '

' Yes, mother.   Is there anything I can do for you ? '

' No, thank you.'   Still she did not move.

' Joan's out,' she said.   Then she went on quickly, ' I wish you'd tell me if there were any-thing——'

' Why, of course.'   He laughed.   ' What exactly do you mean ? '

' Nothing, dear.   Only I like to know about your plans.'

' Plans ?   I haven't any.'

' No, but I always think you may be going away suddenly.   Perhaps I could help you.   I know it isn't very much that I can do, but anything you told me I think I could help you about . . . I'd like to help you.'

He could see that she had been resolving for some time to speak to him, and that this little appeal was the result of a desperate determination.   He was touched.

' That's all right, mother.   I suppose father and you think I oughtn't to be hanging around here doing nothing.'

' Oh, your father hasn't said anything to me. I don't know what he thinks. But I should miss you if you went. It is nice for us having you, although, of course, it must seem slow to you here.'

He stood back against the wall, looking past her out through the window that showed the grey sky of a misty day.

' Well, it's true that I've got to settle about doing something soon. I can't be home like this for ever. There's a man I know in London wants me to go in for a thing with him. . . .'

' What kind of a thing, dear ? '

' It's to do with the export trade. Travelling about. I should like that. I'm a bit restless, I'm afraid. I should want to put some money into it, of course, but the governor will let me have something. . . . He wants me to go into Parliament.'

' Parliament ? '

' Yes,' Falk laughed. ' That's his latest idea. He was talking about it the other night. Of course, that's foolishness. It's not my line at all. I told him so.'

' I wouldn't like you to go away altogether,' she repeated. ' It would make a great difference to me.'

' Would it really ? ' He had a strange mysterious impulse to speak to her about Annie Hogg. The thought of his mother and Annie Hogg together showed him at once how impossible that was. They were in separate worlds. He was suddenly angry at the difficulties that life was making for him without his own wish. ' Oh, I'll be here some time yet, mother,' he said. ' Well, I must get along now. I've got an appointment with a fellow.'

She smiled and disappeared into her room.

All the way into Seatown he was baffled and

irritated by this little conversation. It seemed that you could not disregard people by simply determining to disregard them. All the time behind you and them some force was insisting on places being taken, connections being formed. One was simply a bally pawn . . . a bally pawn. . . .

But what was his mother thinking ? Had some one been talking to her ? Perhaps already she knew about Annie. But what could she know ? Girls like Annie were outside her ken. What could his mother know about life ? The day did not help his dissatisfaction. The fog had not descended upon the town, but it had sent as its forerunner a wet sea mist, dim and intangible, depressing because it removed all beauty and did not leave even challenging ugliness in its place.

On the best of days Seatown was not beautiful. I have read in books romantic descriptions of Glebeshire coves, Glebeshire towns with the romantic Inn, the sanded floor, fishermen with gold rings in their ears and strange oaths upon their lips. In one book I remember there was a fine picture of such a place, with beautiful girls dancing and mysterious old men telling mysterious tales about ghosts and goblins, and, of course, somewhere in the distance some one was singing a chanty, and the moon was rising, and there was a nice little piece of Glebeshire dialect thrown in. All very pretty . . . Seatown cannot claim such prettiness. Perhaps once long ago, when there were only the Cathedral, the Castle, the Rock, and a few cottages down by the river, when, at nighttide, strange foreign ships came up from the sea, when the woods were wild forest and the downs were bare and savage, Seatown had its romance, but that was long ago. Seatown, in these latter days, was a place of bad drainage, bad drinking, bad living and bad dying. The men who haunted its dirty narrow little streets were loafers and idlers and castaways. The women were, most of them, no better than they should be, and the children were the most slatternly and ill-bred in the whole of Glebeshire. Small credit to the Canons and the Town Councillors and the prosperous farmers that it was so, but in their defence it might be urged that it needed a very valiant Canon and the most fearless of Town Councillors to disturb that little nest. And the time came when it was disturbed. . . .

Even the Pol, a handsome river enough out beyond the town in the reaches of the woods, was no pretty sight at low tide when there was nothing to see but a thin, sluggish grey stream · filtering through banks of mud to its destination the sea. At high tide the river beat up against the crazy stone wall that bordered Pennicent Street ; and on the further side there were green fields and a rising hill with a feathery wood to crown it. From the river, coming up through the green banks, Seatown looked picturesque, with its disordered cottages scrambling in confusion at the tail of the rock and the Cathedral and Castle nobly dominating it. That distant view is the best thing to be said for Seatown.

To-day, in the drizzling mist, the place was horribly depressing. Falk plunged down into Bridge Street as into a damp stuffy well. Here some of the houses had once been fine ; there were porticoes and deep-set doors and bow-windows, making them poor relations of the handsome bene-volent Georgian houses in Orange Street. The street, top-tilting down to the river, was slovenly with dirt and carelessness. Many of the windows were broken, their panes stuffed with paper, washing hung from house to house. The windows that were not broken were hermetically sealed and filled with grimy plants and ferns, and here and there a photograph of an embarrassed sailor or a smiling married couple or an overdressed young woman placed face outward to the street. Bridge Street tumbled with a dirty absent-mindedness into Pennicent Street. This, the main thoroughfare of Seatown, must have been once a handsome cobbled walk by the river-side. The houses, more than in Bridge Street, showed by their pillared doorways and their faded red-brick that they had once been gentlemen's residences, with gardens, perhaps, running to the river's edge and a fine view of the meadows and woods beyond. To-day all was shrouded in a mist that was never stationary, that seemed alive in its shifting movement, revealing here a window, there a door, now a chimney-pot, now steps that seemed to lead into air, and the river, now at full tide and lapping the stone wall, seemed its drunken bewildered voice.

'Bally pawns, that's what we are,' Falk muttered again. It seemed to be the logical conclusion of the thoughts that had worried him, like flies, during his walk. Some one lurched against him as he stayed for a moment to search for the inn. A hot spasm of anger rose in him, so sudden and fierce that he was frightened by it, as though he had seen his own face in a mirror. But he said nothing. 'Sorry,' said a voice, and shadow faded into shadow.

He found ' The Dog and Pilchard' easily enough. Just beyond it the river was caught into a kind of waterfall by a ridge of stone that projected almost into mid-stream. At high tide it tumbled over this

obstruction with an astonished splash and gurgle.
Even when the river was at its lowest there was a
dim chattering struggle at this point.   Falk always
connected this noise with the inn and the power or
enchantment of the inn that held him — ' Black
Enchantment,' perhaps.   He was to hear that
struggling chatter of the river until his dying
day.

He pushed through the passage and turned to
the right into the bar.   A damp day like this always
served Hogg's trade.   The gas was lit and sizzled
overhead with a noise as though it commented
ironically on the fatuity of the human beings beneath it.   The room was full, but most of the men—
seamen, loafers, a country man or two—crowded up
to the bar.   Falk crossed to a table in the corner
near the window, his accustomed seat.   No one
seemed to notice him, but soon Hogg, stout and
smiling, came over to him.   No one had ever seen
Samuel Hogg out of temper—no, never, not even
when there had been fighting in the place and he
had been compelled to eject men, by force of arms,
through the doors and windows.   There had not
been many fights there.   Men were afraid of him,
in spite of his imperturbable good temper.   Men
said of him that he would stick at nothing, although
what exactly was meant by that no one knew.

He had a good word for every one ; no crime or
human failing could shock him.   He laughed at
everything.   And yet men feared him.   Perhaps
for that very reason.   The worst sinner has some
kind of standard of right and wrong.   Himself he
may not keep it, but he likes to see it there.   ' Oh,
he's deep,' was Seatown's verdict on Samuel Hogg,
and it is certain that the late Mrs. Hogg had not

been, in spite of her husband's good temper, a happy woman.

He came up to Falk now, smiling, and asked him what he would have. 'Nasty day,' he said. Falk ordered his drink. Dimly through the mist and thickened air the Cathedral chimes recorded the hour. Funny how you could hear them in every nook and corner of Polchester.

'Likely turn to rain before night,' Hogg said, as he turned back to the bar. Falk sat there watching. Some of the men he knew, some he did not, but to-day they were all shadows to him. Strange how, from the moment that he crossed the threshold of that place, hot, burning excitement and expectation lapped him about, swimming up to him, engulfing him, swamping him body and soul. He sat there drowned in it, not stirring, his eyes fixed upon the door. There was a good deal of noise, laughter, swearing, voices raised and dropped, forming a kind of skyline, and above this a voice telling an interminable tale.

Annie Hogg came in, and at once Falk's throat contracted and his heart hammered in the palms of his hands. She moved about, talking to the men, fetching drinks, unconcerned and aloof as she always was. Seen there in the mist of the overcrowded and evil-smelling room, there was nothing very remarkable about her. Stalwart and resolute and self-possessed she looked ; sometimes she was beautiful, but not now. She was a woman at whom most men would have looked twice. Her expression was not sullen nor disdainful ; in that, perhaps, there was something fine, because there was life, of its own kind, in her eyes, and independence in the carriage of her head.

Falk never took his eyes from her. At that moment she came down the room and saw him. She did not come over to him at once, but stopped and talked to some one at another table. At last she was beside him, standing up against his table and looking over his head at the window behind him.

' Nasty weather, Mr. Brandon,' she said. Her voice was low and not unpleasant ; although she rolled her r's her Glebeshire accent was not very strong, and she spoke slowly as though she were trying to choose her words.

' Yes,' Falk answered. ' Good for your trade, though.'

' Dirty weather always brings them in,' she said. He did not look at her.

' Been busy to-day ? '

' Nothing much this morning,' she answered. ' I've been away at my aunt's, out to Borheddon, these last two days.'

' Yes. I saw you were not here,' he said. ' Did you have a good time ? '

' Middling,' she answered. ' My aunt's been terrible bad with bronchitis this winter. Poor soul, it'll carry her off one of these days, I reckon.'

' What's Borheddon like ? ' he asked.

' Nothing much. Nothing to do, you know. But I like a bit of quiet just for a day or two. How've you been keeping, Mr. Brandon ? '

' Oh, I'm all right. I shall be off to London to look for a job one of these days.'

He looked up at her suddenly, sharply, as though he wanted to catch her interest. But she showed no emotion.

' Well, I expect this is slow for you, a little place like this. Plenty going on in London, I expect.'

' Yes. Do you ever think you'd like to go there ? '

' Daresay I shall one of these days. Never know your luck. But I'm not terrible anxious. . . . Well, I must be getting on.'

He caught her eyes and held them.

' Come back for a moment when you're less busy. I've got something I want to say to you.'

Very slightly the colour rose in her dark cheek.

' All right,' she said.

When she had gone he drew a deep breath, as though he had surmounted some great and sudden danger. He felt that if she had refused to come he would have risen and broken everything in the place. Now, as though he had, by that little con- versation with her, reassured himself about her, he looked around the room. His attention was at once attracted by a man who was sitting in the further corner, his back against the wall, opposite to him.

This was a man remarkable for his extreme thinness, for the wild lock of black hair that fell over his forehead and almost into his eyes, and for a certain sort of threadbare and dissolute distinction which hung about him. Falk knew him slightly. His name was Edmund Davray, and he had lived in Polchester now for a considerable number of years. He was an artist, and had arrived in the town one summer on a walking tour through Glebeshire. He had attracted attention at once by the quality of his painting, by the volubility of his manner, and by his general air of being a person of considerable distinction. His surname was French, but no one knew anything with any certainty about him. Some- thing attracted him in Polchester, and he stayed. He soon gave it out that it was the Cathedral that fascinated him ; he painted a number of remarkable sketches of the nave, the choir, Saint Margaret's Chapel, the Black Bishop's Tomb. He had a ' show ' in London and was supposed to have done very well out of it. He disappeared for a little, but soon returned, and was to be found in the Cathedral most days of the week.

At first he had a little studio at the top of Orange Street. At this time he was rather popular in Polchester society. Mrs. Combermere took him up and found him audacious and amusing. His French name gave a kind of piquancy to his audacity; he was unusual ; he was striking. It was right for Polchester to have an artist and to stick him up in the very middle of the town as an emblem of taste and culture. Soon, however, he began to decline. It was whispered that he drank, that his morals were ' only what you'd expect of an artist,' and that he was really ' too queer about the Cathedral.' One day he told Miss Dobell that the amount that she knew about literature would go inside a very small pea, and he was certainly ' the worse for liquor ' at one of Mrs. Combermere's tea-parties. He did not, however, give them time to drop him ; he dropped himself, gave up his Orange Street studio, lived, no one knew where, neglected his appearance, and drank quite freely whenever he could get anything to drink. He now cut everybody, rather than allowed himself to be cut.

He was in the Cathedral as often as ever, and Lawrence and Cobbett, the Vergers, longed to have an excuse for expelling him, but he always behaved himself there and was in nobody's way. He was finally regarded as ' quite mad,' and was seen to talk aloud to himself as he walked about the streets.

' An unhappy example,' Miss Dobell said, ' of the artistic temperament, that wonderful gift, gone wrong.'

Falk had seen him often before at ' The Dog and Pilchard,' and had wondered at first whether Annie Hogg was the attraction. It was soon clear, however, that there was nothing in that. He never looked at the girl nor, indeed, at any one else in the place. He simply sat there moodily staring in front of him and drinking.

To-day it was clear that Falk had caught his attention. He looked across the room at him with a queer defiant glance, something like Falk's own. Once it seemed that he had made up his mind to come over and speak to him.

He half rose in his seat, then sank back again. But his eyes came round again and again to the corner where Falk was sitting.

The Cathedral chimes had whispered twice in the room before Annie returned.

' What is it you're wanting ? ' she asked.

' Come outside and speak to me.'

' No, I can't do that. Father's watching.'

' Well, will you meet me one evening and have a talk ? '

' What about ? '

' Several things.'

' It isn't right, Mr. Brandon. What's a gentleman like you want with a girl like me ? '

' I only want us to get away a little from all this noise and filth.'

Suddenly she smiled.

' Well, I don't mind if I do. After supper's a good time. Father goes up the town to play billiards. After eight.'

' When ? '

' What about to-morrow evening ? '

' All right.   Where ? '

' Up to the Mill.   Five minutes up from here.'

' I'll be there,' he said.

' Don't let father catch 'ee — that's all,' she smiled down at him.   ' You'm a fule, Mr. Brandon, to bother with such as I.'   He said nothing and she walked away.   Very shortly after, Davray got up from his seat and came over to Falk's corner.   It was obvious that he had been drinking rather heavily.   He was a little unsteady on his feet.

' You're young Brandon, aren't you ? ' he asked.

In ordinary times Falk would have told him to go to the devil, and there would have been a row, but to-day he was caught away so absolutely into his own world that any one could speak to him, any one laugh at him, any one insult him, and he would not care.   He had been meditating for weeks the advance that he had just taken ; always when one meditates for long over a risk it swells into gigantic proportions.   So this had been ; that simple sentence asking her to come out and talk to him had seemed an impossible challenge to every kind of fate, and now, in a moment, the gulf had been jumped . . . so easy, so strangely easy. . . .

From a great distance Davray's words came to him, and in the dialogue that followed he spoke like a somnambulist.

' Yes,' he said, ' my name's Brandon.'

' I knew, of course,' said Davray.   ' I've seen you about.'   He spoke with great swiftness, the words tumbling over one another, not with eagerness, but rather with a kind of supercilious carelessness.   ' Beastly hole, isn't this ?   Wonder why one comes

here. Must do something in this rotten town.
I've drunk enough of this filthy beer. What do
you say to moving out?'

Falk looked up at him.

'What do you say?' he asked.

'Let's move out of this. If you're walking up
the town I'll go with you.'

Falk was not conscious of the man, but it was
quite true that he wanted to get out of the place
now that his job in it was done. He got up without
a word and began to push through the room. He
was met near the door by Hogg.

'Goin', Mr. Brandon? Like to settle now or
leave it to another day?'

'What's that?' said Falk, stopping as though
some one had touched him on the shoulder. He
seemed to see the large smiling man suddenly in
front of him outlined against a shifting wall of mist.

'Payin' now or leavin' it? Please yourself, Mr.
Brandon.'

'Oh—paying!' He fumbled in his pocket,
produced half-a-crown, gave it to Hogg without
looking at him and went out. Davray followed,
slouching through the room and passage with the
conceited over-careful walk of a man a little tipsy.

Outside, as they went down the street still
obscured with the wet mist, Davray poured out a
flow of words to which he seemed to want no
answer.

'I hope you didn't mind my speaking to you
like that—a bit unceremonious. But to tell you
the truth I'm lonely sometimes. Also, if you want
to know the whole truth and nothing but the
truth, I'm a bit tipsy too. Generally am. This air
makes one feel queer after that stinking hole, doesn't

it ? if you can call this air. I've seen you there a lot lately and often thought I'd like to talk to you. You're the only decent-looking fellow in the whole of this town, if you'll forgive my saying so. Isn't it a bloody hole ? But of course you think so too. I can see it in your face. I suppose you go to that pub after that girl. I saw you talking to her. Well, each man to his taste. I'd never interfere with any man's pleasure. I loathe women myself, always have. They never appealed to me a little bit. In Paris the men used to wonder what I was after. I was after Ambition in those days. Funny thing, but I thought I was going to be a great painter once. Queer what one can trick oneself into believing—so I might have been if I hadn't come to this beastly town. Hope I'm not boring you. . . .'

He stopped as though he had suddenly realised that his companion had not said a word. They were pushing now up the hill into the market-place and the mist was now so thick that they could scarcely see one another's face. Falk was thinking. 'To-morrow evening. . . . What do I want ? What's going to happen ? What do I want ? '

The silence made him conscious of his companion.

'What do you say ? ' he asked.

'Hope I'm not boring you.'

'No, that's all right. Where are we ? '

'Just coming into the market.'

'Oh, yes.'

'If I talk a lot it's because I haven't had any one to talk to for weeks. Not that I want to talk to any one. I despise the lot of them. Conceited set of ignorant parrots. . . . Whole place run by

women and what can you expect ? You're not
staying here, I suppose. I heard you'd had enough
of Oxford and I don't wonder. No place for a
man, beautiful enough but spoilt by the people.
Damn people—always coming along and spoiling
places. Now there's the Cathedral, most wonderful
thing in England, but does any one know it ? Not
a bit of it. You'd think they fancied that the
Cathedral owes *them* something—about as much
sense of beauty as a cockroach.'

They were pressing up the High Street now
There was no one about. It was a town of ghosts.
By the Arden Gate Falk realised where he was and
halted.

' Hullo ! we're nearly home. . . . Well . . .
good afternoon, Mr. Davray.'

' Come into the Cathedral for a moment,'
Davray seemed to be urgent about this. ' Have
you ever been up into the King Harry Tower ? I
bet you haven't.'

' King Harry Tower ? . . . ' Falk stared at
the man. What did the fellow want him to do ?
Go into the Cathedral ? Well, why not ? Stupid
to go home just now—nothing to do there but
think, and people would interrupt. . . . Think
better out of doors. But what was there to think
about ? He was not thinking, simply going round
and round. . . . Who was this fellow anyway ?

' As you like,' he said.

They crossed the Precincts and went through
the West door into the Cathedral. The nave was
full of dusky light and very still. Candles glimmered behind the great choir-screen and there were
lamps by the West door. Seen thus, in its half-
dark, the nave bore full witness to the fact that

Polchester has the largest Cathedral in Northern
Europe.   It is certainly true that no other building
in England gives the same overwhelming sense of
length.

In full daylight the nave perhaps, as is the case
with all English Cathedrals, lacks colour and seems
cold and deserted.   In the dark of this spring
evening it was full of mystery, and the great columns
of the nave's ten bays, rising unbroken to the roof
groining, sprang, it seemed, out of air, superbly,
intolerably inhuman.

The colours from the tombs and the brasses
glimmered against the grey, and the great rose-
coloured circle of the West window flung pale
lights across the cold dark of the flags and pillars.

The two men were held by the mysterious
majesty of the place.   Falk was lifted right out of
his own preoccupied thoughts.

He had never considered the Cathedral except
as a place to which he was dragged for services
against his will, but to-night, perhaps because of
his own crisis, he seemed to see it all for the first
time.   He was conscious now of Davray and was
aware that he did not like him and wished to be
rid of him—' an awful-looking tout ' he thought
him, ' with his greasy long hair and his white long
face and his spindle legs.'

' Now we'll go up into King Harry,' Davray
said.   But at that moment old Lawrence came
bustling along.   Lawrence, over seventy years of
age, had grown stout and white-haired in the
Cathedral's service.   He was a fine figure in his
purple gown, broad-shouldered, his chest and
stomach of a grand protuberance, his broad white
flowing beard a true emblem of his ancient dignity.

He was the most autocratic of Vergers and had been allowed now for many years to do as he pleased. The only thorn in his flesh was Cobbett, the junior Verger, who, as he very well realised, was longing for him to die, that he might step into his shoes. 'I do believe,' he was accustomed to say to Mrs. Lawrence, a little be-bullied woman, 'that that man will poison me one of these fine days.'

His autocracy had grown on him with the size and whiteness of his beard, and there were many complaints—rude to strangers, sycophantic to the aristocracy, greedy of tips, insolent and conceited, he was an excellent example of the proper spirit of the Church Militant. He had, however, his merits. He loved small children and would have allowed them to run riot on the Cathedral greens had he not been checked, and he had a pride in the Cathedral that would drive him to any sacrifice in his defence of it.

It was natural enough that he should hate the very sight of Davray, and when that gentleman appeared he hung about in the background hoping that he might catch him in some crime. At first he thought him alone.

'Oh, Verger,' Davray said, as though he were speaking to a beggar who had asked of him alms. 'I want to go up into King Harry. You have the key, I think.'

'Well you can't, sir,' said Lawrence with considerable satisfaction. ''Tis after hours.' Then he saw Falk.

'Oh I beg your pardon, Mr. Brandon, sir. I didn't realise. Do you want to go up the Tower, sir?'

'We may as well,' said Falk.

' Of course for you, sir, it's different. Strangers
have to keep certain hours. This way, sir.'

They followed the pompous old man across the
nave, up the side aisle, past ' tombs and monuments
and gilded knights,' until they came to the King
Harry Chapel. This was to the right of the choir,
and before the screen that railed it off from the rest
of the church there was a notice saying that this
Chapel had been put aside for private prayer and
it was hoped that no one would talk or make any
noise, were some one meditating or praying there.
The little place was infinitely quiet, with a special
air of peace and beauty as though all the prayers
and meditations that had been offered there had
deeply sanctified it ; Lawrence pushed open the
door of the screen and they crossed the flagged floor.
Suddenly into the heart of the hush there broke the
Cathedral chimes, almost, as it seemed, directly
above their heads, booming, echoing, dying with
lingering music back into the silence. At the
corner of the Chapel there was a little wooden
door ; Lawrence unlocked it and pushed it open.
' Mind how you go, sir,' he said, speaking to Falk
as though Davray did not exist. ' 'Tis a bit difficult
with the winding stair.'

The two men went forward into the black
darkness, leaving the dusky light behind them.
Davray led the way and Falk followed, feeling with
his arms the black walls on either side of him,
knocking with his legs against the steps above him.
Here there was utter darkness and no sound. He
had suddenly a half-alarmed, half-humorous suspicion that Davray was suddenly going to turn round
upon him and push him down the stair or stick a
knife into him—the fear of the dark. ' After all,

what am I doing with this fellow?' he thought.
'I don't know him. I don't like him. I don't
want to be with him.'

'That's better,' he heard Davray say. There
was a glimmer, then a shadow of grey light, finally
they had stepped out into what was known as the
Whispering Gallery, a narrow railed platform that
ran the length of the Chapel and beyond to the
opposite Tower. They did not stop there. They
pushed up again by more winding stairs, black for
a space, then lit by a window, then black again. At
last, after what had seemed a long journey, they were
in a little, spare, empty room with a wooden floor.
One side of this little room was open and railed in.
Looking down, the floor of the nave seemed a vast
distance below. You seemed here to be flying in
glory. The dim haze of the candles just touched
the misty depth with golden colour. Above them
the great roof seemed close and menacing. Everywhere pillars and buttresses rose out of space. The
great architect of the building seemed here to have
his true kingdom, so vast was the depth and the
height and the grandeur. The walls and the roof
and the pillars that supported it were alive with
their own greatness, scornful of little men and their
little loves. The hush was filled with movement
and stir and a vast business. . . .

The two men leaned on the rails and looked
down. Far below, the white figured altar, the brass
of the Black Bishop's tomb, the glitter of Saint
Margaret's screen struck in little points of dull gold
like stars upon a grey inverted sky.

Davray turned suddenly upon his companion.
'And it's men like your father,' he said, 'who think
that this place is theirs. . . . Theirs! Presumption!

But they'll get it in the neck for that. This place can bide its time. Just when you think you're its master it turns and stamps you out.'

Falk said nothing. Davray seemed irritated by his silence. 'You wait and see,' he said. 'It amuses me to see your governor walking up the choir on Sundays as though he owned the place. Owned it! Why, he doesn't realise a stone of it! Well, he'll get it. They all have who've tried his game. Owned it!'

'Look here,' said Falk, 'don't you say anything about my father——that's none of your business. He's all right. I don't know what the devil I came up here for——thinking of other things.'

Davray too was thinking of other things.

'You wonderful place!' he whispered. 'You beautiful place! You've ruined me, but I don't care. You can do what you like with me. You wonder! You wonder!'

Falk looked at him. The man was mad. He was holding on to the railing, leaning forward, staring. . . .

'Look here, it isn't safe to lean like that. You'll be tumbling over and breaking your neck if you're not careful.'

But Davray did not hear him. He was lost in his own dreams. Falk despised dreams although just now he was himself in the grip of one. Besides the fellow was drunk.

A sudden disgust of his companion overtook him.

'Well, so long,' he said. 'I must be getting home!'

He wondered for a moment whether it were safe to leave the fellow there. 'It's his own look-out,' he thought, and as Davray said no more he left him.

Back once more in the King Harry Chapel, he looked up. But he could see no one and could hear no sound.

CHAPTER VII

RONDER'S DAY

RONDER had now spent several months in Polchester and was able to come to an opinion about it, and the opinion that he had come to was that he could be very comfortable there. His aunt, who in spite of her sharpness, never was sure how he would take anything, was a little surprised when he told her this. But then she was never certain what were the secret springs from which he derived that sense of comfort that was the centre of his life. She should have known by now that he derived it from two things—luxury and the possibility of intrigue.

Polchester could not have appeared to any casual observer a luxurious town, but it had for Ronder exactly that combination of beauty and mystery that obtained for him his sensation.

He did not analyse it as yet further than that— he knew that those two things were there ; he might investigate them at his leisure.

In that easy, smiling fashion that he had developed from his earliest days as the surest protection for his own security and ease, he arranged everything around him to assure his tranquillity. Everything was not as yet arranged ; it might take him six months, a year, two years for that arrangement . . . but he knew now that it would be done.

The second element in his comfort, his love of intrigue, would be satisfied here simply because everything was not, as yet, as he would have it. He would have hated to have tumbled into the place and found it just as he required it. He liked to have things to move, to adjust, to arrange, just as when he entered a room he always, if he had the power, at once altered the chairs, the cushions. It was towards this final adjustment that his power of intrigue always worked. Once everything was adjusted he sank back luxuriously and surveyed it— and then, in all probability, was quickly tired of it and looked for new fields to conquer.

He could not remember a time when he had not been impelled to alter things for his comfort. He did not wish to be selfish about this, he was quite willing for every one else to do the same—indeed, he watched them with geniality and wondered why on earth they didn't. As a small boy at Harrow he had, with an imperturbable smile and a sense of humour that, in spite of his rotund youth and a general sense amongst his elders that he was 'cheeky,' won him popularity, worked always for his own comfort.

He secured it and, first as fag and afterwards as House-prefect, finally as School-prefect, did exactly what he wanted with everybody.

He did it by being, quite frankly, all things to all men, although never with sycophancy nor apparent falseness. He amused the bored, was confidential with the wicked, upright with the upright, and sympathetic with the unfortunate.

He was quite genuine in all these things. He

was deeply interested in humanity, not for humanity's sake but his own. He bore no man any grudge, but if any one was in his way he worked hard until they were elsewhere. That removal attained, he wished them all the luck in the world.

He was ordained because he thought he could deal more easily with men as a parson. 'Men always take clergymen for fools,' he told his aunt, 'and so they sometimes are . . . but not always.' He knew he was not a fool, but he was not conceited. He simply thought that he had hit upon the one secret of life and could not understand why others had not done the same. Why do people worry so ? was the amused speculation. 'Deep emotions are simply not worth while,' he decided on his coming of age. He liked women but his sense of humour prevented him from falling in love. He really did understand the sensual habits and desires of men and women but watched them from a distance through books and pictures and other men's stories. He was shocked by nothing—nor did he despise mankind. He thought that mankind did on the whole very well considering its difficulties. He was kind and often generous ; he bore no man alive or dead any grudge. He refused absolutely to quarrel—' waste of time and temper.'

His one danger was lest that passion for intrigue should go deeper than he allowed anything to go. Playing chess with mankind was to him, he declared, simply a means to an end. Perhaps once it had been so. But, as he grew older, there was a danger that the end should be swallowed by the means.

This danger he did not perceive ; it was his one blindness. Finally he believed with La Rochefoucauld that 'Pity is a passion which is wholly useless to a well-constituted mind.'

At any rate he discovered that there was in Polchester a situation exactly suited to his powers. The town, or the Cathedral part of it, was dominated by one man, and that man a stupid, autocratic, retrogressive, good-natured child. He bore that child not the slightest ill-will, but it must go or, at any rate, its authority must be removed. He did, indeed, like Brandon, and through most of this affair he did not cease to like him, but he, Ronder, would never be comfortable so long as Brandon was there, he would never be free to take the steps that seemed to him good, he would be interfered with and patronised. He was greatly amused by Brandon's patronage, but it really was not a thing that could be allowed to remain.

If he saw, as he made his plans, that the man's heart and soul, his life, physical and spiritual, were involved—well he was sorry. It simply proved how foolish it was to allow your heart and soul to be concerned in anything.

He very quickly perceived that the first thing to be done was to establish relations with the men who composed the Chapter. He watched, he listened, he observed, then, at the end of some months, he began to move.

Many men would have considered him lazy. He never took exercise if he could avoid it, and it was Polchester's only fault that it had so many hills. He always had breakfast in bed, read the papers there and smoked a cigarette. Every morning he had a bath as hot as he could bear it—and he could bear it very hot indeed. Much of his best thinking was done there.

When he came downstairs he reserved the first hour for his own reading, reading, that is, that had nothing to do with any kind of work, that was purely for his own pleasure. He allowed nothing whatever to interfere with this—Gautier and Flaubert, La Bruyère and Montaigne were his favourite authors, but he read a great deal of English, Italian, and Spanish, and had a marvellous memory. He enjoyed too, erotic literature and had a fine collection of erotic books and prints shut away in a cabinet in his study. He found great fascination in theological books : he laughed at many of them, but kept an open mind—atheistic and materialistic dogmas seemed to him as absurd as orthodox ones. He read too a good deal of philosophy but, on the whole, he despised men who gave themselves up to philosophy more than any other human beings. He felt that they lost their sense of humour so quickly, and made life unpleasant for themselves.

After his hour of reading he gave himself up to the work of the day. He was the most methodical of men : the desk in his study was full of little drawers and contrivances for keeping things in order. He had a thin vase of blue glass filled with flowers, a small Chinese image of green jade, a photograph of the Blind Homer from the Naples Museum in a silver frame, and a little gold clock ; all these things had to be in their exactly correct positions. Nothing worried him so much as dust or any kind of disorder. He would sometimes stop in the middle of his work and cross the room in the soft slippers of brown kid that he always wore in his study, and put some picture straight or move some ornament from one position to another. The books that stretched along one wall from floor to ceiling were arranged most carefully according to their subjects. He disliked to see some books projecting further from the shelf than others, and, with a little smile of protest, as though he were giving them a kindly scolding, he would push them into their right places.

Let it not be supposed, however, that he was idle during these hours. He could accomplish an astonishing amount of work in a short time, and he was never idle except by deliberate intention.

When luncheon time arrived he was ready to be charming to his aunt, and charming to her he was. Their relations were excellent. She understood him so well that she left his schemes alone. If she did not entirely approve of him—and she entirely approved of nobody—she loved him for his good company, his humour, and his common sense. She liked it too that he did not mind when she chose to allow her irony to play upon him. He cared nothing for any irony.

At luncheon they felt a very agreeable intimacy. There was no need for explanations ; half allusions were enough. They could enjoy their joke without emphasising it and sometimes even without expressing it. Miss Ronder knew that her nephew liked to hear all the gossip. He collected it, tied it into little packets, and put them away in the little mechanical contrivances with which his mind was filled. She told him first what she heard, then her authorities, finally her own opinions. He thoroughly enjoyed his meal.

He had, by now, very thoroughly mastered the Cathedral finances. They were not complicated and were in good order, because Hart-Smith had been a man of an orderly mind. Ronder very quickly discovered that Brandon had had his fingers considerably in the old pie. 'And now there'll be a new pie,' he said to himself, 'baked by me.' . . . He traced a number of stupid and conservative decisions to Brandon's agency. There was no doubt that many things needed a new urgency and activity.

People had had to fight desperately for money when they should have been given it at once ; on the other hand, the Cathedral had been well looked after——it was rather dependent bodies like the School, the Almshouses, and various livings in the Chapter grant that had suffered.

Anything that could possibly be considered a novelty had been fought and generally defeated. 'There will be a lot of novelties before I've finished with them,' Ronder said to himself.

He started his investigations by paying calls on Bentinck-Major and Canon Foster. Bentinck-Major lived at the top of Orange Street, in a fine house with a garden, and Foster lived in one of four tumble-down buildings behind the Cathedral, known from time immemorial as Canon's Yard.

The afternoon of his visit was about three days after a dinner-party at the Castle. He had seen and heard enough at that dinner to amuse him for many a day ; he considered it to have been one of the most entertaining dinners at which he had ever been present. It had been here that he had heard for the first time of the Pybus St. Anthony living. Brandon had been present, and he observed Brandon's nervousness, and gathered enough to realise that this would be a matter of considerable seriousness. He was to know a great deal more about it before the afternoon was over.

As he walked through the town on the way to Orange Street he came upon Ryle, the Precentor. Ryle looked the typical clergyman, tall but not too tall, here a smile and there a smile, with his soft black hat, his trousers too baggy at the knees, his boots and his gold watch-chain both too large.

He cared, with serious devotion, for the Cathedral music and sang the services beautifully, but he would have been able to give more time to his work were he not so continuously worrying as to whether people were vexed with him or no. His idea of Paradise was a place where he could chant eternal services and where everybody liked him. He was a good man, but weak, and therefore driven again and again into insincerity. It was as though there was for ever in front of him the consciousness of some secret in his past life that must on no account be discovered ; but, poor man, he had no secret at all.

' Well, Precentor, and how are you ? ' said Ronder, beaming at him over his spectacles.

Ryle started. Ronder had come behind him. He liked the *look* of Ronder. He always preferred fat men to thin ; they were much less malicious, he thought.

' Oh, thank you, Canon Ronder — very well, thank you. I didn't see you. Quite spring weather. Are you going my way ? '

' I'm off to see Bentinck-Major.'

' Oh, yes, Bentinck-Major. . . .'

Ryle's first thought was—' Now is Bentinck-Major likely to have anything to say against me this afternoon ? '

' I'm going up Orange Street too. It's the High School Governors' meeting, you know.'

' Oh, yes, of course.'

The two men started up the hill together. Ronder surveyed the scene around him with pleasure. Orange Street always satisfied his aesthetic sense. It was the street of the doctors, the solicitors, the dentists, the bankers, and the wealthier old maids of Polchester. The grey stone was of a charming age, the houses with their bow-windows, their pillared porches, their deep-set doors, their gleaming old-fashioned knockers, spoke eloquently of the day when the great Janes, Elizabeths and D'Arcys, Mrs. Morrises and Misses Bates found the world in a tea-cup, when passions were solved by matrimony and ambitions by the possession of a carriage and a fine pair of bays. But more than this was the way that the gardens and lawns and orchards ran unchecked in and out, up and down, here breaking into the street, there crowding a church with apple-trees, seeming to speak, at every step, of leisure and sunny days and lives free of care.

Ronder had never seen anything so pretty ; something seemed to tell him that he would never see anything so pretty again.

Ryle was not a good conversationalist, because he had always before him the fear that some one might twist what he said into something really unpleasant, but, indeed, he found Ronder so agreeable that, as he told Mrs. Ryle when he got home, ' he never noticed the hill at all.'

' I hope you won't think me impertinent,' said Ronder, ' but I must tell you how charmed I was with the way that you sang the service on Sunday. You must have been complimented often enough before, but a stranger always has the right, I think, to say something. I'm a little critical, too, of that kind of thing, although, of course, an amateur . . . but—well, it was delightful.'

Ryle flushed with pleasure to the very tips of his over-large ears.

' Oh, really, Canon. . . . But indeed I hardly know what to say. You're too good. I do my poor best, but I can't help feeling that there is danger of one's becoming stale. I've been here a great many years now and I think some one fresh . . .'

' Well, often,' said Ronder, ' that *is* a danger. I know several cases where a change would be all for the better, but in your case there wasn't a trace of staleness. I do hope you won't think me pre-sumptuous in saying this. I couldn't help myself. I must congratulate you, too, on the choir. How do you find Brockett as an organist ? '

' Not quite all one would wish,' said Ryle eagerly—and then, as though he remembered that some one might repeat this to Brockett, he added hurriedly, ' Not that he doesn't do his best. He's an excellent fellow. Every one has their faults. It's only that he's a *little* too fond of adventures on his own account, likes to add things on the spur of the moment . . . a little *fantastic* sometimes.'

' Quite so,' said Ronder gravely. ' That's rather what I'd thought myself. I noticed it once or twice last Sunday. But that's a fault on the right side. The boys behave admirably. I never saw better behaviour.'

Ryle was now in his element. He let himself go, explaining this, defending that, apologising for one thing, hoping for another. Before he knew where he was he found himself at the turning above the monument that led to the High School.

' Here we part,' he said.

'Why, so we do,' cried Ronder.

'I do hope,' said Ryle nervously, 'that you'll come and see us soon. Mrs. Ryle will be delighted. . . .'

'Why, of course I will,' said Ronder. 'Any day you like. Good-bye. Good-bye,' and he went to Bentinck-Major's.

One look at Bentinck-Major's garden told a great deal about Bentinck-Major. The flower-beds, the trim over-green lawn, the neat paths, the trees in their fitting places, all spoke not only of a belief in material things but a desire also to demonstrate that one so believed. . . .

One expected indeed to see the Bentinck-Major arms over the front-door. They were there in spirit if not in fact.

'Is the Canon in ?' Ronder asked of a small and gaping page-boy.

He was in, it appeared. Would he see Canon Ronder ? The page-boy disappeared and Ronder was able to observe three family-trees framed in oak, a large china bowl with visiting-cards, and a huge round-faced clock that, even as he waited there, pompously announced the half-hour. Presently the Canon, like a shining Ganymede, came flying into the hall.

'My dear Ronder ! But this is delightful. A little early for tea, perhaps. Indeed, my wife is, for the moment, out. What do you say to the library ?'

Ronder had nothing to say against the library, and into it they went. A fine room with books in leather bindings, high windows, an oil painting of the Canon as a smart young curate, a magnificent writing-table, *The Spectator* and *The Church Times* near the fireplace, and two deep leather arm-chairs. Into these last two the clergymen sank.

Bentinck-Major put his fingers together, crossed his admirable legs, and looked interrogatively at his visitor.

'I'm lucky to catch you at home,' said Ronder. 'This isn't quite the time to call, I'm afraid. But the fact is that I want some advice.'

'Quite so,' said his host.

'I'm not a very modest man,' said Ronder, laughing. 'In fact, to tell you the truth, I don't believe very much in modesty. But there *are* times when it's just as well to admit one's incompetence. This is one of them——'

'Why, really, Canon,' said Bentinck-Major, wishing to give the poor man encouragement.

'No, but I mean what I say. I don't consider myself a stupid man, but when one comes fresh into a place like this there are many things that one *can't* know, and that one must learn from some one wiser than oneself if one's to do any good.'

'Oh, really, Canon,' Bentinck-Major repeated. 'If there's anything I can do——'

'There is. It isn't so much about the actual details of the work that I want your advice. Hart-Smith has left things in excellent condition, and I only hope that I shall be able to keep everything as straight as he has done. What I really want from you is some sort of bird's-eye view as to the whole situation. The Chapter, for instance. Of course, I've been here for some months now and have a little idea as to the people in the place, but you've been here so long that there are many things that you can tell me.'

'Now, for instance,' said Bentinck-Major, looking very wise and serious. 'What kind of things?'

'I don't want you to tell me any secrets,' said Ronder. 'I only want your opinion, as a man of the world, as to how things stand—what really wants doing, who, beside yourself, are the leading men here and in what directions they work. I needn't say that this conversation is confidential.'

'Oh, of course, of course.'

'Now, I don't know if I'm wrong, but it seems from what I've seen during the short time that I've been here that the general point of view is inclined to be a little too local. I believe you rather feel that yourself, although I may be prejudiced, coming straight as I have from London.'

'It's odd that you should mention that, Canon,' said Bentinck-Major. 'You've put your finger on the weak spot at once. You're only saying what I've been crying aloud for the last ever so many years. A voice in the wilderness I've been, I'm afraid—a voice in the wilderness, although perhaps I *have* managed to do a little something. But there's no doubt that the men here, excellent though they are, are a *little* provincial. What else can you expect? They've been here for years. They have not had, most of them, the advantage of mingling with the great world. That I should have had a little more of that opportunity than my fellows here is nothing to my credit, but it does, beyond question, give one a wider view—a wider view. There's our dear Bishop for instance—a saint, if ever there was one. A saint, Ronder, I assure you. But there he is, hidden away at Carpledon—out of things, I'm afraid, although of course he does his best. Then there's Sampson.

Well, I hardly need to tell you that he's not quite
the man to make things hum. *Not* by his own fault
I assure you. He does his best, but we are as we're
made . . . yes. We can only use the gifts that
God has given us, and God has not, undoubtedly,
given the Dean *quite* the gifts that we need here.'

He paused and waited. He was a cautious man
and weighed his words.

'Then there's Brandon,' said Ronder, smiling.
'There, if I may say so, is a splendid character, a
man who gives his whole life and energy for the
good of the place—who spares himself nothing.'

There was a little pause. Bentinck-Major took
advantage of it to look graver than ever.

'He strikes you like that, does he?' he said at
last. 'Well, in many ways I think you're right.
Brandon is a good friend of mine—I may say that
he thoroughly appreciates what I've done for this
place. But he is—*quite* between ourselves—how
shall I put it?—just a *little* autocratic. Perhaps
that's too strong a word, but he *is*, some think, a
little too inclined to fancy that he runs the Cathedral !
That, mind you, is only the opinion of some here,
and I don't know that I should entirely associate
myself with it, but perhaps there is *something* in it.
He is, as you can see, a man of strong will and, again
between ourselves, of a considerable temper. This
will not, I'm sure, go further than ourselves ? '

'Absolutely not,' said Ronder.

'Things have been a little slack here for several
years, and although I've done my own little best,
what is one against so many, if you understand what
I mean ? '

'Quite,' said Ronder.

'Well, nobody could call Brandon an unenergetic

man—quite the reverse. And, to put it frankly, to oppose him one needs courage. Now I may say that I've opposed him on a number of occasions but have had no backing. Brandon, when he's angry, is no light opponent, and the result has been that he's had, I'm afraid, a great deal of his own way.'

' You're afraid ? ' said Ronder.

Bentinck-Major seemed a little nervous at being caught up so quickly. He looked at Ronder suspiciously. His voice was sharper than it had been.

' Oh, I like Brandon—don't make any mistake about that. He and I together have done some excellent things here. In many ways he's admirable. I don't know what I'd have done sometimes without his backing. All I mean is that he is perhaps a little hasty sometimes.'

' Quite,' said Ronder. ' I can't tell you how you've helped me by what you've told me. I'm sure you're right in everything you've said. If you were to give me a tip then, you'd say that I couldn't do better than follow Brandon. I'll remember that.'

' Well, no,' said Bentinck-Major rather hastily. ' I don't know that I'd quite say that either. Brandon is often wrong. I'm not sure either that he has quite the influence he had. That silly little incident of the elephant the other day—you heard that, didn't you ?—well, a trivial thing, but one saw by the way that the town took it that the Archdeacon isn't *quite* where he was. I agree with him entirely in his policy—to keep things as they always have been. That's the only way to save our Church, in my opinion. As soon as they tell me an idea's new, that's enough for me. . . . I'm down on it at once. But what I *do* think is that his diplomacy is often faulty. He rushes at things like a bull—exactly like a bull. A little too confident always. No, if you won't think me conceited—and I believe I'm a modest man—you couldn't do better than come to me—talk things over with me, you know. I'm sure we'll see alike about many things.'

' I'm sure we will,' said Ronder. ' Thank you very much. As you've been so kind I'm sure you won't mind my asking you a few questions. I hope I'm not keeping you from anything.'

' Not at all. Not at all,' said Bentinck-Major very graciously, and stretching his plump little body back into the arm-chair. ' Ask as many questions as you like and I'll do my best to answer them.'

Ronder did then, during the next half-hour, ask a great many questions, and he received a great many answers. The answers may not have told him overmuch about the things that he wanted to know, but they did tell him a great deal about Bentinck-Major.

The clock struck four.

Ronder got up.

' You don't know how you've helped me,' he said. ' You've told me exactly what I wanted to know. Thank you so very much.'

Bentinck-Major looked gratified. He had, in fact, thoroughly enjoyed himself.

' Oh, but you'll stay and have some tea, won't you ? '

' I'm afraid I can't do that. I've got a pretty busy afternoon still in front of me.'

' My wife will be so disappointed.'

' You'll let me come another day, won't you ? '

'Of course. Of course.'

The Canon himself accompanied his guest into the hall and opened the front door for him.

'Any time—any time—that I can help you.'

'Thank you so very much. Good-bye.'

'Good-bye. Good-bye.'

So far so good, but Ronder was aware that his next visit would be quite another affair—and so indeed it proved.

To reach Canon's Yard from Orange Street, Ronder had to go down through Green Lane past the Orchards, and up by a steep path into Bodger's Street and the small houses that have clustered for many years behind the Cathedral. Here once was Saint Margaret's Monastery, utterly swept away, until not a stone remained, by Henry VIII.'s servants. Saint Margaret's only memory lingers in the Saint Margaret's Hostel for Women at the top of Bodger's Street, and even that has now a worn and desolate air as though it also were on the edge of departure. In truth, this part of Polchester is neglected and forgotten ; it has not sunk like Seatown into dirt and degradation, it has still an air of romance and colour, but the life is gone from it.

Canon's Yard is behind the Hostel and is a little square, shut-in, cobbled place with tall thin houses closing it in and the Cathedral towers overhanging it. Rooks and bells and the rattle of carts upon the cobbles make a perpetual clatter here, and its atmosphere is stuffy and begrimed. When the Cathedral chimes ring they echo from house to house, from wall to wall, so that it seems as though the bells of a hundred Cathedrals were ringing here. Nevertheless from the high windows of the Yard there is a fine view of orchards and hills and distant woods—a view not to be despised.

The house in which Canon Foster had his rooms is one of the oldest of all the houses. The house was kept by one Mrs. Maddis, who had 'run' rooms for the clergy ever since her first marriage, when she was a pretty blushing girl of twenty. She was now a hideous old woman of eighty, and the house was managed by her married daughter, Mrs. Crumpleton. There were three floors and there should have been three clergymen, but for some time the bottom floor had been empty and the middle apartments were let to transient tenants. They were at this moment inhabited by a retired sea-captain.

Foster reigned on the top floor and was quite oblivious of neighbours, landladies, tidiness, and the view—he cared, by nature, for none of these things. Ronder climbed up the dirty dark staircase and knocked on the old oak door that had upon it a dirty visiting-card with Foster's name. When he ceased his climb and the noise of his footsteps fell away there was a great silence. Not a sound could be heard. The bells were not chiming, the rooks were not cawing (it was not as yet their time), nor was the voice of Mrs. Crumpleton to be heard, shrill and defiant, as was too often the case. The house was dead ; the town was dead ; had the world itself suddenly died, like a candle whose light is put out, Foster would not have cared.

Ronder knocked three times with the knob of his walking-stick. The man must be out. He was about to turn away and go when the door suddenly opened, as though by a secret life of its own, and the pale face and untidy person of the Canon, like the apparition of a surprised and indignant *revenant*, was apparent.

'May I come in for a moment?' said Ronder. 'I won't keep you long.'

Foster stared at his visitor, said nothing, opened the door a little wider, and stood aside. Ronder accepted this as an invitation and came in.

'You'd better come into the other room,' said Foster, looking about him as though he had been just ruthlessly awakened from an important dream. They passed through a little passage and an untidy sitting-room into the study. This was a place piled high with books, and its only furniture was a deal table and two straw-bottomed chairs. At the table Foster had obviously been working. Books lay about it and papers, and there was also a pile of manuscript. Foster looked around him, caught his large ears in his fingers and cracked them, and then suddenly said:

'You'd better sit down. What can I do for you?'

Ronder sat down. It was at once apparent that, whatever the state of the rooms might be, his reluctant host was suddenly very wide awake indeed. He felt, what he had known from the very first meeting, that he was in contact here with a man of brain, of independence, of character. His capacity for amused admiration, that was one of the strongest things in him, was roused to the full. Another thing that he had also by now perceived was that Foster was not that type, by now so familiar to us in the pages of French and English fiction, of the lost and bewildered old clergyman whose long nose has been for so many years buried in dusty books that he is unable to smell the real world. Foster was neither lost nor bewildered. He was very much all there.

What could he do for Ronder? Ronder was, for a moment, uncertain. Here, he was happy to think, he must go with the greatest care. He did not smile as he had smiled upon Bentinck-Major. He spoke to Foster as to an equal.

' I can see you're busy,' he said. ' All the same I'm not going to apologise for coming. I'll tell you frankly that I want your help. At the same time I'll tell you that I don't care whether you give it me or no.'

' In what way can I help you?' asked Foster coldly.

' There's to be a Chapter Meeting in a few days' time, isn't there? Honestly I haven't been here quite long enough yet to know how things stand. Questions may come up, although there's nothing very important this time, I believe. But there may be important things brewing. Now you've been here a great many years and you have your opinion of how things should go. I want your idea of some of the conditions.'

' You've come to spy out the land, in fact?'

' Put it that way if you like,' said Ronder seriously, ' although I don't think spying is exactly the word. You're perfectly at liberty, I mean, to tell anybody that I've been to see you and to repeat to anybody what I say. It simply is that I don't care to take on all the work that's being shoved on to my shoulders without getting the views of those who know the place well.'

' Oh, if it's my views you want,' cried Foster, suddenly raising his voice and almost shouting, ' they're easy enough to discover. They are simply

that everything here is abominable, going to wrack
and ruin. . . . Now you know what *I* think.'

He looked down at his manuscript as much as to
say, ' Well, good afternoon.'

' Going to ruin in what way ? ' asked Ronder.

' In the way that the country is going to ruin—
because it has turned its back upon God.'

There was a pause. Suddenly Foster flung out,
' Do you believe in God, Canon Ronder ? '

' I think,' said Ronder, ' the fact that I'm in the
position I'm in——'

' Nonsense,' interrupted Foster. ' That's anybody's answer. You don't look a spiritual man.'

' I'm fat, if that's what you mean,' said Ronder,
smiling. ' That's my misfortune.'

' If I've been rude,' said Foster more mildly,
' forgive me. I *am* rude these days. I've given up
trying not to be. The truth is that I'm sick to the
heart with all their worldliness, shams, lies, selfishness, idleness. You may be better than they. You
may not. I don't know. If you've come here
determined to wake them all up and improve things,
then I wish you God-speed. But you won't do it.
You needn't think you will. If you've come like
the rest to get what you can out of it, then I don't
think you'll find my company good for you.'

' I certainly haven't come to wake them up,' said
Ronder. ' I don't believe that to be my duty.
I'm not made that way. Nor can I honestly believe
things to be as bad as you say. But I do intend,
with God's help, to do my best. If that's not good
enough for you, then you must abandon me to my
fate.'

Foster seemed to appreciate that. He nodded
his head.

'That's honest at any rate,' he said. 'It's the first honest thing I've heard here for a long time except from the Bishop. To tell you the truth, I had thought you were going to work in with Brandon. One more of his sheep. If that were to be so the less we saw of one another the better.'

'I have not been here long enough,' said Ronder, 'to think of working in with anybody. And I don't wish to take sides. There's my duty to the Cathedral. I shall work for that and let the rest go.'

'There's your duty to God,' said Foster vehemently. 'That's the thing that everybody here's forgotten. But you don't sound as though you'd go Brandon's way. That's something in your favour.'

'Why should one go Brandon's way?' Ronder asked.

'Why? Why? Why? Why do sheep huddle together when the dog barks at their heels? . . . But I respect him. Don't you mistake me. He's a man to be respected. He's got courage. He cares for the Cathedral. He's a hundred years behind, that's all. He's read nothing, he knows nothing, he's a child—and does infinite harm. . . .' He looked up at Ronder and said quite mildly, 'Is there anything more you want to know?'

'There's talk,' said Ronder, 'about the living at Pybus St. Anthony. It's apparently an important place, and when there's an appointment I should like to be able to form an opinion about the best man——'

'What ! is Morrison dead?' said Foster eagerly.

'No, but very ill, I believe.'

'Well, there's only one possible appointment for that place, and that is Wistons.'

'Wistons?' repeated Ronder.

'Yes, yes,' said Foster impatiently, 'the author of *The New Apocalypse*—the rector of St. Edward's, Hawston.'

Ronder remembered. 'A stranger?' he said. 'I thought that it would have to be some one in the diocese.'

Foster did not hear him. 'I've been waiting for this—to get Wistons here—for years,' he said. 'A wonderful man—a great man. He'll wake the place up. We *must* have him. As to local men, the more strangers we let in here the better.'

'Brandon said something about a man called Forsyth—Rex Forsyth?'

Foster smiled grimly. 'Yes—he would,' he said, 'that's just his kind of appointment. Well, if he tries to pull that through there'll be such a battle as this place has never seen.'

Ronder said slowly, 'I like your idea of Wistons. That sounds interesting.'

Foster looked at him with a new intensity.

'Would you help me about that?' he asked.

'I don't know quite where I am yet,' said Ronder, 'but I think you'll find me a friend rather than an enemy, Foster.'

'I don't care what you are,' said Foster. 'So far as my feelings or happiness go, nothing matters. But to have Wistons here—in this place. . . . Oh, what we could do! What we could do!'

He seemed to be lost in a dream. Five minutes later he roused himself to say good-bye. Ronder once more at the top of the stairs felt about him again the strange stillness of the house.

CHAPTER VIII

SON—FATHER

FALK BRANDON was still, in reality, a boy. He, of course, did not know this and would have been very indignant had any one told him so ; it was nevertheless the truth.

There is a kind of confidence of youth that has great charm, a sort of assumption of grown-up manners and worldly ways that is accompanied with an ingenuous belief in human nature, a naïve trust in human goodness. One sees it sometimes in books, in stories that are like a charade acted by children dressed in their elders' clothes, and although these tales are nothing but fairy stories in their actual relation to life, the sincerity of their belief in life, and a kind of freshness that comes from ignorance, give them a power of their own.

Falk had some of this charm and power just as his father had, but whereas his father would keep it all his days, Falk would certainly lose it as he learnt more and went more into the world. But as yet he had not lost it.

This emotion that had now gained such control over him was the first real emotion of his life, and he did not know in the least how to deal with it.

He was like a man caught in a baffling fog. He did not know in the least whether he were in love with this girl, he did not know what he wanted to do with her, he sometimes fancied that he hated her, he could not see her clearly either mentally or physically; he only knew that he could not keep away from her, and that with every meeting he approached more nearly the moment when he would commit some desperate action that he would probably regret for the rest of his life.

But although he could not see her clearly he could see sharply enough the other side of the situation—the practical, home, filial side. It was strange how, as the affair advanced, he was more and more conscious of his father. It was as though he were an outsider, a friend of his father's, but no relation to the family, who watched a calamity approach ever more closely and was powerless to stop it. Although he was only a boy he realised very sufficiently his father's love for him and pride in him. He realised, too, his father's dependence upon his dignity and position in the town, and, last and most important of all, his father's passionate devotion to the Cathedral. All these things would be bruised were he, Falk, involved in any local scandal. Here he saw into himself and, with a bitterness and humility that were quite new to him, despised himself. He knew, as though he saw future events passing in procession before him, that if such a scandal did break out he would not be able to stay in the place and face it—not because he himself feared any human being alive, but because he could not see his father suffer under it.

Well, then, since he saw so clearly, why not abandon it all? Why not run away, obtain some

kind of work in London and leave Polchester until
the madness had passed away from him?

He could not go.

He would have been one of the first to scorn
another man in such a position, to mock his weakness and despise him. Well, let that be so. He
despised himself, but—he could not go.

He was always telling himself that soon the
situation would clear and that he would then know
how to act. Until that happened he must see her,
must talk to her, must be with her, must watch her.
They had had, by now, a number of meetings, always
in the evening by the river, when her father was away,
up in the town.

He had kissed her twice. She had been quite
passive on each occasion, watching him ironically
with a sort of dry amusement. She had given him
no sign that she cared for him, and their conversation
had always been bare and unsatisfactory. Once
she had said to him with sudden passion:

' I want to get away out of this.' He had asked
her where she wanted to go.

' Anywhere—London.' He had asked her whether
she would go with him.

' I would go with any one,' she had said. Afterwards she added : ' But you won't take me.'

' Why not ?' he had asked.

' Because I'm not in love with you.'

' You may be—yet.'

' I'd be anything to get away,' she had replied.

On a lovely evening he went down to see her,
determined that this time he would give himself
some definite answer. Just before he turned down
to the river he passed Samuel Hogg. That large
and smiling gentleman, a fat cigar between his lips,

was sauntering, with a friend, on his way to Murdock's billiard tables.

'Evenin', Mr. Brandon.'

'Good evening, Hogg.'

'Lovely weather.'

'Lovely.'

The shadows, faintly pink on the rise of the hill, engulfed his fat body. Falk wondered as he had before now done many times, How much does he know? What's he thinking? What does he want? . . . The river, at high tide, very gently lapped the side of the old wall. Its colour to-night was pure crystal green, the banks and the hills smoky grey behind it. Tiny pink clouds ran in little fleets across the sky, chasing one another in and out between the streamers of smoke that rose from the tranquil chimneys. Seatown was at rest this evening, scarcely a sound came from the old houses; the birds could be heard calling from the meadows beyond the river. The pink clouds faded into a rosy shadow, then that in its turn gave way to a sky faintly green and pointed with stars. Grey mist enveloped the meadows and the river, and the birds cried no longer. There was a smell of onions and rank seaweed in the air.

Falk's love-story pursued at first its usual realistic course. She was there near the waterfall waiting for him; they had very little to say to one another. She was depressed to-night, and he fancied that she had been crying. She was not so attractive to him in such a mood. He liked her best when she was intolerant, scornful, aloof. To-night, although she showed no signs of caring for him, she surrendered herself absolutely. He could do what he liked with her. But he did not want to do anything with her.

She leaned over the Seatown wall looking desolately in front of her.

At last she turned round to him and asked him what she had asked him before :

' What do you come after me for ? '

' I don't know,' he said.

' It isn't because you love me.'

' I don't know.'

' *I* know—there's no mistakin' it when it's there. I've lain awake a lot o' nights wondering what you're after. You must have your reasons. You take a deal o' trouble.'

Then she put her hand on his. It was the first time that she had ever, of her own accord, touched him.

' I'm gettin' to like you,' she said. ' Seein' so much of you, I suppose. You're only a boy when all's said. And then, somehow or another, men don't go after me. You're the only one that ever has. They say I'm stuck-up. . . . Oh, man, but I'm unhappy here at home ! '

' Well, then—you'd better come away with me— to London.'

Even as he said it he would have caught the words back. What use for them to go ? Nothing to live on, no true companionship . . . there could be only *one* end to that.

But she shook her head.

' No—if you cared for me enough, mebbe I'd go. But I don't know that we'd be together long if we did. I want my own life, my own, own, own life ! I can look after myself all right. . . . I'll be off by myself alone one day.'

Then suddenly he wanted her as urgently as he had ever done.

' No, you must never do that,' he said. ' If you go it must be with me. You must have some one to look after you. You don't know what London's like.'

He caught her in his arms and kissed her passionately, and she seemed to him a new woman altogether, created by her threat that she would go away alone.

She passively let him kiss her, then with a little turn in his arms and a little sigh she very gently kissed him of her own will.

' I believe I could care for 'ee,' she said softly. ' And I want to care for some one terrible bad.'

They were nearer in spirit than they had ever been before ; an emotion of simple human companionship had crept into the unsettled disturbance and quieted it and deepened it. She wore in his eyes a new aspect, something wise and reasonable and comfortable. She would never be quite so mysterious to him again, but her hold on him now was firmer. He was suddenly sorry for her as well as for himself.

For the first time he left her that night with a sense that comradeship might grow between them.

But as he went back up the hill he was terribly depressed and humiliated. He hated and despised himself for longing after something that he did not really want. He had always, he fancied, done that, as though there would never be time enough in life for all the things that he would wish to test and to reject.

When he went to bed that night he was in rebellion with all the world, but before he fell asleep Annie Hogg seemed to come to him, a gentler, kinder spirit, and to say to him, ' It'll be all right.

. . . I'll look after 'ee. . . . I'll look after 'ee,'
and he seemed to sink to sleep in her arms.

Next morning Falk and Joan had breakfast alone
with their father, a headache having laid Mrs.
Brandon low. Falk was often late for breakfast,
but to-day had woken very early, had got up and
gone out and walked through the grey mist, turning
his own particular trouble over and over in his mind.
To-day Annie had faded back from him again ;
that tenderness that he had felt for her last night
seemed to have vanished, and he was aware only of
a savage longing to shake himself free of his burden.
He had visions this morning of going up to London
and looking for work. . . .

Joan saw that to-day was a ' Chapter morning '
day. She always knew by her father's appearance
when there was to be a Chapter Meeting. He had
then an extra gloss, an added splendour, and also an
added importance. He really was the smartest old
thing, she thought, looking at him this morning
with affectionate pride. He looked as though he
spent his time in springing in and out of cold baths.

The importance was there too. He had the
Glebeshire Morning News propped up in front of
him, and every now and then he would poke his
fine head up over it and look at his children and the
breakfast-table and give them a little of the world's
news. In former days it had been only at the risk
of their little lives that they had spoken to one
another. Now, although restrictions had broken
down, they would always hear, if their voices were
loud :

' Come, children . . . come, come. Mayn't
your father read the newspaper in quiet ? Plenty
of time to chatter during the rest of the day.'

He would break forth into little sentences and exclamations as he read. ' Well, that's settled Burnett's hash.—Serve him right, too. . . . Dear, dear, five shillings a hundred now. Phillpott's going to St. Lummen ! What an appointment ! . . .' and so on.

Sometimes he would grow so deeply agitated that he would push the paper away from him and wave vaguely about the table with his hands as though he were learning to swim, letting out at the same time little snorts of indignation and wonder :

' The fools ! The idiots ! Savage, of all men ! Fancy listening to him ! Well, they'll only get what they deserve for their weakness. I wrote to Benson, too—might as well have written to a rhinoceros. Toast, please, Joan !—Toast, toast. Didn't you hear me ? Savage ! What can they be thinking of ? Yes, and butter. . . . Of course I said butter.'

But on ' Chapter Days ' it was difficult for the newspaper to disturb him. His mind was filled with thoughts for the plan and policy of the morning. It was unfortunately impossible for him ever to grasp two things at the same time, and this made his reasoning and the development of any plan that he had rather slow. When the Chapter was to be an important one he would not look at the newspaper at all and would eat scarcely any break-fast. To-day, because the Chapter was a little one, he allowed himself to consider the outside world. That really was the beginning of his mis-fortune, because the paper this morning contained a very vivid picture of the loss of the *Drummond Castle*. That was an old story by this time, but here was some especial account that provided new

details and circumstances, giving a fresh vivid horror
to the scene even at this distance of time.

Brandon tried not to read the thing. He made
it a rule that he would not distress himself with the
thought of evils that he could not cure. That is
what he told himself, but indeed his whole life was
spent in warding off and shutting out and refusing
to listen.

He had told himself many years ago that it was a
perfect world and that God had made it and that God
was good. To maintain this belief it was necessary
that one should not be ' Presumptuous.' It was
' Presumptuous ' to imagine for a moment about
any single thing that it was a ' mistake.' If anything *were* evil or painful it was there to ' try and
test ' us. . . . A kind of spring - board over the
waters of salvation.

Once, some years ago, a wicked atheist had
written an article in a magazine manifesting how
evil nature was, how the animals preyed upon one
another, how everything from the tiniest insect to
the largest elephant suffered and suffered and suffered. How even the vegetation lived a short life
of agony and frustration, and then fell into foul
decay. . . . Brandon had read the article against
his will, and had then hated the writer of it with so
deep a hatred that he would have had him horse-
whipped, had he had the power. The article upset
him for days, and it was only by asserting to himself
again and again that it was untrue, by watching
kittens at play and birds singing on the branches
and roses bursting from bud to bloom, that he could
reassure himself.

Now to-day here was the old distress back again.
There was no doubt but that those men and women

on the *Drummond Castle* had suffered in order to win quite securely for themselves a crown of glory. He ought to envy them, to regret that he had not been given the same chance, and yet—and yet——

He pushed the paper impatiently away from him. It was good that there was nothing important to be discussed at Chapter this morning, because really he was not in the mood to fight battles. He sighed. Why was it always he that had to fight battles ? He had indeed the burden of the whole town upon his shoulders. And at that secretly he felt a great joy. He was glad—yes, he was glad that he had. . . .

As he looked over at Joan and Falk he felt tenderly towards them. His reading then about the *Drummond Castle* made him anxious that they should have a good time and be happy. It might be better for them that they should suffer ; nevertheless; if they *could* be sure of heaven and at the same time not suffer too badly he would be glad.

Suddenly then, across the breakfast-table, a picture drove itself in front of him—a picture of Joan with her baby-face, struggling in the water. . . . She screamed ; she tried to catch on to the side of a boat with her hand. Some one struck her. . . .

With a shudder of disgust he drove it from him.

' Pah ! ' he cried aloud, getting up from the table.

' What is it, father ? ' Joan asked.

' People oughtn't to be allowed to write such things,' he said, and went to his study.

When an hour later he sallied forth to the Chapter Meeting he had recovered his equanimity. His mind now was nailed to the business on hand. Most innocently as he crossed the Cathedral Green he strutted, his head up, his brow stern, his hands crossed behind his back. The choristers coming in from the choir-school practice in the Cathedral passed him in a ragged line. They all touched their mortar-boards and he smiled benignly upon them, reserving a rather stern glance for Brockett, the organist, of whose musical eccentricities he did not at all approve.

Little remained now of the original Chapter House, which had once been a continuation of Saint Margaret's Chapel. Some extremely fine Early Norman arches which were once part of the Chapter House are still there and may be seen at the southern end of the Cloisters. Here, too, are traces of the dormitory and infirmary which formerly stood there. The present Chapter House consists of two rooms adjoining the Cloisters, once a hall used by the monks as a large refectory. There is still a timber roof of late thirteenth-century work, and this is supposed to have been once part of the old pilgrims' or strangers' hall. The larger of the two rooms is reserved for the Chapter Meetings, the smaller being used for minor meetings and informal discussions.

The Archdeacon was a little late as, I am afraid, he liked to be when he was sure that others would be punctual. Nothing, however, annoyed him more than to find others late when he himself was in time. There they all were, and how exactly he knew how they would all be !

There was the long oak table, blotting-paper and writing materials neatly placed before each seat, there the fine walls in which he always took so great a pride, with the portraits of the Polchester Bishops in grand succession upon them. At the head of the table was the Dean, nervously with anxious smiles looking about him. On the right was Brandon's seat; on the left Witheram, seriously approaching the business of the day as though his very life depended upon it; then Bentinck-Major, his hands looking as though they had been manicured; next to him Ryle, laughing obsequiously at some fashionable joke that Bentinck-Major had delivered to him; opposite to him Foster, looking as though he had not had a meal for a week and badly shaved with a cut on his chin; and next to *him* Ronder.

At the bottom of the table was little Bond, the Chapter Clerk, sucking his pencil.

Brandon took his place with dignified apologies for his late arrival.

' Let us ask God for His blessing on our work to-day,' said the Dean.

A prayer followed, then general rustling and shuffling, blowing of noses, coughing and even, from the surprised and consternated Ryle, a sneeze —then the business of the day began. The minutes of the last meeting were read, and there was a little amiable discussion. At once Brandon was conscious of Ronder. Why? He could not tell and was the more uncomfortable. The man said nothing. He had not been present at the last meeting and could therefore have nothing to say to this part of the business. He sat there, his spectacles catching the light from the opposite windows so that he seemed to have no eyes. His chubby body, the position in which he was sitting, hunched up, leaning forward on his arms, spoke of perfect and almost sleepy content. His round face and fat cheeks gave him the air of a man to whom business was a tiresome and unnecessary interference with the pleasures of life.

Nevertheless, Brandon was so deeply aware of Ronder that again and again, against his will, his eyes wandered in his direction. Once or twice Brandon said something, not because he had anything really to say, but because he wanted to impress himself upon Ronder. All agreed with him in the complacent and contented way that they had always agreed. . . .

Then his consciousness of Ronder extended and gave him a new consciousness of the other men. He had known for so long exactly how they looked and the words that they would say, that they were, to him, rather like the stone images of the Twelve Apostles in the niches round the West Door. To-day they jumped in a moment into new life. Yesterday he could have calculated to a nicety the attitude that they would have ; now they seemed to have been blown askew with a new wind. Because he noticed these things it does not mean that he was generally perceptive. He had always been very sharp to perceive anything that concerned his own position.

Business proceeded and every one displayed his own especial characteristics. Nothing arose that concerned Ronder. Every one's personal opinion about every one else was clearly apparent. It was a fine thing, for instance, to observe Foster's scorn and contempt whilst Bentinck-Major explained his little idea about certain little improvements that he, as Chancellor, might naturally suggest, or Ryle's attitude of goodwill to all and sundry as he apologised for certain of Brockett's voluntaries and assured Brandon on one side that ' something should be done about it,' and agreed with Bentinck-Major on the other that it was indeed agreeable to hear sometimes music a little more advanced and original than one usually found in Cathedrals.

Brandon sniffed something of incipient rebellion in Bentinck-Major's attitude and looked across the table severely. Bentinck-Major blinked and nervously examined his nails.

'Of course,' said the Archdeacon in his most solemn manner, 'there may be people who wish to turn the Cathedral into a music-hall. I don't say there *are*, but there *may* be. In these strange times nothing would astonish me. In my own humble opinion what was good enough for our fathers is good enough for us. However, don't let my opinion influence any one.'

'I assure you, Archdeacon,' said Bentinck-Major. Witheram earnestly assured every one that he was certain that there need be no alarm. They could trust the Precentor to see. . . . There was a general murmur. Yes, they *could* trust the Precentor.

This little matter being settled, the meeting was very near an agreeable conclusion and the Dean was beginning to congratulate himself on an early return to his botany—when, unfortunately, there cropped up the question of the garden-roller.

This matter of the garden-roller was a simple one enough. The Cathedral School had some months ago requested the Chapter to allow it to purchase for itself a new garden-roller. Such an article was seriously needed for the new cricket-field. It was true that the School already possessed two garden-rollers, but one of these was very small—'quite a baby one,' Dennison the headmaster explained pathetically—and the other could not possibly cover all the work that it had to do. The School grounds were large ones.

The matter, which was one that mainly concerned the Treasury side of the Chapter, had been discussed at the last meeting, and there had been a good deal of argument about it.

Brandon had then vetoed it, not because he cared in the least whether or no the School had a garden-roller, but because, Hart-Smith having left and Ronder being not yet with them, he was in charge, for the moment, of the Cathedral funds. He liked to feel his power, and so he refused as many things as possible. Had it not been only a temporary glory—had he been permanent Treasurer—he would in all probability have acted in exactly the opposite way and allowed everybody to have everything.

' There's the question of the garden-roller,' said Witheram, just as the Dean was about to propose that they should close with a prayer.

' I've got it here on the minutes,' said the Chapter Clerk severely.

' Oh, dear, yes,' said the Dean, looking about him rather piteously. ' Now what shall we do about it ? '

' Let 'em have it,' said Foster, glaring across at Brandon and shutting his mouth like a trap.

This was a direct challenge. Brandon felt his breast charged with the noble anger that always filled it when Foster said anything.

' I must confess,' he said, covering, as he always did when he intended something to be final, the Dean with his eye, ' that I thought that this was quite definitely settled at last Chapter ; I understood—I may of course have been mistaken—that we considered that we could not afford the thing and that the School must wait.'

' Well, Archdeacon,' said the Dean nervously (he knew of old the danger-signals in Brandon's

flashing eyes), ' I must confess that I hadn't thought
it *quite* so definite as that.   Certainly we discussed
the expense of the affair.'

' I think the Archdeacon's right,' said Bentinck-
Major, who wanted to win his way back to favour
after the little mistake about the music.   ' It *was*
settled, I think.'

' Nothing of the kind,' said Foster fiercely.
' We settled nothing.'

' How does it read on the minutes ? ' asked the
Dean nervously.

' Postponed until the next meeting,' said the
Clerk.

' At any rate,' said Brandon, feeling that this
absurd discussion had gone on quite long enough,
' the matter is simple enough.   It can be settled
immediately.   Any one who has gone into the
matter at all closely will have discovered first that
the School doesn't *need* a roller—they've enough
already—secondly, that the Treasury cannot possibly at the present moment afford to buy a new one.'

' I really must protest, Archdeacon,' said Foster,
' this is going too far.   In the first place, have you
yourself gone into the case ? '

Brandon paused before he answered.   He felt
that all eyes were upon him.   He also felt that
Foster had been stirred to a new strength of hostility
by some one—he fancied he knew by whom.   Moreover, *had* he gone into it ?   He was aware with a
stirring of impatience that he had not.   He had
intended to do so, but time had been short, the
matter had not seemed of sufficient importance. . . .

' I certainly have gone into it,' he said, ' quite as
far as the case deserves.   The facts are clear.'

' The facts are *not* clear,' said Foster angrily.

' I say that the School should have this roller and that we are behaving with abominable meanness in preventing it ' ; and he banged his fist upon the table.

' If that charge of meanness is intended personally . . .' said Brandon angrily.

' I assure you, Archdeacon . . .' said Ryle. The Dean raised a hand in protest.

' I don't think,' he said, ' that anything here is ever intended personally. We must never forget that we are in God's House. Of course, this is an affair that really should be in the hands of the Treasury. But I'm afraid that Canon Ronder can hardly be expected in the short time that he's been with us to have investigated this little matter.'

Every one looked at Ronder. There was a pleasant sense of drama in the affair. Brandon was gazing at the portraits above the table and pretending to be outside the whole business ; in reality, his heart beat angrily. His word should have been enough, in earlier days *would* have been. Everything now was topsy-turvy. . . .

' As a matter of fact,' said Ronder, ' I *have* gone into the matter. I saw that it was one of the most urgent questions on the Agenda. Unimportant though it may sound, I believe that the School cricket will be entirely held up this summer if they don't secure their roller. They intend, I believe, to get a roller by private subscription if we refuse it to them, and that, gentlemen, would be, I cannot help feeling, rather ignominious for us. I have been into the question of prices and have examined some catalogues. I find that the expense of a good garden-roller is really *not* a very great one. One that I think the Treasury could sustain without serious inconvenience. . . .'

' You think then, Canon, that we should allow the roller ? ' said the Dean.

' I certainly do,' said Ronder.

Brandon felt the impression that had been created. He knew that they were all thinking amongst themselves : ' Well, *here's* an efficient man ! '

He burst out :

' I'm afraid that I cannot agree with Canon Ronder. If he will allow me to say so, he has not been, as yet, long enough in the place to know how things really stand. I have nothing to say against Dennison, but he has obviously put his case very plausibly, but those who have known the School and its methods for many years have perhaps a prior right of judgment over Canon Ronder, who's known it for so short a time.'

' Absurd. Absurd,' cried Foster. ' It isn't a case of knowing the School. It's simply a question of whether the Chapter can afford it. Canon Ronder, who is Treasurer, says that it can. That ought to be enough for anybody.'

The atmosphere was now very warm indeed. There was every likelihood of several gentlemen speaking at once. Witheram looked anxious, Bentinck-Major malicious, Ryle nervous, Foster triumphant, and Brandon furious. Only Ronder seemed unconcerned.

The Dean, distress in his heart, raised his hand.

' As there seems to be some difference of opinion in this matter,' he said, ' I think we had better vote upon it. Those in favour of the roller being granted to the School please signify.'

Ronder, Foster and Witheram raised their hands.

' And those against ? ' said the Dean.

Brandon, Ryle and Bentinck-Major were against.

'I'm afraid,' said the Dean, smiling anxiously, 'that it will be for me to give the casting vote.' He paused for a moment. Then, looking straight across the table at the Clerk, he said :

'I think I must decide *for* the roller. Canon Ronder seems to me to have proved his case.'

Every one, except possibly Ronder, was aware that this was the first occasion for many years that any motion of Brandon's had been defeated. . . .

Without waiting for any further business the Archdeacon gathered together his papers and, looking neither to right nor left, strode from the room.

BOOK II

THE WHISPERING GALLERY

CHAPTER I

THE cloud seemed to creep like smoke from the funnel of the Cathedral tower. The sun was setting in a fiery wreath of bubbling haze, shading in rosy mist the mountain of grey stone. The little cloud, at first in the shadowy air light green and shaped like a ring, twisted spirally, then, spreading, washed out and lay like a pool of water against the smoking sunset.

Green like the Black Bishop's ring. . . . Lying there, afterwards, until the orange had faded and the sky, deserted by the sun, was milk-white. The mists descended. The Cathedral chimes struck five. February night, cold, smoke-misted, enwrapped the town.

I

At a quarter to five Evensong was over and Cobbett was putting out the candles in the choir. Two figures slowly passed down the darkening nave.

Outside the West door they paused, gazing at the splendour of the fiery sky.

' It's cold, but there'll be stars,' Ronder said.

Stars. Cold. Brandon shivered. Something was wrong with him. His heart had clap-clapped during the Anthem as though a cart with heavy wheels had rumbled there. He looked suspiciously at Ronder. He did not like the man, confidently standing there addressing the sky as though he owned it. He would have liked the sunset for himself.

'Well, good - night, Canon,' brusquely. He moved away.

But Ronder followed him.

'One moment, Archdeacon. . . . Excuse me. . . . I have been wanting an opportunity. . . .'

Brandon paused. The man was nervous. Brandon liked that.

'Yes?' he said.

The rosy light was fading. Strange that little green cloud rising like smoke from the tower. . . .

'At the last Chapter we were on opposite sides. I want to say how greatly I've regretted that. I feel that we don't know one another as we should. I wonder if you would allow me . . .'

The light was fading—Ronder's spectacles shone, his body in shadow.

'. . . to see something more of you—to have a real talk with you?'

Brandon smiled grimly to himself in the dusk. This fool! He was afraid then. He saw himself hatless in Bennett's shop; outside, the jeering crowd.

'I'm afraid, Canon Ronder, that we shall never see eye to eye here about many things. If you will allow me to say so, you have perhaps not been here quite long enough to understand the real needs of this diocese. You must go slowly here—more slowly than perhaps you are prepared for. We are not Modernists here.'

The spectacles, alone visible, answered : 'Well,

let us discuss it then.   Let us talk things over.
Let me ask you at once, Have you something
against me, something that I have done unwittingly ?
I have fancied lately a personal note. . . . I am
absurdly sensitive, but if there *is* anything that I
have done, please let me apologise for it.   I want
you to tell me.'

Anything that he had done ?   The Archdeacon
smiled grimly to himself in the dusk.

' I really don't think, Canon, that talking things
over will help us.   There is really nothing to discuss.
. . . Good-night.'

The green cloud was gone.   Ronder, invisible
now, remained in the shadow of the great door.

2

Beside the river, above the mill, a woman's body
was black against the gold-crested water.   She
leaned over the little bridge, her body strong, confident in its physical strength, her hands clasped,
her eyes meditative.

No need for secrecy to-night.   Her father was
in Drymouth for two days.   Quarter to five.   The
chimes struck out clear across the town.   Hearing
them she looked back and saw the sky a flood of
red behind the Cathedral.   She longed for Falk
to-night, a new longing.   He was better than she
had supposed, far far better.   A good boy, tender
and warm-hearted.   To be trusted.   Her friend.
At first he had stood to her only for a means of
freedom.   Freedom from this horrible place, from
this horrible man, her father, more horrible than
any others knew.   Her mother had known.   She
shivered, seeing that body, heavy-breasted, dull

white, as, stripped to the waist, he bent over the
bed to strike. Her mother's cry, a little moan.
. . . She shivered again, staring into the sunset for
Falk. . . .

He was with her. They leant over the bridge
together, his arm around her. They said very little.

She looked back.

' See that strange cloud ? Green. Ever seen a
green cloud before ? Ah, it's peaceful here.'

She turned and looked into his face. As the
dusk came down she stroked his hair. He put his
arm round her and held her close to him.

3

The lamps in the High Street suddenly flaring
beat out the sky. There above the street itself the
fiery sunset had not extended ; the fair watery space
was pale egg-blue ; as the chimes so near at hand
struck a quarter to five the pale colour began slowly
to drain away, leaving ashen china shades behind it,
and up to these shades the orange street-lights
extended, patronising, flaunting.

But Joan, pausing for a moment under the Arden
Gate before she turned home, saw the full glory of
the sunset. She heard, contending with the chimes,
the last roll of the organ playing the worshippers
out of that mountain of sacrificial stone.

She looked up and saw a green cloud, faintly
green like early spring leafage, curl from the tower
smoke-wise ; and there, lifting his hat, pausing at
her side, was Johnny St. Leath.

She would have hurried on ; she was not happy.
Things were not right at home. Something wrong
with father, with mother, with Falk. Something

wrong, too, with herself. She had heard in the town the talk about this girl who was coming to the Castle for the Jubilee time, coming to marry Johnny. Coming to marry him because she was rich and handsome. Lovely. Lady St. Leath was determined. . . .

So she would hurry on, murmuring ' Good evening.' But he stopped her. His face was flushed. Andrew heaved eagerly, hungrily, at his side.

' Miss Brandon. Just a moment. I want to speak to you. Lovely evening, isn't it ? . . . You cut me the other day. Yes, you did. In Orange Street.'

' Why ? '

She tried to speak coldly.

' We're friends. You know we are. Only in this beastly town no one can be free. . . . I only want to tell you if I go away—suddenly—I'm coming back. Mind that. You're not to believe anything they say—anything that any one says. I'm coming back. Remember that. We're friends. You must trust me. Do you hear ? '

And he was gone, striding off towards the Cathedral, Andrew panting at his heels.

The light was gone too—going, going, gone.

She stayed for a moment. As she reached her door the wind rose, sifting through the grass, rising to her chin.

4

The two figures met, unconsciously, without spoken arrangement, pushed towards one another by destiny, as they had been meeting now continuously during the last weeks.

Almost always at this hour ; almost always at

this place.   On the sandy path in the green hollow below the Cathedral, above the stream, the hollow under the opposite hill, the hill where the field was, the field where they had the Fair.

Down into this green depth the sunset could not strike, and the chimes, telling over so slowly and so sweetly the three-quarters, filtered down like a memory, a reiteration of an old promise, a melody almost forgotten.   But above her head the woman, looking up, could see the rose change to orange and could watch the cloud, like a pool of green water, extend and rest, lying like a sheet of glass behind which the orange gleamed.

They met always thus, she coming from the town as though turning upwards through the tangled path to her home in the Precincts, he sauntering slowly, his hands behind his back, as though he had been wandering there to think out some problem. . . .

Sometimes he did not come, sometimes she could not.   They never stayed more than ten minutes there together.   No one from month to month at that hour crossed that desolate path.

To-day he began impetuously.   'If you hadn't come to-night, I think I would have gone to find you.   I *had* to see you.   No, I had nothing to say. Only to see you.   But I am so lonely in that house. I always knew I was lonely—never more than when I was married—but now. . . . If I hadn't these ten minutes most days I'd die, I think. . . .'

They didn't touch one another, but stood opposite gazing, face into face.

'What are we to do?' he said.   'It can't be wicked just to meet like this and to talk a little.'

'I'd like you to know,' she answered, 'that you and my son—you are all I have in the world.   The

two of you. And my son has some secret from
me. I have been so lonely too. But I don't feel
lonely any more. Your friendship for me. . . .'

'Yes, I am your friend. Think of me like that.
Your friend from the first moment I saw you—you
so quiet and gentle and unhappy. I realised your
unhappiness instantly. No one else in this place
seemed to notice it. I believe God meant us to be
friends, meant me to bring you happiness—a
little. . . .'

'Happiness?' She shivered. 'Isn't it cold to-
night? Do you see that strange green cloud?
Ah, now it is gone. All the light is going. . . .
Do you believe in God?'

He came closer to her. His hand touched her
arm.

'Yes,' he answered fiercely. 'And He means
me to care for you.' His hand, trembling, stroked
her arm. She did not move. His hand, shaking,
touched her neck. He bent forward and kissed
her neck, her mouth, then her eyes.

She leant her head wearily for an instant on his
shoulder, then, whispering good-night, she turned
and went quietly up the path.

CHAPTER II

SOULS ON SUNDAY

I MUST have been thirteen or fourteen years of age—it may have been indeed in this very year '97—when I first read Stevenson's story of *Treasure Island*. It is the fashion, I believe, now with the Clever Solemn Ones to despise Stevenson as a writer of romantic Tushery.

All the same, if it's realism they want I'm still waiting to see something more realistic than Pew or Long John Silver. Realism may depend as truly on a blind man's tap with his stick upon the ground as on any number of adulteries.

In those young years, thank God, I knew nothing about realism and read the tale for what it was worth. And it was worth three hundred bags of gold. Now, on looking back, it seems to me that the spirit that overtook our town just at this time was very like the spirit that seized upon Dr. Livesey, young Hawkins and the rest when they discovered the dead Buccaneer's map. This is no forced parallel. It was with a real sense of adventure that the Whispering began about the Brandons and Ronder and the Pybus St. Anthony living and the rest of it. Where did the Whispering start? Who can ever tell?

Our Polchester Whispering was carried on and fostered very largely by our servants. As in every village and town in Glebeshire, the intermarrying that had been going on for generations was astonishing. Every servant-maid, every errand-boy, every gardener and coachman in Polchester was cousin, brother or sister to every other servant-maid, errand-boy, gardener and coachman. They made, these people, a perfect net about our town.

The things that they carried from house to house, however, were never the actual things ; they were simply the material from which the actual things were made. Nor was the construction of the actual tale positively malicious ; it was only that our eyes were caught by the drama of life and we could not help but exclaim with little gasps and cries at the wonderful excitement of the history that we saw. Our treasure-hunting was simply for the fun of the thrill of the chase, not at all that we wished harm to a soul in the world. If, on occasion, a slight hint of maliciousness did find its place with us, it was only because in this insecure world it is delightful to re-affirm our own security as we watch our neighbours topple over. We do not wish them to ' topple,' but if somebody has got to fall we would rather it were not ourselves.

Brandon had been for so long so remarkable a figure in our world that the slightest stir of the colours in his picture was immediately noticeable. From the moment of Falk's return from Oxford it was expected that something ' would happen.'

It often occurs that a situation between a number of people is vague and indefinite, until a certain moment, often quite undramatic and negative in itself, arrives, when the situation suddenly fixes itself and stands forward, set full square to the world, as a definite concrete fact.　There was a certain Sunday in the April of this year that became for the Archdeacon and a number of other people such a definite crisis—and yet it might quite reasonably have been said at the end of it that nothing very much had occurred.

Everything seemed to happen in Polchester on Sundays.　For one thing more talking was done on Sunday than on all the other days of the week together.　Then the Cathedral itself came into its full glory on that day.　Every one gathered there, every one talked to every one else before parting, and the long spaces and silences and pauses of the day allowed the comments and the questions and the surmises to grow and swell and distend into gigantic images before night took every one and stretched them upon their backs to dream.

What the Archdeacon liked was an ' off ' Sunday, when he had nothing to do save to walk majestically into his place in the choir stall, to read, perhaps, a Lesson, to talk gravely to people who came to have tea with him after the Sunday Evensong, to reflect lazily, after Sunday supper, his long legs stretched out in front of him, a pipe in his mouth, upon the goodness and happiness and splendour of the Cathedral and the world and his own place in it. Such a Sunday was a perfect thing—and such a Sunday April the 18th ought to have been . . . alas ! it was not so.

It began very early, somewhere about seven in the morning, with a horrible incident.　The rule on Sundays was that the maid knocked at half-past six on the door and gave the Archdeacon and his wife their tea.　The Archdeacon lay luxuriously drinking it until exactly a quarter to seven, then he sprang out of bed, had his cold bath, performed his exercises, and shaved in his little dressing-room. At about a quarter past seven, nearly dressed, he returned into the bedroom, to find Mrs. Brandon also nearly dressed. On this particular day while he drank his tea his wife appeared to be sleeping ; that did not make him bound out of bed any the less noisily —after twenty years of married life you do not worry about such things ; moreover it was quite time that his wife bestirred herself. At a quarter past seven he came into the bedroom in his shirt and trousers, humming ' Onward, Christian Soldiers.' It was a fine spring morning, so he flung up the window and looked out into the Precincts, fresh and dewy in the morning sun, silent save for the inquisitive reiteration of an early jackdaw. Then he turned back, and, to his amazement, saw that his wife was lying, her eyes wide open, staring in front of her.

' My dear ! ' he cried. ' Aren't you well ? '

' I'm perfectly well,' she answered him, her eyes maintaining their fixed stare. The tone in which she said these words was quite new—it was not submissive, it was not defensive, it was indifferent.

She must be ill. He came close to the bed.

' Do you realise the time ? ' he asked. ' Twenty minutes past seven. I'm sure you don't want to keep me waiting.'

She didn't answer him. Certainly she must be ill. There was something strange about her eyes.

' You *must* be ill,' he repeated. ' You look ill. Why didn't you say so ? Have you got a headache ? '

' I'm not ill. I haven't got a headache, and I'm not coming to Early Service.'

' You're not ill, and you're not coming . . . ' he stammered in his amazement. ' You've forgotten. There isn't late Celebration.'

She gave him no answer, but turned on her side, closing her eyes.

He came right up to the bed, frowning down upon her.

' Amy—what does this mean ? You're not ill, and yet you're not coming to Celebration ? Why ? I insist upon an answer.'

She said nothing.

He felt that anger, of which he had tried now for many years to beware, flooding his throat.

With tremendous self-control he said quietly : ' What is the matter with you, Amy ? You must tell me at once.'

She did not open her eyes but said in a voice so low that he scarcely caught the words :

' There is nothing the matter. I am not ill, and I'm not coming to Early Service.'

' Why ? '

' Because I don't wish to go.'

For a moment he thought that he was going to bend down and lift her bodily out of the bed. His limbs felt as though they were prepared for such an action.

But to his own surprised amazement he did nothing, he said nothing. He looked at the bed, at the hollow where his head had been, at her head with her black hair scattered on the pillow, at her closed eyes, then he went away into his dressing-room. When he had finished dressing he came back into the bedroom, looked across at her, motion-less, her eyes still closed, lying on her side, felt the silence of the room, the house, the Precincts broken only by the impertinent jackdaw.

He went downstairs.

Throughout the Early Celebration he remained in a condition of amazed bewilderment. From his position just above the altar-rails he could see very clearly the Bishop's Tomb ; the morning sun reflected in purple colours from the East window played upon its blue stone. It caught the green ring and flashed splashes of fire from its heart. His mind went back to that day, not so very long ago, when, with triumphant happiness, he had seemed to share in the Bishop's spirit, to be dust of his dust, and bone of his bone. That had been the very day, he remembered, of Falk's return from Oxford. Since that day everything had gone wrong for him— Falk, the Elephant, Ronder, Foster, the Chapter. And now his wife ! Never in all the years of his married life had she spoken to him as she had done that morning. She must be on the edge of a serious illness, a very serious illness. Strangely a new concern for her, a concern that he had never felt in his life before, arose in his heart. Poor Amy—and how tiresome if she were ill, the house all at sixes and sevens ! With a shock he realised that his mind was not devotional. He swung himself back to the service, looking down benevolently upon the two rows of people waiting patiently to come in their turn to the altar steps.

At breakfast, however, there Mrs. Brandon was, looking quite her usual self, in the Sunday dress of grey silk, making the tea, quiet as she always was, answering questions submissively, patiently, ' as the wife of an Archdeacon should.' He tried to show her by his manner that he had been deeply shocked, but, unfortunately, he had been shocked, annoyed, indignant on so many occasions when there had been no real need for it, that to-day, when there was the occasion, he felt that he made no impression.

The bells pealed for morning service, the sun shone ; as half-past ten approached, little groups of people crossed the Precincts and vanished into the mouth of the great West door. Now were Lawrence and Cobbett in their true glory—Lawrence was in his fine purple robe, the Sunday silk one. He stood at the far end of the nave, just under the choir-screen, waiting for the aristocracy, for whom the front seats were guarded with cords which only he might untie. How deeply pleased he was when some unfortunate stranger, ignorant in the ways of the Cathedral, walked, with startling clatter, up the whole length of the shining nave and endeavoured to penetrate one of these sacred defences ! Majestic-ally — staff in hand, he came forward, shook his snow-white head, looking down upon the intrusive one more in sorrow than in anger, spoke no word, but motioned the audacity back down the nave again to the place where Cobbett officiated. Back, clatter, clatter, blushing and confused, he retreated, watched, as it seemed to him, by a thousand sarcastic and cynical eyes. The bells slipped from their jangling peal into a solemn single note. The Mere People were in their places at the back of the nave, the Great Ones leaving their entrance until the very last moment. There was a light in the organ-loft ; very softly Brockett began his volun-tary—clatter, clatter, clatter, and the School arrived, the small boys, swallowed by their Eton collars, first, filing into their places to the right of the screen, then the middle boys, a little indifferent and careless, then the Fifth and Sixth in their 'stick-up' collars, haughty and indifferent indeed.

Dimly, on the other side of the screen, the School boys in their surplices could be seen settling into their places between the choir and the altar.

A rustling of skirts, and the aristocracy entered in ones and twos from the side doors that opened out of the Cloisters. For some of them—for a very few—Lawrence had his confidential smile. For Mrs. Sampson, for instance—for Mrs. Combermere, for Mrs. Ryle and Mrs. Brandon.

A very special one for Mrs. Brandon because of his high opinion of her husband. She was nothing very much—'a mean little woman,' he thought her—but the Archdeacon had married her. That was enough.

Joan was with her, conscious that every one must be noticing her — the D'Arcy girls and Cynthia Ryle and Gladys Sampson, they would all be looking and criticising. Rustle, rustle, rustle — here was an event indeed! Lady St. Leath was come, and with her in attendance Johnny and Hetty. Lawrence hurried forward, disregarding Mrs. Brandon, who was compelled to undo her cord for herself. He led Lady St. Leath forward with a ceremony, a dignity, that was marvellous to see. She moved behind him as though she owned the Cathedral, or rather could have owned it had she thought it worth her while. All the little boys in the Upper Third and Lower Fourth turned their necks in their Eton collars and watched. What a bonnet she was wearing! All the colours of the rainbow, odd, indeed, perched there on the top of her untidy white hair!

Every one settled down ; the voluntary was louder, the single note of the bell suddenly more urgent. Ladies looked about them. Ellen Stiles saw Miss Dobell—smile, smile. Joan saw Cynthia Ryle—smile, smile. Lawrence, with the expression of the Angel Gabriel waiting to admit into heaven a new troop of repentant sinners, stood expectant. The sun filtered in dusty ladders of coloured light and fell in squares upon the empty spaces of the nave.

The bell suddenly ceased, a long melodious and melancholy ' Amen ' came from somewhere far away in the purple shadow. Every one moved ; a noise like a little uncertain breeze blew through the Cathedral as the congregation rose ; then the choir filed through, the boys, the men, the Precentor, old Canon Morphew and older Canon Bartholomew, Canon Rogers, his face bitter and discontented, Canon Foster, Bentinck-Major, last of all, Arch-deacon Brandon. They had filed into their places in the choir, they were kneeling, the Precentor's voice rang out. . . .'

The familiar sound of Canon Ryle's voice re-called Mrs. Brandon to time and place. She was kneeling, her gloved hands pressed close to her face. She was looking into thick dense darkness, a darkness penetrated with the strong scent of Russia leather and the faint musty smell that always seemed to rise from the Cathedral hassocks and the wood-work upon which she leant. Until Ryle's voice roused her she had been swimming in space and eternity ; behind her, like a little boat bobbing dis-tressfully in her track, was the scene of that early morning with which that day had opened. She saw herself, as it were, the body of some quite other

woman, lying in that so familiar bedroom and saying
' No '—saying it again and again and again. ' No.
No. No.'

Why had she said ' No,' and was it not in reality
another woman who had said it, and why had he
been so quiet ? It was not his way. There had
been no storm. She shivered a little behind her
gloves.

' Dearly beloved brethren,' began the Precentor,
pleading, impersonal.

Slowly her brain, like a little dark fish striking
up from deep green waters, rose to the surface of
her consciousness. What she was then most surely
aware of was that she was on the very edge of something ; it was a quite physical sensation, as though
she had been walking over mist-soaked downs and
had suddenly hesitated, to find herself looking down
along the precipitances of jagged black rock. It
was ' jagged black rock ' over which she was now
peering.

The two sides of the choir were now rivalling
one another over the psalms, hurling verses at one
another with breathless speed, as though they
said : ' Here's the ball. Catch. Oh, you *are*
slow ! '

In just that way across the field of Amy Brandon's
consciousness two voices were shouting at one
another.

One cried : ' See what she's in for, the foolish
woman ! She's not up to it. It will finish her.'

And the other answered : ' Well, she *is* in for
it ! So it's no use warning her any longer. She
wants it. She's going to have it.'

And the first repeated : ' It never pays ! It
never pays ! It never pays ! '

And the second replied : ' No, but nothing can stop her now. Nothing l '

Could nothing stop her ? Behind the intricacies of one of Smart's most elaborate ' Te Deums,' with clenched hands and little shivers of apprehension, she fought a poor little battle.

' We praise Thee, O God. We acknowledge Thee to be the Lord. . . .'

' The goodly fellowship of the prophets praise Thee. . . .' A boy's voice rose, ' Thou didst not abhor the Virgin's womb. . . .'

Let her step back now while there was yet time. She had her children. She had Falk. Falk l She looked around her, almost expecting him to be at her side, although she well knew that he had long ago abandoned the Cathedral services. Ah, it wasn't fair l If only he loved her, if only any one loved her, any one whom she herself could love. If any one wanted her !

Lawrence was waiting, his back turned to the nave. As the last words of the ' Te Deum ' rose into a shout of triumphant confidence he turned and solemnly, his staff raised, advanced, Archdeacon Brandon behind him. Now, as always, a little giggle of appreciation ran down the nave as the Archdeacon marched forward to the Lectern. The tourists whispered and asked one another who that fine - looking man was. They craned their necks into the aisle. And he *did* look fine, his head up, his shoulders back, his grave dignity graciously at their service. At their service and God's.

The sight of her husband inflamed Mrs. Brandon. She stared at him as though she were seeing him for the first time, but in reality she was not seeing him as he was now, but rather as he had been that

morning bending over her bed in his shirt and
trousers. That movement that he had made as
though he would lift her bodily out of the bed.

She closed her eyes. His fine rich voice came
to her from a long way off. Let him boom as
loudly as he pleased, he could not touch her any
more. She had escaped, and for ever. She saw,
then, Morris as she had seen him at that tea-party
months ago. She recovered that strange sense that
she had had (and that he had had too, as she knew)
of being carried out right away from one's body
into an atmosphere of fire and heat and sudden cold.
They had no more been able to avoid that look that
they had exchanged than they had been able to
escape being born. Let it then stay at that. She
wanted nothing more than that. Only that look
must be exchanged again. She was hungry, starving
for it. She *must* see him often, continually. She
must be able to look at him, touch the sleeve of his
coat, hear his voice. She must be able to do
things for him, little simple things that no one else
could do. She wanted no more than that. Only
to be near to him and to see that he was cared for . . .
looked after. Surely that was not wrong. No one
could say. . . .

Little shivers ran continually about her body, and
her hands, clenched tightly, were damp within her
gloves.

The Precentor gave out the words of the Anthem,
' Little children, love one another.'

Every one rose—save Lady St. Leath, who settled
herself magnificently in her seat and looked about
her as though she challenged anybody to tell her
that she was wrong to do so.

Yes, that was all Amy Brandon wanted. Who

could say that she was wrong to want it ? The little battle was concluded.

Old Canon Foster was preaching to-day. Always at the conclusion of the Anthem certain ruffians, visitors, tourists, clattered out. No sermon for them. They did not matter very greatly because they were far away at the back of the nave, and nobody need look at them ; but on Foster's preaching days certain of the aristocracy also retired, and this was disconcerting because their seats were prominent ones and their dresses were of silk. Often Lady St. Leath was one of these, but to-day she was sunk into a kind of stupor and did not move. Mrs. Combermere, Ellen Stiles and Mrs. Sampson were the guilty ones.

Rustle of their dresses, the heavy flop of the side Cloister door as it closed behind them, and then silence once more and the thin angry voice of Canon Foster, ' Let us pray.'

Out in the grey Cloisters it was charming. The mild April sun flooded the square of grass that lay in the middle of the thick rounded pillars like a floor of bright green glass.

The ladies stood for a moment looking out into the sunny silence. The Cathedral was hushed behind them ; Ellen Stiles was looking very gay and very hideous in a large hat stifled with flowers, set sideways on her head, and a bright purple silk dress pulled in tightly at the waist, rising to high puffed shoulders. Her figure was not suited to the fashion of the day.

Mrs. Sampson explained that she was suffering from one of the worst of her nervous headaches and that she could not have endured the service another moment. Miss Stiles was all eager solicitude.

'I *am* so sorry. I know how you are when you get one of those things. Nothing does it any good, does it? I know you've tried everything, and it simply goes on for days and days, getting worse and worse. And the really terrible part of them is that, with you, they seem to be constitutional. No doctors can do anything—when they're constitutional. There you are for the rest of your days!'

Mrs. Sampson gave a little shiver.

'I must say, Dr. Puddifoot seems to be very little use,' she moaned.

'Oh! Puddifoot!' Miss Stiles was contemptuous. 'He's past his work. That's one comfort about this place. If any one's ill he dies. No false hopes. At least, we know where we are.'

They walked through the Martyr's Passage out into the full sunlight of the Precincts.

'What a jolly day!' said Mrs. Combermere, 'I shall take my dogs for a walk. By the way, Ellen,' she turned round to her friend, 'how did Miss Burnett's tea-party go? I haven't seen you since.'

'Oh, it was too funny!' Miss Stiles giggled. 'You never saw such a mixture, and I don't think Miss Burnett knew who any one was. Not that she had much time to think, poor dear, she was so worried with the tea. Such a maid as she had you never saw!'

'A mixture?' asked Mrs. Combermere. 'Who were they?'

'Oh, Canon Ronder and Bentinck - Major and Mrs. Brandon and—Oh, yes! actually Falk Brandon!'

' Falk Brandon there ? '

' Yes, wasn't it the strangest thing ?   I shouldn't
have thought he'd have had time——   However,
you told me not to, so I won't——'

' Whom did you talk to ? '

' I talked to Miss Burnett most of the time.   I
tried to cheer her up.   No one else paid the least
attention to her.'

' She's a very stupid person, it seems to me,' Mrs.
Sampson murmured.   ' But of course I know her
very slightly.'

' Stupid ! '   Miss Stiles laughed.   ' Why, she
hasn't an idea in her head.   I don't believe that she
knows it's Jubilee Year.   Positively ! '

A little wind blew sportively around Miss Stiles'
large hat.   They all moved forward.

' The funny thing was——'   Miss Stiles paused
and looked apprehensively at Mrs. Combermere.
' I know you don't like scandal, but of course this
isn't scandal—there's nothing in it——'

' Come on, Ellen.   Out with it,' said Mrs.
Combermere.

' Well, Mrs. Brandon and Mr. Morris.   I caught
the oddest look between them.'

' Look !   What do you mean ? ' asked Mrs.
Combermere sharply.   Mrs. Sampson stood still,
her mouth a little open, forgetting her neuralgia.

' Of course it was nothing.   All the same, they
were standing at the window saying something,
looking at one another, well, positively as though
they had known one another intimately for years.   I
assure you——'

Mrs. Combermere turned upon her.   ' Of all
the nasty minds in this town, Ellen, you have the
nastiest.   I've told you so before.   People can't

even look at one another now. Why, you might as
well say that I'd been gazing at your Ronder when
he came to tea the other day.'

'Perhaps I shall,' said Miss Stiles, laughing.
'It would be a delightful story to spread. Seriously,
why not make a match of it ? You'd just suit one
another.'

'Once is enough for me in a life-time,' said Mrs.
Combermere grimly. 'Now, Ellen, come along.
No more mischief. Leave poor little Morris alone.'

'Mrs. Brandon and Mr. Morris !' repeated
Mrs. Sampson, her eyes wide open. 'Well, I do
declare.'

The ladies separated, and the Precincts was
abandoned for a time to its beautiful Sunday peace
and calm.

CHAPTER III

THE MAY-DAY PROLOGUE

MAY is the finest month of all the year in Glebe-shire. The days are warm but not too hot, the sky is blue but not too blue, the air is soft but with a touch of sharpness. The valleys are pressed down and overflowing with flowers, the cuckoo cries across the glassy waters of blue harbours, and the gorse is honey-scented among the rocks.

May-day in Polchester this year was warm and bright, with a persistent cuckoo somewhere in the Dean's garden, and a very shrill-voiced canary in Miss Dobell's open window. The citizens of Polchester were suddenly aware that summer was close upon them. Doors were flung open and the gardens sinuously watered, summer clothes were dragged from their long confinement and anxiously over-looked, Mr. Martin, the stationer, hung a row of his coloured Polchester views along a string across his window, the dark, covered ways of the market-place quivered and shone with pots of spring flowers, and old Simon's water-cart made its first trembling and shaking appearance down the High Street.

All this was well enough and customary enough, but what marked this spring from any other spring that had ever been was that it was Jubilee Year. It was on this warm May-day that Polchester people realised suddenly that the Jubilee was not far away. The event had not quite the excitement and novelty that the Jubilee of 1887 had had ; there was, perhaps, in London and the larger towns, something of a sense of repetition. But Polchester was far from the general highway, and, although the picture of the wonderful old lady, now nearly eighty years of age, was strong before every one's vision, there was a deep determination to make this year's celebration a great Polchester affair, to make it the celebration of Polchester men and Polchester history and Polchester progress.

The programme had been long arranged—the great Service in the Cathedral, the Ball in the Assembly Rooms, the Flower Show in the St. Leath Castle grounds, the Torchlight Procession, the Croquet Tournament, the School-children's Tea and the School Cricket-match. A fine programme, and the Jubilee Committee, with the Bishop, the Mayor, and the Countess of St. Leath for its presidents, had already held several meetings.

Nevertheless, Glebeshire has a rather languishing climate. Polchester has been called by its critics 'a lazy town,' and it must be confessed that everything in connection with the Jubilee had been jogging along very sleepily until of a sudden this warm May-day arrived and every one sprang into action. The Mayor called a meeting of the town branch of the Committee, and the Bishop out at Carpledon summoned his ecclesiastics, and Joan found a note from Gladys Sampson beckoning her to the Sampson house to do her share of the glorious work. It had been decided by the Higher Powers that it would be a charming thing for some of the younger Polchester ladies to have in charge the working of two of the flags that were to decorate the Assembly Room walls on the night of the Ball. Gladys Sampson, who, unlike her mother, never suffered from headaches, and was a strong, determined, rather masculine girl, soon had the affair in hand, and the party was summoned.

I would not like to say that Polchester had a more snobbish spirit than other Cathedral towns, but there is no doubt that, thirty years ago, the lines were drawn very clearly indeed between the 'Cathedral' and the 'Others.'

'Cathedral' included not only the daughters of the Canons and what Mr. Martin, in his little town guide-book, called 'General Ecclesiastical Phenomena,' but also the two daughters of Puddifoot's sister, Grace and Annie Trudon; the three daughters of Roger McKenzie, the town lawyer; little Betty Callender, the only child of old, red-faced Major Callender; Mary and Amy Forrester, daughters of old Admiral Forrester; and, of course, the St. Leath girls.

When Joan arrived, then, in the Deanery dining-room, there was a fine gathering. Very unsophisticated they would all have been considered by the present generation. Lady Rose and Lady Mary, who were both of them nearer forty than thirty, had of course had some experience of London, and had been even to Paris and Rome. Of the 'Others,' at this time, only Betty Callender, who had been born in India, and the Forresters had been farther, in all their lives, than Drymouth. Their lives were bound, and happily bound, by the Polchester horizon. They lived in and for and by the local excitements, talks, croquet, bicycling (under proper guardianship), Rafiel or Buquay or Clinton in the summer,

and the occasional (very, very occasional) perform-
ances of amateur theatricals in the Assembly Rooms.

Moreover, they were happy and contented and
healthy. For many of them *Jane Eyre* was still a
forbidden book and a railway train a remarkable
adventure.

Polchester was the world and the world was
Polchester. They were at least a century nearer
to Jane Austen's day than they were to George
the Fifth's.

Joan saw, with relief, so soon as she entered the
room, that the St. Leath women were absent. They
overawed her and were so much older than the others
there that they brought constraint with them and
embarrassment.

Any stranger, coming suddenly into the room,
must have felt its light and gaiety and happiness.
The high wide dining-room windows were open and
looked, over sloping lawns, down to the Pol and up
again to the woods beyond. The trees were faintly
purple in the spring sun, daffodils were nodding on
the lawn, and little gossamer clouds of pale orange
floated like feathers across the sky. The large
dining-room table was cleared for action, and Gladys
Sampson, very serious and important, stood at the
far end of the room under a very bad oil-painting of
her father, directing operations. The girls were
dressed for the most part in white muslin frocks,
high in the shoulders and pulled in at the waist and
tight round the neck—only the McKenzie girls,
who rode to hounds and played tennis beautifully
and had, all three of them, faces of glazed red brick,
were clad in the heavy Harris tweeds that were just
then beginning to be so fashionable.

Joan, who only a month or two ago would have

been devoured with shyness at penetrating the fastnesses of the Sampson dining-room, now felt no
shyness whatever but nodded quite casually to
Gladys, smiled at the McKenzies, and found a place
between Cynthia Ryle and Jane D'Arcy.

They all sat, bathed in the sunshine, and looked
at Gladys Sampson. She cleared her throat and
said in her pounding heavy voice—her voice was
created for Committees : ' Now all of you know
what we're here for. We're here to make two
banners for the Assembly Rooms and we've got to
do our very best. We haven't got a great deal of
time between now and June the Twentieth, so we
must work, and I propose that we come here every
Tuesday and Friday afternoon, and when I say *here*
I mean somebody or other's house, because of course
it won't be always here. There's cutting up to do
and sewing and plenty of work really for everybody,
because when the banners are done there are the
flags for the school-children. Now if any one has any
suggestions to make I shall be very glad to hear them.'

There was at first no reply to this and every one
smiled and looked at the portrait of the Dean.
Then one of the McKenzie girls remarked in a deep
bass voice :

' That's all right, Gladys. But who's going to
decide who does what ? Very decent of you to ask
us but we're not much in the sewing line—never
have been.'

' Oh,' said Gladys, ' I've got people's names down
for the different things they're to do and any one
whom it doesn't suit has only got to speak up.'

Soon the material was distributed and groups
were formed round the room. A chatter arose like
the murmur of bees. The sun as it sank lower

behind the woods turned them to dark crimson and the river pale grey. The sun fell now in burning patches and squares across the room, and the dim yellow blinds were pulled half-way across the windows. With this the room was shaded into a strong coloured twilight and the white frocks shone as though seen through glass. The air grew cold beyond the open windows, but the room was warm with the heat that the walls had stolen and stored from the sun.

Joan sat with Jane D'Arcy and Betty Callender. She was very happy to be at rest there ; she felt secure and safe. Because in truth during these last weeks life had been increasingly difficult—difficult not only because it had become, of late, so new and so strange, but also because she could not tell what was happening. Family life had indeed become of late a mystery, and behind the mystery there was a dim sense of apprehension, apprehension that she had never felt in all her days before. As she sank into the tranquillity of the golden afternoon glow, with the soft white silk passing to and fro in her hands, she tried to realise for herself what had been occurring. Her father was, on the whole, simple enough. He was beginning to suffer yet again from one of his awful obsessions. Since the hour of her earliest childhood she had watched these obsessions and dreaded them.

There had been so many, big ones and little ones. Now the Government, now the Dean, now the Town Council, now the Chapter, now the Choir, now some rude letter, now some impertinent article in a paper. Like wild fierce animals these things had from their dark thickets leapt out upon him, and he had proceeded to wrestle with them in the full presence of

his family.   Always, at last, he had been victorious
over them, the triumph had been publicly announced,
' Te Deums ' sung, and for a time there had been
peace.   It was some while since the last obsession,
some ridiculous action about drainage on the part
of the Town Council.   But the new one threatened
to make up in full for the length of that interval.

Only just before Falk's unexpected return from
Oxford Joan had been congratulating herself on
her father's happiness and peace of mind.   She
might have known the omens of that dangerous
quiet.   On the very day of Falk's arrival Canon
Ronder had arrived too.

Canon Ronder !   How Joan was beginning to
detest the very sound of the name !   She had
hated the man himself as soon as she had set eyes
upon him.   She had scented, in some instinctive
way, the trouble that lay behind those large round
glasses and that broad indulgent smile.   But now !
Now they were having the name ' Ronder ' with
their breakfast, their dinner, and their tea.   Into
everything apparently his fat fingers were inserted ;
her father saw his rounded shadow behind every
door, his rosy cheeks at every window.

And yet it was very difficult to discover what
exactly it was that he had done !   Now, whatever
it might be that went wrong in the Brandon house,
in the Cathedral, in the town, her father was certain
that Ronder was responsible—but proof.   Well,
there wasn't any.   And it was precisely this absence
of proof that built up the obsession.

Everywhere that Ronder went he spoke en-
thusiastically about the Archdeacon.   These compliments came back to Joan again and again.   ' If
there's one man in this town I admire——'   ' What

would this town be without——' 'We're lucky, indeed, to have the Archdeacon——' And yet was there not behind all these things a laugh, a jest, a mocking tone, something that belonged in spirit to that horrible day when the elephant had trodden upon her father's hat?

She loved her father, and she loved him twice as dearly since one night when on driving up to the Castle he had held her hand. But now the obsession had killed the possibility of any tenderness between them; she longed to be able to do something that would show him how strongly she was his partisan, to insult Canon Ronder in the market-place, to turn her back when he spoke to her—and, at the same time, intermingled with this hot championship was irritation that her father should allow himself to be obsessed by this. He who was so far greater than a million Ronders !

The situation in the Brandon family had not been made any easier by Falk's strange liking for the man. Joan did not pretend that she understood her brother or had ever been in any way close to him. When she had been little he had seemed to be so infinitely above her as to be in another world, and now that they seemed almost of an age he was strange to her like some one of foreign blood. She knew that she did not count in his scheme of life at all, that he never thought of her nor wanted her. She did not mind that, and even now she would have been tranquil about him had it not been for her mother's anxiety. She could not but see how during the last weeks her mother had watched every step that Falk took, her eyes always searching his face as though he were keeping some secret from her. To Joan, who never believed that people could plot and plan and lead double lives, this all seemed unnatural and exaggerated.

But she knew well enough that her mother had never attempted to give her any of her confidence. Everything at home, in short, was difficult and confused. Nobody was happy, nobody was natural. Even her own private history, if she looked into it too closely, did not show her any very optimistic colours. She had not seen Johnny St. Leath now for a fortnight, nor heard from him, and those precious words under the Arden Gate one evening were beginning already to appear a dim unsubstantial dream. However, if there was one quality that Joan Brandon possessed in excess of all others, it was a simple fidelity to the cause or person in front of her.

Her doubts came simply from the wonder as to whether she had not concluded too much from his words and built upon them too fairy-like a castle.

With a gesture she flung all her wonders and troubles out upon the gold-swept lawn and trained all her attention to the chatter among the girls around her. She admired Jane D'Arcy very much ; she was so ' elegant.' Everything that Jane wore became her slim straight body, and her pale pointed face was always a little languid in expression, as though daily life were an exhausting affair and not intended for superior persons. She had been told, from a very early day, that her voice was ' low and musical,' so she always spoke in whispers which gave her thoughts an importance that they might not otherwise have possessed. Very different was little Betty Callender, round and rosy like an apple, with freckles on her nose and bright blue eyes. She

laughed a great deal and liked to agree with everything that any one said.

'If you ask me,' said Jane in her fascinating
whisper, 'there's a lot of nonsense about this old
Jubilee.'

'Oh, do you think so?' said Joan.

'Yes. Old Victoria's been on the throne long
enough. 'Tis time we had somebody else.'

Joan was very much shocked by this and said so.

'I don't think we ought to be governed by *old*
people,' said Jane. 'Every one over seventy ought
to be buried whether they wish it or no.'

Joan laughed aloud.

'Of course they wouldn't wish it,' she said.

Laughter came, now here, now there, from
different parts of the room. Every one was very
gay from the triple sense that they were the elect
of Polchester, that they were doing important work,
and that summer was coming.

Jane D'Arcy tossed her head.

'Father says that perhaps he'll be taking us to
London for it,' she whispered.

'I wouldn't go if any one offered me,' said Joan.
'It's Polchester I want to see it at, not London.
Of course I'd love to see the Queen, but it would
probably be only for a moment, and all the rest
would be horrible crowds with nobody knowing
you. While here! Oh! it will be lovely!'

Jane smiled. 'Poor child. Of course you know
nothing about London. How should you? Give
me a week in London and you can have your old
Polchester for ever. What ever happens in Polchester? Silly old croquet parties and a dance
in the Assembly Rooms. And *never* any one
new.'

'Well, there *is* some one new,' said Betty
Callender, ' I saw her this morning.'

'Her? Who?' asked Jane, with the scorn of
one who has already made up her mind to despise.

'I was with mother going through the market
and Lady St. Leath came by in an open carriage.
She was with her. Mother says she's a Miss
Daubeney from London—and oh! she's perfectly
lovely! and mother says she's to marry Lord St.
Leath——'

'Oh! I heard she was coming,' said Jane, still
scornfully. 'How silly you are, Betty! You think
any one lovely if she comes from London.'

'No, but she was,' insisted Betty, 'mother said
so too, and she had a blue silk parasol, and she was
just sweet. Lord St. Leath was in the carriage
with them.'

'Poor Johnny!' said Jane. 'He always has to
do just what that horrible old mother of his tells
him.'

Joan had listened to this little dialogue with
what bravery she could. Doom then had been pro-
nounced? Sentence had fallen? Miss Daubeney
had arrived. She could hear the old Countess's voice
again. 'Claire Daubeney—Monteagle's daughter—
such a nice girl—Johnny's friend——'

Johnny's friend! Of course she was. Nothing
could show to Joan more clearly the difference
between Joan's world and the St. Leath world than
the arrival of this lovely stranger. Although Mme.
Sarah Grand and others were at this very moment
forcing that strange figure, the New Woman, upon
a reluctant world, Joan belonged most distinctly to
the earlier generation. She trembled at the thought
of any publicity, of any thrusting herself forward,

of any, even momentary, rebellion against her position. Of course Johnny belonged to this beautiful creature ; she had always known, in her heart, that her dream was an impossible one. Nevertheless the room, the sunlight, the white dresses, the long shining table, the coloured silks and ribbons, swam in confusion around her. She was suddenly miserable. Her hands shook and her upper lip trembled. She had a strange illogical desire to go out and find Miss Daubeney and snatch her blue parasol from her startled hands and stamp upon it.

'Well,' said Jane, 'I don't envy any one who marries Johnny—to be shut up in that house with all those old women !'

Betty shook her head very solemnly and tried to look older than her years.

The afternoon was drawing on. Gladys came across and closed the windows.

'I think that's about enough to-day,' she said. 'Now we'll have tea.'

Joan's great desire was to slip away and go home. She put her work on the table, fetched her coat from the other end of the room.

Gladys stopped her. 'Don't go, Joan. You must have tea.'

'I promised mother——' she said.

The door opened. She turned and found herself close to the Dean and Canon Ronder.

The Dean came forward, nervously rubbing his hands together as was his custom. 'Well, children,' he said, blinking at them. Ronder stood, smiling, in the doorway. At the sight of him Joan was filled with hatred—vehement, indignant hatred ; she had never hated any one before, unless possibly it was Miss St. Clair, the French mistress. Now, from what source she did not know, fear and passion flowed into her. Nothing could have been more amiable and genial than the figure that he presented.

As always, his clothes were beautifully neat and correct, his linen spotless white, his black boots gleaming.

He beamed upon them all, and Joan felt, behind her, the response that the whole room made to him. They liked him ; she knew it. He was becoming popular.

He had towards them all precisely the right attitude ; he was not amiable and childish like the Dean, nor pompous like Bentinck-Major, nor sycophantic like Ryle. He did not advance to them but became, as it were, himself one of them, understanding exactly the way that they wanted him.

And Joan hated him ; she hated his red face and his neatness and his broad chest and his stout legs —everything, everything ! She also feared him. She had never before, although for long now she had been conscious of his power, been so deeply aware of his connection with herself. It was as though his round shadow had, on this lovely afternoon, crept forward a little and touched with its dim grey for the first time the Brandon house.

' Canon Ronder,' Gladys Sampson cried, ' come and see what we've done.'

He moved forward and patted little Betty Callender on the head as he passed. ' Are you all right, my dear, and your father ? '

It appeared that Betty was delighted. Suddenly he saw Joan.

' Oh, good evening, Miss Brandon.' He altered his tone for her, speaking as though she were an equal.

Joan looked at him ; colour flamed in her cheeks. She did not reply, and then feeling as though in an instant she would do something quite disgraceful, she slipped from the room.

Soon, after gently smiling at the parlourmaid, who was an old friend of hers because she had once been in service at the Brandons', she found herself standing, a little lost and bewildered, at the corner of Green Lane and Orange Street. Lost and bewildered because one emotion after another seemed suddenly to have seized upon her and taken her captive. Lost and bewildered almost as though she had been bewitched, carried off through the shining skies by her captor and then dropped, deserted, left, in some unknown country.

Green Lane in the evening light had a fairy air. The stumpy trees on either side with the bright new green of the spring seemed to be concealing lamps within their branches. So thick a glow suffused the air that it was as though strangely coloured fruit, purple and orange and amethyst, hung glittering against the pale yellow sky, and the road running up the hill was like pale wax.

On the other side Orange Street tumbled pell-mell into the roofs of the town. The monument of the fierce Georgian citizen near which Joan was standing guarded with a benevolent devotion the little city whose lights, stealing now upon the air, sprinkled the evening sky with a jewelled haze. No sound broke the peace; no one came nor went; only the trees of the Lane moved and stirred very faintly as though assuring the girl of their friendly company.

Never before had she so passionately loved her town. It seemed to-night when she was disturbed by her new love, her new fear, her new worldly knowledge, to be eager to assure her that it was with her in all her troubles, that it understood that she must pass into new experiences, that it knew, none better indeed, how strange and terrifying that first realisation of real life could be, that it had itself suffered when new streets had been thrust upon it and old loved houses pulled down and the river choked and the hills despoiled, but that everything passes and love remains and homeliness and friends.

Joan felt more her own response to the town than the town's reassurance to her, but she was a little comforted and she felt a little safer.

She argued as she walked home through the Market Place and up the High Street and under the Arden Gate into the quiet sheltered Precincts, why should she think that Ronder mattered? After all might not he be the good fat clergyman that he appeared? It was more perhaps a kind of jealousy because of her father that she felt. She put aside her own little troubles in a sudden rush of tenderness for her family. She wanted to protect them all and make them happy. But how could she make them happy if they would tell her nothing? They still treated her as a child, but she was a woman now. Her love for Johnny. She had admitted that to herself. She stopped on the path outside the decorous strait-laced houses and put her cool gloved hand up to her burning cheek.

She had known for a long time that she loved him, but she had not told herself. She must conquer that, stamp upon it. It was foolish, hopeless. . . . She ran up the steps of their house as though something pursued her.

She let herself in and found the hall dusky and

obscure. The lamp had not yet been lit. She heard a voice :

' Who's that ? '

She looked up and saw her mother, a little, slender figure, standing at the turn of the stairs holding in her hand a lighted candle.

' It's I, mother, Joan. I've just come from Gladys Sampson.'

' Oh ! I thought it would be Falk. You didn't pass Falk on your way ? '

' No, mother dear.'

She went across to the little cupboard where the coats were hung. As she poked her head into the little dark, musty place, she could feel that her mother was still standing there, listening.

CHAPTER IV

THE GENIAL HEART

RONDER was never happier than when he was wishing well to all mankind.

He could neither force nor falsify this emotion. If he did not feel it he did not feel it, and himself was the loser. But it sometimes occurred that the weather was bright, that his digestion was functioning admirably, that he liked his surroundings, that he had agreeable work, that his prospects were happy—then he literally beamed upon mankind and in his fancy showered upon the poor and humble largesse of glittering coin. In such a mood he loved every one, would pat children on the back, help old men along the road, listen to the long whinings of the reluctant poor. Utterly genuine he was ; he meant every word that he spoke and every smile that he bestowed.

Now, early in May and in Polchester he was in such a mood. Soon after his arrival he had discovered that he liked the place and that it promised to suit him well, but he had never supposed that it could develop into such perfection. Success already was his, but it was not success of so swift a kind that plots and plans were not needed. They were very much needed. He could remember no time in his past life when he had had so admirable a combination of difficulties to overcome. And they were difficulties of the right kind. They centred around a figure whom he could really like and admire. It would have been very unpleasant had he hated Brandon or despised him. Those were uncomfortable emotions in which he indulged as seldom as possible.

What he liked, above everything, was a fight, when he need have no temptation towards anger or bitterness. Who could be angry with poor Brandon? Nor could he despise him. In his simple blind confidence and self-esteem there was an element of truth, of strength, even of nobility.

Far from despising or hating Brandon, he liked him immensely—and he was on his way utterly to destroy him.

Then, as he approached nearer the centre of his drama, he noticed, as he had often noticed before, how strangely everything played into his hands. Without undue presumption it seemed that so soon as he determined that something ought to occur and began to work in a certain direction, God also decided that it was wise and pushed everything into its right place. This consciousness of Divine partnership gave Ronder a sense that his opponents were the merest pawns in a game whose issue was already decided.

Poor things, they were helpless indeed! This only added to his kindly feelings towards them, his sense of humour, too, was deeply stirred by their own unawareness of their fate—and he always liked any one who stirred his sense of humour.

Never before had he known everything play so immediately into his hands as in this present case.

Brandon, for instance, had just that stupid obstinacy that was required, the town had just that ignorance of the outer world and cleaving to old traditions.

And now, how strange that the boy Falk had on several occasions stopped to speak to him and had at last asked whether he might come and see him !

How lucky that Brandon should be making this mistake about the Pybus St. Anthony living !

Finally, although he was completely frank with himself and knew that he was working, first and last, for his own future comfort, it did seem to him that he was also doing real benefit to the town. The times were changing. Men of Brandon's type were anachronistic ; the town had been under Brandon's domination too long. New life was coming—a new world—a new civilisation.

Ronder, although no one believed less in Utopias than he, did believe in the Zeitgeist—simply for comfort's sake if for no stronger reason. Well, the Zeitgeist was descending upon Polchester, and Ronder was its agent. Progress ? No, Ronder did not believe in Progress. But in the House of Life there are many rooms ; once and again the furniture is changed.

One afternoon early in May he was suddenly aware that everything was moving more swiftly upon its appointed course than he, sharp though he was, had been aware. Crossing the Cathedral Green he encountered Dr. Puddifoot. He knew that the Doctor had at first disliked him but was quickly coming over to his side and was beginning to consider him as ' broad-minded for a parson and knowing a lot more about life than you would suppose.' He saw precisely into Puddifoot's brain and watched the thoughts dart to and fro as though

they had been so many goldfish in a glass bowl.
He also liked Puddifoot for himself ; he always
liked stout, big, red-faced men ; they were easier
to deal with than the thin severe ones. He knew
that the time would very shortly arrive when Puddifoot would tell him one of his improper stories.
That would sanctify the friendship.

'Ha ! Canon !' said Puddifoot, puffing like a
seal. 'Jolly day !'

They stood and talked, then, as they were both
going into the town, they turned and walked towards
the Arden Gate. Puddifoot talked about his health ;
like many doctors he was very timid about himself
and eager to reassure himself in public. 'How are
you, Canon ? But I needn't ask—looking splendid.
I'm all right myself—never felt better really. Just a
twinge of rheumatics last night, but it's nothing.
Must expect something at my age, you know—
getting on for seventy.'

'You look as though you'll live for ever,' said
Ronder, beaming upon him.

'You can't always tell from us big fellows.
There's Brandon now, for instance — the Archdeacon.'

'Surely there isn't a healthier man in the kingdom,' said Ronder, pushing his spectacles back into
the bridge of his nose.

'Think so, wouldn't you ? But you'd be wrong.
A sudden shock, and that man would be nowhere.
Given to fits of anger, always tried his system too
hard, never learnt control. Might have a stroke
any day for all he looks so strong !'

'Really, really ! Dear me !' said Ronder.

'Course these are medical secrets in a way.
Know it won't go any farther. But it's curious.

isn't it? Appearances are deceptive — damned deceptive. That's what they are. Brandon's brain's never been his strong point. Might go any moment.'

'Dear me, dear me,' said Ronder. 'I'm sorry to hear that.'

'Oh, I don't mean,' said Puddifoot, puffing and blowing out his cheeks like a cherub in a picture by Sir Joshua Reynolds, 'that he'll die to-morrow, you know — or have a stroke either. But he ain't as secure as he looks. And he don't take care of himself as he should.'

Outside the Library Ronder paused.

'Going in here for a book, Doctor. See you later.'

'Yes, yes,' said Puddifoot, his eyes staring up and down the street, as though they would burst out of his head. 'Very good — very good. See you later then,' and so went blowing down the hill.

Ronder passed under the gloomy portals of the Library and found his way, through faith rather than vision, up the stone stairs that smelt of mildew and blotting-paper, into the high dingy room. He had had a sudden desire the night before to read an old story by Bage that he had not seen since he was a boy — the violent and melancholy *Hermsprong*.

It had come to him, as it were, in his dreams — a vision of himself rocking in a hammock in his uncle's garden on a wonderful summer afternoon, eating apples and reading *Hermsprong*, the book discovered, he knew not by what chance, in the dusty depths of his uncle's library. He would like to read it again. *Hermsprong*! the very scent of the skin of the apple, the blue-flecked tapestry of light between the high boughs came back to him. He was a boy again. . . .   He was brought up sharply by meeting the little red-rimmed eyes of Miss Milton. Red-rimmed to-day surely with recent weeping. She sat humped up on her chair, glaring out into the room.

'It's all right, Miss Milton,' he said, smiling at her. 'It's an old book I want. I won't bother you. I'll look for myself.'

He passed into the further dim secrecies of the Library, whither so few penetrated. Here was an old ladder, and, mounted upon it, he confronted the vanished masterpieces of Holcroft and Radcliffe, Lewis and Jane Porter, Clara Reeve and Mackenzie, old calf-bound ghosts who threw up little clouds of sighing dust as he touched them with his fingers. He was happily preoccupied with his search, balancing his stout body precariously on the trembling ladder, when he fancied that he heard a sigh.

He stopped and listened; this time there could be no mistake. It was a sigh of prodigious intent and meaning, and it came from Miss Milton. Impatiently he turned back to his books ; he would find his Bage as quickly as possible and go. He was not at all in the mood for lamentations from Miss Milton. Ah ! there was *Barham Downs*. *Hermsprong* could not be far away. Then suddenly there came to him quite unmistakably a sob, then another, then two more, finally something that horribly resembled hysterics. He came down from his ladder and crossed the room.

'My dear Miss Milton !' he exclaimed. 'Is there anything I can do ? '

She presented a strange and unpoetic appearance, huddled up in her wooden armchair, one fat leg crooked under her, her head sinking into her ample bosom, her whole figure shaking with convulsive grief, the chair creaking sympathetically with her.

Ronder, seeing that she was in real distress, hurried up to her.

' My dear Miss Milton, what is it ? '

For a while she could not speak ; then raised a face of mottled purple and white, and, dabbing her cheeks with a handkerchief not of the cleanest, choked out between her sobs :

' My last week—Saturday—Saturday I go—disgrace—ugh, ugh—dismissed—Archdeacon.'

' But I don't understand,' said Ronder, ' who goes ? Who's disgraced ? '

' I go ! ' cried Miss Milton, suddenly uncurling her body and her sobs checked by her anger.—' I shouldn't have given way like this, and before you, Canon Ronder. But I'm ruined—ruined !— and for doing my duty ! '

Her change from the sobbing, broken woman to the impassioned avenger of justice was so immediate that Ronder was confused. ' I still don't understand, Miss Milton,' he said. ' Do you say you are dismissed, and, if so, by whom ? '

' I *am* dismissed !   I *am* dismissed ! ' cried Miss Milton. ' I leave here on Saturday. I have been librarian to this Library, Canon Ronder, for more than twenty years. Yes, twenty years. And now I'm dismissed like a dog with a month's notice.'

She had collected her tears and, with a marvellous rapidity, packed them away. Her eyes, although red, were dry and glittering ; her cheeks were of a pasty white marked with small red spots of indignation. Ronder, looking at her and her dirty hands, thought that he had never seen a woman whom he disliked more.

But, Miss Milton,' he said, ' if you'll forgive
me, I still don't understand. Under whom do you
hold this appointment ? Who have the right to
dismiss you ? and, whoever it was, they must have
given some reason.'

Miss Milton was now the practical woman,
speaking calmly, although her bosom still heaved
and her fingers plucked confusedly with papers on
the table in front of her. She spoke quietly, but
behind her words there were so vehement a hatred,
bitterness, and malice that Ronder observed her with
a new interest.

' There is a Library Committee, Canon Ronder,'
she said. ' Lady St. Leath is its president. It has
in its hands the appointment of the librarian. It
appointed me more than twenty years ago. It has
now dismissed me with a month's notice for what
it calls—what it *calls*, Canon Ronder—"abuse and
neglect of my duties." Abuse ! Neglect ! Me !
about whom there has never been a word of complaint until—until——'

Here again Miss Milton's passions seemed to
threaten to overwhelm her. She gathered herself
together with a great effort.

' I know my enemy, Canon Ronder. Make no
mistake about that. I know my enemy. Although,
what have *I* ever done to him I cannot imagine.
A more inoffensive person——'

' Yes.—But,' said Canon Ronder gently, ' tell me,
if you can, exactly with what they charge you. Perhaps I can help you. Is it Lady St. Leath who——'

' No, it is *not* Lady St. Leath,' broke in Miss
Milton vehemently. ' I owe Lady St. Leath much
in the past. If she has been a little imperious at
times, that after all is her right. Lady St. Leath

is a perfect lady. What occurred was simply this. Some months ago I was keeping a book for Lady St. Leath that she especially wished to read. Miss Brandon, the daughter of the Archdeacon, came in and tried to take the book from me, saying that her mother wished to read it. I explained to her that it was being kept for Lady St. Leath; nevertheless, she persisted and complained to Lord St. Leath, who happened to be in the Library at the time; he, being a perfect gentleman, could of course do nothing but say that she was to have the book.

' She went home and complained, and it was the Archdeacon who brought up the affair at a Committee meeting and insisted on my dismissal. Yes, Canon Ronder, I know my enemy and I shall not forget it.'

' Dear me,' said Canon Ronder benevolently, ' I'm more than sorry. Certainly it sounds a little hasty, although the Archdeacon is the most honourable of men.'

' Honourable! Honourable!' Miss Milton rose in her chair. ' Honourable! He's so swollen with pride that he doesn't know what he is. Oh! I don't measure my words, Canon Ronder, nor do I see any reason why I should.

' He has ruined my life. What have I now at my age to go to? A little secretarial work, and less and less of that. But it's not *that* of which I complain. I am hurt in the very depths of my being, Canon Ronder. In my pride and my honour. Stains, wounds that I can never forget!'

It was so exactly as though Miss Milton had just been reading *Hermsprong* and was quoting from it that Ronder looked about him, almost expecting to see the dusty volume.

'Well, Miss Milton, perhaps I can put a little work in your way.'

'You're very kind, sir,' she said. 'There's more than I in this town, sir, who're glad that you've come among us, and hope that perhaps your presence may lead to a change some day amongst those in high authority.'

'Where are you living, Miss Milton?' he asked.

'3 St. James' Lane,' she answered. 'Just behind the Market and St. James' Church. Opposite the Rectory. Two little rooms, my windows looking on to Mr. Morris'.'

'Very well, I'll remember.'

'Thank you, sir, I'm sure. I'm afraid I've forgotten myself this morning, but there's nothing like a sense of injustice for making you lose your self-control. I don't care who hears me. I shall not forgive the Archdeacon.'

'Come, come, Miss Milton,' said Ronder. 'We must all forgive and forget.'

Her eyes narrowed until they almost disappeared.

'I don't wish to be unfair, Canon Ronder,' she said. 'But I've worked for more than twenty years like an honourable woman, and to be turned out.— Not that I bear Mrs. Brandon any grudge, coming down to see Mr. Morris so often as she does. I daresay she doesn't have too happy a time if all were known.'

'Now, now,' said Ronder. 'This won't do, Miss Milton. You won't make your case better by talking scandal, you know. I have your address. If I can help you I will. Good afternoon.'

Forgetting *Hermsprong*, having now more important things to consider, he found his way down the steps and out into the air.

On every side now it seemed that the Archdeacon was making some blunder. Little unimportant blunders perhaps, but nevertheless cumulative in their effect ! The balance had shifted. The Powers of the Air, bored perhaps with the too-extended spectacle of an Archdeacon successful and triumphant, had made a sign. . . .

Ronder, as he stood in the spring sunlight, glancing up and down the High Street, so full of colour and movement, had an impulse as though it were almost a duty to go and warn the Archdeacon. ' Look out ! Look out ! There's a storm coming ! ' *Warn* the Archdeacon ! He smiled. He could imagine to himself the scene and the reception his advice would have. Nevertheless, how sad that undoubtedly you cannot make an omelette without first breaking the eggs ! And this omelette positively *must* be made !

He had intended to do a little shopping, an occupation in which he delighted because of the personal victories to be won, but suddenly now, moved by what impulse he could not tell, he turned back towards the Cathedral. He crossed the Green, and almost before he knew it he had pushed back the heavy West door and was in the dark, dimly coloured shadow. The air was chill. The nave was scattered with lozenges of purple and green light. He moved up the side aisle, thinking that now he was here he would exchange a word or two with old Lawrence. No harm would be done by a little casual amiability in that direction.

Before he realised, he was close to the Black Bishop's Tomb. The dark grim face seemed to-day to wear a triumphant smile beneath the black beard. A shaft of sunlight played upon the marble like a searchlight upon water; the gold of the iron-work and the green ring and the tracery on the scrolled borders jumped under the sunlight like living things.

Ronder, moved as always by beauty, smiled as though in answer to the dead Bishop.

'Why! you're the most alive thing in this Cathedral,' he thought to himself.

'Pretty good bit of work, isn't it?' he heard at his elbow. He turned and saw Davray, the painter. The man had been pointed out to him in the street; he knew his reputation. He was inclined to be interested in the man, in any one who had a wider, broader view of life than the citizens of the town. Davray had not been drinking for several weeks; and always towards the end of one of his sober bouts he was gentle, melancholy, the true artist in him rising for one last view of the beauty that there was in the world before the inevitable submerging.

He had, on this occasion, been sober for a longer period than usual; he felt weak and faint, as though he had been without food, and his favourite vice, that had been approaching closer and closer to him during these last days, now leered at him, leaning towards him from the other side of the gilded scrolls of the tomb.

'Yes, it's a very fine thing.' He cleared his throat. 'You're Canon Ronder, are you not?'

'Yes, I am.'

'My name's Davray. You've probably heard of me as a drunkard who hangs about the town doing no good. I'm quite sure you don't want to speak to me or know me, but in here, where it's so quiet and so beautiful, one may know people whom it wouldn't be nice to know outside.'

Ronder looked at him. The man's face, worn

now and pinched and sharp, must once have had its
fineness.

'You do yourself an injustice, Mr. Davray,'
Ronder said. 'I'm very glad indeed to know
you.'

'Well, of course, you parsons have got to know
everybody, haven't you? And the sinners especially. That's your job. But I'm not a sinner
to-day. I haven't drunk anything for weeks,
although don't congratulate me, because I'm certainly not going to hold out much longer. There's
no hope of redeeming me, Canon Ronder, even if
you have time for the job.'

Ronder smiled.

'I'm not going to preach to you,' he said, 'you
needn't be afraid.'

'Well, let's forget all that. This Cathedral is
the very place, if you clergymen had any sense of
proportion, where you should be ashamed to preach.
It laughs at you.'

'At any rate the Bishop does,' said Ronder,
looking down at the tomb.

'No, but all of it,' said Davray. Instinctively
they both looked up. High above them, in the
very heart of the great Cathedral tower, a mist,
reflected above the windows until it was coloured a
very faint rose, trembled like a sea about the black
rafters and rounded pillars. Even as they looked
some bird flew twittering from corner to corner.

'When I'm worked up,' said Davray, 'which
I'm not to-day, I just long to clear all you officials
out of it. I laugh sometimes to think how important you think yourselves and how unimportant
you really are. The Cathedral laughs too, and once
and again stretches out a great lazy finger and just

flicks you away as it would a spider's web. I hope you don't think me impertinent.'

'Not in the least,' said Ronder; 'some of us even may feel just as you do about it.'

'Brandon doesn't.' Davray moved away. 'I sometimes think that when I'm properly drunk one day I'll murder that man. His self-sufficiency and conceit are an insult to the Cathedral. But the Cathedral knows. It bides its time.'

Ronder looked gravely at the melancholy ineffective figure with the pale pointed beard, and the weak hands. 'You speak very confidently, Mr. Davray,' he said. 'As with all of us, you judge others by yourself. When you know what the Cathedral's attitude to yourself is, you'll be able to see more clearly.'

'To myself!' Davray answered excitedly. 'It has none! To myself? Why, I'm nobody, nothing. It doesn't have to begin to consider me. I'm less than the dung the birds drop from the height of the tower. But I'm humble before it. I would let its meanest stone crush the life out of my body, and be glad enough. At least I know its power, its beauty. And I adore it! I adore it!'

He looked up as he spoke; his eyes seemed to be eagerly searching for some expected face.

Ronder disliked both melodrama and sentimentality. Both were here.

'Take my advice,' he said, smiling. 'Don't think too much about the place. . . . I'm glad that we met. Good afternoon.'

Davray did not seem to have noticed him; he was staring down again at the Bishop's Tomb. Ronder walked away. A strange man! A strange day! How different people were! Neither better nor worse, but just different. As many varieties as there were particles of sand on the seashore.

How impossible to be bored with life! Nevertheless, entering his own home he was instantly bored. He found there, having tea with his aunt and sitting beneath the Hermes, so that the contrast made her doubly ridiculous, Julia Preston. Julia Preston was to him the most boring woman in Polchester. To herself she was the most important. She was a widow and lived in a little green house with a little green garden in the Polchester outskirts. She was as pretty as she had been twenty years before, exactly the same, save that what nature had, twenty years ago, done for the asking, it now did under compulsion. She believed the whole world in love with her and was therefore a thoroughly happy woman. She had a healthy interest in the affairs of her neighbours, however small they might be, and believed in 'Truth, Beauty, and the Improvement of the Lower Classes.'

'Dear Canon Ronder, how nice this is!' she exclaimed. 'You've been hard at work all the afternoon, I know, and want your tea. How splendid work is! I often think what *would* life be without it!'

Ronder, who took trouble with everybody, smiled, sat down near to her and looked as though he loved her.

'Well, to be quite honest, I haven't been working very hard. Just seeing a few people.'

'Just seeing a few people!' Mrs. Preston used a laugh that was a favourite of hers because she had once been told that it was like 'a tinkling bell.' 'Listen to him! As though that weren't the hardest thing in the world. Giving out! Giving out ! What is so exhausting, and yet what so worth while in the end ? Unselfishness ! I really sometimes feel that is the true secret of life.'

' Have one of those little cakes, Julia,' said Miss Ronder drily. She, unlike her nephew, bothered about very few people indeed. ' Make a good tea.'

' I will, as you want me to, dear Alice,' said Mrs. Preston. ' Oh, thank you, Canon Ronder ! How good of you ; ah, there ! I've dropped my little bag. It's under that table. Thank you a thousand times ! And isn't it strange about Mrs. Brandon and Mr. Morris ? '

' Isn't what strange ? ' asked Miss Ronder, regarding her guest with grim cynicism.

' Oh well — nothing really, except that every one's asking what they can find in common. They're always together. Last Monday Aggie Combermere met her coming out of the Rectory, then Ellen Stiles saw them in the Precincts last Sunday afternoon, and I saw them myself this morning in the High Street.'

' My dear Mrs. Preston,' said Ronder, ' why *shouldn't* they go about together ? '

' No reason at all,' said Mrs. Preston, blushing very prettily, as she always did when she fancied that any one was attacking her. ' I'm sure that I'm only too glad that poor Mrs. Brandon has found a friend. My motto in life is, Let us all contribute to the happiness of one another to the best of our strength.

' Truly, that's a thing we can *all* do, isn't it ? Life isn't too bright for some people, I can't help thinking. And courage is the thing. After all, it isn't life that is important but simply how brave you are.

' At least that's my poor little idea of it. But it

does seem a little odd about Mrs. Brandon. She's always kept so much to herself until now.'

'You worry too much about others, dear Julia,' said Miss Ronder.

'Yes, I really believe I do. Why, there's my bag gone again ! Oh, how good of you, Canon ! It's under that chair. Yes. I do. But one can't help one's nature, can one ? I often tell myself that it's really no credit to me being unselfish. I was simply born that way. Poor Jack used to say that he wished I *would* think of myself more ! I think we were meant to share one another's burdens. I really do. And what Mrs. Brandon can see in Mr. Morris is so odd, because *really* he isn't an interesting man.'

'Let me get you some more tea,' said Ronder.

'No, thank you. I really must be going. I've been here an unconscionable time. Oh ! there's my handkerchief. How silly of me ! Thank you so much ! '

She got up and prepared to depart, looking so pretty and so helpless that it was really astonishing that the Hermes did not appreciate her.

'Good-bye, dear Canon. No, I forbid you to come out. Oh, well, if you will. I hear everywhere of the splendid work you're doing. Don't think it flattery, but I do think we needed you here. What we have wanted is a message—something to lift us all up a little. It's so easy to see nothing but the dreary round, isn't it ? And all the time the stars are shining. . . . At least that's how it seems to me.'

The door closed ; the room was suddenly silent. Miss Ronder sat without moving, her eyes staring in front of her.

Soon Ronder returned.

Miss Ronder said nothing. She was the one human being who had power to embarrass him. She was embarrassing him now.

'Aren't things strange?' he said. 'I've seen four different people this afternoon. They have all of their own accord instantly talked about Brandon, and abused him. Brandon is in the air. He's in danger.'

Miss Ronder looked her nephew straight between the eyes.

'Frederick,' she said, 'how much have you had to do with this?'

'To do with this? To do with what?'

'All this talk about the Brandons.'

'I! Nothing at all.'

'Nonsense. Don't tell me. Ever since you set foot in this town you've been determined that Brandon should go. Are you playing fair?'

He got up, stood opposite her, legs apart, his hands crossed behind his broad back.

'Fair? Absolutely.'

Her eyes were full of distress. 'Through all these years,' she said, 'I've never truly known you. All I know is that you've always got what you wanted. You're going to get what you want now. Do it decently.'

'You needn't be afraid,' he said.

'I *am* afraid,' she said. 'I love you, Fred; I have always loved you. I'd hate to lose that love. It's one of my most precious possessions.'

He answered her slowly, as though he were thinking things out. 'I've always told you the truth,' he said; 'I'm telling you the truth now. Of course I want Brandon to go, and of course he's going. But I haven't to move a finger in the matter. It's all advancing without my agency. Brandon is ruining himself. Even if he weren't, I'm quite square with him. I fought him openly at the Chapter Meeting the other day. He hates me for it.'

' And you hate *him*.'

' *Hate* him ? Not the least in the world. I admire and like him. If only he were in a less powerful position and were not in my way, I'd be his best friend. He's a fine fellow—stupid, blind, conceited, but finer made than I am. I like him better than any man in the town.'

' I don't understand you ; ' she dropped her eyes from his face. ' You're extraordinary.'

He sat down again as though he recognised that the little contest was closed.

' Is there anything in this, do you think ? This chatter about Mrs. Brandon and Morris.'

' I don't know. There's a lot of talk beginning. Ellen Stiles is largely responsible, I fancy.'

' Mrs. Brandon and Morris ! Good Lord ! Have you ever heard of a man called Davray ? '

' Yes, a drunken painter, isn't he ? Why ? '

' I talked to him in the Cathedral this afternoon. He has a grudge against Brandon, too. . . . Well, I'm going up to the study.'

He bent over, kissed her forehead tenderly and left the room.

Throughout that evening he was uncomfortable, and when he was uncomfortable he was a strange being. His impulses, his motives, his intentions were like a sheaf of corn bound tightly about by his sense of comfort and well-being. When that sense was disturbed everything fell apart and he seemed to be facing a new world full of elements that he always denied. His aunt had a greater power of disturbing him than had any other human being. He knew that she spoke what she believed to be the truth ; he felt that, in spite of her denials, she knew him. He was often surprised at the eagerness with which he wanted her approval.

As he sat back in his chair that evening in Bentinck-Major's comfortable library and watched the other, this sense of discomfort persisted so strongly that he found it very difficult to let his mind bite into the discussion. And yet this meeting was immensely important to him. It was the first obvious result of the manœuvring of the last months. This was definitely a meeting of Conspirators, and all of those engaged in it, with one exception, knew that that was so. Bentinck-Major knew it, and Foster and Ryle and Rogers. The exception was Martin, a young Minor Canon, who had the living of St. Joseph's-in-the-Fields, a slum parish in the lower part of the town.

Martin had been invited because he was the best clergyman in Polchester. Young though he was, every one was already aware of his strength, integrity, power with the men of the town, sense of humour and intelligence. There was, perhaps, no man in the whole of Polchester whom Ronder was so anxious to have on his side.

He was a man with a scorn of any intrigue, deeply religious, but human and impatient of humbug.

Ronder knew that he was the Polchester clergyman beyond all others who would in later years come to great power, although at present he had nothing save his Minor Canonry and small living.

He was not perhaps a deeply read man, he was of no especial family nor school and had graduated at Durham University. In appearance he was commonplace, thin, tall, with light sandy hair and mild good-tempered eyes. It had been Ronder's intention that he should be invited. Foster, who was more responsible for the meeting than any one, had protested.

'Martin—what's the point of Martin?'

'You'll see in five years' time,' Ronder had answered.

Now, as Ronder looked round at them all, he moved restlessly in his chair.

Was it true that his aunt was changing her opinion of him? Would he have to deal, during the coming months, with persistent disapproval and opposition from her? And it was so unfair. He had meant absolutely what he said, that he liked Brandon and wished him no harm. He *did* believe that it was for the good of the town that Brandon should go. . . .

He was pulled up by Foster, who was asking him to tell them exactly what it was that they were to discuss. Instinctively he looked at Martin as he spoke. As always, with the first word there came over him a sense of mastery and happiness, a desire to move people like pawns, a readiness to twist any principle, moral and ethical, if he might bend it to his purpose. Instinctively he pitched his voice, formed his mouth, spread his hands upon the broad arms of his chair exactly as an actor fills in his part.

'I object a little,' he said, laughing, 'to Foster's suggestion that I am responsible for our talking here. I've no right to be responsible for anything

when I've been in the place so short a time. All
the same, I don't want to pretend to any false
modesty. I've been in Polchester long enough to
be fond of it, and I'm going to be fonder of it still
before I've done. I don't want to pretend to any
sentimentality either, but there are broader issues
than merely the fortunes of this Cathedral in danger.

'Because I feel the danger, I intend to speak out
about it, and get any one on my side I can. When
I find that Canon Foster who has been here so long
and loves the Cathedral so passionately and so
honestly, if I may say so, feels as I do, then I'm
only strengthened in my determination. I don't care
who says that I've no right to push myself forward
about this. I'm not pushing myself forward.

'As soon as some one else will take the cause
in hand I'll step back, but I'm not going to see the
battle lost simply because I'm afraid of what people
will say of me. . . . Well, this is all fine words.
The point simply is that, as every one knows, poor
Morrison is desperately ill and the living of Pybus
St. Anthony may fall vacant at any moment. The
appointment is a Chapter appointment. The living
isn't anything very tremendous in itself, but it has
been looked upon for years as *the* jumping-off place
for preferment in the diocese. Time after time
the man who has gone there has become the most important influence here. Men are generally chosen,
as I understand it, with that in view. These are, of
course, all commonplaces to you, but I'm recapitu-
lating them because it makes my point the stronger.
Morrison, with all his merits, was not out of the way
intellectually. This time we want an exceptional
man.

'I've only been here a few months, but I've

noticed many things, and I will definitely say that the Cathedral is at a crisis in its history. Perhaps the mere fact that this is Jubilee Year makes us all more ready to take stock than we would otherwise have been. But it is not only that. The Church is being attacked from all sides. I don't believe that there has ever been a time when the west of England needed new blood, new thought, new energy more than it does at this time. The vacancy at Pybus will offer a most wonderful opportunity to bring that force among us. I should have thought every one would realise that.

'It happens, however, that I have discovered on first-hand evidence that there is a strong resolve on the part of most important persons in this town (I will mention no names) to fill the living with the most unsatisfactory, worthless and conservative influence that could possibly be found anywhere. If that influence succeeds I don't believe I'm exaggerating when I say that the progress of the religious life here is flung back fifty years. One of the greatest opportunities the Chapter can ever have had will have been missed. I don't think we can regard the crisis as too serious.'

Foster broke in : ' Why *not* mention names, Canon ? We've no time to waste. It's all humbug pretending we don't know whom you mean. It's Brandon who wants to put young Forsyth into Pybus whom we're fighting. Let's be honest.'

' No. I won't allow that,' Ronder said quickly. ' We're fighting no personalities. Speaking for myself, there's no one I admire more in this town than Brandon. I think him reactionary and opposed to new ideas, and a dangerous influence here, but there's no personal feeling in any of this. We've got to keep personalities out of this. There's something bigger than our own likes and dislikes in this.'

'Words! Words,' said Foster angrily. 'I hate Brandon. You hate him, Ronder, for all you're so circumspect. It's true enough that we don't want young Forsyth at Pybus, but it's truer still that we want to bring the Archdeacon's pride down. And we're going to.'

The atmosphere was electric. Rogers' thin and bony features were flushed with pleasure at Foster's denunciation. Bentinck-Major rubbed his soft hands one against the other and closed his eyes as though he were determined to be a gentleman to the last; Martin sat upright in his chair, his face puzzled, his gaze fixed upon Ronder; Ryle, the picture of nervous embarrassment, glanced from one face to another, as though imploring every one not to be angry with him—all these sharp words were certainly not his fault.

Ronder was vexed with himself. He was certainly not at his best to-night. He had realised the personalities that were around him, and yet had not steered his boat among them with the dexterous skill that was usually his.

In his heart he cursed Foster for a meddling, cantankerous fanatic.

Rogers broke in. 'I must say,' he exclaimed in a strange shrill voice like a peacock's, 'that I associate myself with every word of Canon Foster's. Whatever we may pretend in public, the great desire of our hearts is to drive Brandon out of the place. The sooner we do it the better. It should have been done long ago.'

Martin spoke. 'I'm sorry,' he said. 'If I had known that this meeting was to be a personal attack

on the Archdeacon, I never would have come. I
don't think the diocese has a finer servant than
Archdeacon Brandon. I admire him immensely.
He has made mistakes. So do we all of course.
But I have the highest opinion of his character, his
work and his importance here, and I would like
every one in the room to know that before we go
any further.'

'That's right. That's right,' said Ryle, smiling
around nervously upon every one. 'Canon Martin
is right, don't you think? I hope nobody here will
say that I have any ill feeling against the Archdeacon.
I haven't, indeed, and I shouldn't like any one to
charge me with it.'

Ronder struck in then, and his voice was so
strong, so filled with authority, that every one looked
up as though some new figure had entered the room.

'I should like to emphasise at once,' he said, 'so
that no one here or anywhere else can be under
the slightest misapprehension, that I will take part
in nothing that has any personal animus towards
anybody. Surely this is a question of Pybus and
Forsyth and of nothing else at all. I have not
even anything against Mr. Forsyth; I have never
seen him—I wish him all the luck in life. But we
are fighting a battle for the Pybus living and for
nothing more nor less than that.

'If my own brother wanted that living and was
not the right man for it I would fight him. The
Archdeacon does not see the thing at present as we
do; it is possible that very shortly he may. As
soon as he does I'm behind him.'

Foster shook his head. 'Have it your own way,'
he said. 'Everything's the same here—always
compromise. Compromise! Compromise! I'm

sick of the cowardly word. We'll say no more of Brandon for the moment then. He'll come up again, never fear. He's not the sort of man to avoid spoiling his own soup.'

'Very good,' said Bentinck-Major in his most patronising manner. 'Now we are all agreed, I think. You will have noticed that I've been waiting for this moment to suggest that we should come to business. Our business, I believe, is to obtain what support we can against the gift of the living to Mr. Forsyth and to suggest some other candidate . . . hum, haw . . . yes, other candidate.'

'There's only one possible candidate,' Foster brought out, banging his lean fist down upon the table near to him. 'And that's Wistons of Hawston. It's been the wish of my heart for years back to bring Wistons here. We don't know, of course, if he would come, but I think he could be persuaded. And then—then there'd be hope once more ! God would be served ! His Church would be a fitting Tabernacle ! . . .'

He broke off. Amazing to see the rapt devotion that now lighted up his ugly face until it shone with saintly beauty. The harsh lines were softened, the eyes were gentle, the mouth tender. 'Then indeed,' he almost whispered, 'I might say my " Nunc Dimittis " and go.'

It was not he alone who was stirred. Martin spoke eagerly : 'Is that the Wistons of the *Four Creeds* ?—the man who wrote *The New Apocalypse* ?'

Foster smiled. 'There's only one Wistons,' he said, pride ringing in his voice as though he were speaking of his favourite son, 'for all the world.'

'Why, that would be magnificent,' Martin said,

' if he'd come. But would he? I should think that very doubtful.'

' I think he would,' said Foster softly, still as though he were speaking to himself.

' Why, that, of course, is wonderful!' Martin looked round upon them all, his eyes glowing. ' There isn't a man in England——' He broke off. ' But surely if there's a *real* chance of getting Wistons nobody on the Chapter would dream of proposing a man like Forsyth. It's incredible!'

' Incredible!' burst in Foster. ' Not a bit of it! Do you suppose Brandon—I beg pardon for mentioning his name, as we're all so particular—do you suppose Brandon wouldn't fight just such a man? He regards him as dangerous, modern, subversive, heretical, anything you please. Wistons! Why, he'd make Brandon's hair stand on end!'

' Well,' said Martin gravely, ' if there's any real chance of getting Wistons into this diocese I'll work for it with my coat off.'

' Good,' said Bentinck-Major, tapping with a little gold pencil that he had been fingering, on the table. ' Now we are all agreed. The next question is, what steps are we to take?'

They all looked instinctively at Ronder. He felt their glances. He was happy, assured, comfortable once more. He was master of them. They lay in his hand for him to do as he would with them. His brain now moved clearly, smoothly, like a beautiful shining machine. His eyes glowed.

' Now, it's occurred to me——' he said. They all drew their chairs closer.

CHAPTER V

FALK BY THE RIVER

Upon that same evening when the conspirators met in Bentinck-Major's handsome study Mrs. Brandon had a ridiculous fit of hysterics.

She had never had hysterics before ; the fit came upon her now when she was sitting in front of her glass brushing her hair. She was dressing for dinner and could see her reflection, white and thin, in the mirror before her. Suddenly the face in the glass began to smile and it became at that same instant another face that she had never seen before.

It was a horrid smile and broke suddenly into laughter. It was as though the face had been hit by something and cracked then into a thousand pieces.

She laughed until the tears poured down her cheeks, but her eyes protested, looking piteously and in dismay from the studied glass. She knew that she was laughing with shrill high cries, and behind her horror at her collapse there was a desperate protesting attempt to calm herself, driven, above all, upon her agitated heart by the fear lest her husband should come in and discover her.

The laughter ceased quite suddenly and was

followed by a rush of tears. She cried as though her heart would break, then, with trembling steps, crossed to her bed and lay down. Very shortly she must control herself because the dinner-bell would ring and she must go. To stay and send the conventional excuse of a headache would bring her husband up to her, and although he was so full of his own affairs that the questions that he would ask her would be perfunctory and absent-minded, she felt that she could not endure, just now, to be alone with him.

She lay on her bed shivering and wondering what malign power it was that had seized her. Malign it was, she did not for an instant doubt. She had asked, did ask, for so little. Only to see Morris for a moment every day. To see him anywhere in as public a place as you please, but to see him, to hear his voice, to look into his eyes, to touch his hand (soft and gentle like a woman's hand)—that had been now for months an absolute necessity. She did not ask more than that, and yet she was aware that there was no pause in the accumulating force of the passion that was seizing her. She was being drawn along by two opposite powers—the tenderness of protective maternal love and the ruthlessness of the lust for possession.

She wanted to care for him, to watch over him, to guard him, to do everything for him, and also she wanted to feel her hold over him, to see him move, almost as though he were hypnotised, towards her.

The thought of him, the perpetual incessant thought of him, ruled out the thought of every one else in the world—save only Falk. She scarcely now considered her husband at all; she never for an instant wondered whether people in the town were talking. She saw only Morris and her future with Morris—only that and Falk.

Upon Falk now everything hung. She had made a kind of bargain. If Falk stayed and loved her and cared for her she would resist the power that was drawing her towards Morris. Now, a million times more than before she had met Morris, she must have some one for whom she could care. It was as though a lamp had been lit and flung a great track of light over those dark, empty earlier years. How could she ever have lived as she did? The hunger, the desperate, eager, greedy hunger was roused in her. Falk could satisfy it, but, if he would not, then she would hesitate no longer.

She would seize Morris as a tiger seizes its prey. She did not disguise that from herself. As she lay now, trembling, upon her bed, she never hesitated to admit to herself that the thought of her domination over Morris was her great glory. She had never dominated any one before. He followed her like a man in a dream, and she was not young, she was not beautiful, she was not clever. . . .

It was her own personal, personal, personal triumph. And then, on that, there swept over her the flood of her tenderness for him, how she longed to be good to him, to care for him, to mend and sew and cook and wash for him, to perform the humblest tasks for him, to nurse him and protect him. She knew that the end of this might be social ruin for both of them! . . . Ah, well, then, he would only need her the more! She was quieter now—the trembling ceased. How strange the way that during these months they had been meeting, so often without their own direct agency at all! She

recalled every moment, every gesture, every word.
He seemed already to be part of herself, moving
within herself.

She sat up on her bed; moved back to her glass.
She bathed her face, slipped on her dress, and went
downstairs.

They were a family party at dinner, but, of course,
without Falk. He was always out in the evening
now.

Joan talked, chattered on. The meal was soon
over. The Archdeacon went to his study, and the
two women sat in the drawing-room, Joan by the
window, Mrs. Brandon, hidden in a high arm-chair,
near the fireplace. The clock ticked on and the
Cathedral bells struck the quarters. Joan's white
dress beyond the circle of lamp-light was a dim
shadow. Mrs. Brandon turned the pages of her
book, her ears straining for the sound of Falk's
return.

As she sat there, so inattentively turning the
pages of her book, the foreboding sense of some
approaching drama flooded the room. For how
many years had she lived from day to day and
nothing had occurred—so long that life had been
unconscious, doped, inert. Now it had sprung into
vitality again with the sudden frantic impertinence
of a Jack-in-the-Box. For twenty years you are dry
on the banks, half-asleep, stretching out lazy fingers
for food, slumbering, waking, slumbering again.
Suddenly a wave comes and you are swept off—
swept off into what disastrous sea ?

She did not think in pictures, it was not her way,
but to-night, half-terrified, half-exultant, in the long
dim room she waited, the pressure of her heart
beating up into her throat, listening, watching Joan

furtively, seeing Morris, his eternal shadow, itching with its long tapering fingers to draw her away with him beyond the house. No, she would be true with herself. It was he who would be drawn away. The power was in her, not in him. . . .

She looked wearily across at Joan. The child was irritating to her as she had always been. She had never, in any case, cared for her own sex, and now, as so frequently with women who are about to plunge into some passionate situation, she regarded every one she saw as a potential interferer. She despised women as most women in their secret hearts do, and especially she despised Joan.

'You'd better go up to bed, dear. It's half-past ten.'

Without a word Joan got up, came across the room, kissed her mother, went to the door. Then she paused.

'Mother,' she said, hesitating, and then speaking timidly, 'is father all right?'

'All right, dear?'

'Yes. He doesn't look well. His forehead is all flushed, and I overheard some one at the Sampsons' say the other day that he wasn't well really, that he must take great care of himself. Ought he to?'

'Ought he what?'

'To take great care of himself.'

'What nonsense!' Mrs. Brandon turned back to her book impatiently. 'There never was any one so strong and healthy.'

'He's always worrying about something. It's his nature.'

'Yes, I suppose so.'

Joan vanished. Mrs. Brandon sat, staring before her, her mind running with the clock—tick-tick-

tick-tick—and then suddenly jumping at the mellow liquid gurgle that it sometimes gave. Would her husband come in and say good-night?

How she had grown, during these last weeks, to loathe his kiss! He would stand behind her chair, bending his great body over her, his red face would come down, then the whiff of tobacco, then the rough pressure on her cheek, the hard, unmeaning contact of his lips and hers. His beautiful eyes would stare beyond her, absently into the room. Beautiful! Why, yes, they were famous eyes, famous the diocese through. How well she remembered those years, long ago, when they had seemed to speak to her of every conceivable tenderness and sweetness, and how, when he thus had bent over her, she had stretched up her hand and found the buttons of his waistcoat and pushed her fingers in, stroking his shirt and feeling his heart thump, thump, and so warm beneath her touch.

Life! Life! What a cheat! What a cheat! She jumped from her chair, letting the book drop upon the floor, and began to pace the room. And why should not this, too, cheat her once again? With the tenderness, the poignancy with which she now looked upon Morris so once she had looked upon Brandon. Yes, that might be. She would cheat herself no longer. But she was older now. This was the last chance to live—definitely, positively the last. It was not the desire to be loved, this time, that drove her forward so urgently as the desire to love. She knew that, because Falk would do. If Falk would stay, would let her care for him and mother him and be with him, she would drive Morris from her heart and brain.

Yes, she almost cried aloud in the dark room. 'Give me Falk and I will leave the other. Give me my own son. That's my right—every mother's right. If I am refused it, it is just that I should take what I can get instead.'

'Give him to me! Give him to me!' One thing at least was certain. She could never return to the old lethargy. That first meeting with Morris had fired her into life. She could not go back and she was glad that she could not. . . .

She stopped in the middle of the room to listen. The hall-door closed softly ; suddenly the line of light below the door vanished. Some one had turned down the hall-lamp. She went to the drawing-room door, opened it, looked out, crying softly :

'Falk! Falk!'

'Yes, mother.' He came across to her. He was holding a lighted candle in his hand. 'Are you still up?'

'Yes, it isn't very late. Barely eleven. Come into the drawing-room.'

They went back into the room. He closed the door behind him, then put the candle down on to a small round table ; they sat in the candle-light, one on either side of the table.

He looked at her and thought how small and fragile she looked and how little, anyway, she meant to him.

How much most mothers meant to their sons, and how little she had ever meant to him! He had always taken his father's view of her, that it was necessary for her to be there, that she naturally did her best, but that she did not expect you to think about her.

' You ought to be in bed,' he said, wishing that she would release him.

For the first time in her life she spoke to him spontaneously, losing entirely the sense that she had always had, that both he and his father would go away and leave her if she were tiresome.

To-night he would *not* go away—not until she had struck her bargain with him.

' What have you been up to all these weeks, Falk ? ' she asked.

' Up to ? ' he repeated. Her challenge was un-expected.

' Yes ; of course I know you're up to something, and you *know* that I know.   You must tell me.   I'm your mother and I ought to be told.'

He knew at once as soon as she spoke that she was the very last person in the world to whom he wished to tell anything.   He was tired, dead tired, and wanted to go to bed, but he was arrested by the urgency in her voice.   What was the matter with her ?   So intent had he been, for the past months, on his own affairs that he had not thought of his mother at all.   He looked across the table at her— a little insignificant woman, colourless, with no personality.   And yet to-night something was happening to her.   He felt all the impatience of a man who is closely occupied with his own drama but is forced, quite against his will, to consider some one else.

' There isn't anything to tell you, mother. Really there is not.   I've just been kicking my heels round this blasted town for the last few months and I'm restless.   I'll be going up to London very shortly.'

' Why need you ? ' she asked him.   The candle

flame seemed to jump with the sharpness of her voice.

'Why need I? But of course I must. I ask you, *is* this a place for *any one* to settle down in?'

'I don't know why it shouldn't be. I should have thought you could be very happy here. There are so many things you could do.'

'What, for instance?'

'You could be a solicitor, or go into business, or—or—why, you'd soon find something.'

He got up, taking the candle in his hand.

'Well, if that's your idea, mother, I'm sorry, but you can just put it out of your head once and for all. I'd rather be buried alive than stay in this hole. I *would* be buried alive if I stayed.'

She looked up at him. He was so tall, so handsome, *and so distant*—some one who had no connection with her at all. She too got up, putting her little hand on his arm.

'Then are we, all of us, to count for nothing at all?'

'Of course you count,' he answered impatiently, irritated by the pressure of her fingers on his coat. 'You'll see plenty of me. But you can't possibly expect me to live here. I've completely wasted my beautiful young life so far—now apparently you want me to waste the rest of it.'

'Then,' she said, coming nearer to him and dropping her voice, 'take me with you.'

'Take you with me!' He stepped back from her. He could not believe that he had heard her correctly. 'Take *you* with me?'

'Yes.'

'Take you with me?'

' Yes, yes, yes.'

It was the greatest surprise of his life. He stared at her in his amazement, putting the candle back upon the table.

' But why ? '

' Why ? . . . Why do you think ? . . . Because I love you and want to be with you.'

' Be with me ? Leave this ? Leave Polchester ? . . . Leave father ? '

' Yes, why not ? Your father doesn't need me any longer. Nobody wants me here. Why shouldn't I go ? '

He came close to her, giving her now all his attention, staring at her as though he were seeing her for the first time in his life.

' Mother, aren't you well ? . . . Aren't you happy ? '

She laughed. ' Happy ? Oh, yes, so happy that I'd drown myself to-night if that would do any good.'

' Here, sit down.' He almost pushed her back into her chair. ' We've got to have this out. I don't know what you're talking about. You're unhappy ? Why, what's the matter ? '

' The matter ? Oh, nothing ! ' she answered. ' Nothing at all, except for the last ten years I've hated this place, hated this house, hated your father.'

' Hated father ? '

He stared at her as though she had in a moment gone completely mad.

' Yes, why not ? ' she answered quietly. ' What has he ever done that I should feel otherwise ? What attention has he ever paid to me ? When has he ever considered me except as a sort of convenient housekeeper and mistress whom he pays to keep near him ? Why shouldn't I hate him ? You're very young, Falk, and it would probably surprise you to know how many quiet stay-at-home wives there are who hate their good, honest, well-meaning husbands.'

He drew a deep breath.

' What's father ever done,' he said, ' to make you hate him ? '

She should have realised then, from the sound in his voice, that she was, in her preoccupation with her own affairs, forgetting one of the principal elements in the whole case, his love for his father.

' It isn't what he's done,' she answered. ' It's what he hasn't done. Whom has he ever considered but himself ? Isn't his conceit so big that he can't *see* any one but himself ? Why should we go on pretending that he's so great and wonderful ? Do you suppose that any one can live for twenty years and more with your father and not see how small and selfish and mean he is ? How he——'

' You're not to say that,' Falk interrupted her angrily. ' Father may have his faults—so has every one—but we've got worse ones. He isn't mean and he isn't small. He may seem conceited, but that's only because he cares so for the Cathedral and knows what he's done for it. He's the finest man I know anywhere. He doesn't see things as I do—I don't suppose that father and son ever do see alike—but that needn't prevent me from admiring him. Why, mother, what's come over you ? You can't be well. Leave father ! Why, it would be terrible ! Think of the talk there'd be ! Why, it would ruin father here. He'd never get over it.'

She saw then the mistake that she had made. She looked across at him beseechingly.

'You're right, Falk. I didn't mean that, I don't mean that. But I'm so unhappy that I don't know what I'm saying. All I want is to be with you. It wouldn't hurt father if I went up to London with you for a little. What I really want is a holiday. I could come back after a month or two refreshed. I'm tired.'

Suddenly while she was speaking the ironical contrast hit him. Here was he amazed at his mother for daring to contemplate a step that would do his father harm, while he, he who professed to love his father, was about to do something that would cause the whole town to talk for a year. But that was different. Surely it was different. He was young and must make his own life. He must be allowed to marry whom he would. It was not as though he were intending to ruin the girl. . . .

Nevertheless, this sudden comparison bewildered and shocked him.

He leant across the table to her. 'You must never leave father—never,' he said. 'You mustn't think of it. He wants you badly. He mayn't show it exactly as you want it. Men aren't demonstrative as women are, but he'd be miserable if you went away. He loves you in his own fashion, which is just as good as yours, only different. You must *never* leave him, mother, do you hear?'

She saw that she was defeated, entirely and completely. She cried to the Powers:

'You've refused me what I ask. I go my own way, then.'

She got up, kissed him on the forehead and said: 'I daresay you're right, Falk. Forget what I've said. I didn't mean most of it. Good-night, dear.'

She went out, quietly closing the door behind her.

Falk did not sleep at all that night. This was only one of many sleepless nights, but it was the worst of them. The night was warm, and a faint dim colour lingered behind the tree-tops of the garden beyond his open window. First he lay under the clothes, then upon the top of his bed, then stripped, plunging his head into a basin of water, then, naked save for his soft bedroom slippers, paced his room. . . . His head was a flaming fire. The pale light seemed for an instant to vanish, and the world was dark and silent. Then, at the striking of the Cathedral clock, as though it were a signal upon some stage, the light slowly crept back again, growing ever stronger and stronger. The birds began to twitter ; a cock crew. A bar of golden light broken by the squares and patterns of the dark trees struck the air.

The shock of his mother's announcement had been terrific. It was not only the surprise of it, it was the sudden light that it flung upon his own case. He had gone, during these last weeks, so far with Annie Hogg that it was hard indeed to see how there could be any stepping back. They had achieved a strange relationship together : one not of comradeship, nor of lust, nor of desire, nor of affection, having a little of all these things but not much of any of them, and finally resembling the case of two strangers, shipwrecked, hanging on to a floating spar of wood that might bring them into safety.

She was miserable ; he was miserable ; whether she cared for him he could not tell, nor whether he cared for her. The excitement that she created in him was intense, all-devouring, but it was not an excitement of lust. He had never done more than kiss her, and he was quite ready that it should remain so. He intended, perhaps, to marry her, but of that he could not be sure.

But he could not leave her ; he could not keep away from her although he was seldom happy when he was with her. Slowly, gradually, through their meetings there had grown a bond. He was more naturally himself with her than with any other human being. Although she excited him she also tranquillised him. Increasingly he admired and respected her—her honesty, independence, reserve, pride. Perhaps it was upon that that their alliance was really based—upon mutual respect and admiration. There had been never, from the very first moment, any deception between them. He had never been so honest with any one before—certainly not with himself. His desire, beyond everything else in life, was to be honest : to pretend to no emotion that he did not truly feel, to see exactly how he felt about life, and to stand up before it unafraid and uncowed. Honesty seemed to him the greatest quality in life ; that was why he had been attracted to Ronder. And yet life seemed to be for ever driving him into false positions. Even now he was contemplating running away with this girl. Until to-night he had fancied that he was only contemplating it, but his conversation with his mother had shown him how near he was to a decision. Nevertheless, he would talk to Ronder and to his father, not, of course, telling them everything, but catching perhaps from them some advice that would seem to him so true that it would guide him.

Finally, when the gold bar appeared behind the

trees he forced himself into honesty with his father. How could he have meant so sincerely that his mother must not hurt his father when he himself was about to hurt him?

And this discovery had not lessened his determination to take the step. Was he, then, utterly hypocritical? He knew he was not.

He could look ahead of his own affair and see that in the end his father would admit that it had been best for him. They all knew—even his mother must in her heart have known—that he was not going to live in Polchester for ever. His departure for London was inevitable, and it simply was that he would take Annie with him. That would be for a moment a blow to his father, but it would not be so for long. And in the town his father would win sympathy; he, Falk, would be condemned and despised. They would say: 'Ah, that young Brandon. He never was any good. His father did all he could, but it was no use. . . .' And then in a little time there would come the news that he was doing well in London, and all would be right.

He looked to his talk with Ronder. Ronder would advise well. Ronder knew life. He was not provincial like these others. . . .

Suddenly he was cold. He went back to bed and slept dreamlessly.

Next evening, as half-past eight was striking, he was at his customary post by the river, above 'The Dog and Pilchard.'

A heavy storm was mounting up behind the Cathedral, black clouds being piled tier on tier as though some gigantic shopman were shooting out rolls of carpet for the benefit of some celestial purchaser. The Cathedral shone in the last flash of the fleeing light with a strange phantasmal silver sheen ; once more it was a ship sailing high before the tempest.

Down by the river the dusk was grey and sodden. The river, flowing sullenly, was a lighter dark between the line of houses and the bending fields. The air was so heavy that men seemed to walk with bending backs as though the burden was more than they could sustain. This section of the river had become now to Falk something that was part of himself. The old mill, the group of trees beside it, the low dam over which the water fell with its own peculiar drunken gurgle, the pathway with its gritty stony surface, so that it seemed to grind its teeth in protest at every step that you took, on the left the town piled high behind you with the Cathedral winged and dominant and supreme, the cool sloping fields beyond the river, the dark bend of the wood cutting the horizon—these things were his history and he was theirs.

There were many other places to which they might have gone, other times that they might have chosen, but circumstances and accident had found for them always this same background. He had long ago ceased to consider whether any one was watching them or talking about them. They were, neither of them, cowards, although to Annie her father was a figure of sinister power and evil desire. She hated her father, believed him capable of in-finite wickedness, but did not fear him enough to hesitate to face him. Nevertheless, it was from him that she was chiefly escaping, and she gave to Falk a curious consciousness of the depths of malice and vice that lay hidden behind that smiling face, in the secret places of that fat jolly body. Falk was certain now that Hogg knew of their meetings ; he suspected that he had known of them from the first. Hogg had his faults, but they did not frighten Falk, who was, indeed, afraid of no man alive save only himself.

The other element in the affair that increased as the week passed was Falk's consciousness of the strange spirit of nobility that there was in Annie. Although she stirred him so deeply she did not blind him as to her character. He saw her exactly for what she was—uneducated, ignorant, limited in all her outlook, common in many ways, sometimes surly, often superstitious ; but through all these things that strain of nobility ran, showing itself in many unexpected places, calling to him like an echo from some high, far-distant source. Because of it he was beginning to wonder whether after all the alliance that was beginning to spring up between them might not be something more permanent and durable than at first he had ever supposed it could be. He was beginning to wonder whether he had not been fortunate far beyond his deserts. . . .

On this thunder-night they met like old friends who had known one another for many years and between whom there had never been anything but comradeship. They did not kiss, but simply touched hands and moved up through the gathering dark to the little bridge below the mill. From here they felt the impact of the chattering water rising to them and falling again like a comment on their talk.

' It'll not be many more times,' Annie said, ' we'll be coming here.'

I

'Why ?' Falk asked.

'Because I'm going up to London whether you come or no—and *soon* I'm going.'

He admired nothing in her more than the clear-cut decision of her mind, which moved quietly from point to point, asking no advice, allowing no regrets when the decision was once made.

'What has happened since last time ?'

'Happened ? Nothing. Only father and "The Dog," and drink. I'm through with it.'

'And what would you do in London if you went up alone ?'

She flung up her head suddenly, laughing. 'You think I'm helpless, don't you ? Well, I'm not.'

'No, I don't—but you don't know London.'

'A fearsome place, mebbe, but not more dis-gustin' than father.'

There was irritation in his voice as he said :

'Then it doesn't matter to you whether I come with you or not ?'

Her reply was soft. She suddenly put out her hand and took his.

'Of course it matters. We're friends. The best friend I'm likely to find, I reckon. What would I be meeting you for all these months if I didn't care for you ? Just to be admiring the scenery ?—shouldn't like.'

She laughed softly.

She went on : 'I'm ready to go with you or without you. If we go together I'm independent, just as though I went without you. I'm independ-ent of every one—father and you and all. I'll marry you if you want me, or I'll live with you without marrying, or I'll live without you and never see you again. I won't say that leaving you wouldn't hurt. It would, after being with you all these weeks ; but I'd rather be hurt than be dependent.'

He held her hand tightly between his two.

' Folks 'ud say,' she went on, ' that I had no right to be talkin' of going away with you—that I'd be ruining your future and making people look down on you, and all that. Well, that's for you to say. If you think it harms your prospects being with me you needn't see me. I've my own prospects to think of. I'm not going to have any man ashamed of me.'

' You're right to speak of it, and we're right to think of it,' said Falk. ' It isn't my prospects that I've got to think about, but it's my father I wouldn't like to hurt. If we go away together there'll be a great deal of talk here, and it will all fall on my father.'

' Well, then,' she said, tossing her head and taking her hand away from his, ' don't come. *I'm* not asking you. As for your father, he's that proud——' She stopped suddenly. ' No. I'm saying nothing about that. You care for him, and you're right to. As far as that goes, we needn't go together ; you can come up later and join me.'

When she said that, he knew that he couldn't bear the thought of her going alone, and that he had all along been determined in his thought that she should not go alone.

' If you'd say you loved me,' he said, suddenly bending towards her, ' I'd never let you out of my sight again.'

' Oh, yes, you would,' she said ; ' you don't know whether you *do* love me. Many's the time you think you don't. And I don't know whether I love you. Sometimes I think I do. What's love, any-way? I dunno. I think sometimes I'm not made to feel that way towards any one. But what I really meant to say to-night is, that I'm dead sick of this hanging on. I'm going up to a cousin I've got Blackheath way a week from to-night. If you're coming, I'm glad. If you're not—well, I reckon I'll get over it.'

'A week from to-day——' He looked out over the water.

'Aye. That's settled.'

Then, unexpected, as she so often was, she put her arms round his neck and drew his head down to her bosom and let her hand rest on his hair.

'I like to feel you there,' she said. 'It's more a mother I feel to you than a lover.'

She would not let him kiss her, but suddenly moved away from him, into the dark, leaving him where he stood.

When he was half-way home the storm that had been slowly, during the last hour and a half, climbing up above the town, broke. As he was crossing the market-place the rain came down in torrents, dancing upon the uneven cobbles with a kind of excited frenzy, and thickening the air with a curtain of mist. He climbed the High Street, his head down, feeling a physical satisfaction in the fierce soaking that the storm was giving him. The town was shining and deserted. Not a soul about. No sound except the hissing, sneering, chattering whisper of the deluge. He went up to his room and changed, putting on a dinner jacket, and came down to his father's study. It was too late for dinner, but he was not hungry ; he did not know how long it was since he had felt hungry last.

He knocked and went in. He felt a desperate urgency that he must somehow reconcile the interests and happiness of the two people who were then filling all his thoughts—his father and Annie. There must *be* a way. He could feel still the touch of Annie's hand upon his head ; he was more deeply bound to her by that evening's conversation than he had ever been before, but he longed to be able to reassure himself by some contact with his father that he was not going to hurt the old man, that he would be able to prove to him that his loyalty was true and his affection deep.

Small causes produce lasting results, and the lives of many people would have been changed had Falk caught his father that night in another mood.

The Archdeacon did not look up at the sound of the closing door. He was sitting at his big table writing letters, the expression of his face being that of a boy who has been kept in on a fine afternoon to write out the first fifty lines of the *Iliad*. His curly hair was ruffled, his mouth was twisted with disgust, and he pushed his big body about in his chair, kicked out his legs and drew them in as though beneath his concentration on his letters he was longing to spring up, catch his enemy by the throat, roll him over on to the ground and kick him.

' Hullo, governor ! ' Falk said, and settled down into one of the big leather armchairs, produced a pipe from his pocket and slowly filled it.

The Archdeacon went on writing, muttering to himself, biting the end of his quill pen. He had not apparently been aware of his son's entrance, but suddenly he sprang up, pushed back his chair until it nearly fell over, and began to stride up and down the room. He was a fine figure then, throwing up his head, flinging out his arms, apostrophising the world.

'Gratitude ! They don't know what it means. Do you think I'll go on working for them, wearing myself to a shadow, staying up all night—getting up at seven in the morning, and then to have this sort of return ? I'll leave the place. I'll let them make their own mistakes and see how they like that. I'll teach them gratitude. Here am I ; for ten years I've done nothing but slave for the town and the Cathedral. Who's worked for them as I have ? '

'What's the matter, father ? ' Falk asked, watching him from the chair. Every one knows the irritation of coming to some one with matters so urgent that they occupy the whole of your mind, and then discovering that your audience has its own determined preoccupation. 'Always thinking of himself,' Falk considered. 'Fusses about nothing.'

'The matter ? ' His father turned round upon him. 'Everything's the matter. Everything ! Here's this Jubilee business coming on and everything going to ruin. Here am I, who know more about the Cathedral and what's been done in the Cathedral for the last ten years than any one, and they are letting Ryle have a free hand over all the Jubilee Week services without another word to anybody.'

'Well, Ryle is the Precentor, isn't he ? ' said Falk.

'Of course he is,' the Archdeacon answered angrily. 'And what a Precentor ! Every one

knows he isn't capable of settling anything by himself. That's been proved again and again. But
that's only one thing. It's the same all the way
round. Opposition everywhere. It'll soon come to
it that I'll have to ask permission from the Chapter
to walk down the High Street.'

'All the same, father,' Falk said, 'you can't be
expected to have the whole of the Jubilee on your
shoulders. It's more than any one man can possibly
do.'

'I know that. Of course I know that. Ryle's
case is only one small instance of the way the wind's
blowing. Every one's got to do their share, of
course. But in the last three months the place is
changed—the Chapter's disorganised, there's rebellion in the choir, among the Vergers, everywhere.
The Cathedral is in pieces. And why? Who's
changed everything? Why is nothing as it was
three months ago?'

'Oh Lord! what a bore the old man is!'
thought Falk. He was in the last possible mood to
enter into any of his father's complaints. They
seemed now, as he looked across at him, to be miles
apart. He felt, suddenly, as though he did not care
what happened to his father, nor whether his feelings
were hurt or no——

'Well, tell me!' said the Archdeacon, spreading
his legs out, putting his hands behind his back and
standing over his son. 'Who's responsible for the
change?'

'Oh, I don't know!' said Falk impatiently.

'You don't know? No, of course you don't
know, because you've taken no interest in the
Cathedral nor in anything to do with it. All the
same, I should have thought it impossible for any one

to be in this town half an hour and *not* know who's responsible. There's only one man, and that man is Ronder.'

Unfortunately Falk liked Ronder. 'I think Ronder's rather a good sort,' he said. 'A clever fellow, too.'

The Archdeacon stared at him.

'You like him?'

'Yes, father, I do.'

'And of course it matters nothing to you that he should be your father's persistent enemy and do his best to hinder him in everything and every way possible.'

Falk smiled, one of those confident superior smiles that are so justly irritating to any parent.

'Oh come, father,' he said. 'Aren't you rather exaggerating?'

'Exaggerating? Yes, of course you would take the other side. And what do you know about it? There you are, lolling about in your chair, idling week after week, until all the town talks about it——'

Falk sprang up.

'And whose fault is it if I do idle? What have I been wanting except to go off and make a decent living? Whose fault——?'

'Oh, mine, of course!' the Archdeacon shouted. 'Put it all down to me! Say that I begged you to leave Oxford, that I want you to laze the rest of your life away. Why shouldn't you, when you have a mother and sister to support you?'

'Stop that, father.' Falk also was shouting. 'You'd better look out what you're saying, or I'll take you at your word and leave you altogether.'

'You can, for all I care,' the Archdeacon shouted

back.. They stood there facing one another, both of them red in the face, a curious family likeness suddenly apparent between them.

' Well, I will then,' Falk cried, and rushed from the room, banging the door behind him.

CHAPTER VI

FALK'S FLIGHT

RONDER sat in his study waiting for young Falk
Brandon. The books smiled down upon him
from their white shelves; because the spring
evening was chill, a fire glittered and sparkled
and the deep blue curtains were drawn. Ronder
was wearing brown kid slippers and a dark
velvet smoking-jacket. As he lay back in the
deep arm-chair, smoking an old and familiar briar,
his chubby face was deeply contented. His eyes
were almost closed; he was the very symbol of
satisfied happy and kind-hearted prosperity.

He was really touched by young Falk's approach
towards friendship. He had in him a very pleasant
and happy vein of sentiment which he was only
too delighted to exercise so long as no urgent
demands were made upon it. Once or twice
women and men younger than himself *had* made
such urgent demands; with what a hurry, a scurry
and a scamper had he then run from them !

But the more tranquil, easy and unexacting
aspects of sentiment he enjoyed. He liked his
heart to be warmed; he liked to feel that the pressure
of his hand, the welcome of the eye, the smile of
the lip were genuine in him and natural; he liked

to put his hand through the arm of a young eager human being who was full of vitality and physical strength. He disliked so deeply sickness and decay ; he despised them.

Falk was young, handsome and eager, something of a rebel—the greater compliment then that he should seek out Ronder. He was certainly the most attractive young man in Polchester, and, although that was not perhaps saying very much, after all Ronder lived in Polchester and wished to share in the best of every side of its life.

There were, however, further, more actual reasons that Ronder should anticipate Falk's visit with deep interest. He had heard, of course, many rumours of Falk's indiscretions, rumours that naturally gained greatly in the telling, of how he had formed some disgraceful attachment for the daughter of a publican down in the river slums, that he drank, that he gambled, that he was the wickedest young man in Polchester, and that he would certainly break his father's heart.

It was this relation of the boy to his father that interested him most of all. He continued to remark to the little god who looked after his affairs and kept an eye upon him that the last thing that he wanted was to interfere in Brandon's family business, and yet to the same little god he could not but comment on the curious persistency with which that same business would thrust itself upon his interest. ‘ If Brandon's wife, son, and general *ménage* will persist in involving themselves in absurd situations it's not my fault,' he would say. But he was not exactly sorry that they should.

Indeed, to-night, in the warm security of his room, with all his plans advancing towards fulfilment, and life developing just as he would have it, he felt so kindly a pity towards Brandon that he was warm with the desire to do something for him, make him a present, or flatter his vanity, or give way publicly to him about some contested point that was of no particular importance.

When young Falk was ushered in by the maid-servant, Ronder, looking up at him, thought him the handsomest boy he'd ever seen. He felt ready to give him all the advice in the world, and it was with the most genuine warmth of heart that he jumped up, put his hand on his shoulder, found him tobacco, whisky and soda, and the easiest chair in the room.

It was apparent at once that the boy was worked up to the extremity of his possible endurance. Ronder felt instantly the drama that he brought with him, filling the room with it, charging every word and every movement with the implication of it.

He turned about in his chair, struck many matches, pulled desperately at his pipe, stared at Ronder with a curious mixture of shyness and eagerness that betrayed his youth and his sense of Ronder's importance. Ronder began by talking easily about nothing at all, a diversion for which he had an especial talent. Falk suddenly broke in upon him :

'Look here. You don't care about that stuff —nor do I. I didn't come round to you for that. I want you to help me.'

'I'll be very glad to,' Ronder said, smiling, 'if I can.'

'Perhaps you can—perhaps you can't. I don't know you really, of course—I only have my idea of you. But you seem to me much older than I am. Do you know what I mean? Father's as young or younger and so are so many of the others. But you must have made your mind up about life. I want to know what you think of it.'

'That's a tall order,' said Ronder, smiling. 'What one thinks of life! Well, one can't say all in a moment, you know.'

And then, as though he had suddenly decided to take his companion seriously, his face was grave and his round shining eyes wide open.

Falk coloured. 'Perhaps you think me impertinent,' he said. 'But I don't care a damn if you do. After all, isn't it an absurd thing that there isn't another soul in this town you could ask such a question of? And yet there's nothing else so important. A fellow's thought an impossible prig if he mentions such a thing. I expect I seem in a hurry too, but I can tell you I've been irritated for years by not being able to get at it—the truth, you know. Why we're here at all, whether there is some kind of a God somewhere or no. Of course you've got to pretend you think there is, but I want to know what you *really* think and I promise it shan't go a step farther. But most of all I want to know whether you don't think we're meant all of us to be free, and why being free should be the hardest thing of all.'

'You must tell me one thing,' said Ronder. 'Is the impulse that brought you in to see me simply a general one, just because you are interested in life, or is there some immediate crisis that you have to settle? I ask that,' he added, smiling gently, 'because I've noticed that people don't as a rule worry very urgently about life unless they have to make up their minds about which turn in the road they're going to take.'

Falk hesitated ; then he said, speaking slowly, ' Yes, there is something. It's what you'd call a crisis in my life, I suppose. It's been piling up for months—for years if you like. But I don't see why I need bother you with that—it's nobody's business but my own. Although I won't deny that things you say may influence me. You see, I felt the first moment I met you that you'd speak the truth, and speaking the truth seems to me more important than anything else in the world.'

' But,' said Ronder, ' I don't want to influence you blindly. You've no right to ask me to advise you when I don't know what it is I am advising you about.'

' Well then,' said Falk, ' it's simply this—that I want to go up to London and live my own life. But I love my father—it would all be easy enough if I didn't—and he doesn't see things as I do. There are other things too—it's all very complicated. But I don't want you to tell me about my own affairs ! I just want you to say what you think this is all about, what we're here for anyway. You must have thought it all through and come out the other side. You look as though you had.'

Ronder hesitated. He really wished that this had not occurred. He could defeat Brandon without being given this extra weapon. His impulse was to put the boy off with some evasion and so to dismiss him. But the temptation that was always so strong in him to manipulate the power placed in his hands was urging him ; moreover, why should he not say what he thought about life ? It was sincere enough. He had no shame of it. . . .

'I couldn't advise you against your father's wishes,' he said. 'I'm very fond of your father. I have the highest opinion of him.'

Falk moved uneasily in his chair. 'You needn't advise me against him,' he said; 'you can't have a higher opinion of him than I have. I'm fonder of him than of any one in the world; I wouldn't be hesitating at all otherwise. And I tell you I don't want you to advise me on my particular case. It just interests me to know whether you believe in a God and whether you think life means anything. As soon as I saw you I said to myself, "Now I'd like to know what *he* thinks." That's all.'

'Of course I believe in a God,' said Ronder. 'I wouldn't be a clergyman otherwise.'

'Then if there's a God,' said Falk quickly, 'why does He let us down, make us feel that we must be free, and then make us feel that it's wrong to be free because, if we are, we hurt the people we're fond of? Do we live for ourselves or for others? Why isn't it easier to see what the right thing is?'

'If you want to know what I think about life,' said Ronder, 'it's just this—that we mustn't take ourselves too seriously, that we must work our utmost at the thing we're in, and give as little trouble to others as possible.'

Falk nodded his head. 'Yes, that's very simple. If you'll forgive my saying so, that's the sort of thing any one says to cover up what he really feels. That's not what *you* really feel. Anyway it accounts for simply nothing at all. If that's all there is in life——'

'I don't say that's all there is in life,' interrupted Ronder softly, ' I only say that that does for a start—for one's daily conduct I mean. But you've got to rid your head of illusions. Don't expect poetry and magic for ever round the corner. Don't dream of Utopias—they'll never come. Mind your own daily business.'

' Play for safety, in fact,' said Falk.

Ronder coloured a little. ' Not at all. Take every kind of risk if you think your happiness depends upon it. You're going to serve the world best by getting what you want and resting contented in it. It's the discontented and disappointed who hang things up.'

Falk smiled. ' You're pushing on to me the kind of philosophy that I'd like to follow,' he said. ' I don't believe in it for a moment nor do I believe it's what you really think, but I think I'm ready to cheat myself if you give me encouragement enough. I don't want to do any one any harm, but I must come to a conclusion about life and then follow it so closely that I can never have any doubt about any course of action again. When I was a small boy the Cathedral used to terrify me and dominate me too. I believed in God then, of course, and I used to creep in and listen, expecting to hear Him speak. That tomb of the Black Bishop seemed to me the place where He'd most likely be, and I used to fancy sometimes that He did speak from the heart of that stone. But I daresay it was the old Bishop himself.

' Anyway, I determined long ago that the Cathedral has a life of its own, quite apart from any of us. It has more immortality in one stone of its nave than we have in all our bodies.'

' Don't be too sure of that,' Ronder said.

'We have our immortality—a tiny flame, but I believe that it never dies. Beauty comes from it and dwells in it. We increase it or diminish it as we live.'

'And yet,' said Falk eagerly, 'you were urging, just now, a doctrine of what, if you'll forgive my saying so, was nothing but selfishness. How do you reconcile that with immortality?'

Ronder laughed. 'There have only been four doctrines in the history of the world,' he answered, 'and they are all Pursuits. One is the pursuit of Unselfishness. "Little children, love one another. He that seeks to save his soul shall lose it." The second is the opposite of the first—Individualism. "I am I. That is all I know, and I will seek out my own good always because that at least I can understand." The third is the pursuit of God and Mysticism. "Neither I matter nor my neighbour. I give up the world and every one and everything in it to find God." And the fourth is the pursuit of Beauty. "Beauty is Truth and Truth Beauty. That is all we need to know." Every man and woman alive or dead has chosen one of those four or a mixture of them. I would say that there is something in all of them, Charity, Individualism, Worship, Beauty. But finally, when all is said and done, we remain ourselves. It is our own life that we must lead, our own goal for which we are searching. At the end of everything we remain alone, of ourselves, by ourselves, for ourselves. Life is, finally, a lonely journey to a lonely bourne, let us cheat ourselves as we may.'

Ronder sat back in his chair, his eyes half closed. There was nothing that he enjoyed more than

delivering his opinions about life to a fit audience—
and by fit he meant intelligent and responsive.
He liked to be truthful without taking risks, and
he was always the audience rather than the speaker
in company that might be dangerous. He almost
loved Falk as he looked across at him and saw the
effect that his words had made upon him. There
was, Heaven knew, nothing very original in what
he had said, but it had been apparently what the
boy had wanted to hear.

He jumped up from his chair : ' You're right,'
he said. ' We've got to lead our own lives. I've
known it all along. When I've shown them what
I can do, then I'll come back to them. I love my
father, you know, sir ; I suppose some people here
think him tiresome and self-opinionated, but he's
like a boy, you always know where you are with
him. He's no idea what deceit means. He looks
on this Cathedral as his own idea, as though he'd
built it almost, and of course that's dangerous.
He'll have a shock one of these days and see that
he's gone too far, just as the Black Bishop did.
But he's a fine man ; I don't believe any one knows
how proud I am of him. And it's much better I
should go my own way and earn my own living
than hang around him, doing nothing—isn't it ? '

At that direct appeal, at the eager gaze that
Falk fixed upon him, something deep within Ronder
stirred.

Should he not even now advise the boy to stay ?
One word just then might effect much. Falk
trusted him. He was the only human being in
Polchester to whom the boy perhaps had come.
Years afterwards he was to look back to that
moment, see it crystallised in memory, see the

books piled row upon row gleam down upon him, see the blue curtain and hear the crackling fire . . a crisis perhaps to himself as well as to Falk.

He went across to the boy and put his hands on his shoulders.

' Yes,' he said, ' I think it's better for you to go.'

' And about God and Beauty ? ' Falk said, staring for a moment into Ronder's eyes, smiling shyly, and then turning away. ' It's a long search, isn't it ? But as long as there's something there, beyond life, and I know there is, the search is worth it.'

He looked rather wistfully at Ronder as though he expected him to confirm him again. But he said nothing.

Falk went to the door. ' Well, I must go. I'll show them that I was right to go my own way. I want father to be proud of me. This will shock him for a moment, but soon he'll see. I think you'll like to know, sir,' he said, suddenly turning and holding out his hand, ' that this little talk has meant a lot to me. It's just helped me to make up my mind.'

When he had gone Ronder sat in his chair, motionless, for a while ; he jumped up, went to the shelves, and found a book. Before he sat down again he said aloud, as though he were answering some accuser, ' Well, I told him nothing, anyway.'

Falk had, from the moment he left Ronder's door, his mind made up, and now that it *was* made up he wished to act as speedily as possible. And instantly there followed an appeal of the Town, so urgent and so poignant that he was taken by surprise. He had lived there most of his days and

never saw it until now, but every step that he took
soon haunted him. He made his plans decisively,
irrevocably, but he found himself lingering at doors
and at windows, peering over walls, hanging over
the Pol bridge, waiting suddenly as though he expected some message was about to be given to him.

The town was humming with life those days.
The May weather was lovely, softly blue with cool
airs and little white clouds like swollen pin-cushions
drifting lazily from point to point. The gardens were
dazzling with their flowers, the Cathedral Green
shone like glass, and every door-knob and brass
knocker in the Precincts glittered under the sun.

The town was humming with the approaching
Jubilee. It seemed itself to take an active part in
the preparations, the old houses smiling to one
another at the plans that they overheard, and the
birds, of which there were a vast number, flying
from wall to wall, from garden to garden, from
chimney to chimney with the exciting news that
they had gathered.

Every shop in the High Street seemed to whisper
to Falk as he passed : ' Surely you are not going to
leave us. We can offer you such charming things.
We've never been so gay in our lives before as we
are going to be now.'

Even the human beings in the place seemed to
be nicer to him than they had ever been before.
They had never, perhaps, been very nice to him,
regarding him with a quite definite disapproval
even when he was a little boy, because he would go
his own way and showed them that he didn't care
what they thought of him.

Now, suddenly, they were making up to him.
Mrs. Combermere, surrounded with dogs, stopped

him in the High Street and, in a deep bass voice, asked him why it was so long since he had been to see her, and then slapped him on the shoulder with her heavy gloved hand. That silly woman, Julia Preston, met him in Bennett's book shop and asked him to help her to choose a book of poems for a friend.

'Something that shall be both True and Beautiful, Mr. Brandon,' she said. 'There's so little real Beauty in our lives, don't you think?' Little Betty Callender caught him up in Orange Street and chattered to him about her painting, and that pompous Bentinck-Major insisted on his going into the Conservative Club with him, where he met old McKenzie and older Forrester, and had to listen to their golfing achievements.

It may have been simply that every one in the town was beside and above himself over the Jubilee excitements—but it made it very hard for Falk. Nothing to the hardness of everything at home. Here at the last moment, when it was too late to change or alter anything, every room, every old piece of furniture seemed to appeal to him with some especial claim. For ten years he had had the same bedroom, an old low-ceilinged room with queer bulges in the wall, a crooked fireplace and a slanting floor. For years now he had had a wall-paper with an ever-recurrent scene of a church tower, a snowy hill, and a large crimson robin. The robins were faded, and the snowy hill a dingy yellow. There were School groups and Oxford groups on the walls, and the bookcase near the door had his old school prizes and Henty and a set of the Waverley Novels with dark red covers and paper labels.

Hardest of all to leave was the view from the window overlooking the Cathedral Green and the Cathedral. That window had been connected with every incident of his childhood. He had leant out of it when he had felt sick from eating too much, he had gone to it when his eyes were brimming with hot rebellious tears after some scene with his father, he had known ecstatic joys gazing from it on the first day of his return from school, he had thrown things out of it on to the heads of un-suspecting strangers, he had gone to it in strange moods of poetry and romance, and watched the moon like a plate of dull and beaten gold sail above the Cathedral towers, he had sat behind it listening to the organ like a muffled giant whispering to be liberated from grey, confining walls, he had looked out of it on a still golden evening when the stars were silver buttons in the sky after a meeting with Annie; he went to it and gazed, heart-sick, across the Green now when he was about to bid farewell to it for ever.

Heart-sick but resolved, it seemed strange to him that after months of irresolution his mind should now be so firmly composed. He seemed even, prophetically, to foretell the future. What had reassured him he did not know, but for himself he knew that he was taking the right step. For himself and for Annie—outside that, it was as though a dark cloud was coming up enveloping all that he was leaving behind. He could not tell how he knew, but he felt as though he were fleeing from the city of Polchester, and were being driven forward on his flight by powers far stronger than he could control.

He fancied, as he looked out of his window, that

the Cathedral also was aware and, aloof, immortal, waited the inevitable hour.

Coming straight upon his final arrangements with Annie, his reconciliation with his father was ironic. So deeply here were his real affections stirred that he could not consider deliberately his approaching treachery; nevertheless he did not for a moment contemplate withdrawal from it. It was as though two personalities were now in active movement within him, the one old, belonging to the town, to his father, to his own youth, the other new, belonging to Annie, to the future, to ambition, to the challenge of life itself. With every hour the first was moving away from him, reluctantly, stirring the other self by his withdrawal but inevitably moving, never, never to return.

He came, late in the afternoon, into the study and found his father, balanced on the top of a small ladder, putting straight ' Christ's Entry into Jerusalem,' a rather faded copy of Benjamin Haydon's picture that had irritated Falk since his earliest youth by a kind of false theatricality that inhabited it.

Falk paused at the door, caught up by a sudden admiration of his father. He had his coat off, and as he bent forward to adjust the cord the vigour and symmetry of his body was magnificently emphasised. The thick strong legs pressed against the black cloth of his trousers, the fine rounded thighs, the broad back almost bursting the shiny stuff of the waistcoat, the fine neck and the round curly head, these denied age and decay. He was growing perhaps a little stout, the neck was a little too thick for the collar, but the balance and energy and strength of the figure belonged to a man as young as Falk himself. . . .

At the sound of the door closing he turned, and at once the lined forehead, the mouth a little slack, gave the man his age, but Falk was to remember that first picture for the rest of his life with a strange poignancy and deeply affectionate pathos.

They had not met alone since their quarrel ; their British horror of any scene forbade the slightest allusion to it. Brandon climbed down from his ladder and came, smiling, across to his son.

At his happy times, when he was at ease with himself and the world, he had the confident gaiety of a child ; he was at ease now. He put his hand through Falk's arm and drew him across to the table by the window.

' I've had a headache,' he said, rather as a child might complain to his elder, ' for two days, and now it's suddenly gone. I never used to have headaches. But I've been irritated lately by some of the tomfoolery that's been going on. Don't tell your mother ; I haven't said a word to her ; but what do you take when you have a headache ? '

' I don't think I ever have them,' said Falk.

' I'm not going to stuff myself up with all their medicines and things. I've never taken medicine in my life if I was strong enough to prevent them giving it to me, and I'm not going to start it now.'

' Father,' Falk said very earnestly, ' don't let yourself get so easily irritated. You usedn't to be. Everybody finds things go badly sometimes. It's bad for you to allow yourself to be worried. Everything's all right and going to be all right.' (The hypocrite that he felt himself as he said this !)

' You know that every one thinks the world of you here. Don't take things too seriously.'

Brandon nodded his head.

'You're quite right, Falk. It's very sensible of you to mention it, my boy. I usedn't to lose my temper as I do. I must keep control of myself better. But when a lot of chattering idiots start gabbling about things that they understand as much about as——'

'Yes, I know,' said Falk, putting his hand upon his father's arm. 'But let them talk. They'll soon find their level.'

'Yes, and then there's your mother,' went on Brandon. 'I'm bothered about her. Have you noticed anything odd about her this last week or two ?'

That his father should begin to worry about his mother was certainly astonishing enough ! Certainly the first time in all these years that Brandon had spoken of her.

'Mother ? No ; in what way ?'

'She's not herself. She's not happy. She's worrying about something.'

'*You're* worrying, father,' Falk said, 'that's what's the matter. *She's* just the same. You've been allowing yourself to worry about everything. Mother's all right.' And didn't he know in his own secret heart that she wasn't ?

Brandon shook his head. 'You may be right. All the same——'

Falk said slowly : 'Father, what would you say if I went up to London ?' This was a close approach to the subject of their quarrel of the other evening.

'When ? What for ?'

'Oh, at once—to get something to do.'

'No, not now. After the summer we might talk of it.'

He spoke with utter decision, as he had always done to Falk, as though he were five years old and could naturally know nothing about life.

' But, father—don't you think it's bad for me, hanging round here doing nothing ? '

Brandon got up, went across to the little ladder, hesitated a moment, then climbed up.

' I've had this picture twenty years,' he said, ' and it's never hung straight yet.'

' No, but, father,' said Falk, coming across to him, ' I'm a man now, not a boy. I can't hang about any longer—I can't really.'

' We'll talk about it in the autumn,' said Brandon, humming ' Onward, Christian Soldiers,' as he always did, a little out of tune.

' I've got to earn my own living, haven't I ? ' said Falk.

' There ! ' said Brandon, stepping back a little, so that he nearly overbalanced. ' *That's* better. But it won't stay like that for five minutes. It never does.'

He climbed down again, his face rosy with his exertions. ' You leave it to me, Falk,' he said, nodding his head. ' I've got plans for you.'

A sudden sense of the contrast between Ronder and his father smote Falk. His father ! What an infant ! How helpless against that other ! Moved by the strangest mixture of tenderness, regret, pity, he did what he had never in all his life before dreamed of doing, what he would have died of shame for doing, had any one else been there—put his hands on his father's shoulders and kissed him lightly on his cheek.

He laughed as he did so, to carry off his embarrassment.

' I don't hold myself bound, you know, father,' he said. ' I shall go off just when I want to.'

But Brandon was too deeply confused by his son's action to hear the words. He felt a strange, most idiotic impulse to hug his son ; to place himself well out of danger, he moved back to the window, humming ' Onward, Christian Soldiers.'

He looked out upon the Green. ' There are two of those choir-boys on the grass again,' he said. ' If Ryle doesn't keep them in better order, I'll let him know what I think of him. He's always promising and never does anything.'

The last talk of their lives alone together was ended.

He had made all his plans. He had decided that on the day of escape he would walk over to Salis Coombe station, a matter of some two miles ; there he would be joined by Annie, whose aunt lived near there, and to whom she could go on a visit the evening before. They would catch the slow four o'clock train to Drymouth and then meet the express that reached London at midnight. He would go to an Oxford friend who lived in St. John's Wood, and he and Annie would be married as soon as possible. Beyond everything else he wanted this marriage to take place quickly ; once that was done he was Annie's protector, so long as she should need him. She should be free as she pleased, but she would have some one to whom she might go, some one who could legally provide for her and would see that she came to no harm.

The thing that he feared most was lest any ill should come to her through the fact of his caring for her ; he felt that he could let her go for ever the very day after his marriage, so that he knew that she would never come to harm. A certain defiant courage in her, mingled with her ignorance and simplicity, made his protection of her the first thing in his life. As to living, his Oxford friend was concerned with various literary projects, having a little money of his own, and much self-confidence and ambition.

He and Falk had already, at Oxford, edited a little paper together, and Falk had been promised some reader's work in connection with one of the younger publishing houses. In after years he looked back in amazement that he should have ventured on the great London attack with so slender a supply of ammunition—but now, looking forward in Polchester, that question of future livelihood seemed the very smallest of his problems.

Perhaps, deepest of all, something fiercely democratic in him longed for the moment when he might make his public proclamation of his defiance of class.

He meant to set off, simply as he was ; they could send his things after him. If he indulged in any pictures of the future, he did, perhaps, see himself returning to Polchester in a year's time or so, as the editor of the most remarkable of London's new periodicals, received by his father with enthusiasm, and even Annie admitted into the family with approval. Of course, they could not return here to live . . . it would be only a visit. . . . At that sudden vision of Annie and his father face to face, that vision faded ; no, this was the end of the old life. He must face that, set his shoulders square to it, steel his heart to it. . . .

That last luncheon was the strangest meal that

be dragons in the way! Here were no dragons. As he went down the High Street people smiled at him and waved hands. The town sparkled under the afternoon sun. It was market-day, and the old fruit-women under the green umbrella, the toy-man with the clockwork monkeys, the flower-stalls and the vegetable-sellers, all these were here; in the centre of the square, sheep and pigs were penned. Dogs were barking, stout farmers in corduroy breeches walked about arguing and ex-pectorating, and suddenly, above all the clamour and bustle, the Cathedral chimes struck the hour.

He hastened then, striding up Orange Street, past the church and the monument on the hill, through hedges thick with flowers, until he struck off into the Drymouth Road. With every step that he took he stirred child memories. He reached the signpost that pointed to Drymouth, to Clinton St. Mary, to Polchester. This was the landmark that he used to reach with his nurse on his walks. Further than this she, a stout, puffing woman, would never go. He had known that a little way on there was Rocket Wood, a place beloved by him ever since they had driven there for a picnic in the jingle, and he had found it all spotted gold under the fir-trees, thick with moss and yellow with primroses. How many fights with his nurse he had had over that! he clinging to the signpost and screaming that he *would* go on to the Wood, she picking him up at last and carrying him back down the road.

He went on into the wood now and found it again spotted with gold, although it was too late for primroses. It was all soft and dark with pillars of purple light that struck through the fretted blue, and the dark shadows of the leaves. All hushed and no living thing—save the hesitating patter of some bird among the fir-cones. He struck through the wood and came out on to the Common. You could smell the sea finely here—a true Glebeshire smell, fresh and salt, full of sea-pinks and the westerly gales. On the top of the Common he paused and looked back. He knew that from here you had your last view of the Cathedral.

Often in his school holidays he had walked out here to get that view. He had it now in its full glory. When he was a boy it had seemed to him that the Cathedral was like a giant lying down behind the hill and leaning his face on the hill-side. So it looked now, its towers like ears, the great East window shining, a stupendous eye, out over the bending wind-driven country. The sun flashed upon it, and the towers rose grey and pearl-coloured to heaven. Mightily it looked across the expanse of the moor, staring away and beyond Falk's little body into some vast distance, wrapped in its own great dream, secure in its mighty memories, intent upon its secret purposes.

Indifferent to man, strong upon its rock, hiding in its heart the answer to all the questions that tortured man's existence—and yet, perhaps, aware of man's immortality, scornful of him for making so slight a use of that—but admiring him, too, for the tenacity of his courage and the undying resurgence of his hope.

Falk, a black dot against the sweep of sky and the curve of the dark soil, vanished from the horizon.

CHAPTER VII

BRANDON PUTS ON HIS ARMOUR

BRANDON was not surprised when, on the morning after Falk's escape, his son was not present at family prayers. That was not a ceremony that Falk had ever appreciated. Joan was there, of course, and just as the Archdeacon began the second prayer Mrs. Brandon slipped in and took her place.

After the servants had filed out and the three were alone, Mrs. Brandon, with a curious little catch in her voice, said :

'Falk has been out all night ; his bed has not been slept in.'

Brandon's immediate impulse, before he had even caught the import of his wife's words, was : 'There's reason for emotion coming ; see that you show none.'

He sat down at the table, slowly unfolding the *Glebeshire Morning News* that always waited, neatly, beside his plate. His hand did not tremble, although his heart was beating with a strange muffled agitation.

'I suppose he went off somewhere,' he said. 'He never tells us, of course. He's getting too selfish for anything.'

He put down his newspaper and picked up his letters. For a moment he felt as though he could not look at them in the presence of his wife. He glanced quickly at the envelopes. There was nothing there from Falk. His heart gave a little clap of relief.

'At any rate, he hasn't written,' he said. 'He can't be far away.'

'There's another post at ten-thirty,' she answered.

He was angry with her for that. How like her ! Why could she not allow things to be pleasant as long as possible ?

She went on : 'He's taken nothing with him. Not even a hand-bag. He hasn't been back in the house since luncheon yesterday.'

'Oh ! he'll turn up !' Brandon went back to his paper. 'Mustard, Joan, please.' Breakfast over, he went into his study and sat at the long writing-table, pretending to be about his morning correspondence. He could not settle to that ; he had never been one to whom it was easy to control his mind, and now his heart and soul were filled with foreboding.

It seemed to him that for weeks past he had been dreading some catastrophe. What catastrophe ? What could occur ?

He almost spoke aloud. 'Never before have I dreaded. . . .'

Meanwhile he would not think of Falk. He would not. His mind flew round and round that name like a moth round the candle-light. He heard half-past ten strike, first in the dining-room, then slowly on his own mantelpiece. A moment later, through his study door that was ajar, he heard the letters fall with a soft stir into the box, then the sharp ring of the bell.   He sat at his table, his hands clenched.

' Why doesn't that girl bring the letters ?   Why doesn't that girl bring the letters ? ' he was repeating to himself unconsciously again and again.

She knocked on the door, came in and put the letters on his table.   There were only three.   He saw immediately that one was in Falk's handwriting. He tore the envelope across, pulled out the letter, his fingers trembling now so that he could scarcely hold it, his heart making a noise as of tramping waves in his ears.

The letter was as follows :

NORTH ROAD STATION,
DRYMOUTH,
May 23, 1897.

MY DEAR FATHER—I am writing this in the waiting-room at North Road before catching the London train. I suppose that I have done a cowardly thing in writing like this when I am away from you, and I can't hope to make you believe that it's because I can't bear to hurt you that I'm acting like a coward.   You'll say, justly enough, that it looks as though I wanted to hurt you by what I'm doing. But, father, truly, I've looked at it from every point of view, and I can't see that there's anything else for it but this. The first part of this, my going up to London to earn my living, I can't feel guilty about.

It seems to me, truly, the only thing to do.   I have tried to speak to you about it on several occasions, but you have always put me off, and, as far as I can see, you don't feel that there's anything ignominious in my hanging about a little town like Polchester, doing nothing at all for the rest of my life.   I think my being sent down from Oxford as I was gave you the idea that I was useless and would never be any good.   I'm going to prove to you you're wrong, and I know I'm right to take it into my own hands as I'm doing.   Give me a little time and you'll see that I'm right

The other thing is more difficult. I can't expect you to forgive me just yet, but perhaps later on, you'll see that it isn't too bad. Annie Hogg, the daughter of Hogg down in Seatown, is with me, and next week I shall marry her.

I have so far done nothing that you need be ashamed of. I love her, but am not her lover, and she will stay with relations away from me until I marry her. I know this will seem horrible to you, father, but it is a matter for my own conscience. I have tried to leave her and could not, but even if I could I have made her, through my talk, determined to go to London and try her luck there. She loathes her father and is unhappy at home. I cannot let her go up to London without any protection, and the only way I can protect her is by marrying her.

She is a fine woman, father, fine and honourable and brave. Try to think of her apart from her father and her surroundings. She does not belong to them, truly she does not. In all these months she has not tried to persuade me to a mean and shabby thing. She is incapable of any meanness. In all this business my chief trouble is the unhappiness that this will bring you. You will think that this is easy to say when it has made no difference to what I have done. But all the same it is true, and perhaps later on, when you have got past a little of your anger with me, you will give me a chance to prove it. I have the promise of some literary work that should give me enough to live on. I have taken nothing with me ; perhaps mother will pack up my things and send them to me at 5 Parker Street, St. John's Wood.

Father, give me a chance to show you that I will make this right.—Your loving son, FALK BRANDON.

In the little morning-room to the right at the top of the stairs Joan and her mother were waiting. Joan was pretending to sew, but her fingers scarcely moved. Mrs. Brandon was sitting at her writing-table ; her ears were straining for every sound. The sun flooded the room with a fierce rush of colour, and through the wide-open windows the noises of the town, cries and children's voices, and the passing of feet on the cobbles came up. As half-past ten struck the Cathedral bells began to ring for morning service.

'Oh, I can't bear those bells,' Mrs. Brandon cried. 'Shut the windows, Joan.'

Joan went across and closed them. The bells were suddenly removed, but seemed to be the more insistent in their urgency because they were shut away.

The door was suddenly flung open, and Brandon stood there.

'Oh, what is it?' Mrs. Brandon cried, starting to her feet.

He was a man convulsed with anger; she had seen him in these rages before, when his blue eyes stared with an emptiness of vision and his whole body seemed to be twisted as though he were trying to climb to some height whence he might hurl himself down and destroy utterly that upon which he fell.

The letter tumbled from his hand. He caught the handle of the door as though he would tear it from its socket, but his voice, when at last it came, was quiet, almost his ordinary voice.

'His name is never to be mentioned in this house again.'

'What has he done?'

'That's enough. What I say. His name is never to be mentioned again.'

The two women stared at him. He seemed to come down from a great height, turned and went, very carefully closing the door behind him.

He had left the letter on the floor. Mrs. Brandon went and picked it up.

' Oh, mother, what has Falk done ? ' Joan asked. The bells danced all over the room.

Brandon went downstairs, back into his study, closing his door, shutting himself in. He stayed in the middle of the room, saying aloud :

'·Never his name again. . . . Never his name again.' The actual sound of the words echoing back to him lifted him up as though out of very deep water. Then he was aware, as one is in the first clear moment after a great shock, of a number of things at the same time. He hated his son because his son had disgraced him and his name for ever. He loved his son, never before so deeply and so dearly as now. He was his only son, and there was none other. His son had gone off with the daughter of the worst publican in the place, and so had shamed him before them all. Falk (he arrived in his mind suddenly at the name with a little shiver that hurt horribly) would never be there any more, would never be about the house, would never laugh and be angry and be funny any more. (Behind this thought ·was a long train of pictures of Falk as a boy, as a baby, as a child, pictures that he kept back with a great gesture of the will.) In the town they would all be talking, they were talking already. They must be stopped from talking ; they must not know. He must lie ; they must all lie. But how could they be stopped from knowing when he had gone off with the publican's daughter ? They would all know. . . . They would laugh. . . . They would laugh. He would not be able to go down the street without their laughter.

Dimly on that came a larger question. What had happened lately so that his whole life had changed ? He had been feeling it now for weeks, long before this terrible blow had fallen, as though he were surrounded by enemies and mockers and men who wished him ill. Men who wished him ill ! Wished HIM ill ! He who had never done any one harm in all his life, who had only wanted the happiness of others and the good of the place in which he was, and the Glory of God ! God ! . . . His thoughts leapt across a vast gulf. What was God about, to allow this disaster to fall upon him ? When he had served God so faithfully and had had no thought but for His grandeur ? He was in a new world now, where the rivers, the mountains, the roads, the cities were new. For years everything had gone well with him, and then, suddenly, at the lifting of a finger, all had been ill. . . .

Through the mist of his thoughts, gradually, like the sun in his strength, his anger had been rising. Now it flamed forth. At the first it had been personal anger because his son had betrayed and deceived him—but now, for a time, Falk was almost forgotten.

He would show them. They would laugh at him, would they ? They would point at him, would they, as the man whose son had run away with an innkeeper's daughter ? Well, let them point. They would plot to take the power from his hands, to reduce him to impotence, to make him of no account in the place where he had ruled for years. He had no doubt, now that he saw farther into it, that they had persuaded Falk to run away with that girl. It was the sort of weapon that they would be likely to use, the sort of weapon that that man Ronder . . .

At the sudden ringing of that now hated name in his ears he was calm. Yes, to fight that enemy he needed all his control. How that man would rejoice at this that had happened! What a victory to him it would seem to be! Well, it should not be a victory. He began to stride up and down his study, his head up, his chest out. It was almost as though he were a great warrior of old, having his armour put on before he went out to the fight— the greaves, the breast-plate, the helmet, the sword. . . .

He would fight to the last drop of blood in his body and beat the pack of them, and if they thought that this would cause him to hang his head or hide or go secretly, they should soon see their mistake.

He suddenly stopped. The pain that sometimes came to his head attacked him now. For a moment it was so sharp, of so acute an agony, that he almost staggered and fell. He stood there, his body taut, his hands clenched. It was like knives driving through his brain; his eyes were filled with blood so that he could not see. It passed, but he was weak, his knees shook so that he was compelled to sit down, holding his hands on his knees. Now it was gone. He could see clearly again. What was it? Imagination, perhaps. Only the hammering of his heart told him that anything was the matter. He was a long while there. At last he got up, went into the hall, found his hat and went out. He crossed the Green and passed through the Cathedral door.

He went out instinctively, without any deliberate thought, to the Cathedral as to the place that would most readily soothe and comfort him. Always when things went wrong he crossed over to the Cathedral and walked about there. Matins were just concluded and people were coming out of the great West door. He went in by the Saint Margaret door, crossed through the Vestry where Rogers, who had been taking the service, was disrobing, and climbed the little crooked stairs into the Lucifer Room. A glimpse of Rogers' saturnine countenance (he knew well enough that Rogers hated him) stirred some voice to whisper within : ' He knows and he's glad.'

The Lucifer Room was a favourite resort of his, favourite because there was a long bare floor across which he could walk with no furniture to interrupt him, and because, too, no one ever came there. It was a room in the Bishop's Tower that had once, many hundreds of years ago, been used by the monks as a small refectory. Many years had passed now since it had seen any sort of occupation save that of bats, owls and mice. There was a fireplace at the far end that had long been blocked up, but that still showed curious carving, the heads of monkeys and rabbits, winged birds, a twisting dragon with a long tail, and the figure of a saint holding up a crucifix. Over the door was an old clock that had long ceased to tell the hours ; this had a strangely carved wood canopy. Two little windows with faint stained glass gave an obscure light. The subjects of these windows were confused, but the old colours, deep reds and blues, blended with a rich glow that no modern glass could obtain. The ribs and bosses of the vaulting of the room were in faded colours and dull gold. In one corner of the room was an old, dusty, long-neglected harmonium. Against the wall were hanging some wooden figures, large life-sized saints, two male and two female, once outside the building, painted on the

wood in faded crimson and yellow and gold.   Much
of the colour had been worn away with rain and
wind, but two of the faces were still bright and
stared with a gentle fixed gaze out into the dim
air.   Two old banners, torn and thin, flapped
from one of the vaultings.   The floor was worn, and
creaked with every step.   As Brandon pushed
back the heavy door and entered, some bird in a
distant corner flew with a frightened stir across
to the window.   Occasionally some one urged that
steps should be taken to renovate the place and
make some use of it, but nothing was ever done.
Stories connected with it had faded away; no one
now could tell why it was called the Lucifer Room—
and no one cared.

Its dimness and shadowed coloured light suited
Brandon to-day.   He wanted to be where no one
could see him, where he could gather together
the resistance with which to meet the world.   He
paced up and down, his hands behind his back;
he fancied that the old saints looked at him with
kindly affection.

And now, for a moment, all his pride and
anger were gone, and he could think of nothing
but his love for his son.   He had an impulse that
almost moved him to hurry home, to take the next
train up to London, to find Falk, to take him in his
arms and forgive him.   He saw again and again
that last meeting that they had had, when Falk had
kissed him.   He knew now what that had meant.
After all, the boy was right.   He had been in the
wrong to have kept him here, doing nothing.   It
was fine of the boy to take things into his own
hands, to show his independence and to fight for
his own individuality.   It was what he himself

would have done if—then the thought of Annie Hogg cut across his tenderness and behind Annie her father, that fat smiling red-faced scoundrel, the worst villain in the town. At the sudden realisation that there was now a link between himself and that man, and that that link had been forged by his own son, tenderness and affection fled. He could only entertain one emotion at a time, and immediately he was swept into such a fury that he stopped in his walk, lifted his head, and cursed Falk. For that he would never forgive him, for the public shame and disgrace that he had brought upon the Brandon name, upon his mother and his sister, upon the Cathedral, upon all authority and discipline and seemliness in the town.

He suffered then the deepest agony that perhaps in all his life he had ever known. There was no one there to see. He sank down upon the wooden coping that protruded from the old wall and hid his face in his hands as though he were too deeply ashamed to encounter even the dim faces of the old wooden figures.

There was a stir in the room ; the little door opened and closed ; the bird, with a flutter of wings, flew back to its corner. Brandon looked up and saw a faint shadow of a man. He rose and took some steps towards the door, then he stopped because he saw that the man was Davray the painter.

He had never spoken to this man, but he had hated everything that he had ever heard about him. In the first place, to be an artist was, in the Archdeacon's mind, synonymous with being a loose liver and an atheist. Then this fellow was, as all the town knew, a drunkard, an idler, a dissolute waster who had brought nothing upon Polchester but disgrace. Had Brandon had his way he would, long ago, have had him publicly expelled and forbidden ever to return. The thought that this man should be in the Cathedral at all was shocking to him and, in his present mood, quite intolerable. He saw, dim though the light was, that the man was drunk now.

Davray lurched forward a step, then said huskily : 'Well, so your fine son's run away with Hogg's pretty daughter.'

The sense that he had had already that his son's action had suddenly bound him into company with all the powers of evil and destruction rose to its full height at the sound of the man's voice ; but with it rose, too, his self-command. The very disgust with which Davray filled him contributed to his own control and dignity.

'You should feel ashamed, sir,' he said quietly, standing still where he was, 'to be in that condition in this building. Or are you too drunk to know where you are ? '

'That's all right, Archdeacon,' Davray said, laughing. 'Of course I'm drunk. I generally am—and that's my affair. But I'm not so drunk as not to know where I am and not to know who you are and what's happened to you. I know all those things, I'm glad to say. Perhaps I am a little ahead of yourself in that. Perhaps you don't know yet what your young hopeful has been doing.'

Brandon was as still as one of the old wooden saints.

'Then if you are sober enough to know where you are, leave this place and do not return to it until you are in a fit state.'

'Fit ! I like that.' The sense that he was

alone now for the first time in his life with the
man whom he had so long hated infuriated Davray.
'Fit ? Let me tell you this, old cock, I'm twice as
fit to be here as you're ever likely to be. Though
I have been drinking and letting myself go, I'm
fitter to be here than you are, you stuck-up, pompous
fool.'

Brandon did not stir.

'Go home !' he said ; 'go home ! Recover
your senses and ask God's forgiveness.'

'God's forgiveness !' Davray moved a step
forward as though he would strike. Brandon made
no movement. 'That's like your damned cheek.
Who wants forgiveness as you do ? Ask this
Cathedral—ask it whether I have not loved it,
adored it, worshipped it as I've worshipped no
woman. Ask it whether I have not been faithful,
drunkard and sot as I am. And ask it. what it
thinks of you—of your patronage and pomposity
and conceit. When have you thought of the
Cathedral and its beauty, and not always of yourself
and your grandeur ? . . . Why, man, we're sick
of you, all of us from the top man in the place
to the smallest boy. And the Cathedral is sick
of you and your damned conceit, and is going to
get rid of you too, if you won't go of yourself.
And this is the first step. Your son's gone with
a whore to London, and all the town's laughing
at you.'

Brandon did not flinch. The man was close
to him ; he could smell his drunken breath—but
behind his words, drunken though they might be,
was a hatred so intense, so deep, so real, that it
was like a fierce physical blow. Hatred of himself.
He had never conceived in all his life that any one

hated him—and this man had hated him for years, a man to whom he had never spoken before to-day.

Davray, as was often his manner, seemed suddenly to sober. He stood aside and spoke more quietly, almost without passion.

'I've been waiting for this moment for years,' he said; 'you don't know how I've watched you Sunday after Sunday strutting about this lovely place, happy in your own conceit. Your very pride has been an insult to the God you pretend to serve. I don't know whether there's a God or no—there can't be, or things wouldn't happen as they do—but there *is* this place, alive, wonderful, beautiful, triumphant, and you've dared to put yourself above it. . . .

'I could have shouted for joy last night when I heard what your young hopeful had done. "That's right," I said; "that'll bring him down a bit. That'll teach him modesty." I had an extra drink on the strength of it. I've been hanging about all the morning to get a chance of speaking to you. I followed you up here. You're one of us now, Archdeacon. You're down on the ground at last, but not so low as you will be before the Cathedral has finished with you.'

'Go,' said Brandon, 'or, House of God though this is, I'll throw you out.'

'I'll go. I've said my say for the moment. But we'll meet again, never fear. You're one of us now—one of us. Good-night.'

He passed through the door, and the dusky room was still again as though no one had been there. . . .

There is an old German tale, by De la Motte Fouqué, I fancy, of a young traveller who asks his way to a certain castle, his destination. He is given his directions, and his guide tells him that the journey will be easy enough until he reaches a small wood through which he must pass. This wood will be dark and tangled and bewildering, but more sinister than those obstacles will be the inhabitants of it, who, evil, malign, foul and bestial, devote their lives to the destruction of all travellers who endeavour to reach the castle on the hill beyond. And the tale tells how the young traveller, proud of his youth and strength, confident in the security of his armour, nevertheless, when he crosses the dark border of the wood, feels as though his whole world has changed, as though everything in which he formerly trusted is of no value, as though the very weapons that were his chief defence now made him most defenceless. He has in the heart of that wood many perilous adventures, but worst of them all, when he is almost at the end of his strength, is the sudden conviction that he has himself changed, and is himself become one of the foul, gibbering, half-visioned monsters by whom he is surrounded.

As Brandon left the Cathedral there was something of that strange sense with him, a sense that had come to him first, perhaps, in its dimmest and most distant form, on the day of the circus and the elephant, and that now, in all its horrible vigour and confidence, was there close at his elbow. He had always held himself immaculate; he had come down to his fellow-men, loving them, indeed, but feeling that they were of some other clay than his own, and that through no especial virtue of his, but simply because God had so wished it. And now he had stood, and a drunken wastrel had cursed

him and told him that he was detested by all men
and that they waited for his downfall.

It was those last words of Davray's that rang
in his ears : ' You're one of us now.   You're one
of us.'   Drunkard and wastrel though the man was,
those words could not be forgotten, would never
be forgotten again.

With his head up, his shoulders back, he returned
to his house.

The maid met him in the hall.   ' There's a
man waiting for you in the study, sir.'

' Who is it ? '

' Mr. Samuel Hogg, sir.'

Brandon looked at the girl fixedly, but not
unkindly.

' Why did you let him in, Gladys ? '

' He wouldn't take no denial, sir.   Mrs. Brandon
was out and Miss Joan.   He said you were expecting him and 'e knew you'd soon be back.'

' You should never let any one wait, Gladys,
unless I have told you beforehand.'

' No, sir.'

' Remember that in future, will you ? '

' Yes, sir.   I'm sure I'm sorry, sir, but——'

Brandon went into his study.

Hogg was standing beside the window, a faded
bowler in his hand.   He turned when he heard the
opening of the door ;   he presented to the Archdeacon a face of smiling and genial, if coarsened,
amiability.

He was wearing rough country clothes, brown
knickerbockers and gaiters, and looked something
like a stout and seedy gamekeeper fond of the
bottle.

' I'm sure you'll forgive this liberty I've taken,

Archdeacon,' he said, opening his mouth very wide as he smiled—'waiting for you like this; but the matter's a bit urgent.'

'Yes?' said Brandon, not moving from the door.

'I've come in a friendly spirit, although there are men who might have come otherwise. You won't deny that, considering the circumstances of the case.'

'I'll be grateful to you if you'll explain,' said Brandon, 'as quickly as possibly your business.'

'Why, of course,' said Hogg, coming away from the window. 'Why, of course, Archdeacon. Now, whoever would have thought that we, you and me, would be in the same box? And that's putting it a bit mild considering that it's my daughter that your son has run away with.'

Brandon said nothing, not, however, removing his eyes from Hogg's face.

Hogg was all amiable geniality. 'I know it must be against the grain, Archdeacon, having to deal with the likes of me. You've always counted yourself a strike above us country-folk, haven't you, and quite natural too. But, again, in the course of nature we've both of us had children and that, as it turns out, is where we finds our common ground, so to speak—you a boy and me a lovely girl. *Such* a lovely girl, Archdeacon, as it's natural enough your son should want to run away with.'

Brandon went across to his writing-table and sat down.

'Mr. Hogg,' he said, 'it is true that I had a letter from my son this morning telling me that he had gone up to London with your daughter and was intending to marry her as soon as possible. You

will not expect that I should approve of that step.
My first impulse was, naturally enough, to go at
once to London and to prevent his action at all
costs. On thinking it over, however, I felt that
as he had run away with the girl the least that he
could now do was to marry her.

' I'm sure you will understand my feeling when
I say that in taking this step I consider that he has
disgraced himself and his family. He has cut
himself off from his family irremediably. I think
that really that is all that I have to say.'

Behind Hogg's strange little half-closed eyes
some gleam of anger and hatred passed. There
was no sign of it in the geniality of his open
smile.

' Why, certainly, Archdeacon, I can understand
that you wouldn't care for what he has done. But
boys will be boys, won't they ? We've both been
boys in our time, I daresay. You've looked at it
from your point of view, and that's natural enough.
But human nature's human nature, and you must
forgive me if I look at it from mine. She's my only
girl, and a good girl she's been to me, keepin'
herself *to* herself and doing her work and helping
me wonderful. Well, your young spark comes
along, likes the look of her and ruins her. . . .'

The Archdeacon made some movement—

' Oh, you may say what you like, Archdeacon,
and he may tell you what *he* likes, but you and I
know what happens when two young things with
hot blood gets together and there's nobody by.
They may *mean* to be straight enough, but before
they knows where they are, nature's took hold of
them, and there they are. . . . But even supposin'
that 'asn't happened I don't know as I'm much

better off. That girl was the very prop of my business ; she's gone, never to return accordin' to her own account. As to this marryin' business, that may seem to you, Archdeacon, to improve things, but I'm not so sure that it does after all. You may be all very 'igh and mighty in your way, but I'm thinkin' of myself and the business. What good does my girl marryin' your son do to me ? That's what I want to know.'

Brandon's hands were clenched upon the table. Nevertheless he still spoke quietly.

' I don't think, Mr. Hogg,' he said, ' that there's anything to be gained by our discussing this just now. I have only this morning heard of it. You may be assured that justice will be done, absolute justice, to your daughter and yourself.'

Hogg moved to the door.

' Why, certainly, Archdeacon. It is a bit early to discuss things. I daresay we shall be havin' many a talk about it all before it's over. I'm sure I only want to be friendly in the matter. As I said before, we're in the same box, you and me, so to speak. That ought to make us tender towards one another, oughtn't it ? One losing his son and the other his daughter.

' Such a good girl as she was too. Certainly I'll be going, Archdeacon ; leave you to think it over a bit. I daresay you'll see my point of view in time.'

' I think, Mr. Hogg, there's nothing to be gained by your coming here. You shall hear from me.'

' Well, as to that, Archdeacon,' Hogg turned from the half-opened door, smiling, ' that's as may be. One can get further sometimes in a little talk

than in a dozen letters.   And I'm really not much
of a letter-writer.   But we'll see 'ow things go on.
Good-evenin'.'

The talk had lasted but five minutes, and every
piece of furniture in the room, the chairs, the table,
the carpet, the pictures, seemed to have upon it
some new stain of disfigurement.   Even the windows were dimmed.

Brandon sat staring in front of him.   The door
opened again and his wife came in.

' That was Samuel Hogg who has just left
you ? '

' Yes,' he said.

He looked across the room at her and was
instantly surprised by the strangest feeling.   He
was not, in his daily life, conscious of ' feelings '
of any sort—that was not his way.   But the events
of the past two days seemed to bring him suddenly
into a new contact with real life, as though, having
lived in a balloon all this time, he had been
suddenly bumped out of it with a jerk and found
Mother Earth with a terrible bang.   He would
have told you a week ago that there was nothing
about his wife that he did not know and nothing
about his own feelings towards her—and yet, after
all, the most that he had known was to have no
especial feelings towards her of any kind.

But to-day had been beyond possible question
the most horrible day he had ever known, and it
might be that the very horror of it was to force
him to look upon everything on earth with new
eyes.   It had at least the immediate effect now of
showing his wife to him as part of himself, as
some one, therefore, hurt as he was, smirched and
soiled and abused as he, needing care and kindness

as he had never known her need it before. It was
a new feeling for him, a new tenderness.

He greeted and welcomed it as a relief after the
horror of Hogg's presence. Poor Amy! She was
in as bad a way as he now—they were at last in the
same box.

'Yes,' he said, 'that was Hogg.'

Looking at her now in this new way, he was also
able to see that she herself was changed. She
figured definitely as an actor now with an odd white
intensity in her face, with some mysterious purpose
in her eyes, with a resolve in the whole poise of
her body that seemed to add to her height.

'Well,' she said, 'what train are you taking up
to London?'

'What train?' he repeated after her.

'Yes, to see Falk.'

'I am not going to see Falk.'

'You're not going up to him?'

'Why should I go?'

'Why should you go? *You* can ask me that?
. . . To stop this terrible marriage.'

'I don't intend to stop it.'

There was a pause. She seemed to summon
every nerve in her body to her control.

The twitching of her fingers against her dress
was her only movement.

'Would you please tell me what you mean to
do? After all, I am his mother.'

The tenderness that he had felt at first sight of
her was increasing so strangely that it was all he
could do not to go over to her. But his horror of
any demonstration kept him where he was.

'Amy, dear,' he said, 'I've had a dreadful day—
in every way a terrible day. I haven't had time,

as things have gone, to think things out. I want
to be fair. I want to do the right thing. I do
indeed. I don't think there's anything to be
gained by going up to London. One thing only
now I'm clear about. He's got to marry the girl
now he's gone off with her. To do him justice he
intends to do that. He says that he has done her
no harm, and we must take his word for that. Falk
has been many things—careless, reckless, selfish,
but never in all his life dishonourable. If I went
up now we should quarrel, and perhaps something
irreparable would occur. Even though he was
persuaded to return, the mischief is done. He
must be just to the girl. Every one in the town
knows by now that she went with him—her father
has been busy proclaiming the news even though
there has been no one else.'

Mrs. Brandon said nothing. She had made in
herself the horrible discovery, after reading Falk's
letter, that her thoughts were not upon Falk at all,
but upon Morris. Falk had flouted her ; not only
had he not wanted her, but he had gone off with a
common girl of the town. She had suddenly no
tenderness for him, no anger against him, no
thought of him except that his action had removed
the last link that held her.

She was gazing now at Morris with all her eyes.
Her brain was fastened upon him with an intensity
sufficient almost to draw him, hypnotised, there to
her feet. Her husband, her - home, Polchester,
these things were like dim shadows.

' So you will do nothing ? ' she said.

' I must wait,' he said, ' I know that when I act
hastily I act badly. . . . ' He paused, looked at
her doubtfully, then with great hesitation went on :

'We are together in this, Amy.   I've been—I've
been—thinking of myself and my work perhaps
too much in the past.   We've got to see this through
together.'

'Yes,' she answered, 'together.'   But she was
thinking of Morris.

CHAPTER VIII

THE WIND FLIES OVER THE HOUSE

LATER, that day, she went from the house. It was a strange evening. Two different weathers seemed to have met over the Polchester streets. First there was the deep serene beauty of the May day, pale blue faintly fading into the palest yellow, the world lying like an enchanted spirit asleep within a glass bell, reflecting the light from the shining surface that enfolded it. In this light houses, grass, cobbles lay as though stained by a painter's brush, bright colours like the dazzling pigment of a wooden toy, glittering under the shining sky.

This was a normal enough evening for the Polchester May, but across it, shivering it into fragments, broke a stormy and blustering wind, a wind that belonged to stormy January days, cold and violent, with the hint of rain in its murmuring voice. It tore through the town, sometimes carrying hurried and, as it seemed, terrified clouds with it ; for a while the May light would be hidden, the air would be chill, a few drops like flashes of glass would fall, gleaming against the bright colours—then suddenly the sky would be again unchallenged blue, there would be no cloud on the horizon, only the pavements would glitter as though reflecting a glassy dome. Sometimes it would be more than one cloud that the wind would carry on its track—a company of clouds ; they would appear suddenly above the horizon, like white-faced giants peering over the world's rim, then in a huddled confusion they would gather together, then start their flight, separating, joining, merging, dwindling and expanding, swallowing up the blue, threatening to encompass the pale saffron of the lower sky, then vanishing with incredible swiftness, leaving warmth and colour in their train.

Amy Brandon did not see the enchanted town. She heard, as she left the house, the clocks striking half-past six. Some regular subconscious self, working with its accustomed daily duty, murmured to her that to-night her husband was dining at the Conservative Club and Joan was staying on to supper at the Sampsons' after the opening tennis party of the season. No one would need her— as so often in the past no one had needed her. But it was her unconscious self that whispered this to her ; in the wild stream into whose current during these last strange months she had flung herself she was carried along she knew not, she cared not, whither.

Enough for her that she was free now to encompass her desire, the only dominating devastating desire that she had ever known in all her dead, well-ordered life. But it was not even with so active a consciousness as this that she thought this out. She thought out nothing save that she must see Morris, be with Morris, catch from Morris that sense of appeasement from the torture of hunger unsatisfied that never now left her.

In the last weeks she had grown so regardless of

the town's opinion that she did not care how many people saw her pass Morris's door. She had, perhaps, been always regardless, only in the dull security of her life there had been no need to regard them. She despised them all; she had always despised them, for the deference and admiration that they paid her husband if for no other reason. Despised them too, it might be, because they had not seen more in herself, had thought her the dull, lifeless nonentity in whose soul no fires had ever burned.

She had never chattered nor gossiped with them, did not consider gossip a factor in any one's day; she had never had the least curiosity about any one else, whether about life or character or motive.

There is no egoist in the world so complete as the disappointed woman without imagination.

She hurried through the town as though she were on a business of the utmost urgency; she saw nothing and she heard nothing. She did not even see Miss Milton sitting at her half-opened window enjoying the evening air.

Morris himself opened the door. He was surprised when he saw her; when he had closed the door and helped her off with her coat he said as they walked into the drawing-room:

'Is there anything the matter?'

She saw at once that the room was cheerless and deserted.

'Is Miss Burnett here?' she asked.

'No. She went off to Rafiel for a week's holiday. I'm being looked after by the cook.'

'It's cold.' She drew her shoulders and arms together, shivering.

'Yes. It *is* cold. It's these showers. Shall I light the fire?'

'Yes, do.'

He bent down, putting a match to the paper; then when the fire blazed he pushed the sofa forwards.

'Now sit down and tell me what's the matter.'

She could see that he was extremely nervous.

'Have you heard nothing?'

'No.'

She laughed bitterly. 'I thought all the town knew by this time.'

'Knew what?'

'Falk has run away to London with the daughter of Samuel Hogg.'

'Samuel Hogg?'

'Yes, the man of "The Dog and Pilchard" down in Seatown.'

'Run away with her?'

'Yesterday. He sent us a letter saying that he had gone up to London to earn his own living, had taken this girl with him, and would marry her next week.'

Morris was horrified.

'Without a word of warning? Without speaking to you? Horrible! The daughter of that man. . . . I know something about him . . . the worst man in the place.'

Then followed a long silence. The effect on Morris was as it had been on Mrs. Brandon—the actual deed was almost lost sight of in the sudden light that it threw on his passion. From the very first the most appealing element of her attraction to him had been her loneliness, the neglect from which she suffered, the need she had of comfort.

He saw her as a woman who, for twenty years, had had no love, although in her very nature she had hungered for it; and if she had not been treated with actual cruelty, at least she had been so basely neglected that cruelty was not far away. It was not true to say that during these months he had grown to hate Brandon, but he had come, more and more, to despise and condemn him. The effeminacy in his own nature had from the first both shrunk from and been attracted by the masculinity in Brandon.

He could have loved that man, but as the situation had forbidden that, his feeling now was very near to hate.

Then, as the weeks had gone by, Mrs. Brandon had made it clear enough to him that Falk was all that she had left to her—not very much to her even there, perhaps, but something to keep her starved heart from dying. And now Falk was gone, gone in the most brutal, callous way. She had no one in the world left to her but himself. The rush of tenderness and longing to be good to her that now overwhelmed him was so strong and so sudden that it was with the utmost difficulty that he held himself from going to the sofa beside her.

She looked so weak there, so helpless, so gentle.

' Amy,' he said, ' I will do anything in the world that is in my power.'

She was trembling, partly with genuine emotion, partly with cold, partly with the drama of the situation.

' No,' she said, ' I don't want to do a thing that's going to involve you. You must be left out of this. It is something that I must carry through

by myself. It was wrong of me, I suppose, to
come to you, but my first thought was that I must
have companionship. I was selfish——'

'No,' he broke in, 'you were not selfish. I
am prouder that you came to me than I can possibly
say. That is what I'm here for. I'm your friend.
You know, after all these months, that I am. And
what is a friend for?' Then, as though he felt
that he was advancing too dangerously close to
emotion, he went on more quietly :

'Tell me—if it isn't impertinent of me to ask—
what is your husband doing about it?'

'Doing? Nothing.'

'Nothing?'

'No. I thought that he would go up to London
and see Falk, but he doesn't feel that that is necessary.
He says that, as Falk has run away with the girl, the
most decent thing that he can do is to marry her.
He seems very little upset by it. He is a most
curious man. After all these years, I don't understand him at all.'

Morris went on hesitatingly. 'I feel guilty
myself. Weeks ago I overheard gossip about your
son and some girl. I wondered then whether I
ought to say something to you. But it's so difficult
in these cases to know what one ought to do.
There's so much gossip in these little Cathedral
towns. I thought about it a good deal. Finally, I
decided that it wasn't my place to meddle.'

'I heard nothing,' she answered. 'It's always
the family that hears the talk last. Perhaps my
husband's right. Perhaps there is nothing to be
done. I see now that Falk never cared anything
for any of us. I cheated myself. I had to cheat
myself, otherwise I don't know what I'd have done.

And now his doing this has made me suspicious of everything and of every one. Yes, even of a friendship like ours—the greatest thing in my life —now—the only thing in my life.'

Her voice trembled and dropped. But still he would not let himself pass on to that other ground. ' Is there *nothing* I can do ? ' he asked. ' I suppose it would be no good if I were to go up to London and see him ? I knew him a little—— '

Vehemently she shook her head.

' You're not to be involved in this. At least I can do that much—keep you out of it.'

' How is he going to live, then ? '

' He talks about writing. He's utterly confident, of course. He always has been. Looking back now, I despise myself for ever imagining that *I* was of any use to him. I see now that he never needed me—never at all.'

Suddenly she looked across at him sharply.

' How is your sister-in-law ? ' His colour rose.

' My sister-in-law ? '

' Yes.'

' She isn't well.'

' What—— ? '

' It's hard to say. The doctor looked at her and said she needed quiet and must go to the sea. It's her nerves.'

' Her nerves ? '

' Yes, they got very queer. She's been sleeping badly.'

' You quarrelled.'

' She and I ?—yes.'

' What about ? '

' Oh, I don't know. She's getting a little too much for me, I think.'

She looked him in the face.

'No, you know it isn't that. You quarrelled about me.'

He said nothing.

'You quarrelled about me,' she repeated. 'She always disliked me from the beginning.'

'No.'

'Oh yes, she did. Of course I saw that. She was jealous of me. She saw, more quickly than any one else, how much—how much we were going to mean to one another. Speak the truth. You know that *is* the best.'

'She didn't understand,' Morris answered slowly. 'She's stupid in some things.'

'So I've been the cause of your quarrelling, of your losing the only friend you had in your life?'

'No, not of my losing it. I haven't lost her. Our relationship has shifted, that's all.'

'No. No. I know it is so. I've taken away the only person near you.'

And suddenly turning from him to the back of the sofa, hiding her face in her hands, she broke into passionate crying.

He stood for a moment, taut, controlled, as though he was fighting his last little desperate battle. Then he was beaten. He knelt down on the floor beside the sofa. He touched her hair, then her cheek. She made a little movement towards him. He put his arms around her.

'Don't cry. Don't cry. I can't bear that. You mustn't say that you've taken anything from me. It isn't true. You've given me everything . . . everything. Why should we struggle any longer? Why shouldn't we take what has been given to us? Your husband doesn't care. I haven't anybody. Has God given me so much that I should miss this? And has He put it in our hearts if He didn't mean us to take it? I love you. I've loved you since first I set eyes on you. I can't keep away from you any longer. It's keeping away from myself. We're one. We *are* one another—not alone, either of us—any more. . . .'

She turned towards him. He drew her closer and closer to him. With a little sigh of happiness and comfort she yielded to him.

There was only one cloud in the dim green sky, a cloud orange and crimson, shaped like a ship. As the sun was setting, a little wind stirred, the faint aftermath of the storm of the day, and the cloud, now all crimson, passed over the town and died in fading ribbons of gold and orange in the white sky of the far horizon.

Only Miss Milton, perhaps, among all the citizens of the town, waiting patiently behind her open window, watched its career.

CHAPTER IX

THE QUARREL

EVERY one has known, at one time or another in life, that strange unexpected calm that always falls like sudden snow on a storm-tossed country, after some great crisis or upheaval. The blow has seemed so catastrophic that the world must be changed with the force of its fall—but the world is *not* changed ; hours pass and days go by, and no one seems to be aware that anything has occurred . . . it is only when months have gone, and perhaps years, that one looks back and sees that it was, after all, on such and such a day that life was altered, values shifted, the face of the world turned to a new angle.

This is platitudinous, but platitudes are not platitudes when we first make our personal experience of them. There seemed nothing platitudinous to Brandon in his present experiences. The day on which he had received Falk's letter had seemed to fling him neck and crop into a new world—a world dim and obscure and peopled with new and terrifying devils. The morning after, he was clear again, and it was almost as though nothing at all had occurred. He went about the town, and everybody behaved in a normal manner. No sign of those strange menacing figures, the drunken painter, the sinister smiling Hogg ; every one as usual.

Ryle complacent and obedient; Bentinck-Major officious but subservient ; Mrs. Combermere jolly ; even, as he fancied, Foster a little more amiable than usual. It was for this open outside world that he had now for many years been living ; it was not difficult to tell himself that things here were unchanged. Because he was no psychologist, he took people as he found them ; when they smiled they were pleased and when they frowned they were angry.

Because there was a great deal of pressing business he pushed aside Falk's problem. It was there, it was waiting for him, but perhaps time would solve it.

He concentrated himself with a new energy, a new self-confidence, upon the Cathedral, the Jubilee, the public life of the town.

Nevertheless, that horrible day had had its effect upon him. Three days after Falk's escape he was having breakfast alone with Joan.

'Mother has a headache,' Joan said. 'She's not coming down.'

He nodded, scarcely looking up from his paper.

In a little while she said : ' What are you doing to-day, daddy ? I'm very sorry to bother you, but I'm housekeeping to-day, and I have to arrange about meals——'

'I'm lunching at Carpledon,' he said, putting his paper down.

'With the Bishop ? How nice ! I wish I were. He's an old dear.'

'He wants to consult me about some of the Jubilee services,' Brandon said in his public voice.

' Won't Canon Ryle mind that ? '

' I don't care if he does. It's his own fault, for not managing things better.'

' I think the Bishop must be very lonely out there. He hardly ever comes into Polchester now. It's because of his rheumatism, I suppose. Why doesn't he resign, daddy ? '

' He's wanted to, a number of times. But he's very popular. People don't want him to go.'

' I don't wonder.' Joan's eyes sparkled. ' Even if one never saw him at all it would be better than somebody else. He's *such* an old darling.'

' Well, I don't believe myself in men going on when they're past their work. However, I hear he's going to insist on resigning at the end of this year.'

' How old is he, daddy ? '

' Eighty-seven.'

There was always a tinge of patronage in the Archdeacon's voice when he spoke of his Bishop. He knew that he was a saint, a man whose life had been of so absolute a purity, a simplicity, an unfaltering faith and courage, that there were no flaws to be found in him anywhere. It was possibly this very simplicity that stirred Brandon's patronage. After all, we were living in a workaday world, and the Bishop's confidence in every man's word and trust in every man's honour had been at times a little ludicrous. Nevertheless, did any one dare to attack the Bishop, he was immediately his most ardent and ferocious defender.

It was only when the Bishop was praised that he felt that a word or two of caution was necessary.

However, he was just now not thinking of the Bishop ; he was thinking of his daughter. As he looked across the table at her he wondered. What had Falk's betrayal of the family meant to her ? Had she been fond of him ? She had given no sign at all as to how it had affected her. She had her friends and her life in the town, and her family pride like the rest of them. How pretty she looked this morning ! He was suddenly aware of the love and devotion that she had given him for years and the small return that he had made. Not that he had been a bad father—he hurriedly reassured himself ; no one could accuse him of that. But he had been busy, preoccupied, had not noticed her as he might have done. She was a woman now, with a new independence and self-assurance ! And yet such a child at the same time ! He recalled the evening in the cab when she had held his hand. How few demands she ever made upon him ; how little she was ever in the way !

He went back to his paper, but found that he could not fix his attention upon it. When he had finished his breakfast he went across to her. She looked up at him smiling. He put his hand on her shoulder.

'Um—yes. . . . And what are you going to do to-day, dear ? '

' I've heaps to do. There's the Jubilee work-party in the morning. Then there are one or two things in the town to get for mother.' She paused.

He hesitated, then said :

' Has any one—have your friends in the town—said anything about Falk ? '

She looked up at him.

" No, daddy—not a word.'

Then she added, as though to herself, with a little sigh : ' Poor Falk ! '

He took his hand from her shoulder.

' So you're sorry for him, are you ? ' he said angrily.

' Not sorry, exactly,' she answered slowly. ' But —you will forgive him, won't you ? '

' You can be sure,' Brandon said, ' that I shall do what is right.'

She sprang up and faced him.

' Daddy, now that Falk is gone, it's more necessary than ever for you to realise *me*.'

' Realise you ? ' he said, looking at her.

' Yes, that I'm a woman now and not a child any longer. You don't realise it a bit. I said it to mother months ago, and told her that now I could do all sorts of things for her. She *has* let me do a few things, but she hasn't changed to me, not been any different, or wanted me any more than she did before. But you must. You *must*, daddy. I can help you in lots of ways. I can——'

' What ways ? ' he asked her, smiling.

' I don't know. You must find them out. What I mean is that you've got to count on me as an element in the family now. You can't disregard me any more.'

' Have I disregarded you ? '

' Of course you have,' she answered, laughing.

' Well, we'll see,' he said. He bent down and kissed her, then left the room.

He left to catch the train to Carpledon in a self-satisfied mind. He was tired, certainly, and had felt ever since the shock of three days back a certain ' warning ' sensation that hovered over him rather like hot air, suggesting that sudden agonizing pain . . . but so long as the pain did not come. . . . He had thought, half derisively, of seeing old Puddifoot, even of having himself overhauled—but Puddifoot was

an ass. How could a man who talked the nonsense
Puddifoot did in the Conservative Club be anything
of a doctor ? Besides, the man was old. There
was a young man now, Newton. But Brandon
distrusted young men.

He was amused and pleased at the station. He
strode up and down the platform, his hands behind
his broad back, his head up, his top-hat shining, his
gaiters fitting superbly his splendid calves. The
station-master touched his hat, smiled, and stayed
for a word or two. Very deferential. Good
fellow, Curtis. Knew his business. The little
stout rosy-faced fellow who guarded the book-stall
also touched his hat. Brandon stopped and looked
at the papers. Advertisements already of special
Jubilee supplements—' Life of the Good Queen,'
' History of the Empire, 1837–1897.' Piles of
that trashy novel Joan had been talking about,
The Massarenes, by Ouida. Pah ! Stuff and
nonsense. How did people have time for such
things ? ' Yes, Mr. Waller. Fine day. Very
fine May we're having. Ought to be fine for the
Jubilee. Hope so, I'm sure. Disappoint many
people if it's wet. . . .'

He bought the *Church Times* and crossed to the
side-line. No one here but a farmer, a country-
woman and her little boy. The farmer's side-face
reminded him suddenly of some one. Who was it ?
That fat cheek, the faint sandy hair beneath the
shabby bowler. He was struck as though, standing
on a tight-rope in mid-air, he felt it quiver beneath
him. Hogg. . . . He turned abruptly and faced
the empty line and the dusty neglected boarding of
a railway-shed. He must not think of that man,
must not allow him to seize his thoughts. Hogg—

Davray. Had he dreamt that horrible scene in the Cathedral ? Could that have been ? He lifted his hand and, as it were, tore the scene into pieces and scattered it on the line. He had command of his thoughts, shutting down one little tight shutter after another upon the things he did not want to see. *That* he did not want to see, did not want to know.

The little train drew in, slowly, regretfully. Brandon got into the solitary first-class carriage and buried himself in his paper. Soon, thanks to his happy gift of attending only to one question at a time, the subjects that that paper brought up for discussion completely absorbed him. Anything more absurd than such an argument !—as though the validity of Baptism did not absolutely depend . . .

He was happily lost ; the little train steamed out. He saw nothing of the beautiful country through which they passed—country, on this May morning, so beautiful in its rich luxuriant security, the fields bending and dipping to the tree-haunted streams, the hedges running in lines of blue and dark purple like ribbons to the sky, that, blue-flecked, caught in light and shadow a myriad pattern as a complement to its own sun-warmed clouds. Rich and English so utterly that it was almost scornful in its resentment of foreign interference. In spite of the clouds the air was now in its mid-day splendour, and the cows, in clusters of brown, dark and clay-red, sought the cool grey shadows of the hedges.

The peace of centuries lay upon this land, and the sun with loving hands caressed its warm flanks as though here, at least, was some one of whom it might be sure, some one known from old time.

The little station at Carpledon was merely a

wooden shed. Woods running down the hill threatened to overwhelm it ; at its very edge beyond the line, thick green fields slipped to the shining level waters of the Pol. Brandon walked up the hill through the wood, past the hedge and on through the Park to the Palace drive. The sight of that old red thick-set building with its square comfortable windows, its bell-tower, its dovecots, its graceful stolid happy lines, its high old doorway, its tiled roof rosy-red with age, respectability and comfort, its square solemn chimneys behind and between whose self-possession the broad branches of the oaks, older and wiser than the house itself, uplifted their clustered leaves with the protection of their conscious dignity—this house thrilled all that was deepest and most superstitious in his soul.

To this building he would bow, to this house surrender. Here was something that would command all his reverence, a worthy adjunct to the Cathedral that he loved ; without undue pride he must acknowledge to himself that, had fate so willed it, he would himself have occupied this place with a worthy and fitting appropriateness. It seemed, indeed, as he pulled the iron bell and heard its clang deep within the house, that he understood what it needed so well that it must sigh with a dignified relief when it saw him approach.

Appleford the butler, who opened the door, was an old friend of his—an aged, white-locked man, but dignity itself.

' His lordship will be down in a moment,' he said, showing him into the library. Some one else was there, his back to the door. He turned round ; it was Ronder.

When Brandon saw him he had again that sense

that came now to him so frequently, that some plot was in process against him and gradually, step by step, hedging him in. That is a dangerous sense for any human being to acquire, but more especially for a man of Brandon's simplicity, almost naïveté of character.

Ronder ! The very last man whom Brandon could bear to see in that place and at that time ! Brandon's visit to-day was not entirely unengineered. To be honest, he had not spoken quite the truth to his daughter when he had said that the Bishop had asked him out there for consultation. Himself had written to the Bishop a very strong letter, emphasising the inadequacy with which his Jubilee services were being prepared, saying something about the suitability of Forsyth for the Pybus living, and hinting at certain carelessnesses in the Chapter 'due to new and regrettable influences.' It was in answer to this letter that Ponting, the Resident Chaplain, had written saying that the Bishop would like to give Brandon luncheon. It may be said, therefore, that Brandon wished to consult the Bishop rather than the Bishop Brandon. The Archdeacon had pictured to himself a cosy *tête-à-tête* with the Bishop lasting for an hour or two, and entirely uninterrupted. He flattered himself that he knew his dear Bishop well enough by this time to deal with him exactly as he ought to be dealt with. But, for that dealing, privacy was absolutely essential. Any third person would have been, to the last extent, provoking. Ronder was disastrous. He instantly persuaded himself, as he looked at that rubicund and smiling figure, that Ronder had heard of his visit and determined to be one of the party. He could only have heard of it through Ponting. . . .

The Archdeacon's fingers twisted within one another as he considered how pleasant it would be to wring Ponting's long, white and ecclesiastical neck.

And, of course, behind all this immediate situation was his sense of the pleasure and satisfaction that Ronder must be feeling about Falk's scandal. Licking his thick red lips about it, he must be, watching with his little fat eyes for the moment when, with his round fat fingers, he might probe that wound.

Nevertheless the Archdeacon knew by this time Ronder's character and abilities too well not to realise that he must dissemble. Dissembling was the hardest thing of all that a man of the Archdeacon's character could be called upon to perform, but dissemble he must.

His smile was of a grim kind.

'Ha! Ronder; didn't expect to see you here.'

'No,' said Ronder, coming forward and smiling with the utmost geniality. 'To tell you the truth, I didn't expect to find myself here. It was only last evening that I got a note from the Bishop asking me to come out to luncheon to-day. He said that you would be here.'

Oh, so Ponting was not to blame. It was the Bishop himself. Poor old man! Cowardice obviously, afraid of some of the home-truths that Brandon might find it his duty to deliver. A coward in his old age. . . .

'Very fine day,' said Brandon.

'Beautiful,' said Ronder. 'Really looks as though we are going to have good weather for the Jubilee.'

'Hope we do,' said Brandon. 'Very hard on thousands of people if it's wet.'

'Very,' said Ronder. 'I hope Mrs. Brandon is well.'

'To-day she has a little headache,' said Brandon. 'But it's really nothing.'

'Well,' said Ronder. 'I've been wondering whether there isn't some thunder in the air. I've been feeling it oppressive myself.'

'It does get oppressive,' said Brandon, 'this time of year in Glebeshire—especially South Glebeshire. I've often noticed it.'

'What we want,' said Ronder, 'is a good thunderstorm to clear the air.'

'Just what we're not likely to get,' said Brandon. 'It hangs on for days and days without breaking.'

'I wonder why that is,' said Ronder; 'there are no hills round about to keep it. There's hardly a hill of any size in the whole of South Glebeshire.'

'Of course, Polchester's in a hollow,' said Brandon. 'Except for the Cathedral, of course. I always envy Lady St. Leath her elevation.'

'A fine site, the Castle,' said Ronder. 'They must get a continual breeze up there.'

'They do,' said Brandon. 'Whenever I'm up there there's a wind.'

This most edifying conversation was interrupted by the entrance of the Reverend Charles Ponting. Mr. Ponting was very long, very thin and very black, his cadaverous cheeks resembling in their colour nothing so much as good fountain-pen ink. He spoke always in a high, melancholy and chanting voice. He was undoubtedly effeminate in his movements, and he had an air of superior secrecy about the affairs of the Bishop that people sometimes found very trying. But he was a good man and a zealous, and entirely devoted to his lord and master.

'Ha! Archdeacon. . . . Ha! Canon. His lordship will be down in one moment. He has asked me to make his apologies for not being here to receive you. He is just finishing something of rather especial importance.'

The Bishop, however, entered a moment later. He was a little frail man, walking with the aid of a stick. He had snow-white hair, rather thick and long, pale cheeks and eyes of a bright china-blue. He had that quality, given to only a few in this world of happy mediocrities, of filling, at once, any room into which he entered with the strength and fragrance of his spirit. So strong, fearless and beautiful was his soul that it shone through the frail compass of his body with an unfaltering light. No one had ever doubted the goodness and splendour of the man's character. Men might call his body old and feeble and past the work that it was still called upon to perform. They might speak of him as guileless, as too innocent of this world's slippery ways, as trusting where no child of six years of age would have trusted — these things might have been, and were, said ; but no man, woman, or child, looking upon him, hesitated to realise that here was some one who had walked and talked with God and in whom there was no shadow of deceit or evil thought. Old Glasgow Parmiter, the lawyer, the wickedest old man Polchester had ever known, said once of him, ' If there's a hell, I suppose I'm going to it, and I'm sure I don't care. There may be one and there may not. I know there's a heaven. Purcell lives there.'

His voice, which was soft and strong, had at its heart a tiny stammer which came out now and then with a hesitating, almost childish, charm. As he stood there, leaning on his stick, smiling at them, there did seem a great deal of the child about him, and Brandon, Ponting and Ronder suddenly seemed old, wicked and soiled in the world's ways.

'Please forgive me,' he said, 'for not being down when you came. I move slowly now. . . . Luncheon is ready, I know. Shall we go in ?'

The four men crossed the stone-flagged hall into the dining-room where Appleford stood, devoutly, as one about to perform a solemn rite. The dining-room was high-ceilinged with a fireplace of old red brick fronted with black oak beams. The walls were plain whitewash, and they carried only one picture, a large copy of Dürer's " Knight and the Devil." The high, broad windows looked out on to the sloping lawn whose green now danced and sparkled under the sun. The trees that closed it in were purple shadowed.

They sat, clustered together, at the end of a long oak refectory table. The Bishop himself was a teetotaler, but there was good claret and, at the end, excellent port. The only piece of colour on the table was a bowl of dark-blue glass piled with fruit. The only ornament in the room was a beautifully carved silver crucifix on the black oak mantelpiece. The sun danced across the stained floor with every pattern and form of light.

Brandon could not remember a more unpleasant meal in that room ; he could not, indeed, remember ever having had an unpleasant meal there before. The Bishop talked, as he always did, in a most pleasant and easy fashion. He talked about the nectarines and plums that were soon to glorify his garden walls, about the pears and apples in his orchard, about the jokes that old Puddifoot made

when he came over and examined his rheumatic
limbs. He gently chaffed Ponting about his
punctuality, neatness and general dislike of violent
noises, and he bade Appleford to tell the housekeeper, Mrs. Brenton, how especially good to-day
was the fish soufflé. All this was all it had ever
been ; nothing could have been easier and more
happy. But on other days it had always been
Brandon who had thrown back the ball for the
Bishop to catch. Whoever the other guest might
be, it was always Brandon who took the lead, and
although he might be a little ponderous and slow
in movement, he supplied the Bishop's conversational
needs quite adequately.

And to-day it was Ronder ; from the first,
without any ostentation or presumption, with the
utmost naturalness, he led the field. To understand
the full truth of this occasion it must be known
that Mr. Ponting had, for a considerable number
of years past, cherished a deep but private detesta-
tion of the Archdeacon. It was hard to say wherein
that hatred had had its inception—probably in some
old, long-forgotten piece of cheerful patronage on
Brandon's part ; Mr. Ponting was of those who
consider and dwell and dwell again, and he had,
by this time, dwelt upon the Archdeacon so long
and so thoroughly that he knew and resented the
colour of every one of the Archdeacon's waistcoat
buttons. He was, perhaps, quick to perceive
to-day that a mightier than the Archdeacon was
here ; or it may have been that he was well aware
of what had been happening in Polchester during
the last weeks, and was even informed of the
incidents of the last three days.

However that may be, he did from the first

pay an almost exaggerated deference to Ronder's opinion, drew him into the conversation at every possible opportunity, with such interjections as ' How true ! How very true ! Don't you think so, Canon Ronder ? ' or ' What has been your experience in such a case, Canon Ronder ? ' or ' I think, my lord, that Canon Ronder told me that he knows that place well,' and disregarding entirely any remarks that Brandon might happen to make.

No one could have responded more brilliantly to this opportunity than did Ronder ; indeed the Bishop, who was his host at the Palace to-day for the first time, said after his departure, ' That's a most able man, most able. Lucky indeed for the diocese that it has secured him . . . a delightful fellow.'

No one in the world could have been richer in anecdotes than Ronder, anecdotes of precisely the kind for the Bishop's taste, not too worldly, not too clerical, amusing without being broad, light and airy, but showing often a fine scholarship and a wise and thoughtful experience of foreign countries. The Bishop had not laughed so heartily for many a day. ' Oh dear ! Oh dear ! ' he cried at the anecdote of the two American ladies in Siena. ' That's good, indeed . . . that's very good. Did you get that, Ponting ? Dear me, that's perfectly delightful ! ' A little tear of shining pleasure trickled down his cheek. ' Really, Canon, I've never heard anything better.'

Brandon thought Ronder's manners outrageous. Poor Bishop ! He was indeed failing that he could laugh so heartily at such pitiful humour. He tried to show his sense of it all by grimly pursuing his food and refusing even the ghost of a chuckle, but

no one was perceiving him, as he very bitterly saw.
The Bishop, it may be, saw it too, for at last he turned
to Brandon and said:

'But come, Archdeacon. I was forgetting.
You wrote to me s-something about that Jubilee
music in the Cathedral. You find that Ryle is
making rather a m-mess of things, don't you ? '

Brandon was deeply offended. Of what was the
Bishop thinking that he could so idly drag forward
the substance of an entirely private letter, without
asking permission, into the public air ? Moreover,
the last thing that he wanted was that Ronder
should know that he had been working behind
Ryle's back. Not that he was in the least ashamed
of what he had done, but here was precisely the thing
that Ronder would like to use and make something
of. In any case, it was the principle of the thing.
Was Ronder henceforth to be privy to everything
that passed between himself and the Bishop ?

He never found it easy to veil his feelings, and
he looked now, as Ponting delightedly perceived,
like an overgrown sulky schoolboy.

'No, no, my lord,' he said, looking across at
Ponting, as though he would love to set his heel
upon that pale but eager visage. 'You have me
wrong there. I was making no complaint. The
Precentor knows his own business best.'

'You certainly said something in your letter,'
said the Bishop vaguely. 'There was s-something,
Ponting, was there not ? '

'Yes, my lord,' said Ponting. 'There was.
But I expect the Archdeacon did not mean it very
seriously.'

'Do you mean that you find the Precentor
inefficient ? ' said the Bishop, looking at the coffee

with longing and then shaking his head. 'Not to-day, Appleford, alas—not to-day.'

'Oh no,' said Brandon, colouring. 'Of course not. Our tastes differ a little as to the choice of music, that's all. I've no doubt that I am old-fashioned.'

'How do you find the Cathedral music, Canon ?' he asked, turning to Ronder.

'Oh, I know very little about it,' said Ronder, smiling. 'Nothing in comparison with the Arch-deacon. I'm sure he's right in liking the old music that people have grown used to and are fond of. At the same time, I must confess that I haven't thought Ryle too venturesome. But then I'm very ignorant, having been here so short a time.'

'That's right, then,' said the Bishop comfortably. 'There doesn't seem much wrong.'

At that moment Appleford, who had been absent from the room for a minute, returned with a note which he gave to the Bishop.

'From Pybus, my lord,' he said ; 'some one has ridden over with it.'

At the word 'Pybus' there was an electric silence in the room. The Bishop tore open the letter and read it. He half started from his chair with a little exclamation of distress and grief.

'Please excuse me,' he said, turning to them. 'I must leave you for a moment and speak to the bearer of this note. Poor Morrison . . . at last . . . he's gone !—Pybus ! . . .'

The Archdeacon, in spite of himself, half rose and stared across at Ronder. Pybus ! The living at last was vacant.

A moment later he felt deeply ashamed　In

that sunlit room the bright green of the outside
world quivering in pools of colour upon the pure
space of the white walls spoke of life and beauty
and the immortality of beauty.

It was hard to think of death there in such a place,
but one must think of it and consider, too, Morrison,
who had been so good a fellow and loved the world,
and all the things in it, and had thought of heaven
also in the spare moments that his energy left
him.

A great sportsman he had been, with a famous
breed of bull-terrier, and anxious to revive the
South Glebeshire Hunt ; very fine, too, in that last
terrible year when the worst of all mortal diseases
had leapt upon his throat and shaken him with
agony and the imminent prospect of death—shaken
him but never terrified him. Brandon summoned
before him that broad, jolly, laughing figure,
summoned it, bowed to its fortitude and optimism,
then, as all men must, at such a moment, considered
his own end ; then, having paid his due to Morrison,
returned to the great business of the—Living.

They were gathered together in the hall now.
The Bishop had known Morrison well and greatly
liked him, and he could think of nothing but the
man himself. The question of the succession could
not come near him that day, and as he stood, a little
white-haired figure, tottering on his stick in the
flagged hall, he seemed already to be far from the
others, to be caught already half-way along the road
that Morrison was now travelling.

Both Brandon and Ronder felt that it was right
for them to go, although on a normal day they would
have stayed walking in the garden and talking for
another three-quarters of an hour until it was time

to catch the three-thirty train from Carpledon. Mr.
Ponting settled the situation.

'His lordship,' he said, ' hopes that you will let
Bassett drive you into Polchester. There is the
little wagonette ; Bassett must go, in any case, to
get some things. It is no trouble, no trouble at all.'

They, of course, agreed, although for Brandon
at any rate there would be many things in the world
pleasanter than sitting with Ronder in a small
wagonette for more than an hour. He also had no
liking for Bassett, the Bishop's coachman for the
last twenty years, a native of South Glebeshire, with
all the obstinacy, pride and independence that that
definition includes.

There was, however, no other course, and, a
quarter of an hour later, the two clergymen found
themselves opposite one another in a wagonette that
was indeed so small that it seemed inevitable that
Ronder's knees must meet Brandon's and Brandon's
ankles glide against Ronder's.

The Archdeacon's temper was, by this time, at its
worst. Everything had been ruined by Ronder's
presence. The original grievances were bad
enough—the way in which his letter had been flouted,
the fashion in which his conversation had been disregarded at luncheon, the sanctified pleasure that
Ponting's angular countenance had expressed at
every check that he had received; but all these
things mattered nothing compared with the fact
that Ronder was present at the news of Morrison's
death.

Had he been alone with the Bishop then, what
an opportunity he would have had ! How exactly
he would have known how to comfort the Bishop,
how tactful and right he would have been in the

words that he used, and what an opportunity finally
for turning the Bishop's mind in the way it should
go, namely, towards Rex Forsyth !

As his knees, place them where he would,
bumped against Ronder's, wrath bubbled in his
heart like boiling water in a kettle. The very
immobility of Bassett's broad back added to the
irritation.

'It's remarkably small for a wagonette,' said
Ronder at last, when some minutes had passed in
silence. 'Further north this would not, I should
think, be called a wagonette at all, but in Glebeshire
there are special names for everything. And then,
of course, we are both big men.'

This comparison was most unfortunate.
Ronder's body was soft and plump, most unmistakably fat. Brandon's was apparently in magnificent condition. It is well known that a large
man in good athletic condition has a deep, overwhelming contempt for men who are fat and soft.
Brandon made no reply. Ronder was determined
to be pleasant.

'Very difficult to keep thin in this part of the
world, isn't it ? Every morning when I look at
myself in the glass I find myself fatter than I was
the day before. Then I say to myself, " I'll give up
bread and potatoes and drink hot water." Hot
water ! Loathsome stuff. Moreover, have you
noticed, Archdeacon, that a man who diets himself
is a perfect nuisance to all his friends and neighbours ? The moment he refuses potatoes his
hostess says to him, " Why, Mr. Smith, not one of
our potatoes ! Out of our own garden ! " And
then he explains to her that he is dieting, whereupon
every one at the table hurriedly recites long and

dreary histories of how they have dieted at one time or another with this or that success. The meal is ruined for yourself and every one else. Now, isn't it so ? What do you do for yourself when you are putting on flesh ? '

' I am not aware,' said Brandon in his most haughty manner, ' that I *am* putting on flesh.'

' Of course I don't mean just now,' answered Ronder, smiling. ' In any case, the jolting of this wagonette is certain to reduce one. Anyway, I agree with you. It's a tiresome subject. There's no escaping fate. We stout men are doomed, I fancy.'

There was a long silence. After Brandon had moved his legs about in every possible direction and found it impossible to escape Ronder's knees, he said :

' Excuse my knocking into you so often, Canon.'

' Oh, that's all right,' said Ronder, laughing. ' This drive comes worse on you than myself, I fancy. You're bonier . . . What a splendid figure the Bishop is ! A great man—really a great man. There's something about a man of that simplicity and purity of character that we lesser men lack. Something out of our grasp altogether.'

' You haven't known him very long, I think,' said Brandon, who considered himself in no way a lesser man than the Bishop.

' No, I have not,' said Ronder, pleasantly amused at the incredible ease with which he was able to make the Archdeacon rise. ' I've never been to Carpledon before to-day. I especially appreciated his inviting me when he was having so old a friend as yourself.'

Another silence. Ronder looked about him ; the afternoon was hot, and little beads of perspiration formed on his forehead. One trickled down his forehead, another into his eye. The road, early in the year though it was, was already dusty, and the high Glebeshire hedges hid the view. The irritation of the heat, the dust and the sense that they were enclosed and would for the rest of their lives jog along, thus, knee to knee, down an eternal road, made Ronder uncomfortable ; when he was uncomfortable he was dangerous. He looked at the fixed obstinacy of the Archdeacon's face and said :

'Poor Morrison ! So he's gone. I never knew him, but he must have been a fine fellow. And the Pybus living is vacant.'

Brandon said nothing.

'An important decision that will be—I beg your pardon. That's my knee again.

'It's to be hoped that they will find a good man.'

'There can be only one possible choice,' said Brandon, planting his hands flat on his knees.

'Really !' said Ronder, looking at the Archdeacon with an air of innocent interest. 'Do tell me, if it isn't a secret, who that is.'

'It's no secret,' said Brandon in a voice of level defiance. 'Rex Forsyth is the obvious man.'

'Really !' said Ronder. 'That *is* interesting. I haven't heard him mentioned. I'm afraid I know very little about him.'

'Know very little about him !' said Brandon indignantly. 'Why, his name has been in every one's mouth for months !'

'Indeed !' said Ronder mildly. 'But then I am, in many ways, sadly out of things. Do tell me about him.'

'It's not for me to tell you,' said Brandon, looking at Ronder with great severity. 'You can find out anything you like from the smallest boy in the town.' This was not polite, but Ronder did not mind. There was a little pause, then he said very amiably :

'I have heard some mention of that man Wistons.'

'What !' cried Brandon in a voice not very far from a shout. 'The fellow who wrote that abominable book, *The Four Creeds* ? '

'I suppose it's the same,' said Ronder gently, rubbing his knee a little.

'That man !' The Archdeacon bounced in his seat. 'That atheist ! The leading enemy of the Church, the man above any who would destroy every institution that the Church possesses !'

'Come, come ! Is it as bad as that ? '

'As bad as that ? Worse ! Much worse ! I take it that you have not read any of his books.'

'Well, I have read one or two !'

'You *have* read them and you can mention his name with patience ? '

'There are several ways of looking at these things——'

'Several ways of looking at atheism ? Thank you, Canon. Thank you very much indeed. I am delighted to have your opinion given so frankly.'

('What an ass the man is !' thought Ronder. 'He's going to lose his temper here in the middle of the road with that coachman listening to every word.')

'You must not take me too literally, Archdeacon,' said Ronder. 'What I meant was that the question whether Wistons is an atheist can be argued from many points of view.'

'It can not ! It can not !' cried Brandon, now shaking with anger. 'There can be no two points of view. " He that is not with me is against me "——'

'Very well then,' said Ronder. 'It can not. There is no more to be said.'

'There *is* more to be said. There is indeed. I am glad, Canon, that at last you have come out into the open. I have been wondering for a long time past when that happy event was to take place. Ever since you came into this town, you have been subverting doctrine, upsetting institutions, destroying the good work that the Cathedral has been doing for many years past. I feel it my duty to tell you this, a duty that no one else is courageous enough to perform——'

'Really, is this quite the place?' said Ronder, motioning with his hand towards Bassett's broad back, and the massive sterns of the two horses that rose and fell, like tubs on a rocking sea.

But Brandon was past caution, past wisdom, past discipline. He could see nothing now but Ronder's two rosy cheeks and the round gleaming spectacles that seemed to catch his words disdainfully and suspend them there in indifference. 'Excuse me. It is time indeed. It is long past the time. If you think that you can come here, a complete stranger, and do what you like with the institutions here, you are mistaken, and thoroughly mistaken. There are those here who have the interests of the place at heart and guard and protect them. Your conceit has blinded you, allow me to tell you, and it's time that you had a more modest estimate of yourself and doings.'

'This really isn't the place,' murmured Ronder, struggling to avoid Brandon's knees.

'Yes, atheism is nothing to you !' shouted the

Archdeacon. 'Nothing at all ! You had better be careful ! I warn you ! '

' *You* had better be careful,' said Ronder, smiling in spite of himself, ' or you will be out of the carriage.'

That smile was the final insult. Brandon jumped up, rocking on his feet. ' Very well, then. You may laugh as you please. You may think it all a very good joke. I tell you it is not. We are enemies, enemies from this moment. You have been never anything *but* my enemy.'

' Do take care, Archdeacon, or you really *will* be out of the carriage.'

' Very well. I will get out of it. I refuse to drive with you another step. I refuse. I refuse.'

' But you can't walk. It's six miles.'

' I will walk ! I will walk ! Stop and let me get out ! Stop, I say ! '

But Bassett, who, according to his back, was as innocent of any dispute as the small birds on the neighbouring tree, drove on.

' Stop, I say. Can't you hear ? ' The Archdeacon plunged forward and pulled Bassett by the collar. ' Stop ! Stop ! ' The wagonette abruptly stopped.

Bassett's amazed face, two wide eyes in a creased and crumpled surface, peered round.

' It's war, I tell you. War ! ' Brandon climbed out.

' But listen, Archdeacon ! You can't ! '

' Drive on ! Drive on ! ' cried Brandon, standing in the road and shaking his umbrella.

The wagonette drove on. It disappeared over the ledge of the hill.

There was a sudden silence. Brandon's anger

pounded up into his head in great waves of constricting passion. These gradually faded. His knees were trembling beneath him. There were new sounds—birds singing, a tiny breeze rustling the hedges. No living soul in sight. He had suddenly a strange impulse to shed tears. What had he been saying? What had he been doing? He did not know what he had said. Another of his tempers. . . .

The pain attacked his head—like a sword, like a sword.

He found a stone and sat down upon it. The pain invaded him like an active personal enemy. Down the road it seemed to him figures were moving —Hogg, Davray—that other world—the dust rose in little clouds.

What had he been doing? His head! Where did this pain come from?

He felt old and sick and weak. He wanted to be at home. Slowly he began to climb the hill. An enemy, silent and triumphant, seemed to step behind him.

BOOK III

JUBILEE

CHAPTER I

It must certainly be difficult for chroniclers of contemporary history to determine significant dates and to define the beginning and end of succeeding periods. But I fancy that any fellow - citizen of mine, if he thinks for a moment, will agree with me that that Jubilee Summer of 1897 was the last manifestation in our town of the separate individual Polchester spirit, of the old spirit that had dwelt in its streets and informed its walls and roofs for hundreds of years past, something as separate and distinct as the smells of Seatown, the chime of the Cathedral bells, the cawing of the Cathedral rooks in the Precinct Elms.

An interesting and, to one reader at least, a pathetic history might be written of the decline and death of that same spirit—not in Polchester alone, but in many another small English town. From the Boer War of 1899 to the Great War of 1914 stretches that destructive period ; the agents of that destruction, the new moneyed classes, the telephone, the telegram, the motor, and last of all, the cinema.

Destruction ? That is, perhaps, too strong a word. We know that that is simply the stepping from one stage to another of the eternal, the immortal cycle. The little hamlet embowered in its protecting trees, defended by its beloved hills, the Rock rising gaunt and naked in its midst; then the Cathedral, the Monks, the Baron's Castle, the feudal rule; then the mighty Bishops and the vast all-encircling power of the Church; then the new merchant age, the Elizabethan salt of adventure; then the cosy seventeenth and eighteenth centuries, with their domesticities, their little cultures, their comfortable religion, their stay-at-home unimaginative festivities.

Throughout the nineteenth century that spirit lingers, gently repulsing the outside world, reproving new doctrine, repressing new movement . . . and the Rock and the Cathedral wait their hours, watching the great sea that, far on the horizon, is bathing its dykes and flooding the distant fields, knowing that the waves are rising higher and higher, and will at last, with full volume, leap upon these little pastures, these green-clad valleys, these tiny hills. And in that day only the Cathedral and the Rock will stand out above the flood.

And this was a Polchester Jubilee. There may have been some consciousness of that little old woman driving in her carriage through the London streets, but in the main the Town suddenly took possession, cried aloud that these festivities were for Herself, that for a week at least the Town would assert Herself, bringing into Her celebration the Cathedral that was her chief glory, but of whom, nevertheless, she was afraid; the Rock upon which she was built, that never changed, the country that surrounded and supported her, the wild men who had belonged to her from time immemorial, the River that encircled her.

That week seemed to many, on looking back, a strangely mad time, days informed with a wildness for which there was no discernible reason—men and women and children were seized that week with some licence that they loved while it lasted, but that they looked back upon with fear when it was over. What had come over them? Who had been grinning at them?

The strange things that occurred that week seemed to have no individual agent. No one was responsible. But life, after that week, was for many people in the town never quite the same again.

On the afternoon of Thursday, June 17, Ronder stood at the window of his study and looked down upon the little orchard, the blazing flowers, the red garden-wall, and the tree-tops on the descending hill, all glazed and sparkling under the hot afternoon sun. As he looked down, seeing nothing, sunk deeply in his own thoughts, he was aware of extreme moral and spiritual discomfort. He moved back from the window, making with his fingers a little gesture of discontent and irritation. He paced his room, stopping absent-mindedly once and again to push in a book that protruded from the shelves, staying to finger things on his writing-table, jolting against a chair with his foot as he moved. At last he flung himself into his deep leather chair and stared fixedly at an old faded silk fire-guard, with its shadowy flowers and dim purple silk, seeing it not at all.

He was angry, and of all things in the world that he hated, he hated most to be that. He had been angry now for several weeks, and, as though it had been a heavy cold that had descended upon him, he woke up every morning expecting to find that his anger had departed—but it had not departed; it showed no signs whatever of departing.

As he sat there he was not thinking of the Jubilee, the one thought at that time of every living soul in Polchester, man, woman and child—he was thinking of no one but Brandon, with whom, to his own deep disgust, he was at last implacably, remorselessly, angry. How many years ago now he had decided that anger and hatred were emotions that every wise man, at all cost to his pride, his impatience, his self-confidence, avoided. Everything could be better achieved without these weaknesses, and for many years he had tutored and trained himself until, at last, he had reached this fine height of superiority. From that height he had suddenly fallen.

It was now three weeks since that luncheon at Carpledon, and in one way or another the quarrel on the road home—the absurd and ludicrous quarrel—had become known to the whole town. Had Brandon revealed it? Or possibly the coachman? Whoever it was, every one now knew and laughed. Laughed! It was that for which Ronder would never forgive Brandon. The man with his childish temper and monstrous conceit had made him into a ludicrous figure. It was true that they were laughing, it seemed, more at Brandon than at himself, but the whole scene was farcical. But beyond this, that incident, trivial though it might be in itself, had thrown the relationship of the two men into dazzling prominence. It was as though they had been publicly announced as antagonists, and now, stripped and prepared, ringed in by the breathless

Town, must vulgarly afford the roughs of the place the fistic exhibition of their lives. It was the publicity that Ronder detested. He had not disliked Brandon—he had merely despised him, and he had taken an infinite pleasure in furthering schemes and ambitions, a little underground maybe, but all for the final benefit of the Town.

And now the blundering fool had brought this blaze down upon them, was indeed rushing round and screaming at his antagonist, shouting to any one who would hear that Ronder was a blackguard and a public menace. It had been whispered—from what source again Ronder did not know—that it was through Ronder's influence that young Falk Brandon had run off to Town with Hogg's daughter. The boy thought the world of Ronder, it was said, and had been to see him and ask his advice. Ronder knew that Brandon had heard this story and was publicly declaring that Ronder had ruined his son.

Finally the two men were brought into sharp rivalry over the Pybus living. Over that, too, the town, or at any rate the Cathedral section of it, was in two camps. Here, too, Brandon's vociferous publicity had made privacy impossible.

Ronder was ashamed, as though his rotund body had been suddenly exposed in all its obese nakedness before the assembled citizens of Polchester. In this public quarrel he was not in his element; forces were rising in him that he distrusted and feared.

People were laughing . . . for that he would never forgive Brandon so long as he lived.

On this particular afternoon he was about to close the window and try to work at his sermon when some one knocked at his door.

'Come in,' he said impatiently. The maid appeared.

'Please, sir, there's some one would like to speak to you.'

'Who is it?'

'She gave her name as Miss Milton, sir.'

He paused, looking down at his papers. 'She said she wouldn't keep you more than a moment, sir.'

'Very well. I'll see her.'

Fate pushing him again. Why should this woman come to him? How could any one say that any of the steps that he had taken in this affair had been his fault? Why, he had had nothing whatever to do with them!

The sight of Miss Milton in his doorway filled him with the same vague disgust that he had known on the earlier occasions at the Library. To-day she was wearing a white cotton dress, rather faded and crumpled, and grey silk gloves; in one of the fingers there was a hole. She carried a pink parasol, and wore a large straw hat overtrimmed with roses. Her face with its little red-rimmed eyes, freckled and flushed complexion, her clumsy thick-set figure, fitted ill with her youthful dress.

It was obvious enough that fate had not treated her well since her departure from the Library; she was running to seed very swiftly, and was herself bitterly conscious of the fact.

Ronder, looking at her, was aware that it was her own fault that it was so. She was incompetent, utterly incompetent. He had, as he had promised, given her some work to do during these last weeks, some copying, some arranging of letters, and she had mismanaged it all. She was a muddle-headed,

ill-educated, careless, conceited and self-opinionated
woman, and it did not make it any the pleasanter for
Ronder to be aware, as he now was, that Brandon had
been quite right to dismiss her from her Library
post which she had retained far too long.

She looked across the room at him with an
expression of mingled obstinacy and false humility.
Her eyes were nearly closed.

' Good afternoon, Canon Ronder,' she said. ' It
is very good of you to see me. I shall not detain
you very long.'

' Well, what is it, Miss Milton ? ' he said, looking over his shoulder at her. ' I am very busy, as a
matter of fact. All these Jubilee affairs—however,
if I can help you.'

' You can help me, sir. It is a most serious
matter, and I need your advice.'

' Well, sit down there and tell me about it.'

The sun was beating into the room. He went
across and pulled down the blind, partly because it
was hot and partly because Miss Milton was less
unpleasant in shadow.

Miss Milton seemed to find it hard to begin.
She gulped in her throat and rubbed her silk gloves
nervously against one another.

' I daresay I've done wrong in this matter,' she
began—' many would think so. But I haven't come
here to excuse myself. If I've done wrong, there
are others who have done more wrong — yes,
indeed.'

' Please come to the point,' said Ronder impatiently.

' I will, sir. That is my desire. Well, you
must know, sir, that after my most unjust dismissal
from the Library I took a couple of rooms with Mrs.

Bassett who lets rooms, as perhaps you know, sir, just opposite St. James' Rectory, Mr. Morris's.'

' Well ? ' said Ronder.

' Well, sir, I had not been there very long before Mrs. Bassett herself, who is the least interfering and meddling of women, drew my attention to a curious fact, a most curious fact.'

Miss Milton paused, looking down at her lap and at a little shabby black bag that lay upon it.

' Well ? ' said Ronder again.

' This fact was that Mrs. Brandon, the wife of Archdeacon Brandon, was in the habit of coming every day to see Mr. Morris ! '

Ronder got up from his chair.

' Now, Miss Milton,' he said, ' let me make myself perfectly clear. If you have come here to give me a lot of scandal about some person, or persons, in this town, I do not wish to hear it. You have come to the wrong place. I wonder, indeed, that you should care to acknowledge to any one that you have been spying at your window on the movements of some people here. That is a disgraceful action. I do not think there is any need for this conversation to continue.'

' Excuse me, Canon Ronder, there *is* need.' Miss Milton showed no intention whatever of moving from her chair. ' I was aware that you would, in all probability, rebuke me for what I have done. I expected that. At the same time I may say that I was *not* spying in any sense of the word. I could not help it if the windows of my sitting-room looked down upon Mr. Morris's house. You could not expect me, in this summer weather, not to sit at my window.

' At the same time if these visits of Mrs. Brandon's

were all that had occurred I should certainly not
have come and taken up your valuable time with an
account of them ; I hope that I know what is due
to a gentleman of your position better than that. It
is on a matter of real importance that I have come to
you to ask your advice. Some one's advice I must
have, and if you feel that *you* cannot give it me, I
must go elsewhere. I cannot but feel that it is
better for every one concerned that you should
have this piece of information rather than any one
else.'

He noticed how she had grown in firmness and
resolve since she had begun to speak. She now saw
her way to the carrying out of her plan. There
was a definite threat in the words of her last sentence,
and as she looked at him across the shadowy light
he felt as though he saw down into her mean little
soul, filled now with hatred and obstinacy and
jealous determination.

'Of course,' he said severely, 'I cannot refuse
your confidence if you are determined to give it
me.'

'Yes,' she said, nodding her head. 'You have
always been very kind to me, Canon Ronder, as you
have been to many others in this place. Thank
you.' She looked at him almost as severely as he
had looked at her. 'I will be as brief as possible.
I will not hide from you that I have never forgiven
Archdeacon Brandon for his cruel treatment of me.
That, I think, is natural. When your livelihood is
taken away from you for no reason at all, you are not
likely to forget it—if you are human. And I do
not pretend to be more nor less than human. I will
not deny that I saw these visits of Mrs. Brandon's
with considerable curiosity. There was something

hurried and secret in Mrs. Brandon's manner that seemed to me odd. I became then, quite by chance, the friend of Mr. Morris's cook-house-keeper, Mrs. Baker, a very nice woman. That, I think, was quite natural as we were neighbours, so to speak, and Mrs. Baker was herself a friend of Mrs. Bassett's.

' I asked no indiscreet questions, but at last Mrs. Baker confessed to both Mrs. Bassett and myself that she did not like what was going on in Mr. Morris's house, and that she thought of giving notice. When we asked her what she meant she said that Mrs. Brandon was the trouble, that she was always coming to the house, and that she and the reverend gentleman were shut up for hours together by them-selves. She told us, too, that Mr. Morris's sister-in-law, Miss Burnett, had also made objections. We advised Mrs. Baker that it was her duty to stay, at any rate for the present.'

Miss Milton paused. Ronder said nothing.

' Well, sir, things got so bad that Miss Burnett went away to the sea. During her absence Mrs. Brandon came to the house quite regularly, and Mrs. Baker told us that they scarcely seemed to mind who saw them.'

As Ronder looked at her he realised how little he knew about women. He hated to realise this, as he hated to realise any ignorance or weakness in him-self, but in the face of the woman opposite to him there was a mixture of motives—of greed, revenge, yes, and strangely enough, of a virgin's outraged propriety—that was utterly alien to his experience. He felt his essential, his almost inhuman, celibacy more at that moment, perhaps, than he had ever felt it before.

'Well, sir, this went on for some weeks. Miss
Burnett returned, but as Mrs. Baker said, the situation remained very strained. To come to my
point, four days ago I was in one evening paying
Mrs. Baker a visit. Every one was out, although
Mr. Morris was expected home for his dinner.
There was a ring at the bell and Mrs. Baker said,
" You go, my dear." She was busy at the moment
with the cooking. I went and opened the hall-door,
and there was Mrs. Brandon's parlour-maid that I
knew by sight. " I have a note for Mr. Morris,"
she said. " You can give it to me," I said. She
seemed to hesitate, but I told her if she didn't give
it to me she might as well take it away again, because
there was no one else in the house. That seemed to
settle her, so telling me it was something special,
and was to be given to Mr. Morris as soon as
possible, she left it with me and went. She'd never
seen me before, I daresay, and didn't know I didn't
belong to the house.' She paused, then opening
her little eyes wide and staring at Ronder as though
she were seeing him for the first time in her life she
said softly, ' I have the note here.'

She opened her black bag slowly, peered into it,
produced a piece of paper out of it, and shut it with
a sharp little click.

' You've kept it ? ' asked Ronder.

' I've kept it,' she repeated, nodding her head.
' I know many would say I was wrong. But was I ?
That's the question. In any case that is another
matter between myself and my Maker.'

' Please read this, sir.' She held out the paper
to him. He took it and after a moment's hesitation
read it. It had neither date nor address. It ran
as follows :

DEAREST—I am sending this by a safe hand to tell you that I cannot possibly get down to-night. I am so sorry and most dreadfully disappointed, but I will explain everything when we meet to-morrow. This is to prevent your waiting on when I'm not coming.

There was no signature.

'You had no right to keep this,' he said to her angrily. As he spoke he looked at the piece of paper and felt again how strange and foreign to him the whole nature of woman was. The risks that they would take! The foolish mad things that they would do to satisfy some caprice or whim!

'How do you know that this was written by Mrs. Brandon?' he asked.

'Of course I know her handwriting very well,' Miss Milton answered. 'She often wrote to me when I was at the Library.'

He was silent. He was seeing those two in the new light of this letter. So they were really lovers, the drab, unromantic, plain, dull, middle-aged souls! What had they seen in one another? What had they felt, to drive them to deeds so desperate, yes, and so absurd? Was there then a world right outside his ken, a world from which he had been since his birth excluded?

Absent-mindedly he had put the letter down on his table. Quickly she stretched out her gloved hand and took it. The bag clicked over it.

'Why have you brought this to me?' he asked, looking at her with a disgust that he did not attempt to conceal.

'You are the first person to whom I have spoken about the matter,' she answered. 'I have not said anything even to Mrs. Baker. I have had the letter for several days and have not known what is right to do about it.'

'There is only one thing that is right to do about it,' he answered sharply. 'Burn it.'

'And say nothing to anybody about it? Oh, Canon Ronder, surely that would not be right. I should not like people to think that you had given me such advice. To allow the Rector of St. James' to continue in his position, with so many looking up to him, and he committing such sins. Oh, no, sir, I cannot feel that to be right!'

'It is not our business,' he answered angrily. 'It is not our affair.'

'Very well, sir.' She got up. 'It's good of you to give me your opinion. It is not our affair. Quite so. But it *is* Archdeacon Brandon's affair. He should see this letter. I thought that perhaps you yourself might like to speak to him——' she paused.

'I will have nothing to do with it,' he answered, getting up and standing over her. 'You did very wrong to keep the letter. You are cherishing evil passions in your heart, Miss Milton, that will bring you nothing but harm and sorrow in the end. You have come to me for advice, you say. Well, I give it to you. Burn that letter and forget what you know.'

Her complexion had changed to a strange muddy grey as he spoke.

'There are others in this town, Canon Ronder,' she said, 'who are cherishing much the same passions as myself, although they may not realise it. I thought it wise to tell you what I know. As you will not help me, I know now what to do. I am grateful for your advice—which, however, I do not think you wish me to follow.'

With one last look at him she moved softly to the door and was gone. She seemed to him to leave some muddy impression of her personality upon the walls and furniture of the room. He flung up the window, walked about, rubbing his hands against one another behind his back, hating everything around him.

The words of the note repeated themselves again and again in his head.

'Dearest . . . safe hand . . . dreadfully disappointed. . . . Dearest.'

Those two ! He saw Morris, with his weak face, his mild eyes, his rather shabby clothes, his hesitating manner, his thinning hair—and Mrs. Brandon, so mediocre that no one ever noticed her, never noticed anything about her—what she wore, what she said, what she did, anything !

Those two ! Ghosts ! and in love so that they would risk loss of everything—reputation, possessions, family—that they might obtain their desire ! In love as he had never been in all his life !

His thoughts turned, with a little shudder, to Miss Milton. She had come to him because she thought that he would like to share in her revenge. That, more than anything, hurt him, bringing him down to her base, sordid level, making him fellow-conspirator with her, plotting . . . ugh ! How cruelly unfair that he, upright, generous, should be involved like this so meanly.

He washed his hands in the little dressing-room near the study, scrubbing them as though the contact with Miss Milton still lingered there. Hating his own company, he went downstairs, where he found Ellen Stiles, having had a very happy tea with his aunt, preparing to depart.

' Going, Ellen ? ' he asked.

She was in the highest spirits and a hat of vivid green.

' Yes, I must go. I've been here ever so long. We've had a perfectly lovely time, talking all about poor Mrs. Maynard and her consumption. There's simply no hope for her, I'm afraid ; it's such a shame when she has four small children ; but as I told her yesterday, it's really best to make up one's mind to the worst, and there'll be no money for the poor little things after she's gone. I don't know what they'll do.'

' You must have cheered her up,' said Ronder.

' Well, I don't know about that. Like all consumptives she will persist in thinking that she's going to get well. Of course, if she had money enough to go to Davos or somewhere . . . but she hasn't, so there's simply no hope at all.'

' If you are going along I'll walk part of the way with you,' said Ronder.

' That *will* be nice.' Ellen kissed Miss Ronder very affectionately. ' Good-bye, you darling. I have had a nice time. Won't it be awful if it's wet next week ? Simply everything will be ruined. I don't see much chance of its being fine myself. Still you never can tell.'

They went out together. The Precincts were quiet and deserted ; a bell, below in the sunny town, was ringing for evensong. ' Morris's church perhaps,' thought Ronder. The light was stretched like a screen of coloured silk across the bright green of the Cathedral square ; the great Church itself was in shadow, misty behind the sun, and shifting from shade to shade as though it were under water.

When they had walked a little way Ellen said :
' What's the matter ? '

' The matter ? ' Ronder echoed.

' Yes. You're looking worried, and that's so
rare with you that when it happens one's interested.'

He hesitated, looking at her and almost stopping
in his walk. An infernal nuisance if Ellen Stiles
were to choose this moment for the exercise of her
unfortunate curiosity ! He had intended to go
down High Street with her and then to go by way
of Orange Street to Foster's rooms ; but one could
reach Foster more easily by the little crooked
street behind the Cathedral. He would say good-
bye to her here. . . . Then another thought struck
him. He would go on with her.

' Isn't your curiosity terrible, Ellen !' he said,
laughing. ' If you didn't happen to have a kind
heart hidden somewhere about you, you'd be a
perfectly impossible woman. As it is, I'm not sure
that you're not.'

' I think perhaps I am,' Ellen answered, laughing. ' I do take a great interest in other people's
affairs. Well, why not ? It prevents me from being
bored.'

' But not from being a bore,' said Ronder. ' I
hate to be unpleasant, but there's nothing more
tiresome than being asked why one's in a certain
mood. However, leave me alone and I will repay
your curiosity by some of my own. Tell me, how
much are people talking about Mrs. Brandon and
Morris ? '

This time she was genuinely surprised. On so
many occasions he had checked her love of gossip
and scandal and now he was deliberately provoking
it. It was as though he had often lectured her

about drinking too much and then had been discovered by her, secretly tippling.

'Oh, everybody's talking, of course,' she said. 'Although you pretend never to talk scandal you must know enough about the town to know that. They happen to be talking less just at the moment because nobody's thinking of anything but the Jubilee.'

'What I want to know,' said Ronder, 'is how much Brandon is supposed to be aware of—and does he mind?'

'He's aware of nothing,' said Ellen decisively. 'Nothing at all. He's always looked upon his wife as a piece of furniture, neither very ornamental nor very useful, but still his property, and therefore to be reckoned on as stable and submissive. I don't think that in any case he would ever dream that she could disobey him in anything, but as it happens, his son's flight to London and his own quarrel with you entirely possess his mind. He talks, eats, thinks, dreams nothing else.'

'What would he do, do you think,' pursued Ronder, 'if he were to discover that there really *was* something wrong, that she had been unfaithful?'

'Why, is there proof?' asked Ellen Stiles eagerly, pausing for a moment in her excitement.

The sharp note of eagerness in her voice checked him.

'No—nothing,' he said. 'Nothing at all. Of course not. And how should I know if there were?'

'You're just the person who would know,' answered Ellen decisively. 'However many other people you've hoodwinked, you haven't taken *me* in all these years. But I'll tell you this as from one friend to another, that you've made the first mistake in your life by allowing this quarrel with Brandon to become so public.'

He marvelled again, as he had often marvelled before, at her unerring genius for discovering just the thing to say to her friends that would hurt them most. And yet with that she had a kind heart, as he had had reason often enough to know. Queer things, women !

' It's not my fault if the quarrel's become public,' he said. They were turning down the High Street now and he could not show all the vexation that he felt. ' It's Brandon's own idiotic character and the love of gossip displayed by this town.'

' Well, then,' she said, delighted that she had annoyed him and that he was showing his annoyance, ' that simply means that you've been defeated by circumstances. For once they've been too strong for you. If you like that explanation you'd better take it.'

' Now, Ellen,' he said, ' you're trying to make me lose my temper in revenge for my not satisfying your curiosity ; give up. You've tried before and you've always failed.'

She laughed, putting her hand through his arm.

' Yes, don't let's quarrel,' she said. ' Isn't it delightful to-night with the sunlight and the excitement and every one out enjoying themselves ? I love to see them happy, poor things. It's only the successful and the self-important and the patronising that I want to pull down a little. As soon as I find myself wanting to dig at somebody, I know it's because they're getting above themselves. You'd better be careful. I'm not at all sure that success isn't going to your head.'

' Success ? ' he asked.

' Yes. Don't look so innocent. You've been here only a few months and already you're the only man here who counts. You've beaten Brandon in the very first round, and it's absurd of you to pretend to an old friend like myself that you don't know that you have. But be careful.'

The street was shining, wine-coloured, against the black walls that hemmed it in, black walls scattered with sheets of glass, absurd curtains of muslin, brown, shabby, self-ashamed backs of looking-glasses, door-knobs, flower-pots, and collections of furniture, books and haberdashery.

' Suppose you leave me alone for a moment, Ellen,' said Ronder, ' and think of somebody else. What I really want to know is how intimate are you with Mrs. Brandon ? '

' Intimate ? '

' Yes. I mean—could you speak to her ? Tell her, in some way, to be more careful, that she's in danger. Women know how to do these things. I want to find somebody.'

He paused. *Did* he want to find somebody ? Why this strange tenderness towards Mrs. Brandon of which he was quite suddenly conscious ? Was it his disgust of Miss Milton, so that he could not bear to think of any one in the power of such a woman ?

' Warn her ? ' said Ellen. ' Then she *is* in danger.'

' Only if, as you say, every one is talking. I'm sorry for her.'

They had come to the parting of their ways.

' No. I don't know her well enough for that.
She wouldn't take it from me. She wouldn't take
it from anybody. She's prouder than you'd think.
And it's my belief she doesn't care if she *is* in danger.
She'd rather welcome it. That's my belief.'

' Good-bye then. I won't ask you to keep our
talk quiet. I don't suppose you could if you wanted
to. But I *will* ask you to be kind.'

' Why should I be kind ? And you know you
don't want me to be, really.'

' I do want you to be.'

' No, it's part of the game you're playing. Or
if it isn't, you're changing more than you've ever
changed before. Look out ! Perhaps it's you
that's in danger ! '

As he turned up Orange Street he wondered
again what impulse it was that was making him
sorry for Mrs. Brandon. He always wished people
to be happy—life was easier so—but had he even
yesterday been told that he would ever feel concern
for Mrs. Brandon, that supreme symbol of feminine
colourless mediocrity, he would have laughed
derisively.

Then the beauty of the hour drove everything
else from him. The street climbed straight into
the sky, a broad flat sheet of gold, and on its
height the monument, perched against the quivering air, was a purple shaft, its gesture proud,
haughty, exultant. Suddenly he saw in front of
him, moving with quick, excited steps, Mrs.
Brandon, an absurdly insignificant figure against
that splendour.

He felt as though his thoughts had evoked her
out of space, and as though she was there against
her will. Then he felt that he, too, was there against

his will, and that he had nothing to do with either
the time or the place.

He caught her up. She started nervously when
he said, ' Good evening, Mrs. Brandon,' and raised
her little mouse-face with its mild, hesitating, grey
eyes to his. He knew her only slightly and was
conscious that she did not like him. That was
not his affair ; she had become something quite
new to him since he had gained this knowledge of
her—she was provocative, suggestive, even romantic.

' Good evening, Canon Ronder.' She did not
smile nor slacken her steps.

' Isn't this a lovely evening ? ' he said. ' If
we have this weather next week we shall be lucky
indeed.'

' Yes, shan't we—shan't we ? ' she said nervously,
not considering him, but staring straight at the
street in front of her.

' I think all the preparations are made,' Ronder
went on in the genial easy voice that he always
adopted with children and nervous women. ' There
should be a tremendous crowd if the weather's fine.
People already are pouring in from every part of
the country, they tell me—sleeping anywhere, in
the fields and the hedges. This old town will be
proud of herself.'

' Yes, yes.' Mrs. Brandon looked about her as
though she were trying to find a way of escape.
' I'm so glad you think that the weather will be
fine. I'm so glad. I think it will myself. I
hope Miss Ronder is well.'

' Very well, thank you.' What *could* Morris see
in her, with her ill-fitting clothes, her skirt trailing
a little in the dust, her hat too big and heavy for
her head, her hair escaping in little untidy wisps

from under it ? She looked hot, too, and her nose was shiny.

'You're coming to the Ball of course,' he went on, relieved that now they were near the top of the little hill. 'It's to be the best Ball the Assembly Rooms have seen since—since Jane Austen.'

'Jane Austen ?' asked Mrs. Brandon vaguely.

'Well, her time, you know, when dancing was all the rage. We ought to have more dances here, I think, now that there are so many young people about.'

'Yes, I agree with you. My daughter is coming out at the Ball.'

'Oh, is she ? I'm sure she'll have a good time. She's so pretty. Every one's fond of her.'

He waited, but apparently Mrs. Brandon had nothing more to say. There was a pause, then Mrs. Brandon, as though she had been suddenly pushed to it by some one behind her, held out her hand. . . .

'Good evening, Canon Ronder.'

He said good-bye and watched her for a moment as she went up past the neat little villas, her dress trailing behind her, her hat bobbing with every step. He looked up at the absurd figure on the top of the monument, the gentleman in frock-coat and tall hat commemorated there. The light had left him. He was not purple now but a dull grey. He, too, had doubtless had his romance, blood and tears, anger and agony for somebody. How hard to keep out of such things, and yet one must if one is to achieve anything. Keep out of it, detached, observant, comfortable. Strange that in life comfort should be so difficult to attain !

Climbing Green Lane he was surprised to feel

how hot it was. The trees that clustered over his head seemed to have gathered together all the heat of the day. Everything conspired to annoy him ! Bodger's Street, when he turned into it, was, from his point of view, at its very worst, crowded and smelly and rocking with noise. The fields behind Bodger's Street and Canon's Yard sloped down the hill and then up again out into the country beyond.

It was here on this farther hill that the gipsies had been allowed to pitch their caravans, and that the Fair was already preparing its splendours. It was through these gates that the countrymen would penetrate the town's defences, just as on the other side, low down in Seatown on the Pol's banks, the seafaring men, fishermen and sailors and merchantmen, were gathering. Bodger's Street was already alive with the anticipation of the coming week's festivities. Gas-jets were flaming behind hucksters' booths, and all the population of the place was out on the street enjoying the fine summer evening, shouting, laughing, singing, quarrelling. The effect of the street illumined by these uncertain flares that leapt unnaturally against the white shadow of the summer sky was of something mediæval, and that impression was deepened by the overhanging structure of the Cathedral that covered the faint blue and its little pink clouds like a swinging spider's web.

Ronder, however, was not now thinking of the town. His mind was fixed upon his approaching interview with Foster. Foster had just paid a visit, quite unofficial and on a private personal basis, to Wistons, to sound him about the Pybus living and his action if he were offered it.

Ronder understood men very much better than he understood women. He understood Foster so long as ambition and religion were his motives, but there was something else in play that he did not understand. It was not only that Foster did not like him—he doubted whether Foster liked anybody except the Bishop—it was rather perhaps that Foster did not like himself. Now it is the first rule of fanaticism that you should be so lost in the impulse of your inspiration that you should have no power left with which to consider yourself at all. Foster was undoubtedly a fanatic, but he did consider himself and even despised himself. Ronder distrusted self-contempt in a man simply because nothing made him so uncomfortable as those moments of his own when he wondered whether he were all that he thought himself. Those moments did not last long, but he hated them so bitterly that he could not bear to see them at work in other people. Foster was the kind of fanatic who might at any minute decide to put peas in his shoes and walk to Jerusalem ; did he so decide, he would abandon, for that decision, all the purposes for which he might at the time be working. Ronder would certainly never walk to Jerusalem.

The silence and peace of Canon's Yard when he left Bodger's Street was almost dramatic. All that penetrated there was a subdued buzz with an occasional shrill note as it might be on a penny whistle. The Yard was dark, lit only by a single lamp, and the cobbles uneven. Lights here and there set in the crooked old windows were secret and uncommunicative : the Cathedral towers seemed immensely tall against the dusk. It would not be dark for another hour and a half, but in those old rooms with their small casements light was thin and uncertain.

He climbed the rickety stairs to Foster's rooms. As always, something made him pause outside Foster's door and listen. All the sounds of the old building seemed to come up to him ; not human voices and movements, but the life of the old house itself, the creaking protests of stairways, the sighs of reluctant doors, the harping groans of ill-mannered window-frames, the coughs and wheezes of trembling walls, the shudders of ill-boding banisters.

'This house will collapse, the first gale,' he thought, and suddenly the Cathedral chimes, striking the half-hour, crashed through the wall, knocking and echoing as though their clatter belonged to that very house.

The echo died, and the old place recommenced its murmuring.

Foster, blinking like an old owl, came to the door and, without a word, led the way into his untidy room. He cleared a chair of papers and books and Ronder sat down.

'Well ?' said Ronder.

Foster was in a state of overpowering excitement, but he looked to Ronder older and more worn than a week ago. There were dark pouches under his eyes, his cheeks were drawn, and his untidy grey hair seemed thin and ragged——here too long, there showing the skull gaunt and white beneath it. His eyes burnt with a splendid flame ; in them there was the light of eternal life.

'Well ?' said Ronder again, as Foster did not answer his first question.

'He's coming,' Foster cried, striding about the

room, his shabby slippers giving a ghostly tip-tap behind him. 'He's coming! Of course I had never doubted it, but I hadn't expected that he would be so eager as he is. He let himself go to me at once. Of course he knew that I wasn't official, that I had no backing at all. He's quite prepared for things to go the other way, although I told him that I thought there would be little chance of that if we all worked together. He didn't ask many questions. He knows all the conditions well. Since I saw him last he's gained in every way— wiser, better disciplined, more sure of himself— everything that I have never been. . . .' Foster paused, then went on. 'I think never in all my life have I felt affection so go out to another human being. He is a man after my own heart—a child of God, an inheritor of Eternal Life, a leader of men——'

Ronder interrupted him.

'Yes, but as to detail. Did you discuss that? He knew of the opposition?'

Foster waved his hand contemptuously. 'Brandon? What does that amount to? Why, even in the week that I have been away his power has lessened. The hand of God is against him. Everything is going wrong with him. I loathe scandal, but there is actually talk going on in the town about his wife. I could feel pity for the man were he not so dangerous.'

'You are wrong there, Foster,' Ronder said eagerly. 'Brandon isn't finished yet — by no manner of means. He still has most of the town behind him and a big majority with the Cathedral people. He stands for what they think or *don't* think—old ideas, conservatism, every established dogma you can put your hand on, bad music, traditionalism, superstition and carelessness. It is not Brandon himself we are fighting, but what he stands for.'

Foster stopped and looked down at Ronder. 'You'll forgive me if I speak my mind,' he said. 'I'm an older man than you are, and in any case it's my way to say what I think. You know that by this time. You've made a mistake in allowing this quarrel with Brandon to become so personal a matter.'

Ronder flushed angrily.

'Allowing !' he retorted. 'As though that were not the very thing that I've tried to prevent it from becoming. But the old fool has rushed out and shouted his grievances to everybody. I suppose you've heard of the ridiculous quarrel we had coming away from Carpledon. The whole town knows of it. There never was a more ridiculous scene. He stood in the middle of the road and screamed like a madman. It's my belief he *is* going mad ! A precious lot I had to do with that. I was as amiable as possible. But you can't deal with him. His conceit and his obstinacy are monstrous.'

Nothing was more irritating in Foster than the way that he had of not listening to excuses ; he always brushed them aside as though they were beneath notice.

'You shouldn't have made it a personal thing,' he repeated. 'People will take sides—are already doing so. It oughtn't to be between you two at all.'

'I tell you it is not ! ' Ronder answered angrily. Then with a great effort he pulled himself in. 'I don't know what has been happening to me lately,' he said with a smile. ' I've always prided myself on keeping out of quarrels, and in any case I'm not going to quarrel with you. I'm sure you're right. It *is* a pity that the thing's become personal. I'll see what I can do.'

But Foster paid as little attention to apologies as to excuses.

' That's been a mistake,' he said ; ' and there have been other mistakes. You are too personally ambitious, Ronder. We are working for the glory of God and for no private interests whatever.'

Ronder smiled. ' You're hard on me,' he said ; ' but you shall think what you like. I won't allow that I've been personally ambitious, but it's difficult sometimes when you're putting all your energies into a certain direction not to seem to be serving your own ends. I like power—who doesn't ? But I would gladly sacrifice any personal success if that were needed to win the main battle.'

' Win ! ' Foster cried. ' Win ! But we've got to win ! There's never been such a chance for us ! If Brandon wins now our opportunity is gone for another generation. What Wistons can do here if he comes ! The power that he will be ! '

Suddenly there came into Ronder's mind for the first time the thought that was to recur to him very often in the future. Was it wise of him to work for the coming of a man who might threaten his own power ? He shook that from him. He would deal with that when the time came. For the present Brandon was enough. . . .

' Now as to detail . . .' Ronder said.

They sat down at the paper-littered table. For another hour and a half they stayed there, and it would have been curious for an observer to see how, in this business, Ronder obtained an absolute mastery. Foster, the fire dead in his eyes, the light gone, followed him blindly, agreeing to everything, wondering at the clearness, order and discipline of his plans. An hour ago, treading the soil of his own country, he had feared no man, and his feeling for Ronder had been one half-contempt, half-suspicion. Now he was in the other's hands. This was a world into which he had never won right of entry.

The Cathedral chimes struck nine. Ronder got up and put his papers away with a little sigh of satisfaction. He knew that his work had been good.

'There's nothing that we've forgotten. Bentinck-Major will be caught before he knows where he is. Ryle too. Let us get through this next week safely and the battle's won.'

Foster blinked.

'Yes, yes,' he said hurriedly. 'Yes, yes. Good-night, good-night,' and almost pushed Ronder from the room.

'I don't believe he's taken in a word of it,' Ronder thought, as he went down the creaking stairs.

At the top of Bodger's Street he paused. The street was still; the sky was pale green on the horizon, purple overhead. The light was still strong, but, to the left beyond the sloping fields, the woods were banked black and sombre. From the meadow in front of the woods came the sounds of an encampment—women shouting, horses neighing, dogs barking. A few lights gleamed like red eyes. The dusky forms of caravans with their thick-set chimneys, ebony-coloured against the green sky, crouched like animals barking. A woman was singing, men's voices took her up, and the song came rippling across the little valley.

All the stir of an invading world was there.

CHAPTER II

ON that Friday evening, about half-past six o'clock, Archdeacon Brandon, just as he reached the top of the High Street, saw God.

There was nothing either strange or unusual about this. Having had all his life the conviction that he and God were on the most intimate of terms, that God knew and understood himself and his wants better than any other friend that he had, that just as God had definitely deputed him to work out certain plans on this earth, so, at times, He needed his own help and advice, having never wavered for an instant in the very simplest tenets of his creed, and believing in every word of the New Testament as though the events there recorded had only a week ago happened in his own town under his own eyes— all this being so, it was not strange that he should sometimes come into close and actual contact with his Master.

It may be said that it was this very sense of contact, continued through long years of labour and success, that was the original foundation of the Archdeacon's pride. If of late years that pride had grown from the seeds of the Archdeacon's own self-confidence and appreciation, who can blame him?

371

We translate more easily than we know our gratitude to God into our admiration of ourselves.

Over and over again in the past, when he had been labouring with especial fervour, he was aware that, in the simplest sense of the word, God was ' walking with him.' He was conscious of a new light and heat, of a fresh companionship ; he could almost translate into physical form that comradeship of which he was so tenderly aware. How could it be but that after such an hour he should look down from those glorious heights upon his other less favoured fellow-companions ? No merit of his own that he had been chosen, but the choice had been made.

On this evening he was in sad need of comfort. Never in all his past years had life gone so hardly with him as it was going now. It was as though, about three or four months back, he had, without knowing it, stepped into some new and terrible country. One feature after another had changed, old familiar faces wore new unfamiliar disguises, every step that he took now seemed to be dangerous, misfortune after misfortune had come to him, at first slight and even ludicrous, at last with Falk's escape, serious and bewildering. Bewildering ! That was the true word to describe his case ! He was like a man moving through familiar country and overtaken suddenly by a dense fog. Through it all, examine it as minutely as he might, he could not see that he had committed the slightest fault.

He had been as he had always been, and yet the very face of the town was changed to him, his son had left him, even his wife, to whom he had been married for twenty years, was altered. Was it not natural, therefore, that he should attribute all

of this to the only new element that had been introduced into his life during these last months, to the
one human being alive who was his declared enemy,
to the one man who had openly, in the public road,
before witnesses, insulted him, to the man who,
from the first moment of his coming to Polchester,
had laughed at him and mocked and derided him ?

To Ronder ! To Ronder ! The name was
never out of his brain now, lying there, stirring,
twisting in his very sleep, sneering, laughing even
in the heart of his private prayers.

He was truly in need of God that evening, and
there, at the top of the High Street, he saw Him
framed in all the colour and glow and sparkling sunlight of the summer evening, filling him with warmth
and new courage, surrounding him, enveloping him
in love and tenderness.

Cynics might say that it was because the Archdeacon, no longer so young as he had been, was
blown by his climb of the High Street and stood,
breathing hard for a moment before he passed into
the Precincts, lights dancing before his eyes as they
will when one is out of breath, the ground swaying
a little under the pressure of the heart, the noise of
the town rocking in the ears.

That is for the cynics to say. Brandon knew ;
his experiences had been in the past too frequent for
him, even now, to make a mistake.

Running down the hill went the High Street,
decorated now with flags and banners in honour of
the great event ; cutting the sky, stretching from
Brent's the haberdasher's across to Adams' the hairdresser's, was a vast banner of bright yellow silk
stamped in red letters with ' Sixty Years Our Queen.
God bless her ! '

Just beside the Archdeacon, above the door of the bookshop where he had once so ignominiously taken refuge, was a flag of red, white and blue, and opposite the bookseller's, at Gummridge's the stationer's, was a little festoon of flags and a blue message stamped on a white ground : ' God bless Our Queen : Long May She Reign ! '

All down the street flags and streamers were fluttering in the little summer breeze that stole about the houses and windows and doors as though anxiously enquiring whether people were not finding the evening just a little too warm.

People were not finding it at all too warm. Every one was out and strolling up and down, laughing and whistling and chattering, dressed, although it was only Friday, in nearly their Sunday best. The shops were closing, one by one, and the throng was growing thicker and thicker. So little traffic was passing that young men and women were already marching four abreast, arm-in-arm, along the middle of the street. It was a long time —ten years, in fact—since Polchester had seen such gaiety.

This was behind the Archdeacon, in front of him was the dark archway in which the grass of the Cathedral square was framed like the mirrored reflection of evening light where the pale blue and pearl white are shadowed with slanting green. The peace was profound—nothing stirred. There in the archway God stood, smiling upon His faithful servant, only as Brandon approached Him passing into shadow and sunlight and the intense blue of the overhanging sky.

Brandon tried then, as he had often tried before, to keep that contact close to himself, but the ecstatic

moment had passed ; it had lasted, it seemed, on
this occasion a shorter time than ever before. He
bowed his head, stood for a moment under the arch
offering a prayer as simple and innocent as a child
offers at its mother's knee, then with an instantaneous
change that in a more complex nature could have
meant only hypocrisy, but that with him was
perfectly sincere, he was in a moment the hot, angry,
mundane priest again, doing battle with his enemies
and defying them to destroy him.

Nevertheless the transition to-night was not
quite so complete as usual. He was unhappy,
lonely, and in spite of himself afraid, afraid of he
knew not what, as a child might be when its candle
is blown out. And with this unhappiness his
thoughts turned to home. Falk's departure had
caused him to consider his wife more seriously
than he had ever done in all their married life
before. She had loved Falk ; she must be lonely
without him, and during these weeks he had
been groping in a clumsy baffled kind of way
towards some expression to her of the kindness and
sympathy that he was feeling.

But those emotions do not come easily after
many years of disuse ; he was always embarrassed
and self-conscious when he expressed affection. He
was afraid of her, too, thought that if he showed
too much kindness she might suddenly become
emotional, fling her arms around him and cover
his face with kisses—something of that kind.

Then of late she had been very strange ; ever
since that Sunday morning when she had refused
to go to Communion. . . . Strange ! Women are
strange ! As different from men as Frenchmen
are from Englishmen !

But he would like to-night to come closer to her. Dimly, far within him, something was stirring that told him that it had been his own fault that during all these years she had drifted away from him. He must win her back ! A thing easily done. In the Archdeacon's view of life any man had only got to whistle and fast the woman came running !

But to-night he wanted some one to care for him and to tell him that all was well and that the many troubles that seemed to be crowding about him were but imaginary after all.

When he reached the house he found that he had only just time to dress for dinner. He ran upstairs, and then, when his door was closed and he was safely inside his bedroom, he had to pause and stand, his hand upon his heart. How it was hammering ! like a beast struggling to escape its cage. His knees, too, were trembling. He was forced to sit down. After all, he was not so young as he had been.

These recent months had been trying for him. But how humiliating ! He was glad that there had been no one there to see him. He would need all his strength for the battle that was in front of him. Yes, he was glad that there had been no one to see him. He would ask old Puddifoot to look at him, although the man *was* an ass. He drank a glass of water, then slowly dressed.

He came downstairs and went into the drawing-room. His wife was there, standing in the shadow by the window, staring out into the Precincts. He came across the room softly to her, then gently put his hand on her shoulder.

She had not heard his approach. She turned round with a sharp cry and then faced him, staring, her eyes terrified. He, on his side, was so deeply startled by her alarm that he could only stare back at her, himself frightened and feeling a strange clumsy foolishness at her alarm.

Broken sentences came from her : 'What did you—— ? Who—— ? You shouldn't have done that. You frightened me.'

Her voice was sharply angry, and in all their long married life together he had never before felt her so completely a stranger ; he felt as though he had accosted some unknown woman in the street and been attacked by her for his familiarity. He took refuge, as he always did when he was confused, in pomposity.

' Really, my dear, you'd think I was a burglar. Hum—yes. You shouldn't be so easily startled.'

She was still staring at him as though even now she did not realise his identity. Her hands were clenched and her breath came in little hurried gasps as though she had been running.

' No — you shouldn't . . . silly . . . coming across the room like that.'

' Very well, very well,' he answered testily. ' Why isn't dinner ready ? It's ten minutes past the time.'

She moved across the room, not answering him.

Suddenly his pomposity was gone. He moved over to her, standing before her like an overgrown schoolboy, looking at her and smiling uneasily.

' The truth is, my dear,' he said, ' that I can't conceive my entering a room without everybody hearing it. No, I can't indeed,' he laughed boisterously. ' You tell anybody that I crossed a room without your hearing it, and they won't believe you. No, they won't.'

He bent down and kissed her. His touch tickled her cheek, but she made no movement. He felt, as his hand rested on her shoulder, that she was still trembling.

'Your nerves must be in a bad way,' he said. 'Why, you're trembling still! Why don't you see Puddifoot?'

'No—no,' she answered hurriedly. 'It was silly of me——' Making a great effort, she smiled up at him.

'Well, how's everything going?'

'Going?'

'Yes, for the great day. Is everything settled?'

He began to tell her in the old familiar, so boring way every detail of the events of the last few hours.

'I was just by Sharpe's when I remembered that I'd said nothing to Nixon about those extra seats at the back of the nave, so I had to go all the way round——'

Joan came in. His especial need of some one that night, rejected as it had been at once by his wife, turned to his daughter. How pretty she was, he thought, as she came across the room sunlit with the deep evening gold that struck in long paths of light into the darkest shadows and corners.

That moment seemed suddenly the culmination of the advance that they had been making towards one another during the last six months. When she came close to him, he, usually so unobservant, noticed that she, too, was in distress.

She was smiling but she was unhappy, and he suddenly felt that he had been neglecting her and letting her fight her battles alone, and that she needed his love as urgently as he needed hers. He

put his arm around her and drew her to him. The
movement was so unlike him and so unexpected
that she hesitated a little, then happily came closer
to him, resting her head on his shoulder. They
had both, for a moment, forgotten Mrs. Brandon.

' Tired ? ' he asked Joan.

' Yes. I've been working at those silly old
flags all the afternoon. Two of them are not
finished now. We've got to go again to-morrow
morning.'

' Everything ready for the Ball ? '

' Yes, my dress is lovely. Oh, mummy, Mrs.
Sampson says will you let two relations of theirs sit
in our seat on Sunday morning ? She hadn't
known that they were coming, and she's very
bothered about it, and I'll tell her whether they can
in the morning.'

They both turned and saw Mrs. Brandon, who
had gone back to the window and again was looking at the Cathedral, now in deep black shadow.

' Yes, dear. There'll be room. There's only
you and I——'

Joan had in the pocket of her dress a letter.
As they went in to dinner she could hear its paper
very faintly crackle against her hand. It was from
Falk and was as follows :

DEAR JOAN—I have written to father but he hasn't
answered. Would you find out what he thought about my
letter and what he intends to do ? I don't mind owning to
you that I miss him terribly, and I would give anything
just to see him for five minutes. I believe that if he saw
me I could win him over. Otherwise I am very happy
indeed. We are married and live in two little rooms just off
Baker Street. You don't know where that is, do you ?
Well, it's a very good place to be, near the Park, and lots

of good shops and not very expensive. Our landlady is a jolly woman, as kind as anything, and I'm getting quite enough work to keep the wolf from the door. I know more than ever now that I've done the right thing, and father will recognise it, too, one day. How is he? Of course my going like that was a great shock to him, but it was the only way to do it. When you write tell me about his health. He didn't seem so well just before I left. Now, Joan, write and tell me everything. One thing is that he's got so much to do that he won't have much time to think about me.—Your affectionate brother, FALK.

This letter, which had arrived that morning, had given Joan a great deal to think about. It had touched her very deeply. Until now Falk had never shown that he had thought about her at all, and now here he was depending on her and needing her help. At the same time, she had not the slightest guide as to her father's attitude. Falk's name had not been mentioned in the house during these last weeks, and, although she realised that a new relationship was springing up between herself and her father, she was still shy of him and conscious of a deep gulf between them. She had, too, her own troubles, and, try as she might to beat them under, they came up again and again, confronting her and demanding that she should answer them.

Now she put the whole of that aside and con- centrated on her father. Watching him during dinner, he seemed to her suddenly to have become older; there was a glow in her heart as she thought that at last he really needed her. After all, if through life she were destined to be an old maid— and that, in the tragic moment of her youth that was now upon her, seemed her inevitable destiny— here was some one for whom at last she could care.

She had felt before she came down to dinner
that she was old and ugly and desperately un-
attractive.   Across the dinner-table she flung away,
as she imagined for ever, all hopes for beauty and
charm ; she would love her father and he should
love her, and every other man in the world might
vanish for all that she cared.   And had she only
known it, she had never before looked so pretty as
she did that night.   This also she did not know,
that her mother, catching a sudden picture of her
under the candle-light, felt a deep pang of almost
agonising envy.   She, making her last desperate bid
for love, was old and haggard ; the years for her
could only add to that age.   Her gambler's throw
was foredoomed before she had made it.

After dinner, Brandon, as always, retired into
the deepest chair in the drawing-room and buried
himself in yesterday's *Times*.   He read a little, but
the words meant nothing to him.   Jubilee !
Jubilee !   Jubilee !   He was sick of the word.
Surely they were overdoing it.   When the great
day itself came every one would be so tired. . . .

He pushed the paper aside and picked up
Punch.   Here, again, that eternal word—'How to
see the Procession.   By one who has thought it
out.   Of course you must be out early.   As the
traffic. . . .'

Joke.—Jinks : Don't meet you 'ere so often as we used
to, Binks, eh ?
  Binks : Well—no.   It don't run to a Hopera Box *this*
Season, because, you see, we've took a Window for this 'ere
Jubilee.

Then, on one page, 'The Walrus and the Car-
penter : Jubilee Version.'   'In Anticipation of the

Naval Review.' ' Two Jubilees ? ' On the next page an illustration of the Jubilee Walrus. On the next—' Oh, the Jubilee ! ' On the next, Toby M.P.'s ' Essence of Parliament,' with a ' Reed ' drawing of ' A naval Field Battery for the Jubilee.'

The paper fell from his hand. During these last days he had no time to read the paper, and he had fancied, as perhaps every Polcastrian was just then fancying, that the Jubilee was a private affair for Polchester's own private benefit. He felt suddenly that Polchester was a small out-of-the-way place of no account ; was there any one in the world who cared whether Polchester celebrated the Jubilee or not ? Nobody. . . .

He got up and walked across to the window, pulling the curtains aside and looking out at the deep purple dusk that stained the air like wine. The clock behind him struck a quarter past nine. Two tiny stars, like inquisitive mocking eyes, winked at him above the high Western tower. Moved by an impulse that was too immediate and peremptory to be investigated, he went into the hall, found his hat and stick, opened softly the door as though he were afraid that some one would try to stop him, and was soon on the grass in front of the Cathedral, staring about him as though he had wakened from a bewildering dream.

He went across to the little side-door, found his key, and entered the Cathedral, leaving the gargoyle to grin after him, growing more alive, and more malicious too, with every fading moment of the light.

Within the Cathedral there was a strange shadowy glow as though behind the thick cold pillars lights were burning. He found his way, stumbling over the cane-bottomed chairs that were

piled in measured heaps in the side aisle, into the
nave. Even he, used to it as he had been for so
many years, was thrilled to-night. There was a
movement of preparation abroad ; through all the
stillness there was the stir of life. It seemed
to him that the armoured knights and the high-
bosomed ladies, and the little cupids with their
pursed lips and puffing cheeks, and the angels
with their too solid wings were watching him and
breathing round him as he passed. Late though
it was, a dim light from the great East window
fell in broad slabs of purple and green shadow across
the grey ; everything was indistinct ; only the white
marble of the Reredos was like a figured sheet
hanging from wall to wall, and the gilded trumpets
of the angels on the choir-screen stood out dimly
like spider pattern. He felt a longing that the
place should return his love and tenderness. The
passion of his life was here ; he knew to-night, as
he had never before, the life of its own that this
place had, and as he stayed there, motionless in the
centre of the nave, some doubt stole into his heart
as to whether, after all, he and it were one and
indivisible, as for so long he had believed. Take
this away, and what was left to him ? His son had
gone, his wife and daughter were strange to him ;
if this, too, went. . . .

The sudden chill sense of loneliness was awful
to him. All those naked and sightless eyes staring
from those embossed tombs were menacing, scornful,
deriding.

He had never known such a mood, and he
wondered suddenly whether these last months had
affected his brain.

He had never doubted during the last ten years

his power over this and its gratitude to him for what
he had done : now, in this chill and green-hued
air, it seemed not to care for him at all.

He moved up into the choir and sat down in
his familiar stall ; all that he could see—his eyes
seemed to be drawn by some will stronger than his
own—was the Black Bishop's Tomb. The blue
stone was black behind the gilded grating, the
figure was like a moulded shell holding some hidden
form. The light died ; the purple and green
faded from the nave—the East window was dark—
only the white altar and the whiter shadows above
it hovered, thinner light against deeper grey. As
the light was withdrawn the Cathedral seemed to
grow in height until Brandon felt himself minute,
and the pillars sprang from the floor beneath him
into unseen canopied distance. He was cold ; he
longed suddenly, with a strange terror quite new to
him, for human company, and stumbled up and
hurried down the choir, almost falling over the
stone steps, almost running through the long, dark,
deserted nave. He fancied that other steps echoed
his own, that voices whispered, and that figures
thronged beneath the pillars to watch him go. It
was as though he were expelled.

Out in the evening air he was in his own world
again. He was almost tempted to return into the
Cathedral to rid himself of the strange fancies that
he had had, so that they might not linger with him.
He found himself now on the farther side of the
Cathedral, and after walking a little way he was on
the little narrow path that curved down through
the green banks to the river. Behind him was the
Cathedral, to his right Bodger's Street and Canon's
Yard, in front of him the bending hill, the river,

and then the farther slope where the lights of the gipsy encampment sparkled and shone. Here the air was lovely, cool and soft, and the stars were crowding into the summer sky in their myriads. But his depression did not leave him, nor his loneliness. He longed for Falk with a great longing. He could not hold out against the boy for very much longer; but even then, were the quarrel made up, things would not now be the same. Falk did not need him any more. He had new life, new friends, new work.

'It's my nerves,' thought Brandon. 'I *will* go and see Puddifoot.' It seemed to him that some one, and perhaps more than one, had followed him from the Cathedral. He turned sharply round as though he would catch somebody creeping upon him. He turned round and saw Samuel Hogg standing there.

'Evening, Archdeacon,' said Hogg.

Brandon said, his voice shaking with anger: 'What are you following me for?'

'Following you, Archdeacon?'

'Yes, following me. I have noticed it often lately. If you have anything to say to me write to me.'

'Following you? Lord, no! What makes you think of such a thing, Archdeacon? Can't a feller enjoy the evenin' air on such a lovely night as this without being accused of following a gentleman?'

'You know that you are trying to annoy me.' Brandon had pulled himself up, but his hatred of that grinning face with its purple veins, its piercing eyes, was working strongly upon his nerves, so that his hands seemed to move towards it without his own impulsion. 'You have been trying to annoy me for weeks now. I'll stand you no longer. If I have any more of this nuisance I'll put it into the hands of the police.'

Hogg spat out complacently over the grass. ' Now, that *is* an absurd thing,' he said, smiling. ' Because a man's tired and wants some air after his day's work he's accused of being a nuisance. It's a bit thick, that's what it is. Now, tell me, Archdeacon, do you happen to have bought this 'ere town, because if so I should be glad to know it—and so would a number of others too.'

' Very well, then,' said Brandon, moving away. ' If you won't go, I will.'

' There's no need for temper that I can see,' said Hogg. ' No call for it at all, especially that we're a sort of relation now. Almost brothers, seeing as how your son has married my daughter.'

Lower and lower ! Lower and lower !

He was moving in a world now where figures, horrible, obscene and foul, could claim him, could touch him, had their right to follow him.

' You will get nothing from me,' Brandon answered. ' You are wasting your time.'

' Wasting my time ? ' Hogg laughed. ' Not me ! I'm enjoying myself. I don't want anything from you except just to see you sometimes and have a little chat. That's quite enough for me ! I've taken quite a liking to you, Archdeacon, which is as it should be between relations, and, often enough, it isn't so. I like to see a proud gentleman like yourself mixing with such as me. It's good for both of us, as you might say.'

Brandon's anger — always dangerously uncontrolled—rose until it seemed to have the whole of his body in his grasp, swaying it, ebbing and flowing

with swift powerful current through his heart into
his brain. Now he could only see the flushed,
taunting face, the little eyes. . . .

But Hogg's hour was not yet. He suddenly
touched his cap, smiling.

' Well, good evening, Archdeacon. We'll be
meeting again '—and he was gone.

As swiftly as the anger had flowed now it ebbed,
leaving him trembling, shaking, that strange
sharp pain cutting his brain, his heart seeming to
leap into his head, to beat there like a drum, and to
fall back with heavy thud into his chest again.
He stood waiting for calm. He was humiliated,
desperately, shamefully. He could not go on here ;
he must leave the place. Leave it ? Be driven
away by that scoundrel ? Never ! He would face
them all and show them that he was above and
beyond their power.

But the peace of the evening and the glory of
the stars gradually stole into his heart. He had
been wrong, terribly wrong. His pride, his conceit,
had been destroying him. With a sudden flash of
revelation he saw it. He had trusted in his own
power, put himself on a level with the God whom
he served. A rush of deep and sincere humility
overwhelmed him. He bowed his head and prayed.

Some while later he turned up the path towards
home. The whole sky now burnt with stars ;
fires were a dull glow across the soft gulf of grey,
the gipsy fires. Once and again a distant voice
could be heard singing. As he reached the corner
of the Cathedral, and was about to turn up towards
the Precincts, a strange sound reached his ears.
He stood where he was and listened. At first he

could not define what he heard—then suddenly he realised. Quite close to him a man was sobbing.

There is something about the sounds of a man's grief that is almost indecent. This sobbing was pitiful in its abandonment and in its effort to control and stifle.

Brandon, looking more closely, saw the dark shadow of a man's body pressed against the inside buttress of the corner of the Cathedral wall. The shadow crouched, the body all drawn together as though folding in upon itself to hide its own agony.

Brandon endeavoured to move softly up the path, but his step crunched on some twigs, and at the sharp noise the sobbing suddenly ceased. The figure turned.

It was Morris. The two men looked at one another for an instant, then Morris, still like a shadow, vanished swiftly into the dusk.

CHAPTER III

JOAN was in her bedroom preparing for the Ball. It was now only half-past six and the Ball was not until half-past nine, but Mr. Mumphit, the be-curled, the be-scented young assistant from the hairdresser's in the High Street had paid his visit very early because he had so many other heads of so many other young ladies to dress in Polchester that evening. So Joan sat in front of the long looking - glass, a towel still over her shoulders, looking at herself in a state of ecstasy and delight.

It was wrong of her, perhaps, to feel so happy— she felt that deep in her consciousness ; wrong, with all the trouble in the house, Falk gone in disgrace, her father unhappy, her mother so strange; but to-night she could not help herself. The excitement was spluttering and crackling all over the town, the wonderful week upon which the whole country was entering, the Ball, her own coming-out Ball, and the consciousness that He would be there, and, even though He did love another, would be sure to give her at least one dance ; these things were all too strong for her—she was happy, happy, happy—her eyes danced, her toes danced, her very soul danced for sheer delirious joy. Had any one been behind her to look over her shoulder into the glass, he would have seen the reflection in that mirror of one of the prettiest children the wide world could show ; especially childish she looked to-night with her dark hair piled high on her head, her eyes wide with wonder, her neck and shoulders so delicately white and soft. Behind her, on the bed, was the dress, on the dingy carpet a pair of shoes of silver tissue, the loveliest things she had ever had. They were reflected in the mirror, little blobs of silver, and as she saw them the colour mounted still higher in her cheeks. She had no right to them ; she had not paid for them. They were the first things that she had ever, in all her life, bought on credit. Neither her father nor her mother knew anything about them, but she had seen them in Harriott's shop-window and had simply not been able to resist them.

If, after all, she was to dance with Him, that made anything right. Were she sent to prison because she could not pay for them it would not matter. She had done the only possible thing.

And so she looked into the mirror and saw the dark glitter in her hair and the red in her cheeks and the whiteness of her shoulders and the silver blobs of the little shoes, and she was happy—happy with an almost fearful ecstasy.

Mrs. Brandon also was in her bedroom. She was sitting on a high stiff-backed chair, staring in front of her. She had been sitting there now for a long time without making any movement at all. She might have been a dead woman. Her thin hands, with the sharply marked blue veins, were clasped tightly on her lap. She was feeding, feverishly, eagerly feeding upon the thought of Morris.

She would see him that evening, they would talk together, dance together, their hands would burn as they touched ; they would say very little to one another ; they would long, agonize for one another, to be alone together, to be far, far away from everybody, and they would be desperately unhappy.

She wondered, in her strange kind of mouse-in-the-trap trance, about that unhappiness. Was there to be no happiness for her anywhere ? Was she always to want more than she got, was all this passion now too late ? Was it real at all ? Was it not a fever, a phantom, a hallucination ? Did she see Morris ? Did she not rather see something that she must seize to slake her burning feverish thirst ? For one moment she had known happiness, when her arms had gone around him and she had been able to console and comfort him. But comfort him for how long ? Was he not as unhappy as she, and would they not always be unhappy ? Was he not weighed down by the sin that he had committed, that he, as he thought, had caused her to commit ? . . . At that she sprang up from the chair and paced the room, murmuring aloud : ' No, no, I did it. My sin, not his. I will care for him, watch over him—watch over him, care for him. He must be glad. . . .'

She sank down by the bed, burying her face in her hands.

Brandon was in his study finishing his letters. But behind his application to the notes that he was writing his brain was moving like an animal stealthily

investigating an unlighted house. He was thinking
of his wife—and of himself. Even as he was writing
' And therefore it seems to me, my dear Ryle, that
with regard to the actual hour of the service, eight
o'clock——' his inner consciousness was whispering
to him, ' How you miss Falk l How lonely the house
seems without him l You thought you could get
along without love, didn't you ? or, at least, you
were not aware that it played any very great part in
your life. But now that the one person whom you
most sincerely loved is gone, you see that it was not
to be so simply taken for granted, do you not ?
Love must be worked for, sacrificed for, cared for,
nourished and cherished. You want some one to
cherish now, and you are surprised that you should
so want . . . yes, there is your wife—Amy . . .
Amy. . . . You had taken her also for granted.
But she is still with you. There is time.'

His wife was illuminated with tenderness. He
put down his pen and stared in front of him. What
he wanted and what she wanted was a holiday.
They had been too long here in this place. That
was what he needed, that was the explanation of his
headaches, of his tempers, of his obsession about
Ronder.

As soon as this Pybus St. Anthony affair was
settled he would take his wife abroad. Just the
two of them. Another honeymoon after all these
years. Greece, Italy . . . and who knows ? Perhaps he would see Falk on his way through London
returning . . . Falk. . . .

He had forgotten his letters, staring in front of
him, tapping the table with his pen.

There was a knock on the door. The maid
said, ' A lady to see you, sir. She says it's im-

portant '—and, before he could ask her name, some
one else was in the room with him and the door was
closed behind her.

He was puzzled for a moment as to her identity,
a rather seedy, down-at-heels-looking woman. She
was wearing a rather crumpled white cotton dress.
She carried a pink parasol, and on her head was a
large straw hat overburdened with bright red roses.
Ah, yes ! Of course ! Miss Milton—who was
the Librarian. Shabby she looked. Come down
in the world. He had always disliked her. He
resented now the way in which she had almost
forced her way into his room.

She looked across at him through her funny half-
closed eyes.

' I beg your pardon, Archdeacon Brandon,' she
said, ' for entering like this at what must be, I fear,
an unseemly time. My only excuse must be the
urgency of my business.'

' I am very sorry, Miss Milton,' he said sternly ;
' it is quite impossible for me to see you just now
on any business whatever. If you will make an
appointment with me in writing, I will see what can
be done.'

At the sound of his voice her eyes closed still
further. ' I'm very sorry, Archdeacon,' she said.
' I think you would do well to listen to what I am
going to tell you.'

He raised his head and looked at her. At those
words of hers he had once again the sensation of
being pushed down by strong heavy hands into
some deep mire where he must have company with
filthy crawling animals—Hogg, Davray, and now
this woman. . . .

' What do you mean ? ' he asked, disgust

thickening his voice. 'What can *you* have to tell *me*?'

She smiled. She crossed the floor and came close to his desk   Her fingers were on the shabby bag that hung over her arm.

'I was greatly puzzled,' she said, 'as to what was the right thing to do. I am a good and honest woman, Archdeacon, although I was ejected from my position most wrongfully by those that ought to have known better. I have come down in the world through no fault of my own, and there are some who should be ashamed in their hearts of the way they've treated me. However, it's not of them I've to speak to-day.' She paused.

Brandon drew back into his chair. 'Please tell me, Miss Milton, your business as soon as possible. I have much to do.'

'I will.' She breathed hard and continued. 'Certain information was placed in my hands, and I found it very difficult to decide on the justice of my course. After some hesitation I went to Canon Ronder, knowing him to be a just man.'

At the name 'Ronder' the Archdeacon's lips moved, but he said nothing.

'I showed him the information I had obtained. I asked him what I should do. He gave me advice which I followed.'

'He advised you to come to me.'

Miss Milton saw at once that a lie here would serve her well. 'He advised me to come to you and give you this letter which in the true sense of the word belongs to you.'

She fumbled with her bag, opened it, took out a piece of paper.

'I must tell you,' she continued, her eyes never

for an instant leaving the Archdeacon's face, ' that this letter came into my hands by an accident. I was in Mr. Morris's house at the time and the letter was delivered to me by mistake.'

' Mr. Morris,' Brandon repeated. ' What has he to do with this affair ? '

Miss Milton rubbed her gloved hands together. ' Mrs. Brandon,' she said, ' has been very friendly with Mr. Morris for a long time past. The whole town has been talking of it.'

The clock suddenly began to strike the hour. No word was spoken.

Then Brandon said very quietly, ' Leave this house, Miss Milton, and never enter it again. If I have any further trouble with you, the police will be informed.'

' Before I go, Archdeacon,' said Miss Milton, also very quietly, ' you should see this letter. I can assure you that I have not come here for mere words. I have my conscience to satisfy like any other person. I am not asking for anything in return for this information, although I should be perfectly justified in such an action, considering how monstrously I have been treated. I give you this letter and you can destroy it at once. My conscience will be satisfied. If, on the other hand, you don't read it —well, there are others in the town who must see it.'

He took the letter from her.

DEAREST—I am sending this by a safe hand to tell you that I cannot possibly get down to-night. I am so sorry and most dreadfully disappointed, but I will explain everything when we meet to-morrow. This is to prevent your waiting on when I'm not coming.

It was in his wife's handwriting.

'Dearest . . . cannot possibly get down to-night. . . .' In his wife's handwriting. Certainly. Yes. His wife's. And Ronder had seen it.

He looked across at Miss Milton. 'This is not my wife's handwriting,' he said. 'You realise, I hope, in what a serious matter you have become involved—by your hasty action,' he added.

'Not hasty,' she said, moistening her lips with her tongue. 'Not hasty, Archdeacon. I have taken much thought. I don't know if I have already told you that I took the letter myself at the door from the hand of your own maid. She has been to the Library with books. She is well known to me.'

He must exercise enormous, superhuman, self-control. That was his only thought. The tide of anger was rising in him so terribly that it pressed against the skin of his forehead, drawn tight, and threatened to split it. What he wanted to do was to rise and assault the woman standing in front of him. His hands longed to take her! They seemed to have life and volition of their own and to move across the table of their own accord.

He was aware, too, once more, of some huge plot developing around him, some supernatural plot in which all the elements too were involved — earth, sun and sky, and also every one in the town, down to the smallest child there.

He seemed to see behind him, just out of his sight, a tall massive figure directing the plot, a figure something like himself, only with a heavy black beard, cloudy, without form. . . .

They would catch him in their plot as in a net, but he would escape them, and he would escape them by wonderful calm, and self-control, and the absence of all emotion.

So that, although his voice shook a little, it was quietly that he repeated :

'This is not in my wife's handwriting. You know the penalties for forgery.' Then, looking her full in the face, he added, 'Penal servitude.'

She smiled back at him.

'I am sure, Archdeacon, that all I require is a full investigation. These wickednesses are going on in this town, and those principally concerned should know. I have only done what I consider my duty.'

Her eyes lingered on his face. She savoured now during these moments the revenge for which, in all these months, she had ceaselessly longed. He had moved but little, he had not raised his voice, but, watching his face, she had seen the agony pass, like an entering guest, behind his eyes. That guest would remain. She was satisfied.

'I have done my duty, Archdeacon, and now I will wish you good-evening.'

She gave a little bow and retired from the room, softly closing the door behind her.

He sat there, looking at the letter. . . .

The Assembly Rooms seemed to move like a ship on a sunset sea. Hanging from the ceiling were the two great silver candelabra, in some ways the most famous treasure that the town possessed. Fitted now with gas, they were nevertheless so shaded that the light was soft and mellow. Round the room, beneath the portraits of the town's celebrities in their heavy gold frames, the lights were hidden with shields of gold. The walls were ivory white. From the Minstrels' Gallery flags with the arms of the Town, of the Cathedral, of the St. Leath family fluttered once and again faintly. In the Minstrels' Gallery the band was playing just as it had played a hundred years ago. The shining floor was covered with moving figures. Every one was there. Under the Gallery, surveying the world like Boadicea her faithful Britons, was Lady St. Leath, her white hair piled high above her pink baby face, that had the inquiring haughty expression of a cockatoo wondering whether it is being offered a lump of sugar or an insult. On either side of her sat two of her daughters, Lady Rose and Lady Mary, plain and patient.

Near her, in a complacent chattering row, were some of the more important of the Cathedral and County set. There were the Marriotts from Maple Durham, fat, sixty, and amiable; old Colonel Wotherston, who had fought in the Crimea; Sir Henry Byles with his large purple nose; little Major Garnet, the kindest bachelor in the County; the Marquesas, who had more pedigree than pennies; Mrs. Sampson in bright lilac, and an especially bad attack of neuralgia; Mrs. Combermere, sheathed in cloth of gold and very jolly; Mrs. Ryle, humble in grey silk; Ellen Stiles in cherry colour; Mrs. Trudon, Mrs. Forrester and Mrs. D'Arcy, their chins nearly touching over eager confidences; Dr. Puddifoot, still breathless from his last dance; Bentinck-Major, tapping with his patent-leather toe the floor, eager to be at it again; Branston the Mayor and Mrs. Branston, uncomfortable in a kind of dog-collar of diamonds; Mrs. Preston, searching for nobility; Canon Martin; Dennison, the head-master of the School; and many many others.

It was just then a Polka, and the tune was so

alluring, so entrancing, that the whole world rose and fell with its rhythm.

And where was Joan ? Joan was dancing with the Reverend Rex Forsyth, the proposed incumbent of Pybus St. Anthony. Had any one told her a week ago that she would dance with the elegant Mr. Forsyth before a gathering of all the most notable people of Polchester and Southern Glebe-shire, and would so dance without a tremor, she would have derided her informant. But what cannot excitement and happiness do ?

She knew that she was looking nice, she knew that she was dancing as well as any one else in the room—and Johnny St. Leath had asked her for two dances and *then* wanted more, and wanted these with the beautiful Claire Daubeney, all radiant in silver, standing close beside him. What, then, could all the Forsyths in the world matter ? Neverthe-less he *was* elegant. Very smart indeed. Rather like a handsome young horse, groomed for a show. His voice had a little neigh in it ; as he talked over her shoulder he gave a little whinny of pleasure. She found it very difficult to think of him as a clergyman at all.

> You should SEE me DANCE the POLKA,
> Ta-ram-te-tum-te-TA.

Yes, she should. And *he* should. And he was very pleasant when he did not talk.

' You dance—very well—Miss Brandon.'

' Thank you. This is my first Ball.'

' Who would — think that ? Ta-ram-te-tum-te-TA. . . . Jolly tu-une ! '

She caught glimpses of every one as they went round. Mrs. Combermere's cloth of gold, Lady

St. Leath's white hair.   Poor Lady Mary—such a pity that they could not do something for her complexion.   Spotty.   Joan liked her.   She did much good to the poor in Seatown, and it must be agony to her, poor thing, to go down there, because she was so terribly shy.   Her next dance was with Johnny.   She called him Johnny.   And why should she not, secretly to herself?   Ah, there was mother, all alone.   And there was Mr. Morris coming up to speak to her.   Kind of him.   But he *was* a kind man.   She liked him.   Very shy, though. All the nicest people seemed to be shy—except Johnny, who wasn't shy at all.

The music stopped and, breathless, they stayed for a moment before finding two chairs.   Now was coming the time that she so greatly disliked.   Whatever to say to Mr. Forsyth?

They sat down in the long passage outside the ballroom.   The floor ran like a ribbon from under their feet into dim shining distance.   Or rather, Joan thought, it was like a stream, and on either side the dancers were sitting, dabbling their toes and looking self-conscious.

'Do you like it where you are?' Joan asked of the shining black silk waistcoat that gleamed beside her.

'Oh, you know . . .' neighed Mr. Forsyth. 'It's all right, you know.   The old Bishop's kind enough.'

'Bishop Clematis?' said Joan.

'Yes.   There ain't enough to do, you know. But I don't expect I'll be there long.   No, I don't. . . . Pity poor Morrison at Pybus dying like that.'

Joan of course at once understood the allusion.

She also understood that Mr. Forsyth was begging her to bestow upon him any little piece of news that she might have obtained. But that seemed to her mean—spying—spying on her own father. So she only said :

' You're very fond of riding, aren't you ? '

' Love it,' said Mr. Forsyth, whinnying so exactly like a happy pony that Joan jumped. ' Don't you ? '

' I've never been on horseback in my life,' said Joan. ' I'd like to try.'

' Never in your life ? ' Mr. Forsyth stared. ' Why, I was on a pony before I was three. Fact. Good for a clergyman, riding——'

' I think it's nearly time for the next dance,' said Joan. ' Would you kindly take me back to my mother ? '

She was conscious, as they plunged down-stream, of all the burning glances. She held her head high. Her eyes flashed. She was going to dance with Johnny, and they could look as much as they liked.

Mr. Forsyth delivered her to her mother and went cantering off. Joan sat down, smoothed her dress and stared at the vast shiny lake of amber in which the silver candelabra were reflected like little islands. She looked at her mother and was suddenly sorry for her. It must be dull, when you were as old as mother, coming to these dances —and especially when you had so few friends. Her mother had never made many friends.

' Wasn't that Mr. Morris who was talking to you just now ? '

' Yes, dear.'

' I like him. He looks kind.'

' Yes, dear.'

' And where's father ? '

' Over there, talking to Lady St. Leath.'

She looked across, and there he was, so big and
tall and fine, so splendid in his grand clothes.   Her
heart swelled with pride.

' Isn't he splendid, mother, dear ? '

' Who ? '

' Father ! '

' Splendid ? '

' Yes ; doesn't he look splendid to-night ? Better-
looking than all the rest of the room put together ? '
(Johnny wasn't *good - looking*.   Better than *good-
looking*.)

' Oh—look splendid.   Yes.   He's a very handsome man.'

Joan felt once again that little chill with which
she was so often familiar when she talked with her
mother—a sudden withdrawal of sympathy, a pushing Joan away with her hand.

But never mind—there was the music again,
and here, oh here, was Johnny ! Some one had
once called him Tubby in her hearing, and how
indignant she had been ! He was perhaps a little
on the fat side, but strong with it. . . . She went
off with him.   The waltz began.

She sank into sweet delicious waters—waters that
rocked and cradled her, hugged her and caressed
her.   She was conscious of his arm.   She did not
speak nor did he.   Years of utter happiness
passed. . . .

He did not take her, as Mr. Forsyth had done,
into the public glare of the passage, but up a crooked
staircase behind the Minstrels' Gallery into a little
room, cool and shaded, where, in easy-chairs, they
were quite alone.

He was shy, fingering his gloves. She said (just to make conversation):

'How beautiful Miss Daubeney is looking!'

'Do you think so?' said Johnny. 'I don't. I'm sick of that girl. She's the most awful bore. Mother's always shoving her at my head. She's been staying with us for months. She wants me to marry her because she's rich. But we've got plenty, and I wouldn't marry her anyway, not if we hadn't a penny. Because she's a bore, and because'—his voice became suddenly loud and commanding—'I'm going to marry you.'

Something—some lovely bird of Paradise, some splendid coloured breeze, some carpet of magic pattern—came and swung Joan up to a high tree loaded with golden apples. There she swung—singing her heart out. Johnny's voice came up to her.

'Because I'm going to marry you.'

'What?' she called down to him.

'I'm going to marry you. I knew it from the very first second I saw you, that day after Cathedral—from the very first moment I knew it. I wanted to ask you right away at once, but I thought I'd do the thing properly, so I went away, and I've been in Paris and Rome and all over the place, and I've thought of you the *whole* time—every minute. Then mother made a fuss about this Daubeney girl—my not being here and all that—so I thought I'd come home and tell you I was going to marry you.'

'Oh, but you can't.' Joan swung down from her apple-tree. 'You and me? Why, what *would* your mother say?'

'It isn't a case of *would* but *will*,' Johnny said. 'Mother will be very angry—and for a considerable

time. But that makes no difference. Mother's
mother and I'm myself.'

'It's impossible,' said Joan quickly, 'from every
point of view. Do you know what my brother has
done? I'm proud of Falk and love him; but
you're Lord St. Leath, and Falk has married the
daughter of Hogg, the man who keeps a public-
house down in Seatown.'

'I heard of that,' said Johnny. 'But what
does that matter? Do you know what I did last
year? I crossed the Atlantic as a stoker in a
Cunard boat. Mother never knew until I got
back, and *wasn't* she furious! But the world's
changing. There isn't going to be any class
difference soon—none at all. You take my word.
Look at the Americans! They're the people!
We'll be like them one day. . . . But what's all
this?' he suddenly said. 'I'm going to marry
you and you're going to marry me. You love me,
don't you?'

'Yes,' said Joan faintly.

'Well, then. I knew you did. I'm going to
kiss you.' He put his arms around her and kissed
her very gently.

'Oh, how I love you!' he said, 'and how good
I'll be to you!'

'But we must be practical,' said Joan wildly.
'How *can* we marry? Everything's against it.
I've no money. I'm nobody. Your mother——'

'Now you just leave my mother alone. Leave
me to manage her—I know all about that——'

'I won't be engaged to you,' Joan said firmly,
'not for ages and ages—not for a year anyway.'

'That's all right,' said Johnny indifferently.
'You can settle it any way you please—but no

one's going to marry you but me, and no one's going to marry me but you.'

He would have kissed her again, but Mrs. Preston and a young man came in.

'Now you shall come and speak to my mother,' he said to her as they went out. 'There's nothing to be afraid of. Just say "Bo" to her as you would to a goose, and she'll answer all right.'

'You won't say anything——' began Joan.

'About us? All right. That's a secret for the present; but we shall meet *every* day, and if there's a day we don't meet you've got to write. Do you agree?'

Whether she agreed or no was uncertain, because they were now in a cloud of people, and, a moment later, were face to face with the old Countess.

She was pleased, it at once appeared. She was in a gracious mood; people had been pleasant enough —that is, they had been obsequious and flattering. Also her digestion was behaving properly; those new pills that old Puddifoot had given her were excellent. She therefore received Joan very graciously, congratulated her on her appearance, and asked her where her elder sister was. When Joan explained that she had no sister Lady St. Leath appeared vexed with her, as though it had been a piece of obvious impertinence on her part not to produce a sister instantly when she had asked for one. However, Lady Mary was kind and friendly and made Joan sit beside her for a little. Joan thought, 'I'd like to have you for a sister one day, if—if—ever——' and allowed her thoughts to go no farther.

Thence she passed into the company of Mrs. Combermere and Ellen Stiles. It seemed to her——

but it was probably her fancy—that as she came
to them they were discussing something that was
not for her ears.   It seemed to her that they swiftly
changed the conversation and greeted her with
quite an unusual warmth of affection.   For the
first time that evening a sudden little chill of
foreboding, whence she knew not, seemed to touch
her and shade, for an instant, her marvellous
happiness.

Mrs. Combermere was very sweet to her indeed,
quite as though she had been, but now, recovering
from an alarming illness.   Her bass voice, strong
thick hands and stiff wiry hair went so incongruously
with her cloth of gold that Joan could not help
smiling.

' You look very happy, my dear,' Mrs. Combermere said.

' Of course I am,' said Joan.   ' How can I help
it, my first Ball ? '

Mrs. Combermere kicked her trailing garments
with her foot, just like a dame in a pantomime.
' Well, enjoy yourself as long as you can.   You're
looking very pretty.   The prettiest girl in the room.
I've just been saying so to Ellen—haven't I, Ellen ? '

Ellen Stiles was at that moment making herself
agreeable to the Mayoress, who was sitting lonely
and uncomfortable (weighed down with longing
for sleep) on a little gilt chair.

' I was just saying to Mrs. Branston,' Miss
Stiles said, turning round, ' that the time one has
to be careful with children after whooping-cough is
when they seem practically well.   Her little boy
has just been ill with it, and she says he's recovered ;
but that's the time, as I tell her, when nine out of
ten children die—just when you think you're safe.'

'Oh dear,' said Mrs. Branston, turning towards them her full anxious eyes. 'You *do* alarm me, Miss Stiles! And I've been letting Tommy quite loose, as you may say, these last few days—with his appetite back and all, there seemed no danger.'

'Well, if you find him feverish when you get home to-night,' said Ellen, 'don't be surprised. All the excitement of the Jubilee too will be very bad for him.'

At that moment Canon Ronder came up. Joan looked and at once, at the sight of the round gleaming spectacles, the smiling mouth, the full cheeks puffed out as though he were blowing perpetual bubbles for his own amusement, felt her old instinct of repulsion. This man was her father's enemy, and so hers. All the town knew now that he was trying to ruin her father so that he might take his place, that he laughed at him and mocked him.

So fierce did she feel that she could have scratched his cheeks. He was smiling at them all, and at once was engaged in a wordy duel with Mrs. Combermere and Miss Stiles. *They* liked him; every one in the town liked him. She heard his praises sung by every one. Well, she would never sing them. She hated him.

And now he was actually speaking to her. He had the impertinence to ask her for a dance.

'I'm afraid I'm engaged for the next and for the one after that, Canon Ronder,' she said.

'Well, later on then,' he said, smiling. 'What about an extra?'

Her dark eyes scorned him.

'We are going home early,' she said. She pretended to examine her programme. 'I'm afraid I have not one before we go.'

She spoke as coldly as she dared. She felt the eyes of Mrs. Combermere and Ellen Stiles upon her. How stupid of her! She had shown them what her feelings were, and now they would chatter the more and laugh about her fighting her father's battles. Why had she not shown her indifference, her complete indifference?

He was smiling still—not discomforted by her rudeness. He said something—something polite and outrageously kind—and then young Charles D'Arcy came up to carry her off for the Lancers.

An hour later her cup of happiness was completely filled. She had danced, during that hour, four times with Johnny; every one must be talking. Lady St. Leath must be furious (she did not know that Boadicea had been playing whist with old Colonel Wotherston and Sir Henry Byles for the last ever so long).

She would perhaps never have such an hour in all her life again. This thing that he so wildly proposed was impossible—utterly, completely impossible; but what was *not* impossible, what was indeed certain and sure and beyond any sort of question, was that she loved Johnny St. Leath with all her heart and soul, and would so love him until the day of her death. Life could never be purposeless nor mean nor empty for her again, while she had that treasure to carry about with her in her heart. Meanwhile she could not look at him and doubt but that, for the moment at any rate, he loved her—and there was something simple and direct about Johnny as there was about his dog Andrew, that made his words, few and clumsy though they might be, most strangely convincing.

So, almost dizzy with happiness, she climbed the stair behind the Gallery and thought that she would escape for a moment into the little room where Johnny had proposed to her, and sit there and grow calm. She looked in. Some one was there. A man sitting by himself and staring in front of him. She saw at once that he was in some great trouble. His hands were clenched, his face puckered and set with pain. Then she saw that it was her father.

He did not move; he might have been a block of stone shining in the dimness. Terrified, she stood, herself not moving. Then she came forward. She put her hand on his shoulder.

'Oh father—father, what is it?' She felt his body trembling beneath her touch—he, the proudest, finest man in the country. She put her arm round his neck. She kissed him. His forehead was damp with sweat. His body was shaking from head to foot. She kissed him again and again, kneeling beside him.

Then she remembered where they were. Some one might come. No one must see him like that.

She whispered to him, took his hands between hers.

'Let's go home, Joan,' he said. 'I want to go home.'

She put her arm through his, and together they went down the little stairs.

CHAPTER IV

BRANDON had been talking to the Precentor at the
far end of the ballroom, when suddenly Ronder had
appeared in their midst. Appeared the only word !
And Brandon, armoured, he had thought, for every
terror that that night might bring to him, had been
suddenly seized with the lust of murder. A lust
as dominating as any other, that swept upon him
in a hot flaming tide, lapped him from head to foot.
It was no matter, this time, of words, of senses, of
thoughts, but of his possession by some other man
who filled his brain, his eyes, his mouth, his stomach,
his heart ; one second more and he would have
flung himself upon that smiling face, those rounded
limbs ; he would have caught that white throat and
squeezed it—squeezed . . . squeezed. . . .

The room literally swam in a tide of impulse that
carried him against Ronder's body and left him
there, breast beating against breast. . . .

He turned without a word and almost ran from
the place. He passed through the passages, seeing
no one, conscious of neither voices nor eyes, climbing stairs that he did not feel, sheltering in that
lonely little room, sitting there, his hands to his face,
shuddering. The lust slowly withdrew from him,

leaving him icy cold. Then he lifted his eyes and saw his daughter and clung to her—as just then he would have clung to anybody—for safety.

Had it come to this then, that he was mad? All that night, lying on his bed, he surveyed himself. That was the way that men murdered. No longer could he claim control or mastery of his body. God had deserted him and given him over to devils.

His son, his wife, and now God. His loneliness was terrible. And he could not think. He must think about this letter and what he should do. He could not think at all. He was given over to devils.

After Matins in the Cathedral next day one thought came to him. He would go and see the Bishop. The Bishop had come in from Carpledon for the Jubilee celebrations and was staying at the Deanery. Brandon spoke to him for a moment after Matins and asked him whether he might see him for half an hour in the afternoon on a matter of great urgency. The Bishop asked him to come at three o'clock.

Seated in the Dean's library, with its old-fashioned cosiness—its book-shelves and the familiar books, the cases, between the high windows, of his precious butterflies—Brandon felt, for the first time for many days, a certain calm descend upon him. The Bishop, looking very frail and small in the big arm-chair, received him with so warm an affection that he felt, in spite of his own age, like the old man's son.

'My lord,' he began with difficulty, moving his big limbs in his chair like a restless schoolboy, ' it isn't easy for me to come to-day. There's no

one in the world I could speak to except yourself.
I find it difficult even to do that.'

'My son,' said the Bishop gently, 'I am a
very, very old man. I cannot have many more
months to live. When one is as near to death as I
am, one loves everything and everybody, because one
is going so soon. You needn't be afraid.'

And in his heart he must have wondered at the
change in this man who, through so many years
now, had come to him with so much self-confidence
and assurance.

'I have had much trouble lately,' Brandon went
on. 'But I would not have bothered you with that,
knowing as I do all that you have to consider just
now, were it not that for the first time in my life
I seem to have lost control and to be heading toward
some great disaster that may bring scandal not only
on myself but on the Church as well.'

'Tell me your trouble,' said the Bishop.

'Nine months ago I seemed to be at the very
height of my powers, my happiness, my usefulness.'
Brandon paused. Was it really only nine months
back, that other time? 'I had no troubles. I
was confident in myself, my health was good, my
family were happy. I seemed to have many
friends. . . . Then suddenly everything changed.
I don't want to seem false, my lord, in anything
that I may say, but it was literally as though in the
course of a night all my happiness forsook me.

'It began with my boy being sent down from
Oxford. I have only one boy, as I think your
lordship knows. He was—he is, in spite of what
has happened—very dear to me.' Brandon paused.

'Yes, I know,' said the Bishop.

'After that everything began to go wrong.

Little things, little tiny things—one after another.
Some one came to this town who almost at once
seemed to put himself into opposition to me.'
Brandon paused once more.

The Bishop said again : ' Yes, I know.'

' At first,' Brandon went on, ' I didn't realise
this. I was preoccupied with my own work. It
had never, at any time in my life, seemed to me
healthy to consider about other people's minds, what
they were thinking or imagining. There is quite
enough work to do in the world without that. But
soon I was forced to consider this man's opposition
to me. It came before me in a thousand little ways.
The attitude of the Chapter changed to me—
especially noticeable at one of the Chapter Meetings.
I don't want to make my story so long, my lord, that
it will tire you. To cut it short—a day came when
my boy ran off to London with a town girl, the
daughter of the landlord of one of the more
disreputable public-houses. That was a terrible,
devastating blow to me. I have quite literally not
been the same man since. I was determined not
to allow it to turn me from my proper work. I
still loved the boy ; he had not behaved dis-
honourably to the girl. He has now married her
and is earning his living in London. If that had
been the only blow——' He stopped, cleared his
throat, and, turning excitedly towards the Bishop,
almost shouted :

' But it is not ! It is not, my lord ! My
enemy has never ceased his plots for one instant.
It was he who advised my boy to run off with this
girl. He has turned the whole town against me ;
they laugh at me and mock me ! And now he . . .
now he . . .' He could not for a moment find

breath. He exercised an impulse of almost super-human self-control, bringing his body visibly back into bounds again. He went on more quietly :

' We are in opposite camps over this matter of the Pybus living—we are in opposition over almost every question that arises here. He is an able man. I must do him that justice. He can plot. . . he can scheme . . . whereas I . . .' Brandon beat his hands desperately on his knees.

' It is not only this man ! ' he cried, ' not only this ! It is as though there were some larger conspiracy, something from Heaven itself. God has turned His face away from me when I have served Him faithfully all my days. No one has served Him more whole-heartedly than I. He has been my only thought, His glory my only purpose. Nine months ago I had health, I had friends, I had honour. I had my family—now my health is going, my friends have forsaken me, I am mocked at by the lowest men in the town, my son has left me, my—my . . .'

He broke off, bending his face in his hands.

The Bishop said : ' My dear friend, you are not alone in this. We have all been tried, like this—tested——'

' Tested ! ' Brandon broke out. ' Why should I be tested ? What have I done in all my life that is not acceptable to God ? What sin have I committed ? What disloyalty have I shown ? But there is something more that I must tell you, my lord—the reason why I have come to you to-day. Canon Ronder and I—you must have known of whom I have been speaking—had a violent quarrel one afternoon on the way home after lunching with you at Carpledon. This quarrel became, in one way or another, the town's property. Ronder affected to like me, but it was impossible now for him to hide his real intentions towards me. This thing began to be an obsession with me. I tried to prevent this. I knew what the danger of such obsessions can be. But there was something else. My wife——' he paused—went on. 'My wife and I, my lord, have lived together in perfect happiness for twenty years. At least it had seemed to me to be perfect happiness. She began to behave strangely. She was not herself. Undoubtedly the affair of our son disturbed her desperately. She seemed to avoid me, to escape from me when she could. This, coming with my other troubles, made me feel as though I were in some horrible dream, as though the very furniture of our home and the appearance of the streets were changing. I began to be afraid sometimes that I might be going mad. I have had bad headaches that have made it difficult for me to think. Then, only last night, a woman brought me a letter. I wish you most earnestly to believe, my lord, that I believe my wife to be absolutely loyal to me—loyal in every possible sense of the word. The letter purported to be in her handwriting. And in this matter also Canon Ronder had had some hand. The woman admitted that she had been first to Canon Ronder and that he had advised her to bring it to me.'

The Bishop made a movement.

'You will, of course, say nothing of this, my lord, to Canon Ronder. I have come privately to ask your prayers for me and to have your counsel. I am making no complaint against Canon Ronder. I must see this thing through by myself. But last night, when my mind was filled with this letter, I

found myself suddenly next to Canon Ronder, and
I had a murderous impulse that was so fierce and
sudden in its power that I——' He broke off,
shuddering ; then cried, suddenly stretching out
his hands :

'Oh, my lord, pray for me, pray for me !
Help me ! I don't know what I do—I am given
over to the powers of Hell !'

A long silence followed. Then the Bishop said :
'You have asked me to say nothing to Canon
Ronder, and of course I must respect your confidence. But the first thing that I would say to you
is that I think that what you feared has happened
—that you have allowed this thought of him to
become an obsession to you. The ways of God are
mysterious and past our finding out ; but all of us,
in our lives, have known that time when everything has suddenly turned against us—our work,
those whom we love, our health, even our belief in
God Himself. My dear, dear friend, I myself have
known that several times in my own life. Once,
when I was a young man, I lost an appointment on
which my whole heart was set, and lost it, as it
seemed, through an extreme injustice. It turned
out afterwards that my losing that was one of the
most fortunate things for me. Once my dear
wife and I seemed to lose all our love for one
another, and I was assailed with most desperate
temptation—and the end of that was that we loved
and understood one another as we had never done
before. Once—and this was the most terrible
period in my life, and it continued over a long time
—I lost, as it seemed, completely all my faith in
God. I came out of that believing only in the
beauty of Christ's life, clinging to that, and saying

to myself, " Such a friend have I—then life is not all lost to me "—and slowly, gradually, I came back into touch with Him and knew Him as I had never known Him before, and, through Him, once again God the Father. And now, even in my old age, temptation is still with me. I long to die. I am tempted often to look upon men and women as shadows that have no longer any connection with me. I am very weak and feeble and I wish to sleep. . . . But the love of God continues and, through Jesus Christ, the love of men. It is the only truth—love of God, love of man—the rest is fantasy and unreality. Look up, my son, bear this with patience. God is standing at your shoulder and will be with you to the end. This is training for you. To show you, perhaps, that all through life you have missed the most important thing. You are learning through this trouble your need of others, your need to love them, and that they should love you—the only lesson worth learning in life. . . .'

The Bishop came over to Brandon and put his hand on his head. Strange peace came into Brandon's heart, not from the old man's words, but from the contact with him, the touch of his thin trembling hand. The room was filled with peace. Ronder was suddenly of little importance. The Cathedral faded. For a time he rested.

For the rest of that day, until the evening, that peace stayed with him. With it still in his heart he came, late that night, into their bedroom. Mrs. Brandon was in bed, awake, staring in front of her, not moving. He sat down in the chair beside the bed, stretched out his hand, and took hers.

'Amy, dear,' he said, 'I want us to have a little talk.'

Her little hand lay still and hot in his large cool one.

'I've been very unhappy,' he went on with difficulty, 'lately about you—I have seen that you yourself are not happy. I want you to be. I will do anything that is in my power to make you so!'

'You would not,' she said, without looking at him, 'have troubled to think of me had not your own private affairs gone wrong and—had not Falk left us!'

The sound of her hostility irritated him against his will; he beat the irritation down. He felt suddenly very tired, quite exhausted. He had an almost irresistible temptation to go down into his dressing-room, lie on his sofa there, and go instantly to sleep.

'That's not quite fair, Amy,' he said. 'But we won't dispute about that. I want to know why, after our being happy for twenty years, something now has come in between us or seems to have done so; I want to clear that away if I can, so that we can be as we were before.'

Be as they were before! At the strange ludicrous irony of that phrase she turned on her elbow and looked at him, stared at him as though she could not see enough of him.

'Why do you think that there is anything the matter?' she asked softly, almost gently.

'Why, of course I can see,' he said, holding her hand more tightly as though the sudden gentleness in her voice had touched him. 'When one has lived with some one a long time,' he went on rather awkwardly, 'one notices things. Of course

I've seen that you were not happy. And Falk leaving us in that way must have made you very miserable. It made me miserable too,' he added, suddenly stroking her hand a little.

She could not bear that and very quietly withdrew her hand.

'Did it really hurt you, Falk's going?' she asked, still staring at him.

'Hurt me?' he cried, staring back at her in utter astonishment. 'Hurt me? Why—why——'

'Then why,' she went on, 'didn't you go up to London after him?'

The question was so entirely unexpected that he could only repeat:

'Why. . . .'

'Oh, well, it doesn't matter now,' she said, wearily turning away.

'Perhaps I did wrong. I think perhaps I've done wrong in many ways during these last years. I am seeing many things for the first time. The truth is I have been so absorbed in my work that I've thought of nothing else. I took it too much for granted that you were happy because I was happy. And now I want to make it right. I do indeed, Amy. Tell me what's the matter.'

She said nothing. He waited for a long time. Her immobility always angered him. He said at last more impatiently.

'Please tell me, Amy, what you have against me.'

'I have nothing against you.'

'Then why are things wrong between us?'

'Are things wrong?'

'You know they are—ever since that morning when you wouldn't come to Holy Communion.'

'I was tired that morning.'

'It is more than tiredness,' he said, with sudden impatience, beating upon the counterpane with his fist. 'Amy—you're not behaving fairly. You must talk to me. I insist on it.'

She turned once more towards him.

'What is it you want me to say?'

'Why you're unhappy.'

'But if I am not unhappy?'

'You are.'

'But suppose I say that I am not?'

'You are. You are. You are!' he shouted at her.

'Very well, then, I am.'

'Why are you?'

'Who *is* happy really? At any rate for more than a moment. Only very thoughtless and silly people.'

'You're putting me off.' He took her hand again. 'I'm to blame, Amy—to blame in many ways. But people are talking.'

She snatched her hand away.

'People talking? Who? . . . But as though that mattered.'

'It *does* matter. It has gone far—much farther than I thought.'

She looked at him then, quickly, and turned her face away again.

'Who's talking? And what are they saying?'

'They are saying——' He broke off. What *were* they saying? Until the arrival of that horrible letter he had not realised that they were saying anything at all.

'Don't think for a single moment, Amy, that I pay the slightest attention to any of their talk. I would not have bothered you with any of this had it not been for something else—of which I'll speak in a moment. If everything is right between *us*— between you and me—then it doesn't matter if the whole world talks until it's blue in the face.'

'Leave it alone, then,' she said. 'Let them talk.'

Her indifference stung him. She didn't care, then, whether things were right between himself and her or no? It was the same to her. She cared so little for him. . . . That sudden realisation struck him so sharply that it was as though some one had hit him in the back. For so many years he had taken it for granted . . . taken something for granted that was not to be so taken. Very dimly some one was approaching him—that dark, misty, gigantic figure—blotting out the light from the windows. That figure was becoming day by day more closely his companion.

Looking at her now more intently, and with a new urgency, he said :

'Some one brought me a letter, Amy. They said it was a letter of yours.'

She did not move nor stir. Then, after a long silence, she said, 'Let me see it.'

He felt in his pocket and produced it. She stretched out her hand and took it. She read it through slowly. 'You think that I wrote this ?' she asked.

'No, I know that you did not.'

'To whom was it supposed to be written ?'

'To Morris of St. James'.'

She nodded her head. 'Ah, yes. We're friends. That's why they chose him. Of course it's a forgery,' she added—'a very clever one.'

'What I don't understand,' he said eagerly, at his heart the strangest relief that he did not dare to stop to analyse, ' is why any one should have troubled to do this—the risk, the danger——'

' You have enemies,' she said. ' Of course you know that. People who are jealous.'

' One enemy,' he answered fiercely. ' Ronder. The woman had been to him with this letter before she came to me.'

' The woman ! What woman ? '

' The woman who brought it to me was a Miss Milton—a wretched creature who was once at the Library.'

' And she had been with this to Canon Ronder before she came to you ? '

' Yes.'

' Ah ! '

Then she said very quietly :

' And what do you mean to do about the letter ? '

' I will do whatever you wish me to do. What I would like to do is to leave no step untaken to bring the authors of this forgery to justice. No step. I will——'

' No,' she broke in quickly. ' It is much better to leave it alone. What good can it do to follow it up ? It only tells every one about it. We should despise it. The thing is so obviously false. Why, you can see,' suddenly holding the letter towards him, ' it isn't even like my writing. My s's, my m's—they're not like that——'

' No, no,' he said eagerly. ' I see that they are not. I saw that at once.'

' You knew at once that it was a forgery ? '

' I knew at once. I never doubted for an instant.'

She sighed ; then settled back into the pillow with a little shudder.

'This town,' she said; 'the things they do. Oh! to get away from it, to get away!'

'And we will!' he cried eagerly. 'That's what we need, both of us—a holiday. I've been thinking it over. We're both tired. When this Jubilee is over we'll go abroad — Italy, Greece. We'll have a second honeymoon. Oh, Amy, we'll begin life again. I've been much to blame—much to blame. Give me that letter. I'll destroy it. I know my enemy, but I'll not think of him or of any one but our two selves. I'll be good to you now if you'll let me.'

She gave him the letter.

'Look at it before you tear it up,' she said, staring at him as though she would not miss any change in his features. 'You're sure that it *is* a forgery?'

'Why, of course.'

'It's nothing like my handwriting?'

'Nothing at all.'

'You know that I am devoted to you, that I would never be untrue to you in thought, word or deed?'

'Why, of course, of course. As though I didn't know——'

'And that I'll love to come abroad with you?'

'Yes, yes.'

'And that we'll have a second honeymoon?'

'Yes, yes. Indeed, Amy, we will.'

'Look well at that letter. You are wrong. It is not a forgery. I did write it.'

He did not answer her, but stayed staring at the letter like a boy detected in a theft. She repeated:

'The woman was quite right. I did write that letter.'

Brandon said, staring at her, 'Don't laugh at me. This is too serious.'

' I'm not laughing. I wrote it. I sent it down by Gladys. If you recall the day to her she'll remember.'

She watched his face. It had turned suddenly grey, as though some one had slipped a grey mask over the original features.

She thought, ' Now perhaps he'll kill me. I'm not sorry.'

He whispered, leaning quite close to her as though he were afraid she would not hear.

' You wrote that letter to Morris ? '

' I did.' Then suddenly springing up, half out of bed, she cried, ' You're not to touch him. Do you hear ? You're not to touch him ! It's not his fault. He's had nothing to do with this. He's only my friend. I love him, but he doesn't love me. Do you hear ? He's had nothing to do with this ! '

' You love him ! ' whispered Brandon.

' I've loved him since the first moment I saw him. I've wanted some one to love for years—years and years and years. You didn't love me, so then I hoped Falk would, and Falk didn't, so then I found the first person—any one who would be kind to me. And he was kind—he *is* kind—the kindest man in the world. And he saw that I was lonely, so he let me talk to him and go to him— but none of this is his doing. He's only been kind. He——'

' Your letter says " Dearest," ' said Brandon. ' If you wrote that letter it says " Dearest." '

' That was my foolishness. It was wrong of me. He told me that I mustn't say anything affectionate. He's good and I'm bad. And I'm bad because you've made me.'

Brandon took the letter and tore it into little pieces ; they scattered upon the counterpane.

' You've been unfaithful to me ? ' he said, bending over her.

She did not shrink back, although that strange, unknown, grey face was very close to her. ' Yes. At first he wouldn't. He refused anything. But I would . . . I wanted to be. I hate you. I've hated you for years.'

' Why ? ' His hand closed on her shoulder.

' Because of your conceit and pride. Because you've never thought of me. Because I've always been a piece of furniture to you—less than that. Because you've been so pleased with yourself and well-satisfied and stupid. Yes. Yes. Most because you're so stupid. So stupid. Never seeing anything, never knowing anything and always —so satisfied. And when the town was pleased with you and said you were so fine I've laughed, knowing what you were, and I thought to myself, " There'll come a time when they'll find him out " —and now they have. They know what you are at last. And I'm glad ! I'm glad ! I'm glad ! ' She stopped, her breasts rising and falling beneath her nightdress, her voice shrill, almost a scream.

He put his hands on her thin bony shoulders and pushed her back into the bed. His hands moved to her throat. His whole weight, he now kneeling on the bed, was on top of her.

' Kill me ! Kill me ! ' she whispered. ' I'll be glad.'

All the while their eyes stared at one another inquisitively, as though they were strangers meeting for the first time.

His hands met round her throat. His knees were over her.

He felt her thin throat between his hands and a voice in his ear whispered, 'That's right, squeeze tighter. Splendid! Splendid!'

Suddenly his eyes recognised hers. His hands dropped. He crawled from the bed. Then he felt his way, blindly, out of the room.

CHAPTER V

THE Great Day arrived, escorted sumptuously with skies of burning blue. How many heads looked out of how many windows, the country over, that morning! In Polchester it was considered as only another proof of the esteem in which that city was held by the Almighty. The Old Lady might deserve and did unquestionably obtain divinely condescending weather for her various excursions, but it was nothing to that which the Old Town got and deserved.

Deserved or no, the town rose to the occasion. The High Street was swimming in flags and bunting ; even in Seatown most of the grimy windows showed those little cheap flags that during the past week hawkers had been so industriously selling. From quite early in the morning the squeak and scream of the roundabouts in the Fair could be heard dimly penetrating the sanctities and privacies of the Precincts. But it was the Cathedral bells, pealing, crashing, echoing, rocking, as early as nine o'clock in the morning, that first awoke the consciousness of most of the Polcastrians to the glories of the day.

I suppose that nearly all souls that morning

subconsciously divided the order of the festival into three periods ; in the morning the Cathedral and its service, in the afternoon the social, friendly, man-to-man celebration, and in the evening, torch-light, bonfire, skies ablaze, drink and love.

Certain it is that many eyes turned towards the Cathedral accustomed for many years to look in quite other directions.   There was to be a grand service, they said, with 'trumpets and shawms' and the big drum, and the old Bishop preaching, making, in all probability, his very last public appearance.   Up from the dark mysteries of Sea-town, down from the chaste proprieties of the villas above Orange Street, from the purlieus of the market, from the shops of the High Street, sailors and merchantmen, traders and sea-captains and, from the wild fastnesses of the Fair, gipsies with silver rings in their ears and, perhaps, who can tell ? bells on their dusky toes.

Very early were Lawrence and Cobbett about their duties.   This was, in all probability, Law-rence's last Great Day before the final and all-judging one, and well both he and Cobbett were aware of it.   Cobbett could see himself that morn-ing almost stepping into the old man's shoes, and the old man himself was not well this morning— not well at all.   Rheumatism, gout, what hadn't he got ?—and, above all, that strange, mysterious pain somewhere in his very vitals, a pain that was not precisely a pain, too dull and homely for that, but a warning, a foreboding.

On an ordinary day, in spite of his dislike of allowing Cobbett any of those duties that were so properly his own, he would have stayed in bed, but to-day ?—no, thank you !   On such a day as this he would defy the Devil himself and all his red-hot pincers ! So there he was in his long purple gown, with his lovely snow-white beard, and his gold-topped staff, patronising Mrs. Muffit (who superintended the cleaning) and her ancient servitors, seeing that the places for the Band (just under the choir-screen) and for the extra members of the choir were all in order, and, above all, that the Bishop's Throne up by the altar was guiltless of a speck of dust, of a shadow of a shadow of disorder. Cobbett saw, beyond any question or doubt, death in the old man's face, and suddenly, to his own amazement, was sorry. For years now he had been waiting for the day when he should succeed the tiresome old fool, for years he had cursed him for a thousand pomposities, blunders, tedious garrulities, and now, suddenly, he was sorry. What had come over him ? But he wasn't a bad old man; plucky, too ; you could see how he was suffering. They had, after all, been companions together for so many years. . . .

Quite early in the morning arrivals began— visitors from the country most likely, sitting there at the back of the nave, bathed in the great silence and the dim light, just looking and wondering and expecting. Some of them wanted to move about and examine the brasses and the tombs and the windows—yes, move about with their families, and their bags of sandwiches, and their oranges. But not this morning, oh, dear, no ! They could come in or go out, but if they came in they must stay quiet. Did they but subterraneously giggle, Cobbett was on their tracks in no time.

The light flooded in, throwing great splashes and lakes of blue and gold and purple on to flag and pillar. Great in its strength, magnificent in its beauty, the Cathedral prepared. ◦ . .

Mrs. Combermere walked rather solemnly that morning from her house to the Cathedral. In spite of the lovely morning she was feeling suddenly old. Things like Jubilees do date you—no doubt about it. Nearly fifty. Three-quarters of life behind her and what had she to show for it? An unlucky marriage, much physical health and fun, some friends—but, at the last, lonely—lonely as perhaps every human being in this queer world was. That old woman now preparing to ride in fantastic procession before her worshipping subjects, she was lonely too. Poor, little, lonely, old woman! Well then, Charity to all and sundry —Charity, kindliness, the one and only thing. Aggie Combermere was not a sentimental woman, nor did she see life falsely, but she was suddenly aware, walking under the blazing blue sky, that she had been unkind, for amusement's sake, more often than she need. . . . Well, why not? She was ready to allow people to have a shy at herself —any one who liked. . . . ' 'Ere you are! Old Aunt Sally! Three shies a penny!' And she *was* an Aunt Sally, a ludicrous creature, caring for her dogs more than for any living creature, shovelling food into her mouth for no particular purpose, doing physical exercises in the morning, and *nearly* fifty!

She found then, just as she reached the Arden Gate, that, to her own immense surprise, it was not of herself that, all this time, she had been thinking, but rather of Brandon and the Brandon family. The Brandons! What an extraordinary affair! The Town now was bursting its fat sides with

excitement over it all! The Town was now
generally aware (but how it was aware no one quite
knew) that there was a mysterious letter that Mrs.
Brandon had written to Morris, and that Miss
Milton, librarian who was, had obtained this letter
and had taken it to Ronder. And the next move,
the next! the next! Oh, tell us! Tell us! The
Town stands on tiptoe; its hair on end. Let us
see! Let us see! Let us not miss the tiniest
detail of this extraordinary affair!

And really how extraordinary! First the boy
runs off with that girl; then Mrs. Brandon, the
quietest, dullest woman for years and years, throws
her cap over the mill and behaves like a madwoman;
and Johnny St. Leath, they say, is in love with the
daughter, and his old mother is furious; and
Brandon, they say, wants to cut Ronder's throat.
Ronder! Mrs. Combermere paused, partly to
get her breath, partly to enjoy for an instant the
shining, glittering grass, dotted with figures, stretching like a carpet from the vast greyness of the
Cathedral. Ronder! There was a remarkable man!
Mrs. Combermere was conquered by him, in spite of
herself. How, in seven short months, he had conquered everybody! What an amusing talker, what
a good preacher, what a clever business head! And
yet she did not really like him. His praises now
were in every one's mouth, but she did not *really*
like him. Old Brandon was still her favourite, her
old friend of ten years; but there was no doubt that
he *was* behind the times, Ronder had shown them
that! No use living in the 'Eighties any longer.
But she was fond of him, she did not want him to
be unhappy—and unhappy he was, that any one
could see. Most of all, she did not want him to

do anything foolish—and he might, his temper was strange, he was not so strong as he looked ; he had felt his son's escapade terribly—and now his wife !

'Well, if I had a wife like that,' was Mrs. Combermere's conclusion before she joined Ellen Stiles and Julia Preston, 'I'd let her go off with any one ! Pay any one to take her !'

Ellen was, of course, full of it all. 'My dear, *what* do you think is the latest ! They say that the Archdeacon threatens to poison the whole of the Chapter if they don't let Forsyth have Pybus, and that Boadicea has ordered Johnny to take a voyage to the Canary Islands for his health, and that he says he'll see her shot first ! And Miss Milton is selling the letter for a thousand pounds to the first comer !'

Mrs. Combermere stopped her sharply—' Mind your own business, Ellen. The whole thing now is past a joke. And as to Johnny St. Leath, he shows his good taste. There isn't a sweeter, prettier girl in England than Joan Brandon, and he's lucky if he gets her.'

' I don't want to be ill-natured,' said Ellen Stiles rather plaintively, ' but that family would test anybody's reticence. We'd better go in or old Lawrence will be letting some one have our seats.'

Joan came with her mother slowly across the grass. In her dress was this letter :

DEAREST, DEAREST, *dearest* JOAN—The first thing you have thoroughly to realise is that it doesn't matter *what* you say or what mother says or what any one says. Mother's angry. Of course she is. She's been angry a thousand million times before and will be a thousand million times again. But it doesn't *mean* anything. Mother likes to be

angry, it does her good, and the longer she's angry with you
the better she'll like you, if you understand what I mean.
What I want you to get into your head is that you can't alter
anything.   Of course if you didn't love me it would be
another matter, and you tried to tell me you didn't love me
yesterday just for my good, but you did it so badly that you
had to admit yourself that it was a failure.   Don't talk
about your brother ; he's a fine fellow, and I'm going to
look him up when I'm in London next month.   Don't
talk about not seeing me, because you can't help seeing me
if I'm right in front of you.   I'm no silph.   (The way he
spelt it.)   I'm quite ready to wait for a certain time anyway.
But marry we will, and happy we'll be for ever and ever !—
Your adoring   JOHNNY.

And what was she to do about it ?   She was
certainly very unmodern and inexperienced by the
standards of to-day——on the other hand, she was
a very long way indeed from the Lily Dales and
Eleanor Hardings of Mr. Trollope.   She had not
told her father——that she was resolved to do so soon
as he seemed a little less worried by his affairs ; but
say that she did not love Johnny she had found
that she could not, and as to damaging him by
marrying him, his love for her had strengthened her
own pride in herself.   She did not understand his
love, it was astounding to her after the indifference
with which her own family had always treated her.
But there it was ; he, with all his experience of
life, loved her more than any one else in the world,
so there *must* be something in her.   And she knew
there was ; privately she had always known it.   As
to his mother——well, so long as Johnny loved her
she could face anybody.

So this wonderful morning she was radiantly
happy.   Child as she was, she adored this excitement.   It was splendid of it to be this glorious

time just when she was having her own glorious time ! Splendid of the weather to be so beautiful, of the bells to clash, of every one to wear their best clothes, of the Jubilee to arrange itself so exactly at the right moment ! And could it be only last Saturday that he had spoken to her ? And it seemed centuries, centuries ago !

She chattered eagerly, smiling at Betty Callender, and then at the D'Arcy girls, and then at Mrs. Bentinck-Major. She supposed that they were all talking about her. Well, let them. There was nothing to be ashamed of. Quite the contrary. She did not notice her mother's silence. But she *had* noticed, before they left the house, how ill her mother was looking. A very bad night—another of her dreadful headaches. Her father had not come into breakfast at all. Everything had been wrong at home since that day when Falk had been sent down from Oxford. She longed to put her arms round her father's neck and hug him. Behind her own happiness, ever since the night of the Ball, there had been a longing, an aching urgent longing to pet him, comfort him, make love to him. And she would, too,—as soon as all these festivities were over.

And then suddenly there were Johnny and his mother and his sisters walking towards the West door ! What a situation ! And then there was Johnny breaking away from his own family and hurrying towards them, lifting his hat, smiling !

How splendid he looked and how happy ! And how happy she also was looking had she only known it !

'Good morning, Mrs. Brandon.'

Mrs. Brandon didn't appear to remember him

at all. Then suddenly, as though she had picked her conscience out of her pocket :

' Oh, good morning, Lord St. Leath.'

Joan, out of the corner, saw Boadicea, her head with its absurd bonnet high, striding indignantly ahead.

' What lovely weather, is it not ? '

' Yes, aren't we lucky ?   Good morning, Joan.'

' Good morning.'

' Isn't it a lovely day ? '

' Oh, yes, it is.'

' Are you going to see the Torchlight Procession to-night ? '

' They come through the Precincts, you know.'

' Of course they do.   We're going to have five bonfires all around us.   Mother's afraid they'll set the Castle on fire.'

They both laughed—much too happy to know what they were laughing at.

Mrs. Sampson joined them.   Johnny and Joan walked ahead.   Only two steps and they would be in the Cathedral.

' Did you get my letter ? '

' Yes.'

' I love you, I love you, I love you.'   This in a hoarse whisper.

' Johnny—you mustn't—you know—we can't— you know I oughtn't——'

They passed through into the Cathedral.

Mrs. Bentinck-Major came with Miss Ronder, slowly, across the grass.   It was not necessary for them to hurry because they knew that their seats were reserved for them.   Mrs. Bentinck-Major thought Miss Ronder ' queer ' because of the clever things that she said and of the odd fashion in which she always dressed. To say anything clever was, with Mrs. Bentinck-Major, at once to be classed as ' queer.'

' It *is* hot ! '

Miss Ronder, thin and piky above her stiff white collar, looked immaculately cool. ' A lovely day,' she said, sniffing the colour and the warmth, and loving it.

Mrs. Bentinck-Major was thinking of the Brandon scandal, but it was one of her habits never to let her left-hand voice know what her right-hand brain was doing. Secretly she often wondered about sexual things — what people *really* did, whether they enjoyed what they did, and whether she would have enjoyed the same things had life gone that way with her instead of leading her to Bentinck-Major.

But she never, never spoke of such things. She was thinking now of Mrs. Brandon and Morris. They said that some one had found a letter, a disgraceful letter. How *extraordinary* !

' It's loneliness,' suddenly said Miss Ronder, ' that drives people to do the things they do.'

Mrs. Bentinck-Major started as though some one had struck her in the small of her back. Was the woman a witch ? How amazing !

' I beg your pardon,' she said nervously.

' I was speaking,' said Miss Ronder in her clear incisive voice, ' of one of our maids, who has suddenly engaged herself to the most unpleasing-looking butcher's assistant you can imagine—all spots and stammer. Quite a pretty girl, too. But it's fear of loneliness that does it. Wanting affection.'

Dear me ! Mrs. Bentinck-Major had never

had very much affection from Mr. Bentinck-Major,
and had not very consciously missed it, but then
she had a dog, a spaniel, whom she loved most
dearly.

'We're all lonely—all of us—to the very end,'
said Miss Ronder, as though she was thinking of
some one in especial. And she was. She was
thinking of her nephew. 'I shouldn't wonder if
the Queen isn't feeling more lonely to-day than
she has ever felt in all her life before.'

And then they saw that dreadful man, Davray,
lurching along. *He* was lonely, but then he deserved to be, with his *drink* and all. *Wicked* man!
Mrs. Bentinck-Major shivered. She didn't know
how he dared to go to church. He shouldn't be
allowed. On such a day, too. What would the
Queen herself think, did she know?

The two ladies and Davray passed through the
door at the same time.

And now every one was inside. The great bell
dropped notes like heavy weights into a liquid well.
For the cup of the Cathedral swam in colour, the
light pouring through the great Rose window, and
that multitude of persons seeming to sway like
shadows beneath a sheet of water from amber to
purple, from purple to crimson, from crimson to
darkest green.

Individuality was lost. The Cathedral, thinking
nothing of Kings and Queens, of history, of movement
forward and retrograde, but only of itself and of
the life that it had been given, that it now claimed
for its own, with haughty confidence assumed its
Power . . . the Power of its own Immortality that
is neither man's nor God's.

The trumpets began.   They rang out the Psalm that had been given them, and transformed it into a cry of exultant triumph.   Their notes rose, were caught by the pillars, acclaimed, tossed higher, caught again in the eaves and corners of the great building, swinging backwards and forwards. . . .

'Now listen to My greatness!   You created Me for the Worship of your God!

'And now I am your God!   Out of your forms and ceremonies you have made a new God!   And I, thy God, am a jealous God. . . .'

Ronder read the First Lesson.

'That's Ronder,' the town-people whispered, 'the new Canon.   Oh! he's clever.   You should hear him preach!'

'Reads *beautiful*!' Gladys, the Brandons' maid, whispered to Annie, the kitchen-maid.   'I do like a bit of fine reading.'

By those accustomed to observe it was noticed that Ronder read with very much more assurance than he had done three months ago.   It was as though he knew now where he was, as though he were settled down now and had his place—and it would take some very strong people to shift him from that place.   Oh, yes.   It would!

And Brandon read the Second Lesson.   As usual, when he stepped down from the choir, slowly, impressively, pausing for a moment before he turned to the Lectern, strangers whispered to one another, 'That's a handsome parson, that is.'   He seemed to hesitate again before going up as though he had stumbled over a step.   Very slowly he read the opening words ; slowly he continued.

Puddifoot, looking up across from his seat in the side aisle, thought, 'There's something the matter with him.' Suddenly he paused, looked about him, stared over the congregation as though he were searching for somebody, then slowly again went on and finished.

'Here endeth—the Second Lesson.'

Then, instead of turning, he leaned forward, gripping the Lectern with both hands, and seemed again to be searching for some one.

'Looks as though he were going to have a stroke,' thought Puddifoot. Then very carefully, as though he were moving in darkness, he turned and groped his way downwards. With bent head he walked back into the choir.

Soon they were scattered—every one according to his or her own individuality—the prayers had broken them up, too many of them, too long, and the wooden kneelers so hard. Minds flew like birds about the Cathedral—ideas, gold and silver, black and grey, soapy and soft, hard as iron. The men yawned behind their trumpets, the School played Noughts and Crosses—the Old Lady and her Triumph stepped away into limbo.

And then suddenly it was time for the Bishop's sermon. Every one hoped that it would not be long, passing clouds veiled the light behind the East window and the Roses faded to ashes. The organ rumbled in its crotchety voice as the old man slowly disentangled himself from his throne, and slowly, slowly, slowly advanced down the choir. When he appeared above the nave, and paused for an instant to make sure of the step, all the minds in the Cathedral suddenly concentrated again, the birds flew back, the air was still. At the sight of that very old man, that little bag of shaking bones, all the brief history of the world was suddenly apparent. Greater than Alexander, more beautiful than Helen of Troy, wiser than Gamaliel, more powerful than Artaxerxes, he made the secret of immortal life visible to all.

His hair was white, and his face was ashen grey, and his hands were like bird's claws. Like a child finding its way across its nursery floor he climbed to the pulpit, being now so far distant in heaven that earth was dark to him.

' The Lord be with you.'

' And with Thy Spirit.'

His voice was clear and could be heard by all. He spoke for a very short time. He told them about the Queen, and that she had been good to her people for sixty years, and that she had feared God ; he told them that that goodness was the only secret of happiness ; he told them that Jesus Christ came nearer and nearer, and ever more near, did one but ask Him.

He said, ' I suppose that I shall never speak to you in this place again. I am very old. Some of you have thought, perhaps, that I was too old to do my work here—others have wanted me to stay. I have loved you all very much, and it is lonely to go away from you. Our great and good Queen also is old now, and perhaps she, too, in the middle of her triumph, is feeling lonely. So pray for her, and then pray for me a little, that when I meet God He may forgive me my sins and help me to do better work than I have done here. Life is sad sometimes, and often it is dark, but at the end it is beautiful and wonderful, for which we must thank God.'

He knelt down and prayed, and every one,

Davray and Mrs. Combermere, Ellen Stiles and Morris, Lady St. Leath and Mrs. Brandon, Joan and Lawrence, Ronder and Foster, prayed too.

And then they all, all for a moment utterly united in soul and body and spirit, knelt down and the old man blessed them from the pulpit.

Then they sang ' Now thank we all Our God.'

Afterwards came the Benediction.

CHAPTER VI

TUESDAY, JUNE 22 : II. THE FAIR

As Brandon left the Cathedral Ronder came up to him. Brandon, with bowed head, had turned into the Cloisters, although that was not the quickest way to his home. The two men were alone in the greyness lit from without by the brilliant sun as though it had been a stage setting.

'I beg your pardon, Archdeacon, I must speak to you.'

Brandon raised his head. He stared at Ronder, then said :

'I have nothing to say to you. I do not wish to speak to you.'

'I know that you do not.' Ronder's face was really troubled ; there was an expression in his eyes that his aunt had never seen.

Brandon moved on, looking neither to right nor left.

Ronder continued : 'I know how you feel about me. But to-day—somehow—this service—I feel that I can't allow our quarrel to continue without speaking. It isn't easy for me——' He broke off.

Brandon's voice shook.

'I have nothing to say to you. I do not wish

to say anything to you. You have been my enemy since you first came to this town. My work—my family——'

' I am not your enemy. Indeed, indeed I am not. I won't deny that when I came here I found that you, who were the most important man in the place, thought differently from myself on every important question. You, yourself, who are an honest man, would not have had me back out from what I believed to be my duty. I could do no other. But this personal quarrel between us was most truly not of my own seeking. I have liked and admired you from the beginning. Such a matter as the Pybus living has forced us into opposition, but I am convinced that there are many views that we have in common, that we could be friends working together——'

Brandon stopped.

' Did my son, or did he not, come to see you before he went up to London ? '

Ronder hesitated.

' Yes,' he said, ' he did. But——'

' Did he, or did he not, ask your advice ? '

' Yes, he did. But——'

' Did you advise him to take the course which he afterwards followed ? '

' No, on my honour, Archdeacon, I did not. I did not know what his personal trouble was. I did not ask him and he did not tell me. We talked of generalities——'

' Had you heard, before he came to you, gossip about my son ? '

' I had heard some silly talk——'

' Very well, then.'

' But you *shall* listen to me, Archdeacon. I

scarcely knew your son. I had met him only once before, at some one's house, and talked to him then only for five minutes. He himself asked to come and see me. I could not refuse him when he asked me. I did not, of course, wish to refuse him. I liked the look of him, and simply for his own sake wished to know him better. When he came he was not with me for very long and our talk was entirely about religion, belief, faith in God, the meaning of life, nothing more particular than such things.'

'Did he say, when he left you, that what you had told him had helped him to make up his mind?'

'Yes.'

'Were you, when he talked to you, quite unconscious that he was my son, and that any action that he took would at once affect my life, my happiness?'

'Of course I was aware that he was your son. But——'

'There is another question that I wish to ask you, Canon Ronder. Did some one come to you not long ago with a letter that purported to be written by my wife?'

Again Ronder hesitated.

'Yes,' he said.

'Did she show you that letter?'

'She did.'

'Did she ask your advice as to what she should do with it?'

'She did—I told her——'

'Did you tell her to come with it to me?'

'No. On my life, Archdeacon, no. I told her to destroy it and that she was behaving with the utmost wickedness.'

'Did you believe that that letter was written by my wife?'

'No.'

'Then why, if you believed that this woman was going about the town with a forged letter directed against my happiness and my family's happiness, did you not come to me and tell me of it?'

'You must remember, Archdeacon, that we were not on good terms. We had had a ridiculous quarrel that had, by some means or another, become public property throughout the whole town. I will not deny that I felt sore about that. I did not know what sort of reception I might get if I came to you.'

'Very well. There is a further question that I wish to ask you. Will you deny that from the moment that you set foot in this town you have been plotting against me in respect to the Pybus living? You found out on which side I was standing and at once took the other. From that moment you went about the town, having secret interviews with every sort of person, working them by flattery and suggestion round to your side. Will you deny that?'

Against his will and his absolute determination Ronder's anger began to rise. 'That I have been plotting as you call it,' he said, 'I absolutely and utterly deny. That is an insulting word. That I have been against you in the matter of Pybus from the first has, of course, been known to every one here. I have been against you because of what I believe to be the future good of our Church and of our work here. There has been nothing personal in that matter at all.'

'You lie,' said Brandon, suddenly raising his voice. 'Every word that you have spoken to me this morning has been a lie. You are an enemy of myself and of my Church, and with God's help your plots and falsehoods shall yet be defeated. You may take from me my wife and my children, you may ruin my career here that has been built up through ten years of unfaltering loyalty and work, but God Himself is stronger than your inventions—and God will see to it. I am your enemy, Canon Ronder, to the end, as you are mine. You had better look to yourself. You have been concerned in certain things that the Law may have something to say about. Look to yourself! Look to yourself!'

He strode off down the Cloisters.

People came to luncheon; there had been an invitation of some weeks before. He scarcely recognised them; one was Mr. Martin, another Dr. Trudon, an old Mrs. Purley, a well-established widow, an ancient resident, a Miss Barrester. He scarcely recognised them although he talked so exactly in his accustomed way that no one noticed anything at all. Mrs. Brandon also talked in her accustomed way; that is, she scarcely spoke. Only that afternoon, at tea at the Dean's, Dr. Trudon confided to Julia Preston that he could assure her that all the rumours were false; the Archdeacon had never seemed better . . . funny for him afterwards to remember!

Shadows of a shade! When they left Brandon it was as though they had never been; the echo of their voices died away into the ticking of the clock, the movement of plates, the shifting of chairs.

He shut himself into his study. Here was his stronghold, his fortress. He settled into his chair and the things in the room gathered around him with friendly consoling gestures.

'We are still here, we are your old friends. We know you for what you truly are. We do not change like the world.'

He fell into a deep sleep; he was desperately tired; he had not slept at all last night. He was sunk into deep fathomless unconsciousness. Then he rose from that, climbing up, up, seeing before him a high, black, snow-tipped mountain. The ascent of this he must achieve, his life depended upon it. He seemed to be naked, the wind lashing his body, icy cold, so cold that his breath stabbed him. He climbed, the rocks cut his knees and hands; then, on every side his enemies appeared, Bentinck-Major and Foster, the Bishop's Chaplain, women, even children, laughing, and behind them Hogg and that drunken painter. Their hands were on him, they pulled at his flesh, they beat on his face—then, suddenly, rising like a full moon behind the hill— Ronder !

He woke with a cry; the sun was flooding the room, and at the joy of that great light and of finding himself alone he could have burst into tears of relief.

His thoughts came to him quickly, his brain had been clarified by that sleep, horrible though it had been. He thought steadily now, the facts all arranged before him. His wife had told him, almost with vindictive pride, that she had been guilty of adultery. He did not at present think of Morris at all.

To him adultery was an awful, a terrible sin.

He himself had been physically faithful to his wife, although he had perhaps never, in the true sense of the word, loved her. Because he had been a man of splendid physique and great animal spirits he had, of course, and especially in his earlier days, known what physical temptation was, but the extreme preoccupation of his time with every kind of business had saved him from that acutest lure that idleness brings. Nevertheless, it may confidently be said that, had temptation been of the sharpest and the most aggravating, he would never have, even for a moment, dwelt upon the possibility of yielding to it. To him this was the 'sin against the Holy Ghost.'

He had not indeed the purity of the Saint to whom these sins are simply not realisable; he had the confidence of one who had made his vows to God and, having made them, could not conceive that they should be broken.

And yet, strangely enough, with all the horror that his wife's confession had raised in him there was mingled, against his will, the strangest fear for her. She had lived with him during all these years, he had been her guard, protector, husband.

Her immortal soul now was lost unless in some way he could save it for her. And it was he who should save it. She had suddenly a new poignant importance for him that she had never had before. Her danger was as deadly and as imminent to him as though she had been in peril from wild beasts.

In peril? But she had fallen. He could not save her. Nothing that he could do now could prevent her sin. At that realisation utter despair seized him; he moaned aloud, shutting out the light from his eyes with his hands.

There followed then wild disbelief; what she had told him was untrue, she had said it to anger him, to spite him. He sprang from his chair and moved towards the door. He would find her and tell her that he knew that she had been lying to him, that he did not believe——

Midway he stopped. He knew that she had spoken the truth, that last moment when they had looked at one another had been compounded, built up, of truth. Both a glass and a wall—a glass to reveal absolutely, a wall to divide them, the one from the other, for ever.

His brain, active now like a snake coiling and uncoiling within the flaming spaces of his mind, darted upon Morris. He must find Morris at once—no delay—at once—at once. What to do? He did not know. But he must be face to face with him and deal with him—that wretched, miserable, whining, crying fool. That he—!—HE! . . . But the picture stopped there. He saw now neither Morris nor his wife. Only a clerical hat, a high white collar like a wall, a sniggering laugh, a door closing.

And his headache was upon him again, his heart pounding and leaping. No matter. He must find Morris. Nothing else. He went to the door, opened it, and walked cautiously into the hall as though he had intruded into some one else's house and was there to rob.

As he came into the hall Mrs. Brandon was crossing it, also furtively. They saw one another and stood staring. She would have spoken, but something in his face terrified her, terrified her so desperately that she suddenly turned and stumbled upstairs, repeating some words over and over to herself.   He did not move, but stayed there watching until she had gone.

Something made him change his clothes. ˙ He put on trousers and an old overcoat and a shabby old clerical hat.   He was a long time in his dressing-room, and he was a while before his looking-glass in his shirt and drawers, staring as though he were trying to find himself.

While he looked he fancied that some one was behind him, and he searched for his shadow in the glass, but could find nothing.   He moved cautiously out of the house, closing the heavy hall-door very softly behind him ; the afternoon was advanced, and the faint fair shadows of the summer evening were stealing from place to place.

He had intended to go at once to Morris's house, but his head was now aching so violently that he thought he would walk a little first so that he might have more control.   That was what he wanted, self-control ! self-control !   That was their plot, to make him lose command of himself, so that he should show to every one that he was unfit to hold his position.   He must have perfect control of everything—his voice, his body, his thoughts. And that was why, just now, he must walk in the darker places, in the smaller streets, until soon he would be, outwardly, himself again.   So he chose for his walk the little dark winding path that runs steeply from the Cathedral, along behind Canon's Yard and Bodger's Street, down to the Pol.   It was dark here, even on this lovely summer evening, and no one was about, but sounds broke through ; cries and bells and the distant bray of bands, and from the hill opposite the clash of the Fair.

At the bottom of the path he stood for a while looking down the bank to the river ; here the Pol runs very quietly and sweetly, like a little country river. He crossed it and, still moving like a man in a dream, started up the hill on the other side. He was not, now, consciously thinking of anything at all ; he was aware only of a great pain at his heart and a terrible loneliness. Loneliness ! What an agony ! No one near him, no one to speak to him, every eye mocking him—God as well, far, far away from him, hidden by walls and hills.

As he climbed upward the Fair came nearer to him. He did not notice it. He crossed a path and was at a turnstile. A man asked him for money. He paid a shilling and moved forward. He liked crowds ; he wanted crowds now. Either crowds or no one. Crowds where he would be lost and not noticed.

So many thousands were there, but nevertheless he was noticed. That was the Archdeacon. Who would have thought that he would come to the Fair ? Too grand. But there he was. Yes, that was the Archdeacon. That tall man in the soft black hat. Yes, some noticed him. But many thousands did not. The Fair was packed ; strangers from all the county over, sailors and gipsies and farmers and tramps, women no better than they should be, and shop-girls and decent farmers' wives, and village girls—all sorts ! Thousands, of course, to whom the Archdeacon meant nothing.

And that *was* a Fair, the most wonderful our town had ever seen, the most wonderful it ever was to see ! As with many other things, that Jubilee Fair marked a period. No Fairs again like the good old Fairs—general education has seen to that.

It was a Fair, as there are still to remember, that had in it a strange element of fantasy. All the accustomed accompaniments of Fairs were there— The Two Fat Sisters (outside whose booth a notice was posted begging the public not to prod with umbrellas to discover whether the Fat were Fat or Wadding); Trixie, the little lady with neither arms nor legs, sews and writes with her teeth; the Great Albert, the strongest man in Europe, who will lift weights against all comers; Battling Edwardes, the Champion Boxer of the Southern Counties; Hippo's World Circus, with six monkeys, two lions, three tigers and a rhino; all the pistol-firing, ball-throwing, cocoa-nut contrivances conceivable, and roundabouts at every turn.

All these were there; but behind them, on the outskirts of them and yet in the very heart of them, there were other unaccustomed things.

Some said that a ship from the East had arrived at Drymouth, and that certain jugglers and Chinese and foreign merchants, instead of going on to London as they had intended, turned to Polchester. How do I know at this time of day? How do we, any of us, know how anything gets here, and what does it matter? But there is at this very moment, living in the magnificently renovated Sea-town, an old Chinaman, who came in Jubilee Year, and has been there ever since, doing washing and behaving with admirable propriety, no sign of opium about him anywhere. One element that they introduced was Colour. Our modern Fairs are not very strong in the element of Colour. It is true that one of the roundabouts was a blaze with gilt and tinsel, and in the centre of it, whence comes the music, there were women with brazen faces and bosoms of gold. It is true also that outside the Circus and the Fat Sisters and Battling Edwardes there were flaming pictures with reds and yellows thrown about like temperance tracts, but the modern figures in these pictures spoilt the colour, the photography spoilt it—too much reality where there should have been mystery, too much mystery where realism was needed.

But here, only two yards from the Circus, was a booth hung with strange cloths, purple and yellow and crimson, and behind the wooden boards a man and a woman, with brown faces and busy twirling, twisting, brown hands, were making strange sweets which they wrapped into coloured packets, and on the other side of the Fat Sisters there was a tent with Li Hung above it in letters of gold and red, and inside the tents, boards on trestles, and on the boards a long purple cloth, and on the cloth little toys and figures and images, all of the gayest colours and the strangest shapes, and all as cheap as nothing.

Farther down the lane of booths was the tent of Hayakawa the Juggler. A little boy in primrose-coloured tights turned, on a board outside the tent, round and round and round on his head like a teetotum, and inside, once every half-hour, Hayakawa, in a lovely jacket of gold and silver, gave his entertainment, eating fire, piercing himself with silver swords, finding white mice in his toes, and pulling ribbons of crimson and scarlet out of his ears.

Farther away again there were the Brothers Gomez, Spaniards perhaps, dark, magnificent in figure, running on one wire across the air, balancing sunshades on their noses, leaping, jumping, standing pyramid-high, their muscles gleaming like billiard-balls.

And behind and before and in and out there were strange figures moving through the Fair, strange voices raised against the evening sky, strange smells of cooking, strange songs suddenly rising, dying as soon as heard.

Only a breath away the English fields were quietly lying safe behind their hedges and the English sky changed from blue to green and from green to mother-of-pearl, and from mother-of-pearl to ivory, and stars stabbed, like silver nails, the great canopy of heaven, and the Cathedral bells rang peal after peal above the slowly lighting town.

Brandon was conscious of little of this as he moved on. Even the thought of Morris had faded from him. He could not think consecutively. His mind was broken up like a mirror that had been smashed into a thousand pieces. He was most truly in a dream. Soon he would wake up, out of this noise, away from these cries and lights, and would find it all as he had for so many years known it. He would be sitting in his drawing-room, his legs stretched out, his wife and daughter near to him, the rumble of the organ coming through the wall to them, thinking perhaps of to-morrow's duties, the town quiet all around them, friends and well-wishers everywhere, no terrible pain in his head, happily arranging how everything should be . . . happy . . . happy. . . . Ah! how happy that real life was! When he awoke from his dream he would realise that and thank God for it. When he awoke. . . . He stumbled over something, and, looking up, realised that he was in a very crowded part of the Fair, a fire was blazing somewhere near, gas-jets, although the evening was bright and clear, were flaming, screams and cries seemed to make the very sky rock above his head.

Where was he ? What was he doing here ? Why had he come ? He would go home. He turned.

He turned to face the fire that leapt close at his heel. It was burning at the back of a caravan, in a dark cul-de-sac away from the main thorough-fare ; to its blazing light the bare boards and ugly plankings of the booth, splashed here and there with torn paper that rustled a little in the evening breeze, were all that offered themselves. Near by a horse, untethered, was quietly nosing at the trodden soil.

Behind the caravan the field ran down to a ditch and thick hedging.

Brandon stared at the fire as though absorbed by its light. What did he see there ? Visions per-haps ? Did he see the Cathedral, the Precincts, the quiet circle of demure old houses, his own door, his own bedroom ? Did he see his wife moving hurriedly about the room, opening drawers and shutting them, pausing for a moment to listen, then coming out, closing the door, listening again, then stepping downstairs, pausing for a moment in the hall to lay something on the table, then stepping out into the green wavering evening light ? Or did the flames make pictures for him of the deserted railway-station, the long platform, lit only by one lamp, two figures meeting, exchanging almost no word, pacing for a little in silence the dreary spaces, stepping back as the London express rolled in— such a safe night to choose for escape—then burying themselves in it like rabbits in their burrow ?

Did his vision lead him back to the deserted house, silent save for its ticking clocks, black in that ring of lights and bells and shouting voices ?

Or was he conscious only of the warmth and the

life of the fire, of some sudden companionship with the woman bending over it to stir the sticks and lift some pot from the heart of the flame? He was feeling, perhaps, a sudden peace here and a silence, and was aware of the stars breaking into beauty one by one above his head.

But his peace, if for a moment he had found it, was soon interrupted. A voice that he knew came across to him from the other side of the fire.

' Why, Archdeacon, who would have thought to find you here? '

He looked up and saw, through the fire, the face of Davray the painter.

He turned to go, and at once Davray was at his side.

' No. Don't go. You're in my country now, Archdeacon, not your own. You're not cock of *this* walk, you know. Last time we met you thought you owned the place. Well, you can't think you own this. Fight it out, Mr. Archdeacon, fight it out.'

Brandon answered :

' I have no quarrel with you, Mr. Davray. Nor have I anything to say to you.'

' No quarrel? I like that. I'd knock your face in for twopence, you blasted hypocrite. And I will too. All free ground here.'

Davray's voice was shrill. He was swaying on his legs. The woman looked up from the fire and watched them.

Brandon turned his back to him and saw, facing him, Samuel Hogg and some men behind him.

' Why, good evening, Mr. Archdeacon,' said Hogg, taking off his hat and bowing. ' What a delightful place for a meeting ! '

Brandon said quietly, ' Is there anything you want with me ? ' He realised at once that Hogg was drunk.

' Nothing,' said Hogg, ' except to give you a damned good hiding. I've been waiting for that these many weeks. See him, boys,' he continued, turning to the men behind him. ' 'Ere's this parson who ruined my daughter—as fine a girl as ever you've seen—ruined 'er, he did—him and his blasted son. What d'you say, boys ? Is it right for him to be paradin' round here as proud as a peacock and nobody touchin' him ? Wot d'you say to givin' him a damned good hiding ? '

The men smiled and pressed forward. Davray from the other side suddenly lurched into Brandon. Brandon struck out, and Davray fell and lay where he fell.

Hogg cried, ' Now for 'im, boys ! ' and at once they were upon him. Hogg's face rose before Brandon's, extended, magnified in all its details. Brandon hit out and then was conscious of blows upon his face, of some one kicking him in the back, of himself hitting wildly, of the fire leaping mountains-high behind him, of a woman's cry, of something trickling down into his eye, of sudden contact with warm, naked, sweating flesh, of a small pinched face, the eyes almost closed, rising before him and falling again, of a shout, then sudden silence and himself on his knees groping in darkness for his hat, of his voice far from him murmuring to him, ' It's all right. . . . It's my hat . . . it's my hat I must find.'

He wiped his forehead. The back of his hand was covered with blood.

He saw once again the fire, low now and darkly

illumined by some more distant light, heard the scream of the merry-go-round, stared about him and saw no living soul, climbed to his feet and saw the stars, then very slowly, like a blind man in the dark, felt his way to the field's edge, found a gate, passed through and collapsed, shuddering in the hedge's darkness.

CHAPTER VII

JOAN came home about seven o'clock that evening.
Dinner was at half-past seven, and after dinner she
was going to the Deanery to watch the Torchlight
Procession from the Deanery garden. She had had
the most wonderful afternoon. Mrs. Combermere,
who had been very kind to her lately, had taken her
up to the Flower Show in the Castle grounds, and
there she had had the most marvellous and beautiful
talk with Johnny. They had talked right under his
mother's nose, so to speak, and had settled everything. Yes—simply everything ! They had told
one another that their love was immortal, that
nothing could touch it, nor lessen it, nor twist it—
nothing !

Joan, on her side, had stated that she would
never be engaged to Johnny until his mother con-
sented, and that until they were engaged they must
behave exactly as though they were not engaged,
that is, never see one another alone, never write
letters that might not be read by any one ; but she
had also asserted that no representations on the part
of anybody that she was ruining Johnny, or that she
was a nasty little intriguer, or that nice girls didn't
behave ' so,' would make the slightest difference to

her ; that she knew what she was and Johnny knew what *he* was, and that that was enough for both of them.

Johnny on his side had said that he would be patient for a time under this arrangement, but that the time would not be a very long one, and that she couldn't object to accepting a little ring that he had bought for her, that she needn't wear it, but just keep it beside her to remind her of him.

But Joan had said that to take the ring would be as good as to be engaged, and that therefore she would not take it, but that he could keep it ready for the day of their betrothal.

She had come home, through the lovely evening, in such a state of happiness that she was forced to tell Mrs. Combermere all about it, and Mrs. Combermere had been a darling and assured her that she was quite right in all that she had done, and that it made her, Mrs. Combermere, feel quite young again, and that she would help them in every way that she could, and parting at the Arden Gate, she had kissed Joan just as though she were her very own daughter.

So Joan, shining with happiness, came back to the house. It seemed very quiet after the sun and glitter and laughter of the Flower Show. She went straight up to her room at the top of the house, washed her face and hands, brushed her hair and put on her white frock.

As she came downstairs the clock struck half-past seven. In the hall she met Gladys.

' Please, miss,' said Gladys, ' is dinner to be kept back ? '

' Why,' said Joan, ' isn't mother in ? '

'No, miss, she went out about six o'clock and she hasn't come in.'

'Isn't father in?'

'No, miss.'

'Did she say that she'd be late?'

'No, miss.'

'Oh, well—we must wait until mother comes in.'

'Yes, miss.'

She saw then a letter on the hall-table. She picked it up. It was addressed to her father, a note left by somebody. She thought nothing of that—notes were so often left; the handwriting was exactly like her mother's, but of course it could not be hers. She went into the drawing-room.

Here the silence was oppressive. She walked up and down, looking out of the long windows at the violet dusk. Gladys came in to draw the blinds.

'Didn't mother say *anything* about when she'd be in?'

'No, miss.'

'She left no message for me?'

'No, miss. Your mother seemed in a hurry like.'

'She didn't ask where I was?'

'No, miss.'

'Did she go out with father?'

'No, miss—your father went out a quarter of an hour earlier.'

Gladys coughed. 'Please, miss, Cook and me's wanting to go out and see the Procession.'

'Oh, of course you must. But that won't be until half-past nine. They come past here, you know.'

'Yes, miss.'

Joan picked up the new number of the *Cornhill*

Magazine and tried to settle down. But she was restless. Her own happiness made her so. And then the house was 'queer.' It had the sense of itself waiting for some effort, and holding its breath in expectation.

As Joan sat there trying to read the *Cornhill* serial, and most sadly failing, it seemed to her stranger and stranger that her mother was not in. She had not been well lately; Joan had noticed how white she had looked; she had always a 'headache' when you asked her how she was. Joan had fancied that she had never been the same since Falk had been away. She had a letter in her dress now from Falk. She took it out and read it over again. As to himself it had only good news; he was well and happy, Annie was 'splendid.' His work went on finely. His only sadness was his breach with his father; again and again he broke out about this, and begged, implored Joan to do something. If she did not, he said, he would soon come down himself and risk a row. There was one sentence towards the end of the letter which read oddly to Joan just now. 'I suppose the old man's in his proper element over all the Jubilee celebrations. I can see him strutting up and down the Cathedral as though he owned every stone in it, bless his old heart! I tell you, Joan, I just ache to see him. I do really. Annie's father hasn't been near us since we came up here. Funny! I'd have thought he'd have bothered me long before this. I'm ready for him if he comes. By the way, if mother shows any signs of wanting to come up to town just now, do your best to prevent her. Father needs her, and it's her place to look after him. I've special reasons for saying this. . . .'

What a funny thing for Falk to say ! and the only allusion to his mother in the whole of the letter

Joan smiled to herself as she read it. What d Falk think her power was ? Why, her mother and father had never listened to her for a single moment, nor had he, Falk, when he had been at home. She had never counted at all—to any one save Johnny. She put down the letter and tried to lose herself in the happy country of her own love, but she could not. Her honesty prevented her ; its silence was now oppressive and heavy-weighted. Where *could* her mother be ? And dinner already half an hour late in that so utterly punctual house l What had Falk meant about mother going to London ? Of course she would not go to London— at any rate without father. How could Falk imagine such a thing ?

She began to walk about the room, wondering what she should do about the dinner. More than an hour passed. She must give up the Sampsons, and she was very hungry. She had had no tea at the Flower Show and very little luncheon.

She was about to go and speak to Gladys when she heard the hall door open. It closed. Something—some unexpressed fear or foreboding—kept her where she was. Steps were in the hall, but they were not her father's ; he always moved with determined stride to his study or the stairs. These steps hesitated and faltered as though some one were there who did not know the house.

At last she went into the hall and saw that it was indeed her father now going slowly upstairs.

' Father l' she cried; ' I'm so glad you're in. Dinner's been waiting for hours. Shall I tell them to send it up ? '

He did not answer nor look back. She went to the bottom of the stairs and said again :

' Shall I, father ? '

But still he did not answer. She heard him close his door behind him.

She went back into the drawing-room terribly frightened. There was something in the bowed head and slow steps that terrified her, and suddenly she was aware that she had been frightened for many weeks past, but that she had never owned to herself that it was so.

She waited for a long time wondering what she should do. At last, calling her courage, she climbed the stairs, waited, and then, as though compelled by the overhanging silence of the house, knocked on his dressing-room door.

' Father, what shall we do about dinner ? Mother hasn't come in yet.' There was no answer.

' Will you have dinner now ? ' she asked again.

A voice suddenly answered her as though he were listening on the other side of the door. ' No, no. I want no dinner.'

She went down again, told Gladys that she would eat something, then sat in the lonely dining-room swallowing her soup and cutlet in the utmost haste.

Something was terribly wrong. Her father was covering all the rest of her view—the Jubilee, her mother, even Johnny. He was in great trouble, and she must help him, but she felt desperately her youth, her inexperience, her inadequacy.

She waited again, when she had finished her meal, wondering what she had better do. Oh ! how stupid not to know instantly the right thing and to feel this fear when it was her own father !

She went half-way upstairs, and then stood listening. No sound. Again she waited outside his door. With trembling hand she turned the handle. He faced her, staring at her. On his left temple was a big black bruise, on his forehead a cut, and on his left cheek a thin red mark that looked like a scratch.

' Father, you're hurt ! '

' Yes, I fell down——stumbled over something, coming up from the river.' He looked at her impatiently. ' Well, well, what is it ? '

' Nothing, father—only they're still keeping some dinner—— '

' I don't want anything. Where is your mother ? '

' She hasn't come back.'

' Not come back ? Why, where did she go to ? '

' I don't know. Gladys says she went out about six.'

He pushed past her into the passage. He went down into the hall ; she followed him timidly. From the bottom of the stairs he saw the letter on the table, and he went straight to it. He tore open the envelope and read :

I have left you for ever. All that I told you on Sunday night was true, and you may use that information as you please. Whatever may come to me, at least I know that I am never to live under the same roof with you again, and that is happiness enough for me, whatever other misery there may be in store for me. Now, at last, perhaps, you will realise that loneliness is worse than any other hell, and that's the hell you've made me suffer for twenty years. Look around you and see what your selfishness has done for you. It will be useless to try to persuade me to return to you. I hope to God that I shall never see you again.

AMY.

He turned and said in his ordinary voice, ' Your mother has left me.'

He came across to her, suddenly caught her by the shoulders, and said : ' Now, *you'd* better go, do you hear ?   They've all left me, your mother, Falk, all of them.   They've fallen on me and beaten me. They've kicked me.   They've spied on me and mocked me.   Well, then, you join them.   Do you hear ?   What do you stay for ?   Why do you remain with me ?   Do you hear ?   Do you hear ? '

She understood nothing.   Her terror caught her like the wind.   She crouched back against the bannisters, covering her face with her hand.

' Don't hit me, father.   Please, please don't hit me.'

He stood over her, staring down at her.

' It's a plot, and you must be in it with the others. . . .   Well, go and tell them they've won. Tell them to come and kick me again.   I'm down now.   I'm beaten ; go and tell them to come in— to come and take my house and my clothes.   Your mother's gone—follow her to London, then.'

He turned.   She heard him go into the drawing-room.   Suddenly, although she still did not understand what had happened, she knew that she must follow him and care for him.   He had pulled the curtains aside and thrown up the windows.

' Let them come in !   Let them come in !   I —I——'

Suddenly he turned towards her and held out his arms.

' I can't—I can't any more.'   He fell on his knees, burying his face in the shoulder of the chair. Then he cried :

' Oh, God, spare me now, spare me !   I cannot

bear any more. Thou hast chastised me enough.
Oh, God, don't take my sanity from me—leave me
that. Oh, God, leave me that! Thou hast taken
everything else. I have been beaten and betrayed
and deserted. I confess my wickedness, my
arrogance, my pride, but it was in Thy service.
Leave me my mind. Oh, God, spare me, spare me,
and forgive her who has sinned so grievously against
Thy laws. Oh, God, God, save me from madness,
save me from madness.'

In that moment Joan became a woman. Her
love, her own life, she threw everything away.

She went over to him, put her arms around his
neck, kissed him, fondled him, pressing her cheek
against his.

'Dear, dear father. I love you so. I love you
so. No one shall hurt you. Father dear, father
darling.'

Suddenly the room was blazing with light. The
Torchlight Procession tumbled into the Precincts.
The Cathedral sprang into light ; on all the hills
the bonfires were blazing.

Black figures scattered like dwarfs, pigmies,
giants about the grass. The torches tossed and
whirled and danced.

The Cathedral rose from the darkness, triumphant
in gold and fire.

BOOK IV

THE LAST STAND

CHAPTER I

EVERY one has, at one time or another, known the experience of watching some friend or acquaintance moved suddenly from the ordinary atmosphere of every day into some dramatic region of crisis where he becomes, for a moment, far more than life-size in his struggle against the elements ; he is lifted, like Siegmund in *The Valkyrie*, into the clouds for his last and most desperate duel.

There was something of this feeling in the attitude taken in our town after the Jubilee towards Archdeacon Brandon. As Miss Stiles said (not meaning it at all unkindly), it really was very fortunate for everybody that the town had the excitement of the Pybus appointment to follow immediately the Jubilee drama ; had it not been so, how flat would every one have been ! And by the Pybus appointment she meant, of course, the Decline and Fall of Archdeacon Brandon, and the issue of his contest with delightful, clever Canon Ronder.

The disappearance of Mrs. Brandon and Mr. Morris would have been excitement enough quite by itself for any one year. As every one said, the wives of Archdeacons simply did *not* run away with the clergymen of their town. It was not done. It had never, within any one's living memory, been done before, whether in Polchester or anywhere else.

Clergymen were, of course, only human like any one else, and so were their wives, but at least they did not make a public declaration of their failings ; they remembered their positions, who they were and what they were.

In one sense there had been no public declaration. Mrs. Brandon had gone up to London to see about some business, and Mr. Morris also happened to be away, and his sister-in-law was living on in the Rectory exactly as though nothing had occurred. However, that disguise could not hold for long, and every one knew exactly what had happened—well, if not exactly, every one had a very good individual version of the whole story.

And through it all, above it, behind it and beyond it, towered the figure of the Archdeacon. *He* was the question, he the centre of the drama. There were a hundred different stories running around the town as to what exactly had happened to him during those Jubilee days. Was it true that he had taken Miss Milton by the scruff of her long neck and thrown her out of the house ? Was it true that he had taken his coat off in the Cloisters and given Ronder two black eyes ? (The only drawback to this story was that Ronder showed no sign of bruises.) Had he and Mrs. Brandon fought up and down the house for the whole of a night, Joan assisting ? And, above all, *what* occurred at the Jubilee Fair ? *Had* Brandon been set upon by a lot of ruffians ? Was it true that Samuel Hogg had revenged himself for his daughter's abduction ? No one knew. No one knew anything at all. The only certain thing was that the Archdeacon had a bruise on his temple and a scratch on his cheek, and that he was ' queer,' oh, yes, very queer indeed !

It was finally about this ' queerness ' that the gossip of the town most persistently clung. Many people said that they had watched him ' going queer ' for a long while back, entirely forgetting that only a year ago he had been the most vigorous, healthiest, sanest man in the place. Old Puddifoot, with all sorts of nods, winks and murmurs, alluded to mysterious medical secrets, and ' how much he could tell an' he would,' and that ' he had said years ago about Brandon. . . .' Well, never mind what he had said, but it was all turning out exactly as, for years, he had expected.

Nothing is stranger (and perhaps more fortunate) than the speed with which the past is forgotten. Brandon might have been all his days the odd, muttering, eye-wandering figure that he now appeared. Where was the Viking now ? Where the finest specimen of physical health in all Glebe- shire ? Where the King and Crowned Monarch of Polchester ?

In the dust and debris of the broken past. ' Poor old Archdeacon.' ' A bit queer in the upper storey.' ' Not to be wondered at after all the trouble he's had.' ' They break up quickly, those strong-looking men.' ' Bit too pleased with himself, he was.' ' Ah, well, he's served his time ; what we need are more modern men. You can't deny that he was old-fashioned.'

People were not altogether to be blamed for this sudden sense that they were stepping into a

new period, out of one room into another, so to
speak. The Jubilee was responsible for that. It
did mark a period, and looking back now after all
these years one can see that that impression was a
true one. The Jubilee of '97—the Boer War, the
death of Queen Victoria, the end of the Victorian
Era for Church as well as for State.

And there were other places beside Polchester
that could show their typical figures doomed, as it
were, to die for their Period—no mean nor unworthy death after all.

But no Polcastrian in '97 knew that that service
in the Cathedral, that scratch on the Archdeacon's
cheek, that visit of Mrs. Brandon to London—that
these things were for them the Writing on the
Wall. June 1897 and August 1914 were not,
happily for them, linked together in immortal
significance—their eyes were set on the personal
history of the men and women who were moving
before them. Had Brandon in the pride of his
heart not claimed God as his ally, would men have
died at Ypres ? Can any bounds be placed to one
act of love and unselfishness, to a single deed of
mean heart and malicious tongue ?

It was enough for our town that ' Brandon
and his ways ' were out-of-date, and it was a lucky
thing that as modern a man as Ronder had come
amongst us.

And yet not altogether. Brandon in prosperity
was one thing, Brandon in misfortune quite another.
He had been abominably treated. What had he
ever done that was not actuated absolutely by zeal
for the town and the Cathedral ?

And, after all, had that man Ronder acted
straight ? He was fair and genial enough out-

wardly, but who could tell what went on behind those round spectacles ? There were strange stories of intrigue about. Had he not determined to push Brandon out of the place from the first moment of his arrival ? And as far as this Pybus living went, it was all very well to be modern and advanced, but wasn't Ronder advocating for the appointment a man who laughed at the Gospels and said that there were no such things as snakes and apples in the Garden of Eden ? After all, he was a foreigner, and Brandon belonged to them. Poor old Brandon !

Ronder was in his study, waiting for Wistons. Wistons had come to Polchester for a night to see his friend Foster. It was an entirely private visit, unknown to anybody save two or three of his friends among the clergy. He had asked whether Ronder could spare him half an hour. Ronder was delighted to spare it. . . .

Ronder was in the liveliest spirits. He hummed a little chant to himself as he paced his study, stopping, as was his habit, to touch something on his table, to push back a book more neatly into its row on the shelf, to stare for an instant out of the window into the green garden drenched with the afternoon sun.

Yes, he was in admirable spirits. He had known some weeks of acute discomfort. That phase was over, his talk with Brandon in the Cloisters after the Cathedral service had closed it. On that occasion he had put himself entirely in the right, having been before that, under the eye of his aunt and certain critics in the town, ever so slightly in the wrong. Now he was justified. He had humbled himself before Brandon (when really there was no reason to do so), apologised (when truly there was not the slightest need for it)—Brandon had utterly rejected his apology, turned on him as though he were a thief and a robber—he had done all that he could, more, far more, than his case demanded.

So his comfort, his dear consoling comfort, had returned to him completely. And with it had returned all his affection, his tenderness for Brandon. Poor man, deserted by his wife, past his work, showing as he so obviously did in the Jubilee week that his brain (never very agile) was now quite inert, poor man, poor, poor man! Ronder, as he walked his study, simply longed to do something for Brandon—to give him something, make him a generous present, to go to London and persuade his poor weak wife to return to him, anything, anything to make him happy again.

Too sad to see the poor man's pale face, restless eyes, to watch his hurried, uneasy walk, as though he were suspicious of every man. Everywhere now Ronder sang Brandon's praises—what fine work he had done in the past, how much the Church owed him ; where would Polchester have been in the past without him ?

' I assure you,' Ronder said to Mrs. Preston, meeting her in the High Street, ' the Archdeacon's work may be over, but when I think of what the Church owes him——'

To which Mrs. Preston had said : ' Ah, Canon, how you search for the Beauty in human life ! You are a lesson to all of us. After all, to find Beauty in even the meanest and most disappointing, that is our task ! '

There was no doubt but that Ronder had come magnificently through the Jubilee week. It had in every way strengthened and confirmed his already strong position. He had been everywhere; had added gaiety and sunshine to the Flower Show; had preached a most wonderful sermon at the evening service on the Tuesday; had addressed, from the steps of his house, the Torchlight Procession in exactly the right words; had patted all the children on the head at the Mayor's tea for the townspeople; had enchanted everywhere. That for which he had worked had been accomplished, and accomplished with wonderful speed.

He was firmly established as the leading Churchman in Polchester; only now let the Pybus living go in the right direction (as it must do), and he would have nothing more to wish for.

He loved the place. As he looked down into the garden and thought of the years of pleasant comfort and happiness now stretching in front of him, his heart swelled with love of his fellow human beings. He longed, here and now, to do something for some one, to give some children pennies, some poor old men a good meal, to lend some one his pounds, to speak a good word in public for some one maligned, to——

'Mr. Wistons, sir,' said the maid. When he turned round only his exceeding politeness prevented him from a whistle of astonishment. He had never seen a photograph of Wistons, and the man had never been described to him.

From all that he had heard and read of him, he had pictured him a tall, lean ascetic, a kind of Dante and Savonarola in one, a magnificent figure of protest and abjuration. This man who now came towards him was little, thin, indeed, but almost deformed, seeming to have one shoulder

higher than the other, and to halt ever so slightly
on one foot.   His face was positively ugly, redeemed
only, as Ronder, who was no mean observer, at
once perceived, by large and penetrating eyes.   The
eyes, indeed, were beautiful, of a wonderful softness
and intelligence.

His hair was jet black and thick ; his hand, as
it gripped Ronder's, strong and bony.

' I'm very glad to meet you, Canon Ronder,' he
said.   ' I've heard so much about you.'   His voice,
as Mrs. Combermere long afterwards remarked,
' has a twinkle in it.'   It was a jolly voice, humorous,
generous but incisive, and exceedingly clear.   It
had a very slight accent, so slight that no one could
ever decide on its origin.   The books said that
Wistons had been born in London, and that his
father had been Rector of Lambeth for many
years ; it was also quickly discovered by penetrating
Polcastrians that he had a not very distant French
ancestry.   Was it Cockney ?   ' I expect,' said Miss
Stiles, ' that he played with the little Lambeth
children when he was small '—but no one really
knew. . . .

The two men sat down facing one another, and
Wistons looked strange indeed with his shoulders
hunched up, his thin little legs like two cross-bones,
one over the other, his black hair and pale face.

' I feel rather like a thief in the night,' he said,
' stealing down here.   But Foster wanted me to
come, and I confess to a certain curiosity myself.'

' You would like to come to Pybus if things go
that way ? ' Ronder asked him.

' I shall be quite glad to come.   On the other
hand, I shall not be at all sorry to stay where I am.
Does it matter very much where one is ? '

'Except that the Pybus living is generally considered a very important step in Church preferment. It leads, as a rule, to great things.'

'Great things? Yes. . . .' Wistons seemed to be talking to himself. 'One thing is much like another. The more power one seems to have outwardly, the less very often one has in reality However, if I'm called I'll come. But I wanted to see you, Canon Ronder, for a special purpose.'

'Yes?' asked Ronder.

'Of course I haven't enquired in any way into the probabilities of the Pybus appointment. But I understand that there is very strong opposition to myself; naturally there would be. I also understand that, with the exception of my friend Foster, you are my strongest supporter in this matter. May I ask you why?'

'Why?' repeated Ronder.

'Yes, why? You may say, and quite justly, that I have no right at all to ask you that question. It should be enough for me, I know, to realise that there are certain people here who want me to come. It ought to be enough. But it isn't. It *isn't*. I won't—I can't come here under false pretences.'

'False pretences!' cried Ronder. 'I assure you, dear Mr. Wistons——'

'Oh, yes, I know. I know what you will naturally tell me. But I have caught enough of the talk here—Foster in his impetuosity has been perhaps indiscreet—to realise that there has been, that there still is, a battle here between the older, more conservative body of opinion and the more modern school. It seems to me that I have been made the figure-head of this battle. To that I have

no objection.   It is not for the first time.   But
what I want to ask you, Canon Ronder, with the
utmost seriousness is just this :

'Have you supported my appointment because
you honestly felt that I was the best man for this
particular job, or because—I know you will forgive
me if this question sounds impertinent—you wished
to score a point over some personal adversary ? '

The question *was* impertinent.   There could be
no doubt of it.   Ronder ought at once to resent
any imputation on his honesty.   What right had
this man to lp down into Ronder's motives ?
The Canon stared from behind his glasses into those
very bright and insistent eyes, and even as he stared
there came once again that cold little wind of discomfort, that questioning, irritating wind, that had
been laid so effectively, he thought, for ever to rest.
What was this man about, attacking him like this,
attacking him before, even, he had been appointed ?
Was it, after all, quite wise that Wistons should
come here ?   Would that same comfort, so rightly
valued by Ronder, be quite assured in the future
if Wistons were at Pybus ?   Wouldn't some
nincompoop like Forsyth be perhaps, after all, his
best choice ?

Ronder suddenly ceased to wish to give pennies
to little children or a present to Brandon.   He was,
very justly, irritated.

'Do forgive me if I am impertinent,' said
Wistons quietly, 'but I have to know this.'

'But of course,' said Ronder, 'I consider you
the best man for this appointment.   I should not
have stirred a finger in your support otherwise.'
(Why, something murmured to him, are people
always attributing to you unworthy motives, first

your aunt, then Foster, now this man ?) 'You are quite correct in saying that there is strong opposition to your appointment here. But that is quite natural ; you have only to consider some of your published works to understand that. A battle is being fought with the more conservative elements in the place. You have heard probably that the Archdeacon is their principal leader, but I think I may say that our victory is already assured. There was never any real doubt of the issue. Archdeacon Brandon is a splendid fellow, and has done great work for the Church here, but he is behind the times, out-of-date, and too obstinate to change. Then certain family misfortunes have hit him hard lately, and his health is not, I fear, what it was. His opposition is as good as over.'

'That's a swift decline,' said Wistons. 'I remember only some six months ago hearing of him as by far the strongest man in this place.'

'Yes, it has been swift,' said Ronder, shaking his head regretfully, 'but I think that his position here was largely based on the fact that there was no one else here strong enough to take the lead against him.

'My coming into the diocese—some one, however feeble, you understand, coming in from outside— made an already strong modern feeling yet stronger.'

'I will tell you one thing,' said Wistons, suddenly shooting up his shoulders and darting forward his head. 'I think all this Cathedral intrigue disgusting. No, I don't blame you. You came into the middle of it, and were doubtless forced to take the part you did. But I'll have no lot or hold in it. If I am to understand that I gain the Pybus appointment only through a lot of backstairs intrigue and cabal, I'll let it be known at once that I would not accept that living though it were offered me a thousand times.'

'No, no,' cried Ronder eagerly. 'I assure you that that is not so. There has been intrigue here owing to the old politics of the party who governed the Cathedral. But that is, I hope and pray, over and done with. It is because so many of us want to have no more of it that we are asking you to come here. Believe me, believe me, that is so.'

'I should not have said what I did,' continued Wistons quietly. 'It was arrogant and conceited. Perhaps you cannot avoid intrigue and party feeling among the community of any Cathedral body. That is why I want you to understand, Canon Ronder, the kind of man I am, before you propose me for this post. I am afraid that you may afterwards regret your advocacy. If I were invited to a Canonry, or any post immediately connected with the Cathedral, I would not accept it for an instant. I come, if I come at all, to fight the Cathedral—that is to fight everything in it, round and about it, that prevents men from seeing clearly the figure of Christ.

'I believe, Canon Ronder, that before many years are out it will become clear to the whole world that there are now two religions—the religion of authority, and the religion of the spirit—and if in such a division I must choose, I am for the religion of the spirit every time.'

The religion of the spirit! Ronder stirred, a little restlessly, his fat thighs. What had that to do with it? They were discussing the Pybus appointment. The religion of the spirit! Well, who wasn't for that? As to dogma, Ronder had never laid very great stress upon it. A matter of words very largely. He looked out to the garden, where a tree, scooped now like a great green fan against the blue-white sky, was shading the sun's rays. Lovely ! Lovely ! Lovely like the Hermes downstairs, lovely like the piece of red amber on his writing-table, like the Blind Homer . . . like a scallop of green glass holding water that washed a little from side to side, the sheen on its surface changing from dark shadow to faintest dusk. Lovely ! He stared, transported, his comfort flowing full-tide now into his soul.

'Exactly !' he said, suddenly turning his eyes full on Wistons. 'The Christian Church has made a golden calf of its dogmas. The Calf is worshipped, the Cathedral enshrines it.'

Wistons gave a swift curious stab of a glance. Ronder caught it ; he flushed. 'You think it strange of me to say that ?' he asked. 'I can see that you do. Let me be frank with you. It has been my trouble all my life that I can see every side of a question. I am with the modernists, but at the same time I can understand how dangerous it must seem to the dogmatists to abandon even an inch of the country that Paul conquered for them. I'm afraid, Wistons, that I see life in terms of men and women rather than of creeds. I want men to be happy and at peace with one another. And if to form a new creed or to abandon an old one leads to men's deeper religious happiness, well, then . . .' He waved his hands.

Wistons, speaking again as it were to himself, answered, 'I care only for Jesus Christ. He is overshadowed now by all the great buildings that men have raised for Him. He is lost to our view ;

we must recover Him. Him ! Him ! Only Him ! To serve Him, to be near Him, almost to feel the touch of His hand on one's head, that is the whole of life to me. And now He is hard to come to, harder every year. . . .' He got up. ' I didn't come to say more than that.

' It's the Cathedral, Ronder, that I fear. Don't you yourself sometimes feel that it has, by now, a spirit of its own, a life, a force that all the past years and all the worship that it has had have given it ? Don't you even feel that ? That it has become a god demanding his own rites and worshippers ? That it uses men for its own purposes, and not for Christ's ? That almost it hates Christ ? It is so beautiful, so lovely, so haughty, so jealous !

' " For I, thy God, am a jealous God." . . .' He broke off. ' I could love Christ better in that garden than in the Cathedral. Tear it down and build it up again ! ' He turned restlessly, almost savagely, to Ronder. ' Can you be happy and comfortable and at ease, when you see what Christ might be to human beings and what He is ? Who thinks of Him, who cares for Him, who loves His sweetness and charity and tenderness ? Why is something always in the way, always, always, always ? Love ! Charity ! Doesn't such a place as this Cathedral breed hatred and malice and pride and jealousy? And isn't its very beauty a contempt? . . . And now what right have you to help my appointment to Pybus ? '

Ronder smiled.

' You are what we need here,' he said. ' You shall shake some of our comfort from us—make a new life here for us.'

Wistons was suddenly almost timid. He spoke as though he were waking from some dream.

'Good-bye. . . . Good-bye. No, don't come down. Thank you so much. Thank you. Very kind of you. Good-bye.'

But Ronder insisted on coming down. They shook hands at his door. The figure was lost in the evening sun.

Ronder stood there for a moment gazing at the bright grass, the little houses with their shining knockers, the purple shadow of the Cathedral.

Had he done right? Was Wistons the man? Might he not be more dangerous than . . . ? No, no, too late now. The fight with Brandon must move to its appointed end. Poor Brandon! Poor dear Brandon!

He looked across at the house as on the evening of his arrival from that same step he had looked.

Poor Brandon! He would like to do something for him, some little kindly unexpected act!

He closed the door and softly padded upstairs humming happily to himself that little chant.

CHAPTER II

TWO IN THE HOUSE

A LETTER from Falk to Joan.

DEAR JOAN — Mother has been here. I could get
. thing out of her. I had only one thing to say—that
s. must go back to father. That was the one thing that
she asserted, over and over again, that she never would.
Joan. she was tragic. I felt that I had never seen her
befor never known her. She was thinking of nothing
but M rris. She seemed to see him all the time that she
was in t e room with me. She is going abroad with Morris
at the e d of this week—to South America, I believe.
Mother esn't seem now to care what happens, except
that she w l not go back to father.

She said n odd thing to me at the end—that she had had
her time, he wonderful time, and that she could never be
as unhappy as lonely as she was, and that she would
love him alway (Morris, I suppose), and that he would love
her.

The skunk t t Morris is ! And yet I don't know.
Haven't I been skunk too ? And yet I don't feel a
skunk. If only father would be happy ! Then things
would be better than they've ever been. You don't know
how good Annie is, Joan. How fine and simple and true !
Why are we all such mixtures ? Why can't you ever do
what's right for yourself without hurting other people ?
But I'm not going to wait much longer. If things aren't
better soon I'm coming down whether he'll see me or no.

We *must* make him happy. We're all that he has now. Once this Pybus thing is settled I'll come down. Write to me. Tell me everything. You're a brick, Joan, to take all this as you do. Why did we go all these years without knowing one another?—Your loving brother,

FALK.

A letter from Joan to Falk.

DEAREST FALK—I'm answering you by return because I'm so frightened. If I send you a telegram, come down at once. Mr. Morris's sister-in-law is telling everybody that he only went up to London on business. But she's not going to stay here, I think. But I can't think much even of mother. I can think of no one but father. Oh, Falk, it's been terrible these last three days, and I don't know *what's* going to happen.

I'll try and tell you how it's been. It's just two months now since mother went away. That night it was dreadful. He walked up and down his room all night. Indeed he's been doing that ever since she went. And yet I don't think it's of her that he's thinking most. I'm not sure even that he's thinking of her at all.

He's concentrating everything now on the Pybus appointment. He talks to himself. (You can see by that how changed he is.) He is hurrying round to see people and asking them to the house, and he's so odd with them, looking at them suddenly, suspiciously, as though he expected that they were laughing at him. There's always something in the back of his mind—not mother, I'm sure. Something happened to him that last day of the Jubilee. He's always talking about some one who struck him, and he puts his hand up to feel his forehead, where there was a bruise. He told me that day that he had fallen down, but I'm sure now that he had a fight with somebody.

He's always talking, too, about a 'conspiracy' against him—not only Canon Ronder, but something more general. Poor dear, the worst of it all is, how bewildered he is. You know how direct he used to be, the way he went straight to his point and wasn't afraid of anybody. Now he's always hesitating. He hesitates before he goes out, before he goes upstairs, before he comes into my room. It's just as though he was for ever expecting that there's some one behind the door waiting for him with a hammer. It's so strange how I've changed my feeling about him. I used to think him so strong that he could beat down anybody, and now I feel he wants looking after all the time. Perhaps he never was really strong at all, but it was all on the outside. All the same he's very brave too. He knows all the town's been talking about him, but I think he'd face a whole world of Polchesters if he could only beat Canon Ronder over the Pybus appointment. If Mr. Forsyth isn't appointed to that I think he'll go to pieces altogether. You see, a year ago there wouldn't have been any question about it at all. Of course he would have had his way.

But what makes me so frightened, Falk, is of something happening in the house. Father is so suspicious that it makes me suspicious too. It doesn't seem like the house it was at all, but as though there *were* some one hiding in it, and at night it's awful. I lie awake listening, and I can hear father walking up and down, his room's next to mine, you know. And then if I listen hard enough, I can hear footsteps all over the house—you know how you do in the middle of the night. And there's always some one coming upstairs. This will sound silly to you up in London, but it doesn't seem silly here, I assure you. All the servants feel it, and Gladys is going at the end of the month.

And oh, Falk! I'm so sorry for him! It does seem so strange that everything should have changed for him as it has. I feel his own bewilderment. A year ago he seemed so strong and safe and secure as though he would go on like that for ever, and hadn't an enemy in the world. How could he have? He's never meant harm to any one. Your going away I can understand, but mother, I feel as though I never could speak to her again. To be so cruel to father and to write him such a letter! (Of course I didn't see the letter, but the effect of it on father was terrible.)

He's so lonely now. He scarcely realises me half the time, and you see he never did think very much about me before, so it's very difficult for him to begin now. I'm so inexperienced. It's hard enough running the house now, and having to get another servant instead of Gladys—and I daresay the others will go too now, but that's nothing to waiting all the time for something to happen and watching father every minute. We *must* make him happy again, Falk. You're quite right. It's the only thing that matters. Everything else is less important than that. If only this Pybus affair were over! Canon Ronder is so powerful now. I'm so afraid of him. I do hate him so! The Cathedral, and the town, everything seems to have changed since he came. A year ago they were like father, settled for ever. And now every one's talking about new people and being out-of-date, and changing the Cathedral music and everything! But none of that matters in comparison with father.

I've written a terrible long letter, but it's done me ever so much good. I'm sometimes so tempted to telegraph to you at once. I'm almost sure father would be glad to see you. You were always the one he loved most. But perhaps we'd better wait a little : if things get worse in any way I'll telegraph at once.

I'm so glad you're well, and happy. You haven't in your letters told me anything about the Jubilee in London. Was it very fine? Did you see the Queen? Did she look very happy? Were the crowds very big? Much love from your loving sister, JOAN.

Joan, waiting in the shadowy drawing-room for Johnny St. Leath, wondered whether her father had come in or no.

It wouldn't matter if he had, he wouldn't come into the drawing-room. He would go directly into his study. She knew exactly what he would do. He would shut the door, then a minute later would open it, look into the hall and listen, then close it again very cautiously. He always now did that. And in any case if he did come into the drawing-room and saw Johnny it wouldn't matter. His mind was entirely centred on Pybus, and Johnny had nothing to do with Pybus. Johnny's mother, yes. Had that stout white-haired cockatoo suddenly appeared, she would be clutched, absorbed, utilised to her last white feather. But she didn't appear. She stayed up in her Castle, serene and supreme.

Joan was very nervous. She stood, a little grey shadow in the grey room, her hands twisting and u ⁺twisting. She was nervous because she was going to s ⁺ good-bye to Johnny, perhaps for ever, and she was. 't sure that she'd have the strength to do it.

Suddenly he was there with her in the room, big and clumsy and cheerful, quite unaware apparently that he was never, after this, to see Joan again.

He tried to kiss her but she prevented him. ' No, you must sit over there,' she said, ' and we must never, at least not probably for years and years, kiss one another again.'

He was aware, as she spoke, of quite a new, a different Joan ; he had been conscious of this new Joan on many occasions during these last weeks. When he had first known her she had been a child and he had loved her for her childishness ; now he must meet the woman and the child together, and instinctively he was himself more serious in his attitude to her.

' We could talk much better, Joan dear,' he said, ' if we were close together.'

' No,' she said ; ' then I couldn't talk at all. We mustn't meet alone again after to-day, and we mustn't write, and we mustn't consider ourselves engaged.'

' Why, please ? '

' Can't you see that it's all impossible ? We've

tried it now for weeks and it becomes more
impossible every day. Your mother's absolutely
against it and always will be—and now at home—
here—my mother——'

She broke off. He couldn't leave her like that ;
he sprang up, went across to her, put his arms
around her, and kissed her. She didn't resist him
nor move from him, but when she spoke again her
voice was firmer and more resolved than before.

' No, Johnny, I mean it, I can think of nothing
now but father. So long as he's alive I must stay
with him. He's quite alone now, he has nobody.
I can't even think about you so long as he's like
this, so unwell and so unhappy. It isn't as though
I were very clever or old or anything. I've never
until lately been allowed to do anything all my life,
not the tiniest bit of housekeeping, and now
suddenly it has all come. And if I were thinking
of you, wanting to see you, having letters from you,
I shouldn't attend to this ; I shouldn't be able to
think of it——'

' Do you still love me ? '

' Why, of course. I shall never change.'

' And do you think that I still love you ? '

' Yes.'

' And do you think I'll change ? '

' You may. But I don't want to think so.'

' Well, then, the main question is settled. It
doesn't matter how long we wait.'

' But it *does* matter. It may be for years and
years. You've got to marry, you can't just stay
unmarried because one day you may marry me.'

' Can't I ? You wait and see whether I can't.'

' But you oughtn't to, Johnny. Think of your
family. Think of your mother. You're the only son.'

' Mother can just think of me for once. It will be a bit of a change for her. It will do her good. I've told her whom I want to marry, and she must just get used to it. She admits herself that she can't have anything against you personally, except that you're too young. I asked her whether she wanted me to marry a Dowager of sixty.'

Joan moved away. She walked to the window and looked out at the grey mist sweeping like an army of ghostly messengers across the Cathedral Green. She turned round to him.

' No, Johnny, this time it isn't a joke. I mean absolutely what I say. We're not to meet alone or to write until—father doesn't need me any more. I can't think, I mustn't think, of anything but father now. Nothing that you can say, or any one can say, will make me change my mind about that now. . . . And please go, Johnny, because it's so hard while you're here. And we *must* do it. I'll never change, but you're free to, and you *ought* to. It's your duty to find some one more satisfactory than me.'

But Johnny appeared not to have heard her last words. He had been looking about him, at the walls, the windows, the ceiling—rather as a young dog sniffs some place new to him.

' Joan, tell me. Are you all right here ? You oughtn't to be all alone here like this, just with your father. Can't you get some one to come and stay ? '

' No,' she answered bravely. ' Of course it's all right. I've got Gladys, who's been with us for years.'

' There's something funny,' he said, still looking about him. ' It feels queer to me—sort of un-happy.'

' Never mind that,' she said, hurriedly moving towards the door, as though she had heard footsteps. ' You must go, Johnny. Kiss me once, the last time. And then no letters, no anything, until— until—father's happy again.'

She rested in his arms, suddenly tranquil, safe, at peace. Her hands were round his neck. She kissed his eyes. They clung together, suddenly two children, utterly confident in one another and in their mutual faith.

A hand was on the door. They separated. The Archdeacon came in. He peered into the dusky room.

' Joan ! Joan ! Are you there ? '

She came across to him. ' Yes, father, here I am. And this is Lord St. Leath.'

' How do you do, sir ? ' said Johnny.

' How do you do ? I hope your mother is well.'

' Very well, thank you, sir.'

' That's good, that's good. I have some business to discuss with her. Rather important business ; I may come and see her to-morrow afternoon if she is disengaged. Will you kindly tell her ? '

' Indeed I will, sir.'

' Thank you. Thank you. This room is very dark. Why are there no lights ? Joan, you should have lights. There's no one else here, is there ? '

' No, father.'

Johnny heard their voices echoing in the empty hall as he let himself out.

Brandon shut his study door and looked about him. The lamp on his table was lit, his study had a warm and pleasant air with the books gleaming in their shelves and the fire crackling. (You needed

a fire on these late summer evenings.) Nevertheless, although the room looked comfortable, he did
not at once move into it. He stood there beside
the door, as though he was waiting for something.
He listened. The house was intensely quiet. He
opened the door and looked into the passage.
There was no one there. The gas hissed ever so
slightly, like a whispering importunate voice. He
came back into his room, closing the door very
carefully behind him, went across softly to his
writing-table, sat down, and took up his pen. His
eyes were fixed on the door, and then suddenly he
would jerk round in his chair as though he expected
to catch some one who was standing just behind
him.

Then began that fight that always now must
be waged whenever he sat down at his desk, the
fight to drive his thoughts, like sheep, into the only
pen that they must occupy. He must think now
only of one thing ; there were others—pictures,
ideas, memories, fears, horrors even—crowding,
hovering close about him, and afterwards—after
Pybus—he would attend to them. Only one thing
mattered now. ' Yes, you gibbering idiots, do
your worst ; knock me down. Come on four to
one like the cowards that you are, strike me in the
back, take my wife from me, and ruin my house. I
will attend to all of you shortly, but first—Pybus.'

His lips were moving as he turned over the
papers. *Was* there some one in the room with him ?
His head was aching so badly that it was difficult to
think. And his heart ! How strangely that behaved
in these days ! Five heavy slow beats, then a little
skip and jump, then almost as though it had stopped
beating altogether.

Suitable was not perhaps exactly the word for Forsyth. It was something other than a question of mere suitability. It was a keeping out of the *bad*, as well as a bringing in of the *good*. *Suitable* was not the word that he wanted. What did he want ? The words began to jump about on the paper, and suddenly out of the centre of his table there stretched and extended the figure of Miss Milton. Yes, there she was in her shabby clothes and hat, smirking. . . . He dashed his hand at her and she vanished. He sprang up. This was too bad. He must not let these fancies get hold of him. He went into the hall.

He called out loudly, his voice echoing through the house, ' Joan ! Joan ! '

Almost at once she came. Strange the relief that he felt ! But he wouldn't show it. She must notice nothing at all out of the ordinary.

She sat close to him at their evening meal and talked to him about everything that came into her young head. Sometimes he wished that she wouldn't talk so much ; she hadn't talked so much in earlier days, had she ? But he couldn't remember what she had done in earlier days.

He was very particular now about his food. Always he had eaten whatever was put in front of him with hearty and eager appreciation ; now he seemed to have very little appetite. He was always complaining about the cooking. The potatoes were hard, the beef was underdone, the pastry was heavy. And sometimes he would forget altogether that he was eating, and would sit staring in front of him, his food neglected on his plate.

It was not easy for Joan. Not easy to choose

topics that were not dangerous. And so often he was not listening to her at all. Perhaps at no other time did she pity him so much, and love him so much, as when she saw him staring in front of him, his eyes puzzled, bewildered, piteous, like those of an animal caught in a trap. All her old fear of him was gone, but a new fear had come in its place. Sometimes, in quite the old w ˙ he would rap out suddenly, ' Nonsense—stuff ana nonsense ! . . . As though *he* knew anything about it ! ' or would once again take the whole place, town and Cathedral and all of them, into his charge with something like, ' I knew how to manage the thing. What they would have done without——' But these defiances never lasted. They would fade away into bewilderment and silence.

He would complain continually of his head, putting his hand suddenly up to it, and saying, like a little child :

' My head's so bad. Such a headache ! ' But he would refuse to see Puddifoot ; had seen him once, and had immediately quarrelled with him, and told him that he was a silly old fool and knew nothing about anything, and this when Puddifoot had come with the noblest motives, intending to patronise and condole.

After dinner to-night Joan and he went into the drawing-room. Often, after dinner, he vanished into the study ' to work ' — but to-night he was ' tired, very tired—my dear. So much effort in connection with this Pybus business. What's come to the town I don't know. A year ago the matter would have been simple enough . . . anything so obvious. . . .'

He sat in his old arm-chair, whence for so many

years he had delivered his decisive judgments. No
decisive judgments to-night! He was really tired,
lying back, his eyes closed, his hands twitching ever
so slightly on his knees.

Joan sat near to him, struggling to overcome
her fear. She felt that if only she could grasp that
fear, like a nettle, and hold it tightly in her hand it
would seem so slight and unimportant. But she
could not grasp it. It was compounded of so many
things, of the silence and the dulness, of the
Precincts and the Cathedral, of whispering trees
and steps on the stairs, of her father and something
strange that now inhabited him like a new guest in
their house, of her loneliness and of her longing
for some friend with whom she could talk, of her
ache for Johnny and his comforting, loving smile,
but most of all, strangely, of her own love for her
father, and her desire, her poignant desire, that he
should be happy again. She scarcely missed her
mother, she did not want her to come back ; but
she ached and ached to see once again that happy
flush return to her father's cheek, that determined
ring to his voice, that buoyant confident movement
to his walk.

To-night she could not be sure whether he slept
or no. She watched him, and the whole world
seemed to hold its breath. Suddenly an absurd
fancy seized her. She fought against it for a time,
sitting there, her hands tightly clenched. Then
suddenly it overcame her. Some one was listening
outside the window ; she fancied that she could
see him—tall, dark, lean, his face pressed against
the pane.

She rose very softly and stole across the floor,
very gently drew back one of the curtains and

looked out. It was dark and he could see nothing —only the Cathedral like a grey web against a sky black as ink. A lamp, across the Green, threw a splash of orange in the middle distance—no other light. The Cathedral seemed to be very close to the house.

She closed the curtain and then heard her father call her.

'Joan! Joan! Where are you?'

She came back and stood by his chair. 'I was only looking out to see what sort of a night it was, father dear,' she said.

He suddenly smiled. 'I had a pleasant little nap then,' he said; 'my head's better. There. Sit down close to me. Bring your chair nearer. We're all alone here now, you and I. We must make a lot of one another.'

He had paid so little attention to her hitherto that she suddenly realised now that her loneliness had, during these last weeks, been the hardest thing of all to bear. She drew her chair close to his and he took her hand.

'Yes, yes, it's quite true. I don't know what I should have done without you during these last weeks. You've been very good to your poor, stupid, old father!'

She murmured something, and he burst out, 'Oh, yes, they do! That's what they say! I know how they talk. They want to get me out of the way and change the place—put in unbelievers and atheists. But they shan't—not while I have any breath in my body——' He went on more gently, 'Why, just think, my dear, they actually want to have that man Wistons here. An atheist! A denier of Christ's divinity! Here worshipping in the Cathedral! And when I try to stop it they say I'm mad. Oh yes! They do! I've heard them. Mad. Out-of-date. They've laughed at me—ever since—ever since . . . that elephant, you know, dear . . . that began it . . . the Circus. . . .'

She leaned over him.

' Father dear, you mustn't pay so much attention to what they say. You imagine so much just because you aren't very well and have those head-aches—and—and—because of other things. You imagine things that aren't true. So many people here love you——'

' Love me!' he burst out suddenly, starting up in his chair. ' When they set upon me, five of them, from behind and beat me! There in public with the lights and the singing.' He caught her hand, gripping it. ' There's a conspiracy, Joan. I know it. I've seen it a long time. And I know who started it and who paid them to follow me. Everywhere I go, there they are, following me.

' That old woman with her silly hat, she followed me into my own house. Yes, she did! " I'll read you a letter," she said. " I hate you, and I'll make you cry out over this." They're all in it. He's setting them on. But he shan't have his way. I'll fight him yet. Even my own son——' His voice broke.

Joan knelt at his feet, looking up into his face. ' Father! Falk wants to come and see you! I've had a letter from him. He wants to come and ask your forgiveness—he loves you so much.'

He got up from his chair, almost pushing her away from him. ' Falk! Falk! I don't know any one called that. I haven't got a son——'

He turned, looking at her. Then suddenly put

his arms around her and kissed her, holding her
tight to his breast.

'You're a good girl,' he said. 'Dear Joan !
I'm glad you've not left me too. I love you, Joan,
and I've not been good enough to you. Oh no, I
haven't ! Many things I might have done, and
now it's too late . . . too late. . . .'

He kissed her again and again, stroking her hair,
then he said that he was tired, very tired—he'd sleep
to-night. He went slowly upstairs.

He undressed rapidly, flinging off his clothes as
though they hurt him. As though some one else
had unexpectedly come into the room, he saw himself standing before the long glass in the dressing-
room, naked save for his vest. He looked at himself and laughed.

How funny he looked only in his vest—how
funny were he to walk down the High Street like
that ! They would say he was mad. And yet he
wouldn't be mad. He would be just as he was
now. He pulled the vest off over his head and
continued to stare at himself. It was as though
he were looking at some one else's body. The
long toes, the strong legs, the thick thighs, the
broad hairless chest, the stout red neck—and then
those eyes, surely not his, those strange ironical
eyes ! He passed his hand down his side and felt
the cool strong marble of his flesh. Then suddenly
he was cold and he hurried into his night-shirt and
his dressing-gown.

He sat on his bed. Something deep down in
him was struggling to come up. Some thought
. . . some feeling . . . some name. Falk ! It
was as though a bell were ringing, at a great dis-

tance, in the sleeping town — but ringing only, for him. Falk! The pain, the urgent pain, crept closer. Falk! He got up from his bed, opened his door, looked out into the dark and silent house, stepped forward, carefully, softly, his old red dressing-gown close about him, stumbling a little on the stairs, feeling the way to his study door.

He sat in his arm-chair huddled up. 'Falk! Falk! Oh, my boy, my boy, come back, come back! I want you, I want to be with you, to see you, to touch you, to hear your voice! I want to love you!

'Love—Love! I never wanted love before, but now I want it, desperately, desperately, some one to love me, some one for me to love, some one to be kind to. Falk, my boy. I'm so lone. It's so dark. I can't see things as I did. It's getting darker.

'Falk, come back and help me. . . .'

CHAPTER III

PRELUDE TO BATTLE

THAT night he slept well and soundly, and in the morning woke tranquil and refreshed. His life seemed suddenly to have taken a new turn. As he lay there and watched the sunlight run through the lattices like strands of pale-coloured silk, it seemed to him that he was through the worst. He did what he had not done for many days, allowed the thought of his wife to come and dwell with him.

He went over many of their past years together, and, nodding his head, decided that he had been often to blame. Then the further thought of what she had done, of her adultery, of her last letter, these like foul black water came sweeping up and darkened his mind. . . . No more. No more. He must do as he had done. Think only of Pybus. Fight that, win his victory, and then turn to what lay behind. But the sunlight no longer danced for him, he closed his eyes, turned on his side, and prayed to God out of his bewilderment.

After breakfast he started out. A restless urgency drove him forth. The Chapter Meeting at which the new incumbent of Pybus was to be chosen was now only three days distant, and all the work in connection with that was completed—

but Brandon could not be still. Some members of the Chapter he had seen over and over again during the last months, and had pressed Rex Forsyth's claims upon them without ceasing, but this thing had become a symbol to him now—a symbol of his fight with Ronder, of his battle for the Cathedral, of his championship, behind that, of the whole cause of Christ's Church.

It seemed to him that if he were defeated now in this thing it would mean that God Himself had deserted him. At the mere thought of defeat his heart began to leap in his breast and the flags of the pavement to run before his eyes. But it could not be. He had been tested ; like Job, every plague had been given to him to prove him true, but this last would shout to the world that his power was gone and that the Cathedral that he loved had no longer a place for him. And then—and then——

He would not, he must not, look. At the top of the High Street he met Ryle the Precentor. There had been a time when Ryle was terrified by the Archdeacon; that time was not far distant, but it was gone. Nevertheless, even though the Archdeacon were suddenly old and sick and unimportant, you never could tell but that he might say something to somebody that it would be unpleasant to have said. ' Politeness all the way round ' was Ryle's motto, and a very safe one too. Moreover, Ryle, when he could rise above his alarm for the safety of his own position, was a kindly man, and it really *was* sad to see the poor Archdeacon so pale and tired, the scratch on his cheek, even now not healed, giving him a strangely battered appearance.

And how would Ryle have liked Mrs. Ryle to

leave him? And how would he feel if his son,
Anthony (aged at present five), ran away with the
daughter of a publican? And how, above all, would
he feel did he know that the whole town was talking about him and saying 'Poor Precentor!'? But
perhaps the Archdeacon did *not* know. Strange
the things that people did not know about themselves!—and at that thought the Precentor went
goose-fleshy all over, because of the things that at
that very moment people might be saying about
him and he knowing none of them!

All this passed very swiftly through Ryle's
mind, and was quickly strangled by hearing Brandon
utter in quite his old knock-you-down-if-you-don't-
get-out-of-my-way voice, 'Ha! Ryle! Out early
this morning! I hope you're not planning any
more new-fangled musical schemes for us!'

Oh, well! if the Archdeacon were going to
take that sort of tone with him, Ryle simply wasn't
going to stand it! Why should he? To-day
isn't six months ago.

'That's all right, Archdeacon,' he said stiffly.
'Ronder and I go through a good deal of the music
together now. He's very musical, you know.
Every one seems quite satisfied.' *That* ought to
get him—my mention of Ronder's name. . . . At
the same time Ryle didn't wish to seem to have gone
over to the other camp altogether, and he was just
about to say something gently deprecatory of
Ronder when, to his astonishment, he perceived that
Brandon simply hadn't heard him at all! And then
the Archdeacon took his arm and marched with
him down the High Street.

'With regard to this Pybus business, Precentor,'
he was saying, 'the matter now will be settled

in another three days. I hope every one realises the extreme seriousness of this audacious plot to push a heretic like this man Wistons into the place. I'm sure that every one *does* realise it. There can be no two opinions about it, of course. At the same time——'

How very uncomfortable ! There had been a time when the Precentor would have been proud indeed to walk down the High Street arm-in-arm with the Archdeacon. But that time was past. The High Street was crowded. Any one might see them. They would take it for granted that the Precentor was of the Archdeacon's party. And to be seen thus affectionately linked with the Archdeacon just now, when his family affairs were in so strange a disorder, when he himself was behaving so oddly, when, as it was whispered, at the Jubilee Fair he had engaged in a scuffle of a most disreputable kind. The word ' Drink ' was mentioned.

Ryle tried, ever so gently, to disengage his arm. Brandon's hand was of steel.

' This seems to me,' the Archdeacon was continuing, ' a most critical moment in our Cathedral's history. If we don't stand together now, we— we—— '

The Archdeacon's hand relaxed. His eyes wandered. Ryle detached his arm. How strange the man was ! Why, there was Samuel Hogg on the other side of the street !

He had taken his hat off and was smiling. How uncomfortable ! How unpleasant to be mixed in this kind of encounter ! How Mrs. Ryle would dislike it if she knew !

But his mind was speedily taken off his own

affairs. He was conscious of the Archdeacon, standing at his full height, his eyes, as he afterwards described it a thousand times, ' bursting from his head.' Then, ' before you could count two,' the Archdeacon was striding across the street.

It was a sunny morning, people going about the. ordinary business, every one smiling and happy. Suddenly Ryle saw the Archdeacon stop in front of Hogg ; himself started across the street, urged he knew not by what impulse, saw Hogg's ugly sneering face, saw the Archdeacon's arm shoot out, catch Hogg one, two terrific blows in the face, saw Hogg topple over like a heap of clothes falling from their peg, was in time to hear the Archdeacon crying out, ' You dirty spy ! You'd set upon me from behind, would you ? Afraid to meet me face to face, are you ? Take that, then, and that ! ' And then shout, ' It's daylight ! It's daylight now ! Stand up and face me, you coward ! '

The next thing of which the terrified Ryle was conscious was that people were running up from all sides. They seemed to spring from nowhere. He saw, too, how Hogg, the blood streaming from his face, lay there on his back, not attempting to move. Some were bending down behind him, holding his head, others had their hands about Brandon, holding him back. Errand - boys were running, people were hurrying from the shops, voices raised on every side—a Constable slowly crossed the street—Ryle slipped away——

Joan had gone out at once after breakfast that morning to the little shop, Miss Milligan's, in the little street behind the Precincts, to see whether she could not get some of that really fresh fruit that only Miss Milligan seemed really able to obtain. She was for some little time in the shop, because Miss Milligan always had a great deal to say about her little nephew Benjie, who was at the School as a day-boy and was likely to get a scholarship, and was just now suffering from boils. Joan was a good listener and a patient, so that it was quite late—after ten o'clock—as she hurried back.

Just by the Arden Gate Ellen Stiles met her.

'Oh, you poor child!' she cried; 'aren't you at home? I was just hurrying up to see whether I could be of any sort of help to you!'

'Any help?' echoed Joan, seeing at once, in the nodding blue plume in Ellen's hat, forebodings of horrible disaster.

'What, haven't you heard?' cried Ellen, pitying from the bottom of her heart the child's white face and terrified eyes.

'No! What? Oh, tell me quickly! What has happened? To father——'

'I don't know exactly myself,' said Ellen. 'That's what I was hurrying up to find out. . . . Your father . . . he's had some sort of fight with that horrible man Hogg in the High Street. . . . No, I don't know. . . . But wait a minute. . . .'

Joan was gone, scurrying through the Precincts, the paper bag with the fruit clutched tightly to her.

Ellen Stiles stared after her; her eyes were dim with kindness. There was nothing now that she would not do for that girl and her poor father! Knocked down to the ground they were, and Ellen championed them wherever she went. And now this! Drink or madness—perhaps both! Poor man ! Poor man ! And that child, scarcely out of the cradle, with all this on her shoulders ! Ellen would do anything for them ! She would go round later in the day and see how she could be useful.

She turned away. It was Ronder now who was ' up ' . . . and a little pulling-down would do him no sort of harm. There were a few little things she was longing, herself, to tell him. A few home-truths. Then, half-way down the High Street, she met Julia Preston, and didn't they have a lot to say about it all !

Meanwhile Joan, in another moment, was at her door. What had happened ? Oh, what had happened ? Had he been brought back dying and bleeding ? Had that horrible man set upon him, there in the High Street, while every one was about ? Was the doctor there, Mr. Puddifoot ? Would there perhaps have to be an operation ? This would kill her father. The disgrace. . . . She let herself in with her latchkey and stood in the familiar hall. Everything was just as it had always been, the clocks ticking. She could hear the Cathedral organ faintly through the wall. The drawing-room windows were open, and she could hear the birds, singing at the sun, out there in the Precincts. Everything as it always was. She could not understand. Gladys appeared from the kitchen.

' Oh, Gladys, here is the fruit. . . . Has father come in ? '

' I don't know, miss.'

' You haven't heard him ? '

' No, miss. I've been upstairs, 'elping with the beds.'

' Oh—thank you, Gladys.'

The terror slipped away from her. Then it

was all right. Ellen Stiles had, as usual, exaggerated. After all, she had not been there. She had heard it only at second-hand. She hesitated for a moment, then went to the study door. Outside she hesitated again, then she went in.

To her amazement her father was sitting, just as he had always sat, at his table. He looked up when she entered, there was no sign upon him of any trouble. His face was very white, stone-white, and it seemed to her that for months past the colour had been draining from it, and now at last all colour was gone. A man wearing a mask. She could fancy that he would put up his hands and suddenly slip it from him and lay it down upon the table. The eyes stared through it, alive, coloured, restless.

'Well, Joan, what is it?'

She stammered, 'Nothing, father. I only wanted to see—whether—that——'

'Yes? Is any one wanting to see me?'

'No—only some one told me that you. . . . I thought——'

'You heard that I chastised a ruffian in the town? You heard correctly. I did. He deserved what I gave him.'

A little shiver shook her.

'Is that all you want to know?'

'Isn't there anything, father, I can do?'

'Nothing—except leave me just now. I'm very busy. I have letters to write.'

She went out. She stood in the hall, her hands clasped together. What was she to do? The worst that she had ever feared had occurred. He was mad.

She went into the drawing-room, where the sun was blazing as though it would set the carpet on

fire. What *was* she to do? What *ought* she to
do? Should she fetch Puddifoot or some older
woman like Mrs. Combermere, who would be able
to advise her? Oh no. She wanted no one there
who would pity him. She felt a longing, urgent
desire to keep him always with her now, away from
the world, in some corner where she could cherish
and love him and allow no one to insult and hurt
him. But madness! To her girlish inexperience
this morning's acts could be nothing but madness.
There in the middle of the High Street, with every
one about, to do such a thing! The disgrace of it!
Why, now, they could never stay in Polchester. . . .
This was worse than everything that had gone before.
How they would all talk, Canon Ronder and all of
them, and how pleased they would be!

At that she clenched her hands and drew herself
up as though she were defying the whole of Polchester. They should not laugh at him, they should
not dare! . . .

But meanwhile what immediately was she to do?
It wasn't safe to leave him alone. Now that he had
gone so far as to knock some one down in the
principal street, what might he not do? What
would happen if he met Canon Ronder? Oh!
why had this come? What had they done to deserve
this?

What had *he* done when he had always been so
good?

She seemed for a little distracted. She could
not think. Her thoughts would not come clearly.
She waited, staring into the sun and the colour.
Quietness came to her. Her life was now his.
Nothing counted in her life but that. If they must
leave Polchester she would go with him wherever

he must go, and care for him. Johnny ! For one terrible instant he seemed to stand, a figure of flame, outside there on the sun-drenched grass.

Outside ! Yes, always outside, until her father did not need her any more. Then, suddenly she wanted Johnny so badly that she crumpled up into one of the old armchairs and cried and cried and cried. She was very young. Life ahead of her seemed very long. Yes, she cried her heart out, and then she went upstairs and washed her face and wrote to Falk. She would not telegraph until she was quite sure that she could not manage it by herself.

The wonderful morning changed to a storm of wind and rain. Such a storm ! Down in the basement Cook could scarcely hear herself speak ! As she said to Gladys, it was what you must expect now. They were slipping into Autumn, and before you knew, why, there would be Winter ! Nothing odder than the sudden way the Seasons took you ! But Cook didn't like storms in that house. ' Them Precincts 'ouses, they're that old, they'd fall on top of you as soon as whistle Trefusis ! For her part she'd always thought this 'ouse queer, and it wasn't any the less queer since all these things had been going on in it.' It was at this point that the grocery ' boy ' arrived and supposed they'd 'eard all about it by that time. All about what ? Why, the Archdeacon knocking Samuel 'Ogg down in the 'Igh Street that very morning ! Then, indeed, you could have knocked Cook down, as she said, with a whisper. Collapsed her so, that she had to sit down and take a cup of tea, the kettle being luckily on the boil. Gladys had to sit down and take one too, and there they sat, the grocer's boy dismissed, in the darkening kitchen, their heads close together, and starting at every hiss of the rain upon the coals. The house hung heavy and dark above them. Mad, that's what he must be, and going mad these past ever so many months. And such a fine man too ! But knocking people down in the street, and 'im such a man for his own dignity ! 'Im an Archdeacon too. 'Ad any one ever heard in their lives of an Archdeacon doing such a thing ? Well, that settled Cook. She'd been in the house ten solid years, but at the end of the month she'd be off. To sit in the house with a madman ! Not she ! Adultery and all the talk had been enough, but she had risked her good name and all, just for the sake of that poor young thing upstairs, but madness !—no, that was another pair of shoes.

Now Gladys was peculiar. She'd given her notice, but hearing this, she suddenly determined to stay. That poor Miss Joan ! Poor little worm ! So young and innocent—shut up all alone with her mad father. Gladys would see her through——

' Why, Gladys,' cried Cook, ' what will your young feller you're walkin' with say ? '

' If 'e don't like it 'e can lump it,' said Gladys. ' Lord, 'ow this house does rattle ! '

All the afternoon of that day Brandon sat, never moving from his study-table. He sat exultant. Some of the shame had been wiped away. He could feel again the riotous happiness that had surged up in him as he struck that face, felt it yield before him, saw it fade away into dust and nothingness. That face that had for all these months been haunting him, at last he had banished it, and with it had gone

those other leering faces that had for so long kept
him company. His room was dark, and it was
always in the dark that they came to him—Hogg's,
the drunken painter's, that old woman's in the dirty
dress.

And to-day they did not come. If they came he
would treat them as he had treated Hogg. That
was the way to deal with them !

His heart was bad, fluttering, stampeding,
pounding and then dying away. He walked about
the room that he might think less of it. Never
mind his heart ! Destroy his enemies, that's what
he had to do—these men and women who were the
enemies of himself, his town and his Cathedral.

Suddenly he thought that he would go out. He
got his hat and his coat and went into the rain.
He crossed the Green and let himself into the
Cathedral by the Saint Margaret Chapel door, as he
had so often done before.

The Cathedral was very dark, and he stumbled
about, knocking against pillars and hassocks. He
was strange here. It was as though he didn't know
the place. He got into the middle of the nave, and
positively he didn't know where he was. A faint
green light glimmered in the East end. There
were chairs in his way. He stood still, listening.

He was lost. He would never find his way out
again. *His* Cathedral, and he was lost ! Figures
were moving everywhere. They jostled him and
said nothing. The air was thick and hard to
breathe. Here was the Black Bishop's Tomb. He
let his fingers run along the metal work. How
cold it was ! His hand touched the cold icy beard !
His hand stayed there. He could not remove it.
His fingers stuck.

He tried to cry out, and he could say nothing. An icy hand, gauntleted, descended upon his and held it. He tried to scream. He could not.

He shouted. His voice was a whisper. He sank upon his knees. He fainted, slipping to the ground like a man tired out.

There, half an hour later, Lawrence found him.

CHAPTER IV

THE LAST TOURNAMENT

On the morning of the Chapter Meeting Ronder went in through the West door, intending to cross the nave by the Cloisters. Just as he closed the heavy door behind him there sprang up, close to him, as though from nowhere at all, that horrible man Davray. Horrible always to Ronder, but more horrible now because of the dreadful way in which he had, during the last few months, gone tumbling downhill. There had been, until lately, a certain austerity and even nobility in the man's face. That was at last completely swept away. This morning he looked as though he had been sleeping out all night, his face yellow, his eyes bloodshot, his hair tangled and unkempt, pieces of grass clinging to his well-worn grey flannel suit.

'Good morning, Canon Ronder,' he said.

'Good morning,' Ronder replied severely, and tried to pass on. But the man stood in his way.

'I'm not going to keep you,' he said. 'I know what your business is this morning. I wouldn't keep you from it for a single moment. I know what you're going to do. You're going to get rid of that damned Archdeacon. Finish him for once and all. Stamp on him so that he can never raise

up his beautiful head again. I know. It's fine
work you've been doing ever since you came here,
Canon Ronder. But it isn't you that's been doing
it. It's the Cathedral.'

' Please let me pass,' said Ronder. ' I haven't
any time just now to spare.'

' Ah, that hurts your pride. You like to think
it's you who's been the mighty fine fellow all this
time. Well, it isn't you at all. It's the Cathedral.
The Cathedral's jealous, you know—don't like its
servants taking all the credit to themselves. Pride's
dangerous, Canon Ronder. In a year or two's
time, when you're feeling pretty pleased with yourself, you just look back on the Archdeacon's history
for a moment and consider it. It may have a lesson
for you. Good morning, Canon Ronder. Pleased
to have met you.'

The wretched creature went slithering up the
aisle, chuckling to himself. How miserable to be
drunk at that early hour of the morning ! Ronder
shrugged his shoulders as though he would like to
shake off from them something unpleasant that was
sticking to them. He was not in a good mood this
morning. He was assured of victory—he had no
doubt about it at all—and unquestionably when the
affair was settled he would feel more tranquil about
it. But ever since his talk with Wistons he had
been unsure of the fellow. Was it altogether wise
that he should come here ? His perfect content
seemed to be as far away as ever. Was it always to
be so ?

And then this horrible affair in the High Street
three days ago, how distressing ! The Archdeacon's brain was going, and that was the very
last thing that Ronder had desired. What he had

originally seen was the pleasant picture of Brandon
retiring with his wife and family to a nice Rectory
in the diocese and ending his days—many years
hence it is to be hoped—in a charming old garden
with an oak-tree on the lawn and pigeons cooing
in the sunny air.

But this! Oh, no! not this! Ronder was a
practical man of straight common-sense, but it did
seem to him as though there had been through all
the movement of the last six months some spirit
far more vindictive than himself had ever been.
He had never, from the first moment to the last,
been vindictive. With his hand on his heart he
could say that. He did not like the Cathedral
that morning, it seemed to him cold, hostile, ugly.
The thick stone pillars were scornful, the glass of
the East window was dead and dull. A little
wind seemed to whistle in the roof so far, so far
above his head.

He hurried on, his great-coat hugged about him.
All that he could say was that he did hope that
Brandon would not be there this morning. His
presence could alter nothing, the voting could go
only one way. It would be very painful were he
there. Surely after the High Street affair he would
not come.

Ronder saw with relief when he came into the
Chapter House that Brandon was not present.
They were standing about the room, looking out
into the Cloisters, talking in little groups—the
Dean, Bentinck-Major, Ryle, Foster, and Bond, the
Clerk, a little apart from the others as social decency
demanded. When Ronder entered, two things at
once were plain—one, how greatly during these last
months he had grown in importance with all of

them, and, secondly, how nervous they were all feeling. They all turned towards him.

'Ah, Ronder,' said the Dean, 'that's right. I was afraid lest something should keep you.'

'No—no—what a cold damp day! Autumn is really upon us.'

They discussed the weather, once and again eyeing the door apprehensively. Bentinck-Major took Ronder aside:

'My wife and I have been wondering whether you'd honour us by dining with us on the 25th,' he said. 'A cousin of my wife's, Lady Caroline Holmesby, is to be staying with us just then. It would give us such great pleasure if you and Miss Ronder would join us that evening. My wife is, of course, writing to Miss Ronder.'

'So far as I know, my aunt and I are both free and will be delighted to come,' said Ronder.

'Delightful! That will be delightful! As a matter of fact we were thinking of having that evening a little Shakespeare reading. We thought of *King Lear*.'

'Ah! That's another matter,' said Ronder, laughing. 'I'll be delighted to listen, but as to taking part——'

'But you must! You must!' said Bentinck-Major, catching hold of one of the buttons on Ronder's waistcoat, a habit that Ronder most especially disliked. 'More culture is what our town needs—several of us have been thinking so. It is really time, I think, to start a little Shakespeare reading amongst ourselves—strictly amongst ourselves, of course. The trouble with Shakespeare is that he is so often a little—a little bold, for mixed reading—and that restricts us. Nevertheless, we hope. . . . I do trust that you will join us, Canon Ronder.'

'I make no promises,' said Ronder. 'If you knew how badly I read, you'd hesitate before asking me.'

'We are past our time,' said the Dean, looking at his watch. 'We are all here, I think, but Brandon and Witheram. Witheram is away at Drymouth. He had written to me. How long we should wait——'

'I can hardly believe,' said Ryle nervously, 'that Archdeacon Brandon will be present. He is extremely unwell. I don't know whether you are aware that three nights ago he was found by Lawrence the Verger here in the Cathedral in a fainting fit. He is very unwell, I'm afraid.'

The whole group was immensely interested. They had heard. . . . Fainting? Here in the Cathedral? Yes, by the Bishop's Tomb. He was better yesterday, but it is hardly likely that he will come this morning.

'Poor man!' said the Dean, gently distressed. 'I heard something. . . . That was the result, I'm afraid, of his fracas that morning in the High Street; he must be most seriously unwell.'

'Poor man, poor man!' was echoed by everybody; it was evident also that general relief was felt. He could not now be expected to be present.

The door opened, and he came in. He came hurriedly, a number of papers in one hand, wearing just the old anxious look of important care that they knew so well. And yet how changed he was! Instead of moving at once to his place at the long table he hesitated, looked at Bentinck-

Major, at Foster, then at Bond, half-puzzled, as though he had never seen them before.

'I must apologise, gentlemen,' he said, 'for being late. My watch, I'm afraid, was slow.'

The Dean then showed quite unexpected qualities.

'Will you sit here on my right, Archdeacon?' he said in a firm and almost casual voice. 'We are a little late, I fear, but no matter—no matter. We are all present, I think, save Archdeacon Witheram, who is at Drymouth, and from whom I have received a letter.' They all found their places. Ronder was as usual exactly opposite to Brandon. Foster slouched into his seat with his customary air of absentmindedness. Ryle tried not to look at Brandon, but his eyes were fascinated and seemed to swim in their watery fashion like fish fascinated by a bait.

'Shall we open with prayer,' said the Dean, 'and ask God's blessing on this morning's work?'

They prayed with bent heads. Brandon's head was bent longer than the others.

When he looked up he stared about him as though completely bewildered.

'As you all know,' the Dean said in his softly urgent voice, as though he were pressing them to give him flowers for his collection, 'our meeting this morning is of the first urgency. I will, with your approval, postpone general business until the more ordinary meeting of next week. That is if no one has any objection to such a course?'

No one had any objections.

'Very well, then. As you know, our business this morning is to appoint a successor to poor Morrison at Pybus St. Anthony. Now in ordinary

cases such an appointment is not of the first importance, but in the matter of Pybus, as you all
know, there is a difference. Whether rightly or
wrongly, it has been a tradition in the Diocese that
the Pybus living should be given only to exceptional
men. It has been fortunate in having a succession
of exceptional men in its service—men who, for the
most part, have come to great position in the
Church afterwards. I want you to remember that,
gentlemen, when you are making your decision
this morning. At the same time you must remember that it has been largely tradition that has
given this importance to Pybus, and that the living
has been vacant already too long.'

He paused. Then he picked up a piece of paper
in front of him.

'There have been several meetings with regard
to this living already,' he said, 'and certain names
have been very thoroughly discussed among us.
I think we were last week agreed that two names
stood out from the others. If to-day we cannot
agree on one of those two names, we must then
consider a third. That will not, I hope, be necessary.
The two names most favourably considered by us
are those of the Rev. Rex Forsyth, Chaplain to
Bishop Clematis, and the Rev. Ambrose Wistons
of St. Edward's, Hawston. The first of these two
gentlemen is known to all of us personally, the
second we know chiefly through his writings. We
will first, I think, consider Mr. Wistons. You,
Canon Foster, are, I know, a personal friend of his,
and can tell us why, in your opinion, his would be
a suitable appointment.'

'It depends what you want,' said Foster, frowning around upon every one present; and then

suddenly selecting little Bond as apparently his most dangerous enemy and scowling at him with great hostility, ' if you want to let the religious life of this place, nearly dead already, pass right away. choose a man like Forsyth. But I don't wish to be contentious ; there's been contention enough in this place during these last months, and I'm sick and ashamed of the share I've had in it. I won't say more than this—that if you want an honest, God-fearing man here, who lives only for God and is in his most secret chamber as he is before men, then Wistons is your man. I understand that some of you are afraid of his books. There'll be worse books than his you'll have to face before you're much older. *That* I can tell you ! I said to myself before I came here that I wouldn't speak this morning. I should not have said even what I have, because I know that in this last year I have grievously sinned, fighting against God when I thought that I was fighting for Him. The weapons are taken out of my hands. I believe that Wistons is the man for this place and for the religious life here. I believe that you will none of you regret it if you bring him to this appointment. I can say nothing more.'

What had happened to Foster ? They had, one and all, expected a fighting speech. The discomfort and uneasiness that was already in the room was now greatly increased.

The Dean asked Ronder to say something. Ronder leaned forward, pushing his spectacles back with his fingers. He leaned forward that he might not see Brandon's face.

By chance he had not seen Brandon for more than a fortnight. He was horrified and frightened by the change. The grey-white face, the restless, beseeching, bewildered eyes belonging apparently to some one else, to whom they were searching to return, the long white fingers ceaselessly moving among the papers and tapping the table, were those of a stranger, and in the eyes of the men in that room it was he who had produced him. Yes, and in the eyes of how many others in that town? You might say that had Brandon been a man of real spiritual and moral strength, not Ronder, not even God Himself, could have brought Brandon to this. But was that so? Which of us knows until he is tried? His wife, his son, his body, all had failed him. And now this too. . . . And if Ronder had not come to that town would it have been so? Had it not been a duel between them from the moment that Ronder first set his foot in that place? And had not Ronder deliberately willed it so? What had Ronder said to Brandon's son and to the woman who would ruin Brandon's wife?

All this passed in the flash of a dream through Ronder's brain, perhaps never entirely to leave him again. In that long duel there had been perhaps more than one defeat. He knew that they were waiting for him to speak, but the thoughts would not come. Wistons? Forsyth? . . . Forsyth? Wistons? Who were they? What had they to do with this personal relation of his with the man opposite?

He flushed. He must say something. He began to speak, and soon his brain, so beautifully ordered, began to reel out the words in soft and steady sequence. But his soul watched Brandon's soul.

'My friend, Canon Foster, knows Mr. Wistons

so much better than I do,' he said, ' that it is absurd for me to try and tell you what he should tell you.

' I do regard him as the right man for this place, because I think our Cathedral, that we all so deeply love, is waiting for just such a man. Against his character no one, I suppose, has anything to say. He is known before all the world as a God-fearing Christian. He is no youth; he has had much experience; he is, every one witnesses, lovable and of strong personal charm. It is not his character, but his ideas, that people have criticised. He is a modernist, of course, a man of an enquiring, penetrating mind, who must himself be satisfied of the truth for which he is searching. Can that do us here any harm? I believe not. I think that some of us, if I may say so, are too easily frightened of the modern spirit of enquiry. I believe that we Churchmen should step forward ready to face any challenge, whether of scientists, psychologists or any one else —I think that before long, whether we like it or no, we shall have to do so. Mr. Wistons is, I believe, just the man to help us in such a crisis. His opinions are not precisely the same as those of some of us in this diocese, and I've no doubt that if he came here there would be some disputes from time to time, but I believe those same disputes would do us a world of good. God did not mean us to sit down twiddling our thumbs and never using our brains. He gave us our intelligences, and therefore I presume that He meant us to make some use of them.

' In these matters Mr. Wistons is exactly what we want here. He is a much-travelled man, widely experienced in affairs, excellent at business. No one who has ever met him would deny his sweetness and personal charm. I think myself that we are very fortunate to have a chance of seeing him here——'

Ronder ceased. He felt as though he had been beating thin air with weak ineffective hands. They had, none of them, been listening to him or thinking of him; they had not even been thinking of Wistons. Their minds had been absorbed, held, dominated by the tall broad figure who sat in their midst, but was not one of them.

Brandon, in fact, began to speak almost before Ronder had finished. He did not look up, but stared at his long nervous fingers. He spoke at first almost in a whisper, so that they did not catch the first few words. '. . . Horrified . . .' they heard him say. 'Horrified. . . . So calmly. . . . These present. . . .

'Cannot understand. . . .' Then his words were clearer. He looked up, staring across at Ronder.

'Horrified at this eager acceptance of a man who is a declared atheist before God.' Then suddenly he flung his head back in his old challenging way and, looking round upon them all, went on, his voice now clear, although weak and sometimes faltering:

'Gentlemen, this is perhaps my last appearance at these Chapter Meetings. I have not been very well of late and, as you all know, I have had trouble. You will forgive me if I do not, this morning, express myself so clearly or carefully as I should like.

'But the first thing that I wish to say is that when you are deciding this question this morning you should do your best, before God, to put my own personality out of your minds. I have learnt many things, under God's hand, in the last six months. He has shown me some weaknesses and failings, and I know now that, because of those weaknesses, there are some in this town who would act against anything that I proposed, simply because they would wish me to be defeated. I do implore you this morning not to think of me, but to think only of what will be best—best—best——' He looked around him for a moment bewildered, frowning in puzzled fashion at Ronder, then continued again, ' best for God and the work of His Church.'

' I'm not very well, gentlemen ; my thoughts are not coming very clearly this morning, and that is sad, because I've looked forward to this morning for months past, wishing to fight my very best. . . .' His voice changed. ' Yes, fight ! ' he cried. ' There should be no fight necessary in such a matter. But what has happened to us all in the last year ?

' A year ago there was not one of us who would have considered such an appointment as I am now disputing ? Have you read this man's books ? Have you read in the papers his acknowledged utterances ? Do you know that he questions the Divinity of Christ Himself——'

' No, Archdeacon,' Foster broke in, ' that is not true. You can have no evidence of that.'

Brandon seemed to be entirely bewildered by the interruption. He looked at Foster, opened his mouth as though he would speak, then suddenly put his hand to his head.

' If you will give me time,' he said. ' Give me time. I will prove everything, I will indeed. I beg you,' he said, suddenly turning to the Dean, ' that you will have this appointment postponed for a month. It is so serious a matter that to decide hastily——'

'Not hastily,' said the Dean very gently 'Morrison died some months ago, and I'm afraid it is imperative that we should fill the vacancy this morning.'

'Then consider what you do,' Brandon cried, now half-rising from his chair. 'This man is breaking in upon the cherished beliefs of our Church. Give him a little and he will take everything. We must all stand firm upon the true and Christian ground that the Church has given us, or where shall we be ? This man may be good and devout, but he does not believe what we believe. Our Church —that we love—that we love——' He broke off again.

'You are against me. Every man's hand now is against me. Nevertheless what I say is right and true. What am I ? What are you, any of you here in this room, beside God's truth ? I have seen God, I have walked with God, I shall walk with Him again. He will lead me out of these sore distresses and take me into green pastures——'

He flushed. 'I beg your pardon, gentlemen. I am taking your time. I must say something for Mr. Forsyth. He is young ; he knows this place and loves it ; he cares for and will preserve its most ancient traditions. . . .

'He cares for the things for which we should care. I do commend him to your attention——'

There was a long silence. The rain that had begun a thick drizzle dripped on the panes. The room was so dark that the Dean asked Bond to light the gas. They all waited while this was being done. At last the Dean spoke :

' We are all very grateful to you, Archdeacon, for helping us as you have done. I think, gentlemen, that unless there is some other name definitely to be proposed we had better now vote on these two names.

' Is there any further name suggested ? '

No one spoke.

' Very well, then. I think this morning, contrary to our usual custom, we will record our votes on paper. I have Archdeacon Witheram's letter here advising me of his wishes in this matter.'

Paper and pens were before every one. The votes were recorded and sent up to the Dean. He opened the little pieces of paper slowly.

At last he said :

' One vote has been recorded in favour of Mr. Forsyth, the rest for Mr. Wistons. Mr. Wistons is therefore appointed to the living of Pybus St. Anthony.'

Brandon was on his feet. His body trembled like a tree tottering. He flung out his hands.

' No. . . . No. . . . Stop one moment. You must. You—all of you——

' Mr. Dean—all of you. . . . Oh, God, help me now ! . . . You have been influenced by your feelings about myself. Forget me, turn me away, send me from the town, anything, anything. . . . I beseech you to think only of the good of the Cathedral in this affair. If you admit this man it is the beginning of the end. Slowly it will all be undermined. Belief in Christ, Belief in God Himself. . . . Think of the future and your responsibility to the unborn children when they come to you and say : " Where is our faith ? Why did you take it from us ? Give it back to us ! " Oh, stop for a moment ! Postpone this for only a little while. Don't do this thing ! . . . Gentlemen ! '

They could see that he was ill. His body swayed as though it were beyond his control. His hands were waving, turning, beseeching. . . .

Suddenly tears were running down his cheeks.

' Not this shame ! ' he cried. ' Not this shame ! —kill me—but save the Cathedral ! '

They were on their feet. Foster and Ryle had come round to him. ' Archdeacon, sit down.' ' You're ill.' ' Rest a moment.' With a great heave of his shoulders he flung them off, a chair falling to the ground with the movement.

He saw Ronder.

' You ! . . . my enemy. Are you satisfied now ? ' he whispered. He held out his quivering hand. ' Take my hand. You've done your worst.'

He turned round as though he would go from the room. Stumbling, he caught Foster by the shoulder as though he would save himself. He bent forward, staring into Foster's face.

' God is love, though,' he said. ' You betray Him again and again, but He comes back.'

He gripped Foster's shoulder more tightly. ' Don't do this thing, man,' he said. ' Don't do it. Because Ronder's beaten me is no reason for you to betray your God. . . . Give me a chair. I'm ill.'

He fell upon his knees.

' This . . . Death,' he whispered. Then, looking up again at Foster, ' My heart. That fails me too.'

And, bowing his head, he died.

Printed in Great Britain by R. & R. CLARK, LIMITED, Edinburgh.